DAD —

IT'S BOOK #5!

D

Use Case Driven Object Modeling with UML

Theory and Practice

■ ■ ■

Doug Rosenberg and
Matt Stephens

Apress®

Use Case Driven Object Modeling with UML: Theory and Practice

Copyright © 2007 by Doug Rosenberg and Matt Stephens

ISBN-13 (pbk): 978-1-59059-774-3

ISBN-10 (pbk): 1-59059-774-5

Printed and bound in the United States of America 9 8 7 6 5 4 3 2 1

Lead Editor: Jonathan Gennick
Technical Reviewer: Dr. Charles Suscheck
Editorial Board: Steve Anglin, Ewan Buckingham, Gary Cornell, Jason Gilmore, Jonathan Gennick, Jonathan Hassell, James Huddleston, Chris Mills, Matthew Moodie, Dominic Shakeshaft, Jim Sumser, Matt Wade
Senior Project Manager: Tracy Brown Collins
Copy Edit Manager: Nicole Flores
Assistant Production Director: Kari Brooks-Copony
Senior Production Editor: Laura Cheu
Compositor: Linda Weidemann, Wolf Creek Press
Proofreader: Nancy Riddiough
Indexer: Toma Mulligan
Artist: Kinetic Publishing Services, LLC
Cover Designer: Kurt Krames
Manufacturing Director: Tom Debolski

Distributed to the book trade worldwide by Springer-Verlag New York, Inc., 233 Spring Street, 6th Floor, New York, NY 10013. Phone 1-800-SPRINGER, fax 201-348-4505, e-mail orders-ny@springer-sbm.com, or visit http://www.springeronline.com.

For information on translations, please contact Apress directly at 2560 Ninth Street, Suite 219, Berkeley, CA 94710. Phone 510-549-5930, fax 510-549-5939, e-mail info@apress.com, or visit http://www.apress.com.

The UML model and source code for the example use cases in this book are available to readers at http://www.apress.com and http://www.iconixprocess.com/InternetBookstore.

For Rob, who has the brightest future of anyone I know.
Keep locating your fastball in unhittable spots,
and good things will continue to happen.

—Doug Rosenberg

To Michelle, for her never-ending patience and support.

—Matt

Contents at a Glance

About the Authors xv

About the Technical Reviewer xvii

Acknowledgments xix

Preface xxi

Introduction xxvii

■**CHAPTER 1**   Introduction to ICONIX Process 1

PART 1 ■■■ Requirements Definition

■**CHAPTER 2**   Domain Modeling 23

■**CHAPTER 3**   Use Case Modeling 49

■**CHAPTER 4**   Requirements Review 83

PART 2 ■■■ Analysis, Conceptual Design, and Technical Architecture

■**CHAPTER 5**   Robustness Analysis 101

■**CHAPTER 6**   Preliminary Design Review 143

■**CHAPTER 7**   Technical Architecture 159

PART 3 ■■■ Design and Coding

■**CHAPTER 8**   Sequence Diagrams 185

■**CHAPTER 9**   Critical Design Review 233

■**CHAPTER 10**   Implementation: Getting from Detailed Design to Code 257

■**CHAPTER 11**   Code Review and Model Update 297

PART 4 ■■■ Testing and Requirements Traceability

■CHAPTER 12   Design-Driven Testing 329
■CHAPTER 13   Addressing Requirements 373

PART 5 ■■■ Appendixes

■APPENDIX A   What's New in UML 2.0 395
■APPENDIX B   Spring Bin 409

■INDEX 425

Contents

About the Authors xv

About the Technical Reviewer xvii

Acknowledgments xix

Preface xxi

Introduction xxvii

■CHAPTER 1   **Introduction to ICONIX Process** 1

    ICONIX Process in Theory 2
        Overview: Getting from Use Cases to Source Code 2
        Requirements 4
        Analysis/Preliminary Design 9
        Detailed Design 12
        Implementation 15
    Extensions to ICONIX Process 19
        Persona Analysis 19
        Test-Driven Development (TDD) 19
        Driving Test Cases from the Analysis Model 20
    ICONIX Process in Practice: The Internet Bookstore Example 20
    Summary 20

PART 1 ■■■ Requirements Definition

■CHAPTER 2   **Domain Modeling** 23

    The 10,000-Foot View 24
        What's a Domain Model? 24
        Why Start with the Domain Model Instead of Use Cases? 25
    Domain Modeling in Theory 26
        Top 10 Domain Modeling Guidelines 26
        Internet Bookstore: Extracting the First-Pass Domain Model
            from High-Level Requirements 30
        Internet Bookstore: Second Attempt at the Domain Model 35
        Internet Bookstore: Building Generalization Relationships 37

Domain Modeling in Practice. 39
    Exercises. 39
More Practice. 45
Summary 47

■CHAPTER 3   **Use Case Modeling**. 49

The 10,000-Foot View 49
    Why Do I Need Use Cases in Addition to
        Functional Requirements? 50
    Don't Forget the Rainy-Day Scenarios. 50
    Do an Initial Domain Model Before You Write the Use Cases 50
    Driving Your Design (and Your Tests) from the Use Cases. 51
Use Case Modeling in Theory 51
    Top 10 Use Case Modeling Guidelines. 51
    Organizing Use Cases into Packages: Internet Bookstore. 61
    Use Case Relationship Roundup 67
    Internet Bookstore: Refining Use Cases. 70
    Internet Bookstore: Basic and Alternate Courses 72
    A Couple of Thoughts on Use Case Templates 74
    Use Case or Algorithm? 76
Use Case Modeling in Practice 77
    Exercises. 77
    Exercise Solutions 78
More Practice. 80
Summary 81

■CHAPTER 4   **Requirements Review** 83

Requirements Review in Theory. 84
    Why Review Requirements? 84
    Top 10 Requirements Review Guidelines 85
    Allocating Functional Requirements to Use Cases. 89
Requirements Review in Practice: Internet Bookstore 89
    Removing Everything That's Out of Scope. 90
    Naming Participating Domain Objects 92
    Making Sure You Have All the Alternate Courses 93
    Checking That the Use Case Text Isn't Too Abstract 93
    Changing Passive Voice to Active Voice 95
    Tracing Each Requirement to Its Use Cases 96
Summary 97

PART 2 ■■■ Analysis, Conceptual Design, and Technical Architecture

■CHAPTER 5   Robustness Analysis 101

The 10,000-Foot View 101
    Where Does Robustness Analysis Fit into the Process? 102
    Like Learning to Ride a Bicycle 102
    Anatomy of a Robustness Diagram 103
Robustness Analysis in Theory 104
    Top 10 Robustness Analysis Guidelines. 104
    More About Robustness Diagram Rules. 112
    How Do You Perform Robustness Analysis? 114
    Updating Your Domain (Static) Model 125
Robustness Analysis in Practice 128
    Exercises. 128
    Exercise Solutions 132
More Practice. 140
Summary 141

■CHAPTER 6   Preliminary Design Review 143

Preliminary Design Review in Theory 144
    Why Do a PDR At All? 144
    Top 10 PDR Guidelines 145
Preliminary Design Review in Practice: Internet Bookstore 149
    PDR for the "Write Customer Review" Robustness Diagram 149
    The Finished "Write Customer Review" Robustness Diagram. . . . 155
Summary 157

■CHAPTER 7   Technical Architecture 159

The 10,000-Foot View 160
    What Is Technical Architecture? 160
    What Are the Duties of a Technical Architect? 160
Technical Architecture in Theory. 161
    Top 10 Technical Architecture Guidelines 161
    Architectural Layering. 162
Technical Architecture in Practice: Internet Bookstore 164
    About Spring Framework 164
    Anatomy of Spring Framework 165

The Internet Bookstore Architecture. 172
    Layered Architecture. 172
    Flow of Events 178
    Testability 179
    Web Security. 179
Top 10 Technical Architecture Errors (the "Don'ts") 180
Summary 181

PART 3 ■■■ Design and Coding

■CHAPTER 8   **Sequence Diagrams** 185

The 10,000-Foot View 185
    Sequence Diagrams and Detailed OOD 186
    Sequence Diagram Notation 186
Sequence Diagramming in Theory. 187
    Top 10 Sequence Diagramming Guidelines 187
    How to Draw a Sequence Diagram: Four Essential Steps 195
    Continuing the Internet Bookstore Example 206
    Updating Your Class Diagrams As You Go Along. 210
    Synchronizing the Static and Dynamic Parts of the Model. 211
    Internet Bookstore: Updating the Static Model 211
Sequence Diagramming in Practice. 217
    Exercises. 217
    Exercise Solutions 221
More Practice. 228
Summary 230

■CHAPTER 9   **Critical Design Review**. 233

The 10,000-Foot View 234
Critical Design Review in Theory 235
    Top 10 Critical Design Review Guidelines 235
    Using the Class Diagrams to Find Errors on the
        Sequence Diagrams. 238

Critical Design Review in Practice: Internet Bookstore 238
    CDR for the "Show Book Details" Use Case 238
    CDR for the "Write Customer Review" Use Case 245
    The Updated Bookstore Diagrams 252
Summary 255

■CHAPTER 10 **Implementation: Getting from Detailed Design to Code** 257

The 10,000-Foot View 258
    Programmer-Driven Design 258
    Spring Framework 258
Implementation in Theory: Getting from Design to Code 258
    Top 10 Implementation Guidelines 259
Implementation in Practice: Internet Bookstore 263
    Creating the Database 263
    Preparing the Style Sheet 265
    Mapping Domain (Entity) Classes to Real Classes 266
    Implementing the "Show Book Details" Use Case 268
    Implementing the "Write Customer Review" Use Case 278
More Practice 294
Summary 295

■CHAPTER 11 **Code Review and Model Update** 297

The 10,000-Foot View 298
Code Review and Model Update in Theory 298
    Top 10 Code Review and Model Update Guidelines 299
    Why Are Code Reviews Necessary After All That
        Design Work? 302
Code Review and Model Update in Practice 303
    Code Review and Model Update Checklist 304
    "Show Book Details" Use Case 304
    "Write Customer Review" Use Case 309
    Future Iterations 324
Summary 325

PART 4 ■■■ Testing and Requirements Traceability

■CHAPTER 12 **Design-Driven Testing** 329

Design-Driven Testing in Theory. 330
 Top 10 Design-Driven Testing Guidelines 330
 Different Kinds of Testing 331
 Driving Test Cases from Robustness Diagrams 334
 Using the Agile ICONIX/EA Add-in 336
 Driving Unit Tests from the Test Cases. 338
 A Quick Introduction to JUnit 339
 Writing Effective Unit Tests. 342
Design-Driven Testing in Practice. 343
 Unit Tests for the Internet Bookstore 344
 Top 10 Design-Driven Testing Errors (the "Don'ts"). 369
More Practice. 370
Summary 371

■CHAPTER 13 **Addressing Requirements** 373

Requirements Gathering in Theory. 374
 Top 10 Requirements Gathering Guidelines 374
 Why Bother Tracking Requirements? 377
 Requirements Allocation and Traceability in Theory 378
Requirements Gathering in Practice. 379
 Organizing Requirements in EA: BillyBob 2.0 379
 Using a Visual Modeling Tool to Support Requirements 382
More Practice. 389
Summary 390

PART 5 ■■■ Appendixes

■**APPENDIX A**   **What's New in UML 2.0** 395

    Overview of Changes in UML 2.0 395
        Composite Structure Diagrams 396
        Activity and State Diagrams. 399
        Sequence and Interaction Overview Diagrams. 401
        Timing Diagrams 404
        Component and Deployment Diagrams 406
    What's Still Missing in UML 407

■**APPENDIX B**   **Spring Bin** 409

    Spring in More Detail 409
        A (Very) Brief Example of IoC 409
        Models, Views, and Controllers 412
    Internet Bookstore Design: Spring Details. 414
        "Show Book Details" Use Case 414
        "Write Customer Review" Use Case.......................... 416
    Internet Bookstore Implementation: Spring Details. 417
        Folder Structure 418
        Contents of the war\WEB-INF Folder 418
        Contents of the war\WEB-INF\jsp and
            war\WEB-INF\jsp\include Folders 421
        Java Package Hierarchy 422

■**INDEX** 425

About the Authors

■**DOUG ROSENBERG** is the founder and president of ICONIX Software Engineering, Inc. (www.iconixsw.com). Doug spent the first 15 years of his career writing code for a living before moving on to managing programmers, developing software design tools, and teaching object-oriented analysis and design.

Doug has been providing system development tools and training for nearly two decades, with particular emphasis on object-oriented methods. He developed a unified Booch/Rumbaugh/Jacobson design method in 1993 that preceded Rational's UML by several years. He has produced more than a dozen multimedia tutorials on object technology, including "COMPREHENSIVE COM" and "Enterprise Architect for Power Users," and is the coauthor of *Use Case Driven Object Modeling with UML* (Addison-Wesley, 1999) and *Applying Use Case Driven Object Modeling with UML* (Addison-Wesley, 2001), both with Kendall Scott, as well as *Extreme Programming Refactored: The Case Against XP* (Apress, 2003) with Matt Stephens, and *Agile Development with ICONIX Process* (Apress, 2005) with Matt Stephens and Mark Collins-Cope.

A few years ago, Doug started a second business, an online travel website (www.VResorts.com) that features his virtual reality photography and some innovative mapping software.

■**MATT STEPHENS** is a Java developer, project leader, and technical architect based in Central London. He's been developing software commercially for over 15 years, and has led many agile projects through successive customer releases. He has spoken at a number of software conferences on OO development topics, and his work appears regularly in a variety of software journals.

Matt is the coauthor of *Extreme Programming Refactored: The Case Against XP* (Apress, 2003) with Doug Rosenberg, and *Agile Development with ICONIX Process* (Apress, 2005) with Doug Rosenberg and Mark Collins-Cope.

Catch Matt online at www.softwarereality.com.

About the Technical Reviewer

■**DR. CHARLES SUSCHECK** is an assistant professor of computer information systems at Colorado State University, Pueblo campus. He specializes in software development methodologies and project management, and has over 20 years of professional experience in information technology.

Dr. Suscheck has held the positions of process architect, director of research, principal consultant, and professional trainer at some of the most recognized companies in America. He has spoken at national and international conferences on topics related to project management. Most recently, he's been heavily involved in delivering the "ICONIX Process Roadmap" (as defined by the activity diagrams in this book) via the Eclipse Process Framework.

Acknowledgments

First and foremost, **thanks to Gary Cornell** for picking up this project midstream.

Thanks to Geoff Sparks and the folks at Sparx Systems for building a great product, for tailoring it to support ICONIX Process, and for helping us with the UML 2.0 tutorial in Appendix A.

Thanks to Philip Nortey for his valuable feedback and his contribution to the chapter on design-driven testing; to Chuck Suscheck for his reviews and insights, especially about the student exercises; and to Mark Collins-Cope for his contribution to the architecture chapter.

And thanks, of course, to the Apress team: Gary; our editor, Jonathan Gennick; "The PM," Tracy Brown-Collins (Queen of the 48-hour chapter-editing turnaround deadline), without whose schedule this project would have forever remained in "manuscript paralysis"; "The World's Greatest Copy Editor" (once again), Nicole Flores; Diana Van Winkle for the outstanding design; and our production editor, Laura Cheu.

Preface

Matt's Preface

This book illustrates how to get from use cases to working, maintainable source code in as few steps as possible . . . but without cutting the essential corners. It's also about how to minimize the amount of rework you need to do once you've *gotten* to source code.

Learning by Doing

In this book we've tried to capture the essential qualities of Doug's ICONIX training courses—that is, the "magic qualities" of **learning by doing**. The ICONIX Jumpstart courses are very practical and hands-on; they draw students in by encouraging them to learn new skills by practicing, often on the real projects that they'll be returning to once the course is finished.

This idea of learning by doing has long been recognized as an optimal form of education. Even at the start of the twentieth century, John Dewey, an American psychologist and educational reformer, recognized that learning from experience gives rise to increasing productivity. The key is to engage the brain with practical tasks rather than to fall into the all-too-familiar "study trap" of rote learning. Memorizing long lists of names or API functions might help someone score highly on a test, but it isn't the same as understanding a subject in depth. For one thing, people tend not to retain information for very long if they've simply memorized it.

In this book, we do several things to avoid the "rote learning" trap. We walk through example diagrams, each starting with a blank screen, and show the steps—and, essentially, the thought process—involved in creating the various types of diagrams. Each step in the ICONIX Process finishes with a review. For the review milestones, we've had some fun and created fictional dialogues between a reviewer and a developer, to demonstrate the sorts of issues that reviewers or senior developers should address at each stage. We also highlight the most common (and the most dangerous) mistakes that developers tend to make.

A key part of learning by doing concerns **learning from your mistakes**. From the day we're born, we learn by discovering how *not* to do things, and then trying over and over until we get it right. Experts eventually "perfect" their art because they no longer make mistakes (at least none that they'll admit to!). So again, we've applied the principle in this book and created an Internet Bookstore example that we follow from use cases to source code, making plenty of "deliberate mistakes" along the way, which then get corrected. Also, throughout the book, you'll find workbook exercises, student exercises, and inline exercises within the chapters. (See the "Introduction" section for more information about these different types of exercises.)

The large number of exercises and step-by-step examples should help to explain why this book contains around 400 pages, to describe a process that is essentially "minimal yet sufficient." You could say that it's a 150-page book at heart, but it's packed with an unusual number of exercises and examples. It's safe to say that after reading this book and completing all the exercises, you'll have a thorough, in-depth understanding of use case–driven object modeling!

ICONIX: A Pluggable Process

ICONIX Process is a "cookbook" process in that it describes a series of specific steps that we've found work really well on many different projects. However, it doesn't prescribe the project life-cycle side of things in the way that most other development methodologies do.

So the decision of whether to do just a little bit of up-front modeling before code (one use case at a time) or model all the use cases first before coding is entirely yours to make. You can be as agile (with short iterations and quick, successive releases) or as "waterfall" (first writing all the requirements, then doing all the design, and then writing all the code) as befits your project, and still be following ICONIX Process.[1]

For this reason, the process should plug neatly into other development methodologies, as it covers the analysis and design steps but doesn't make any fixed assumptions about the project life cycle. But however you choose to apply the process to your own projects, we hope you'll start to see positive results very quickly.

Matt Stephens
Software Reality, www.softwarereality.com

Doug's Preface

It was 13 or 14 years ago, somewhere around 1992 or 1993, when one of my first training clients, Dan Mosten of Philip Morris in New York, said to me, "You should write a cookbook on how to design for OO. My people like cookbooks."

At that time, Grady Booch was at Rational, Jim Rumbaugh was at GE writing books about OMT, and Ivar Jacobson was in Sweden working on his Objectory CASE Tool. There was no UML, no Java language, no C#/.NET, and the Internet itself largely existed only in universities. Smalltalk and C++ were the dominant object-oriented (OO) languages. The ancestor of Rational Rose was being developed by Jon Hopkins at Palladio Software as a Booch diagramming tool for the PC. There was no eXtreme Programming (jumping too quickly to code was known as "hacking" back then), and no Agile Manifesto had yet declared tools and process to be second-class citizens.

The More Things Change, the More They Stay the Same

At ICONIX, we were trying to make some sense out of OO analysis and design (like everybody else), and our efforts produced a tool called ObjectModeler, which supported Booch, Rumbaugh (OMT), and Jacobson (Objectory) methods. We got into training because we had to—nobody would buy our object-oriented analysis and design (OOAD) tool if they didn't understand OOAD.

We synthesized what is now known as ICONIX Process (and was originally called "A Unified Object Modeling Approach") from what we felt were the best aspects of the three methodologies that were combined a few years later to form the UML. As we did this, *it seemed clear that the art of driving object models from use cases ought to be the core of our approach*, and

---

1. Most projects benefit from being somewhere between these two extremes. We show how to fit ICONIX Process into an "ideal medium" agile project life cycle in this book's companion volume, *Agile Development with ICONIX Process* (Apress, 2005).

as we gained experience in teaching it to clients, it became obvious that Jacobson's approach (use cases, robustness diagrams, and sequence diagrams) really worked pretty well.

In fact *it continually amazed us how well it worked on a wider and wider range of projects*. Experience in teaching the process convinced us that the "missing link" between requirements and design was the robustness diagram, and when UML was created and this diagram got relegated to an obscure appendix in the UML specification, we were seriously concerned that it would become a lost art form.

Our training business was given a bit of a boost when UML came into existence, as suddenly a lot more people were interested in how to do OOAD using a combined Jacobson/Rumbaugh/Booch approach, while our tools business (being Macintosh-based) didn't fare as well.

So ICONIX became a training company instead of a tools company, and, as our experience delivering training grew, there eventually came an opportunity to write a book: *Use Case Driven Object Modeling* (UCDOM), which I wrote with Kendall Scott. One of the reviewers of that book, Greg Wilson of *Dr. Dobbs Journal*, suggested that we write an example-intensive companion workbook, which we did. *Applying Use Case Driven Object Modeling* (AUCDOM), built around the Internet Bookstore example, was published a few years later.

The Truth About Disambiguation

Meanwhile, we continued to deliver training, year after year, and (as far as we could tell) our clients continued to succeed with it. At least, they kept hiring us back to teach additional classes, which was the best metric we could think of for judging this.

OO technologies such as CORBA and COM appeared on the scene, followed by Java, DCOM, EJBs, C#, and .NET, and our use case–driven approach just kept right on working without skipping a beat. Occasionally we'd sit back and ponder why it hadn't broken, and it seemed like we (following in Ivar Jacobson's footsteps) had hit on a systematic approach that provided the answers to some fundamentally important questions that addressed the issue of how to get from use cases to code. This approach involved things like understanding all the scenarios and user interactions (both sunny- and rainy-day scenarios) before trying to do design; taking a little bit of extra time to disambiguate the behavior requirements before attacking detailed design issues; and focusing on "object discovery" first and "behavior allocation" (assigning operations to classes) later.

As the years went by and the number of training classes grew from dozens to hundreds, it became increasingly obvious that the notion of *disambiguating behavior requirements using robustness diagrams* was one of the most important "fundamental truths" that had emerged from Jacobson's work.

We can state that fundamental truth as follows: *one of the main reasons that programmers get frustrated by attempts to bring analysis and design (and especially use cases) into their projects is that they are generally given vague and ambiguous requirements to design against*. And the reason for so much ambiguity in use cases is that so many of the books and gurus out there preach "abstract, essential, technology-free, and implementation-independent" as the right way to write use cases.

To carry it one small step further, I'll make the following claim: if you hand a programmer an abstract, technology-free, implementation-independent, "essential" use case, that programmer will find the use case to be vague, ambiguous, incomplete, and therefore incorrect.

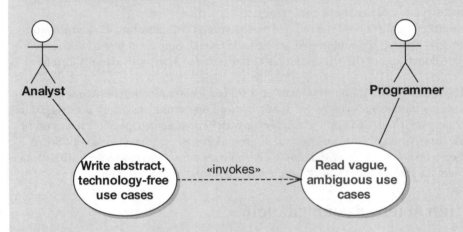

FOOTLOOSE AND TECHNOLOGY-FREE

Without disambiguation, analysts write "essential, abstract, technology-free, and implementation-independent" use cases. The programmers who must read these use cases are, from their perspective, reading "vague, ambiguous, incomplete, and incorrect" use cases.

These use cases don't have enough detail to allow programmers to get to code while driving the OO design from the use cases. So, the use case–driven process doesn't work very well without robustness analysis (a technique we describe in detail in this book).

ICONIX Process seems to resonate better with programmers than many other approaches to use cases and UML/OOAD because it actually *forces the use cases into concrete, tangible, and specific statements of required system behavior* that programmers can deal with efficiently. If there's a secret to all of this, that's it.

What's New

I took a writing detour for a few years (while continuing to deliver training in ICONIX Process) and Matt Stephens and I wrote *Extreme Programming Refactored: The Case Against XP*[2] and *Agile Modeling with ICONIX Process*[3] for Apress. Matt and I discovered that we work pretty well together, so he's joined me for the current effort. Meanwhile, *Use Case Driven Object Modeling* continues to sell and reached somewhere around 45,000 copies, including Chinese, Japanese, and Korean editions the last time I checked.

When we decided to do an update, we determined that there were a number of things that we could do that might justify a new edition (aka this book), including the following:

---

2. See www.softwarereality.com/ExtremeProgrammingRefactored.jsp.

3. See www.softwarereality.com/AgileDevelopment.jsp.

- Merge UCDOM and AUCDOM into a single title, all based around the Internet Bookstore example

- Add student exercises, with the idea that some universities might start using the book as a text

- Create "top 10 to-do" lists, in addition to the "top 10 error" lists we already had

- Carry the Internet Bookstore forward all the way through code and test

- Update the process with a few new tricks we've learned over the years, and fully leverage some advances in modeling tools

- Update the book to be current with the new UML 2.0 specification (and with Ivar Jacobson's new ideas on aspect-oriented programming [AOP])

As you'll see, these goals have resulted in a typical chapter structure that's in three parts: "Theory" (the process explained, using the Internet Bookstore as a running example), "Practice" (workbook exercises), and "More Practice" (student exercises). Matt went ahead and implemented a small Internet bookstore in Java, complete with unit tests driven from the use cases, which has allowed us to extend the book both in breadth and depth over the original titles (thanks, Matt).

We think that we've improved upon the original books in a number of ways, and we hope that you agree and like the result.

Doug Rosenberg
ICONIX, www.iconixsw.com

Introduction

The difference between "theory" and "practice" is that in theory there is no difference between theory and practice, but in practice, there is.

Doug has been using this phrase to open each and every training class for so long now that he's forgotten where he first heard it. Matt did some research and found that it's commonly credited to a Jan L. A. van de Snepscheut, who, in addition to having a wonderful name, was quite a distinguished professor at Caltech.[4]

Matt also found the quote attributed to Yogi Berra, who said, "In theory there is no difference between theory and practice. In practice there is."[5] This makes us wonder if Professor Snepscheut might have been a baseball fan, or if Yogi made a practice of attending lectures at Caltech in the off-season, but no matter—they were both right.

Regardless of who said it first, we like to apply this statement to UML modeling, because, to be blunt, **UML is way too big**. A project trying to ingest all of UML into its working practices resembles a python that has just swallowed a pig. It's going to take an awfully long time to digest, and your project probably can't afford it.

The Unified Modeling Language User Guide by Grady Booch, James Rumbaugh, and Ivar Jacobson (Addison-Wesley, 1998) tells us that "**you can do 80% of your modeling with 20% of the UML**" somewhere after page 400.[6] They would have saved the industry many millions (billions?) of dollars and horrific cases of analysis paralysis (see the upcoming sidebar titled "The Mysterious Case of Analysis Paralysis") if they had said that in the Introduction, but they didn't. To compound the felony, **they never tell us which 20% of UML is the useful part**.

Most people that we meet *usually* want to apply UML in the up-front stages of their project. And most of them *usually* want to start their analysis process with use cases. So, in our search for the **"minimal, yet sufficient" core subset** of UML, we focus on the question, **How do you get from use cases to code?**

So, in *theory*, everything in the UML is useful, but in *practice*, a whole lot of people and projects need to know how to drive an OO software design from use cases. And they also need to know which diagrams from the UML directly help to accomplish this.

This book explains the minimalist, core subset of UML and the thought process behind using it to drive OO software designs from use cases (collectively referred to as ICONIX Process), with an eye toward the practical as opposed to the theoretical. We hope the journey will be both informative and entertaining.

---

4. Read Edgser W. Djikstra's "In Memoriam" for Professor Snepscheut at www.cs.utexas.edu/users/EWD/transcriptions/EWD11xx/EWD1177.html.

5. More Yogi-isms can be found here: http://en.wikiquote.org/wiki/Yogi_Berra. Yogi also said, "It's tough to make predictions, especially about the future," which clearly applies to software cost estimation, and "It was hard to have a conversation with anyone; there were so many people talking," which is applicable to the "all the programmers in one big room" XP working environment.

6. See page 431 of the first edition.

THE MYSTERIOUS CASE OF ANALYSIS PARALYSIS

It was a blustery, cold, rainy night at our flat on Baker Street. The howl of the wind whipping raindrops against the windows could be heard over Holmes' violin as I read the paper in front of the fireplace. Mrs. Hudson had just cleared away the dishes from our late supper of pork pie and beans, when Holmes suddenly paused in the aria he was playing, sat bolt upright in his chair, and exclaimed, "Watson, the game's afoot!"

A few moments later, our good friend Inspector Lestrade from Scotland Yard clattered up the stairs and burst in the doorway, exclaiming, "Thank goodness you're home, Mr. Holmes—you've got to come quickly!"

"Come in, Lestrade. Pray take a seat by the fire and tell us every detail," said Holmes.

"They're all dead, Mr. Holmes, every one of them—the whole project's dead! And no signs of violence, not a mark on any of them!" said Lestrade.

"Who's dead?" I asked.

"The entire staff of Scotland Yard's new automated fingerprint recognition system," Lestrade responded. "The whole technical staff . . . sitting dead right in the conference room . . . as if they'd been frozen to their chairs!"

"Has anything been touched?" asked Holmes.

"No, I've left the strictest instructions that the conference room be completely sealed off until you could inspect it," said Lestrade.

"Most excellent," murmured Holmes. "You are learning, Lestrade. Come along, Watson." Grabbing our coats and hats, we hastened down to Lestrade's waiting hansom cab.

We arrived shortly at Scotland Yard and were escorted to the conference room, where we were confronted by a bizarre and grisly death scene. Still in their seats, but struck down by some mysterious assassin, was the entire staff of the new automated fingerprint recognition project. Holmes walked around the room excitedly, his highly trained senses alert for any sort of clue. He paused at the whiteboard, and again at a stack of UML books on the table.

"You see, Mr. Holmes, they're all dead, and not a mark on any of them. How could a whole project just die like that?" asked Lestrade.

"Elementary, my dear Lestrade. A clear case of that obscure poison from the Amazon jungle known as *analysisparalysisflagrantis*. Perhaps you've seen my monograph on the topic? No? Tut, tut," murmured Holmes.

"But Holmes, how can you be sure?" I queried. "All I can see is these UML books scattered around the table. Here's one called *Fully Dressed Use Cases: The Hallway Closet Approach* by Professor Moriarty. It suggests you should stuff everything you can think of into your use cases, just like you do with the hallway closet," I said.

"You *see*, Watson, but you do not *observe*. Notice the three-day growth of beard on all the corpses, and the scrawls of <<includes>> and <<extends>> on the whiteboards?" asked Holmes.

"Sure enough, Mr. Holmes," said Lestrade. "Even the women have grown beards!"

"Great Scott!" I exclaimed. "Gives me the shivers."

"Analysis paralysis, Watson," said Holmes. "The second fastest killer of software projects, after *DoingTheSimplestThingThatCanPossiblyWork*, and nearly as dangerous. It's caused by a lethal overdose of formality and strict adherence to the UML semantics documentation. Moriarty's been up to his evil tricks again. You see the hollow expressions on the victims' faces, caused by interminable meetings spent debating topics of marginal uselessness. The despair and the anguish. The feverish search for a practical approach instead of highbrow theories. And all so easily avoidable," he sighed. "Come along, Watson, we have arrived too late."

We headed homeward toward Baker Street and the fireplace.

Theory, in Practice

Each chapter in this book starts with the theory, and then explores said theory using the Internet Bookstore project. Over the course of the book, we'll demonstrate, in practice, the theory of getting from use cases to source code, using the Internet Bookstore as the main example throughout.

The practice doesn't stop there, though. This book also contains practical exercises of various types, which we describe here.

Workbook Exercises

It's been clear for some time that the process of reviewing models is critically important and not well understood by many folks. So, in this book, we dissect the design of the Internet Bookstore, step by step, in great detail. This involves showing many common mistakes, and then showing the relevant pieces of the model with their mistakes corrected.

We've been teaching workshops using the Internet Bookstore example for many years, and as a result we have a rich source of classroom UML models with real student mistakes in them. We've collected some of our favorite mistakes—that is, the kinds of mistakes we saw repeated over and over again—and turned these into workbook exercises that you can find at the end of many of the chapters.

The following aspects are common to each set of exercises:

- There's an example diagram, with some errors intentionally left in.

- There's **a corrected version of the diagram a few pages later**. Corrections to the errors presented on the associated "bad" page are explicitly indicated; **explanations of the mistakes are provided in detail**.

Student Exercises

At the end of most chapters in the "More Practice" section, you'll find student exercises to help you to test whether you truly "got" what the chapter is about. These exercises are in the form of more traditional numbered questions, and can thus be assigned as tasks for students.

For this reason, we don't provide the answers to these exercises in the book, although of course it's possible to *learn* the answers by reading and understanding the chapters! We do plan to provide some sort of "teacher's guide" material on the book's website, www.iconixprocess.com. The exact form of this teacher's guide has yet to be determined, so check the website for details.

Inline Exercises Within the Chapters

Getting things right first time is great, but getting something wrong initially and then **learning from your mistakes** is a *much* better way to learn. Because of the way your brain is wired, you end up with a deeper understanding of the subject that way.

As we develop the example Internet Bookstore application through the course of the book, we don't just show the right thing to do next. We slip some "deliberate" mistakes into the diagrams, and then discover and correct them later (usually in the review chapters). However, unlike the "More Practice" exercises (where we do reveal the errors, in great detail), we don't tell you precisely what the mistake is for these inline exercises. Instead, we provide a clue as to the nature of the error, and then invite you to scrutinize the diagram (and the relevant review chapter) and figure out what's wrong with it.

Trying to figure out what's wrong in the diagram is a good way to learn, but there's another element to this. Notice that we didn't say "the answer can be found on page 141" or "check the list of answers at the end of this chapter," as that would be too easy. An important part of the learning process is in searching through the next chapter, looking for the paragraph that reveals the answer. You'll be surprised how well you learn while you're hunting down the solution to a particular problem.

Cool set of premises, aren't they? We're not aware of another book like this one, and we're hoping you'll find it useful in your efforts to apply use case–driven object modeling with UML.

Top 10 Things People Who Use ICONIX Process Like About It

Each chapter in this book kicks off with a top 10 list of guidelines, and the first half of each chapter is structured around its top 10 list. For this Introduction, we've put together a list of the top 10 comments that we've heard from clients who've applied ICONIX Process on their own projects.

10. *The process uses a core subset of UML.*

(We'd rather learn 4 diagrams than 14 . . .)

9. *It actually gets me all the way to code.*

(I have 13 use case books on my shelf that don't get within 50 miles of code.)

8. *It's traceable from one step to the next.*

7. *It addresses both sunny- and rainy-day scenarios.*

(If another one of my programmers tells me they're "Doing The Simplest Thing That Could Possibly Work" [DTSTTCPW], I think I'm gonna scream.)

6. *It assumes that the requirements I'm initially given are vague, ambiguous, incomplete, and incorrect.*

(Have Doug and Matt actually met our business analysts?)

5. *It actually drives the OO design from the use cases.*

(I know RUP says that it's use case–driven, but I get lost somewhere around the Elaboration phase.)

4. *It works well in an "agile" (short iteration, small increment) environment.*

(I wish somebody would write a book on how to do Agile/ICONIX, though.)[7]

---

7. We did: *Agile Development with ICONIX Process* (Apress, 2005).

3. *It doesn't drown me in five-syllable buzzwords.*

(What about multiple polymorphic inheritance, anyway?)[8]

2. *It operates at a tangible level where the use cases talk about what the users are doing on the screens, and there are no huge use case templates.*

(In other words, the use cases aren't abstract, essential, technology-free, or implementation independent.)

1. *It's a practical approach that's been proven to work in the real world, on hundreds of projects.*

---

8. Although we do have fun making up new buzzwords and phrases, like "disintermangling dysfunctional requirements."

CHAPTER 1

Introduction to ICONIX Process

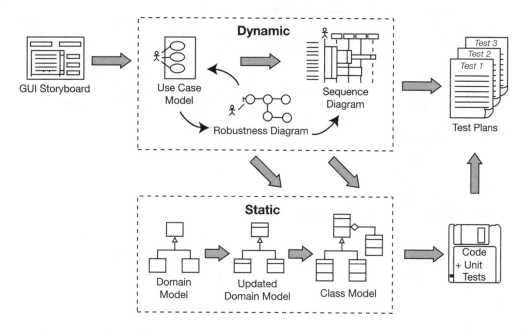

One process is much larger
And the other's way too small
And the full UML that OMG gives you
Is incomprehensible to all . . .

(Sing to the tune of "Go Ask Alice" by Jefferson Airplane)

In theory, every single aspect of the UML is potentially useful, but in practice, there never seems to be enough time to do modeling, analysis, and design. There's always pressure from management to jump to code, to start coding prematurely because progress on software projects tends to get measured by how much code exists. ICONIX Process, as shown in the chapter's opening figure, is a minimalist, streamlined approach that focuses on that area that lies in between use cases and code. Its emphasis is on what needs to happen at that point in the life cycle where you're starting out: you have a start on some use cases, and now you need to do good analysis and design.

WHEN TO USE A COOKBOOK

There's a growing misconception in software development that cookbook approaches to software development don't work. We agree with this to an extent, because analysis and programming are massive, highly complex fields, and the number of different software project types is roughly equal to the number of software projects. However, we firmly believe that analysis and design can—and in fact should—be a specific sequence of repeatable steps. These steps aren't set in stone (i.e., they can be tailored), but it helps to have them there. In a world filled with doubt and uncertainty, it's nice to have a clearly defined sequence of "how-to" steps to refer back to.

Way back in the pre-UML days when Doug first started teaching a unified Booch/Rumbaugh/Jacobson modeling approach (around 1992/1993), one of his early training clients encouraged him to "write a cookbook, because my people like following cookbook approaches." While many have claimed that it's impossible to codify object-oriented analysis and design (OOAD) practices into a simple, repeatable set of steps (and it probably isn't possible in its entirety), ICONIX Process probably comes as close as anything out there to a cookbook approach to OOAD.

While there's still room for significant flexibility within the approach (e.g., adding in state or activity diagrams), ICONIX Process lays down a simple, minimal set of steps that generally lead to pretty good results. These results have proven to be consistent and repeatable over the last 12 years.

ICONIX Process in Theory

In this section we provide an overview of ICONIX Process, showing how all the activities fit together. We'll start with a very high-level view—kind of an overview of the overview—and then we'll examine each activity in more detail. As you're walking through the overview, keep referring back to the process diagram at the start of this chapter, to see how each part fits into the overall process.

Overview: Getting from Use Cases to Source Code

The diagram at the start of this chapter gives an overview of ICONIX Process. (We'll repeat this diagram at the start of each chapter, with the relevant section of the diagram shown in red.) As you can see from the diagram, ICONIX Process is divided into *dynamic* and *static* workflows, which are highly iterative: you might go through one iteration of the whole process for a small batch of use cases (perhaps a couple of packages' worth, which isn't a huge amount given that each use case is only a couple of paragraphs), all the way to source code and unit tests. For this reason, ICONIX Process is well suited to agile projects, where swift feedback is needed on such factors as the requirements, the design, and estimates.

Let's walk through the steps that we'll cover in the course of this book. The items in red correspond with the subtitles in this section (pretty slick, huh?).

As with any project, at some stage early on you begin exploring and defining the requirements. Note that within each phase there's a degree of parallelism, so all the activities in the requirements definition phase go on sort of overlapped and interleaved until they're ready.

■Note There are many different types of requirements (e.g., nonfunctional requirements such as scalability). However, at a process level, we distinguish between *functional requirements* and *behavioral requirements*.

---

1. **REQUIREMENTS**

   a. Functional requirements: Define what the system should be capable of doing. Depending on how your project is organized, either you'll be involved in creating the functional requirements or the requirements will be "handed down from on high" by a customer or a team of business analysts.

   b. Domain modeling: Understand the problem space in unambiguous terms.

   c. Behavioral requirements: Define how the user and the system will interact (i.e., write the first-draft use cases). We recommend that you start with a GUI prototype (storyboarding the GUI) and identify all the use cases you're going to implement, or at least come up with a first-pass list of use cases, which you would reasonably expect to change as you explore the requirements in more depth.

   d. Milestone 1: Requirements Review: Make sure that the use case text matches the customer's expectations. Note that you might review the use cases in small batches, just prior to designing them.

Then in each iteration (i.e., for a small batch of use cases), you do the following.

2. **ANALYSIS/PRELIMINARY DESIGN**

   a. Robustness analysis: Draw a robustness diagram (an "object picture" of the steps in a use case), rewriting the use case text as you go.

   b. Update the domain model while you're writing the use case and drawing the robustness diagram. Here you will discover missing classes, correct ambiguities, and add attributes to the domain objects (e.g., identify that a Book object has a Title, Author, Synopsis, etc.).

   c. Name all the logical software functions (**controllers**) needed to make the use case work.

   d. Rewrite the first draft use cases.

3. Milestone 2: Preliminary Design Review (PDR)

4. **DETAILED DESIGN**

   a. Sequence diagramming: Draw a sequence diagram (one sequence diagram per use case) to show *in detail* how you're going to implement the use case. The primary function of sequence diagramming is to allocate behavior to your classes.

b. Update the domain model while you're drawing the sequence diagram, and add operations[1] to the domain objects. By this stage, the domain objects are really domain classes, or *entities*, and the domain model should be fast becoming a *static model*, or *class diagram*—a crucial part of your detailed design.

c. Clean up the static model.

5. Milestone 3: Critical Design Review (CDR)

6. IMPLEMENTATION

a. Coding/unit testing: Write the code and the unit tests. (Or, depending on your preferences, write the unit tests and then the code.[2])

b. Integration and scenario testing: Base the integration tests on the use cases, so that you're testing both the basic course and the alternate courses.

c. Perform a Code Review and Model Update to prepare for the next round of development work.

For most of the rest of this chapter, we describe these steps in a little more detail. Throughout the rest of the book, we describe these steps in *much* greater detail, and provide lots of examples and exercises to help you understand how best to apply them to your own project.

Requirements

Figure 1-1 shows the steps involved in defining the **behavioral requirements**—that is, drawing the initial domain model and writing the first-draft use cases.

The steps shown in Figure 1-1 are covered in Chapters 2, 3, and 4.

---

1. Also called methods, functions, or messages, depending which programming language you use.

2. For Test-Driven Development (TDD) fans, in Chapter 12 we illustrate a method of incorporating the "test first" approach into ICONIX Process. The result is essentially "Design-Driven Testing."

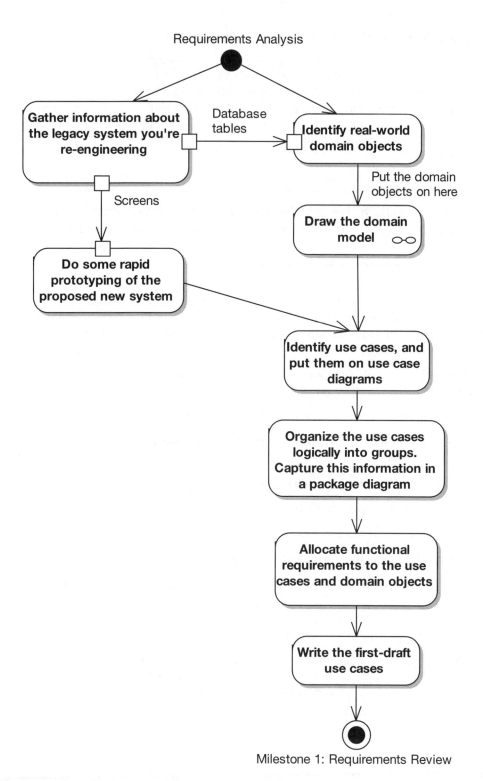

Figure 1-1. *Requirements analysis*

Functional Requirements (What Will the System Be Capable Of?)

Right at the start of the project, somebody (possibly a team of business analysts) will be talking to the customer, end users, and various project stakeholders, and that person (or team) will most likely create a big Microsoft Word document packed to the brim with functional requirements. This is an important document, but it's difficult to create a design from (or to create an accurate estimate from, for that matter), as it tends to be quite unstructured. (Even if every requirement is numbered in a big document-length list, that still doesn't quite count as being structured.)

■**Note** The initial stages of ICONIX Process involve creating a set of unambiguous behavioral requirements (use cases) that are "closer to the metal" than the functional requirements specification, and that *can* be easily designed from.

Creating functional requirements falls just slightly outside the scope of ICONIX Process, but we do offer some advice on the matter.[3] Probably the best way to describe our approach to requirements gathering is to list our **top 10 requirements gathering guidelines**. We describe these in more detail in Chapter 13.

10. Use a modeling tool that supports linkage and traceability between requirements and use cases.

9. Link requirements to use cases by dragging and dropping.

8. Avoid **dysfunctional requirements** by separating functional details from your behavioral specification.

7. Write at least one test case for each requirement.

6. Treat requirements as first-class citizens in the model.

5. Distinguish between different types of requirements.

4. Avoid the "big monolithic document" syndrome.

3. Create estimates from the use case scenarios, not from the functional requirements.

2. Don't be afraid of examples when writing functional requirements.

1. Don't make your requirements a technical fashion statement.

With the functional requirements written (whether by your team or by somebody else), you'll really want to do some additional analysis work, to create a set of **behavioral requirements** (use cases) from which you can create a high-level, preliminary design.

---

3. In Chapter 13, we show how to link your use cases back to the original requirements.

Domain Modeling

Domain modeling is the task of building a project glossary, or a dictionary of terms used in your project (e.g., an Internet bookstore project would include domain objects such as Book, Customer, Order, and Order Item). Its purpose is to make sure everyone on the project understands the problem space in unambiguous terms. The domain model for a project defines the scope and forms the foundation on which to build your use cases. The domain model also provides a common vocabulary to enable clear communication among members of a project team. Expect early versions of your domain model to be wrong; as you explore each use case, you'll "firm up" the domain model as you go.

Here are our **top 10 domain modeling guidelines**. We describe these in more detail in Chapter 2.

10. Focus on real-world (problem domain) objects.

9. Use generalization (is-a) and aggregation (has-a) relationships to show how the objects relate to each other.

8. Limit your initial domain modeling efforts to a couple of hours.

7. Organize your classes around key abstractions in the problem domain.

6. Don't mistake your domain model for a data model.

5. Don't confuse an object (which represents a single instance) with a database table (which contains a collection of things).

4. Use the domain model as a project glossary.

3. Do your initial domain model before you write your use cases, to avoid name ambiguity.

2. Don't expect your final class diagrams to precisely match your domain model, but there should be some resemblance between them.

1. Don't put screens and other GUI-specific classes on your domain model.

Once you have your first-pass domain model, you can use it to write the use cases—that is, to create your **behavioral requirements**, which we introduce in the next section.

Behavioral Requirements (How Will the User and the System Interact?)

ICONIX Process is a scenario-based approach; the primary mechanism for decomposing and modeling the system is on a scenario-by-scenario basis. But when you use ICONIX Process, your goal is to produce an object-oriented design that you can code from. Therefore, you need to link the scenarios to objects. You do this by writing the use cases using the domain model that you created in the previous step.

Storyboarding the GUI

Behavior requirements detail the user's actions and the system's responses to those actions. For the vast majority of software systems, this interaction between user and system takes place via screens, windows, or pages. When you're exploring the behavioral requirements, you capture the usage scenarios in narrative text form in the use cases, and these narratives have come from detailed conversations with customers and end users.

It's notoriously difficult for us humans to picture a proposed system in our mind's eye. So quite often it's easier for the customers and end users to relate to a visual aid, which often takes the form of a sequence of screens. These can be simple line drawings on paper, a Power-Point slide show that sequences through the screens, an HTML prototype with core functionality left out—the exact form doesn't matter much. What's important is that they present a sequence of screens as they will appear to the users within the context of the usage scenarios being modeled.

It's also important that the screen mockups include details about the various buttons, menus, and other action-oriented parts of the UI. It's amazing how often a use case done without this sort of accompanying visual aid will omit alternate course behavior for events like "user clicks Cancel button," and how much better the use cases become when accompanied by a UI storyboard.

Use Case Modeling

Use cases describe the way the user will interact with the system and how the system will respond. Here are our **top 10 use case modeling guidelines**. We describe these in more detail in Chapter 3.

10. Follow the two-paragraph rule.

9. Organize your use cases with actors and use case diagrams.

8. Write your use cases in active voice.

7. Write your use case using an event/response flow, describing both sides of the user/system dialogue.

6. Use GUI storyboards, prototypes, screen mockups, etc.

5. Remember that your use case is really a runtime behavior specification.

4. Write the use case in the context of the object model.

3. Write your use cases using a noun-verb-noun sentence structure.

2. Reference domain classes by name.

1. Reference boundary classes (e.g., screens) by name.

Milestone 1: Requirements Review

Right at the end of Figure 1-1, you'll see the Requirements Review milestone. This vital step ensures that the requirements are sufficiently well understood by both the development team and the customer/users/project stakeholders.

Here are our **top 10 requirements review guidelines**. We describe these in more detail in Chapter 4.

10. Make sure your domain model describes at least 80% of the most important abstractions (i.e., real-world objects) from your problem domain, in nontechnical language that your end users can understand.

9. Make sure your domain model shows the is-a (generalization) and has-a (aggregation) relationships between the domain objects.

8. Make sure your use cases describe both basic and alternate courses of action, in active voice.

7. If you have lists of functional requirements (i.e., "shall" statements), make sure these are not absorbed into and "intermangled" with the active voice use case text.[4]

6. Make sure you've organized your use cases into packages and that each package has at least one use case diagram.

5. Make sure your use cases are written in the context of the object model.

4. Put your use cases in the context of the user interface.

3. Supplement your use case descriptions with some sort of storyboard, line drawing, screen mockup, or GUI prototype.

2. Review the use cases, domain model, and screen mockups/GUI prototypes with end users, stakeholders, and marketing folks, in addition to more technical members of your staff.

1. Structure the review around our "eight easy steps to a better use case" (see Chapter 4).

Once the requirements review is complete, you can move on to the **preliminary design** stage.

Analysis/Preliminary Design

Analysis is about **building the right system**. Design is about **building the system right**. Preliminary design is an intermediate step between analysis and design.

Preliminary design explicitly recognizes something that many people recognize implicitly:

You usually can't fully understand the requirements that you're dealing with unless you do some exploratory design.

Figure 1-2 (which follows on from Figure 1-1) shows the **preliminary design** steps.

---

4. In Chapter 13, we introduce the term "intermangled" to describe use case text that has had functional requirements text mangled into it.

Milestone 1: Requirements Review

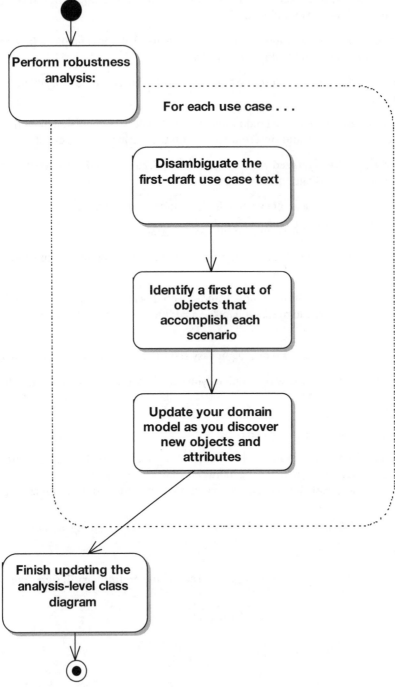

Figure 1-2. *Analysis/preliminary design*

The preliminary design step (aka **robustness analysis**) involves doing the exploratory design you need to understand the requirements, refining and removing ambiguity from (aka disambiguating) those requirements as a result of the exploratory design, and linking the behavior requirements (use case scenarios) to the objects (domain model).

The steps shown in Figure 1-2 are covered in Chapters 5, 6, and 7.

Robustness Analysis

To get from use cases to detailed design (and then to code), you need to link your use cases to objects. Robustness analysis helps you to bridge the gap between analysis and design by doing exactly that. It's a way of analyzing your use case text and identifying a first-guess set of objects for each use case.

Here are our **top 10 robustness analysis guidelines**. We describe these in more detail in Chapter 5.

10. Paste the use case text directly onto your robustness diagram.

9. Take your entity classes from the domain model, and add any that are missing.

8. Expect to rewrite (disambiguate) your use case while drawing the robustness diagram.

7. Make a boundary object for each screen, and name your screens unambiguously.

6. Remember that controllers are only occasionally **real control objects**; they are typically **logical software functions**.

5. Don't worry about the direction of the arrows on a robustness diagram.

4. It's OK to drag a use case onto a robustness diagram if it's invoked from the parent use case.

3. The robustness diagram represents a preliminary conceptual design of a use case, not a literal detailed design.

2. Boundary and entity classes on a robustness diagram will generally become object instances on a sequence diagram, while controllers will become messages.

1. Remember that a robustness diagram is an "object picture" of a use case, whose purpose is to force refinement of both use case text and the object model.

With the preliminary design complete, your use cases should now be thoroughly disambiguated and thus written in the context of the domain model. The domain model itself should have helped to eliminate common issues such as duplicate names for the same item, and the classes on the domain model should also have attributes assigned to them (but not operations, yet).

In theory you should now be ready to start the detailed design, but in practice, it really helps to perform a quick **Preliminary Design Review** (PDR) first.

Milestone 2: Preliminary Design Review

The Preliminary Design Review (PDR) session helps you to make sure that the robustness diagrams, the domain model, and the use case text all match each other. This review is the "gateway" between the preliminary design and detailed design stages, for each package of use cases.

Here are our **top 10 PDR guidelines**. We describe these in more detail in Chapter 6.

10. For each use case, make sure the use case text matches the robustness diagram, using the highlighter test.

9. Make sure that all the entities on all robustness diagrams appear within the updated domain model.

8. Make sure that you can trace data flow between entity classes and screens.

7. Don't forget the alternate courses, and don't forget to write behavior for each of them when you find them.

6. Make sure each use case covers both sides of the dialogue between user and system.

5. Make sure you haven't violated the syntax rules for robustness analysis,

4. Make sure that this review includes both nontechnical (customer, marketing team, etc.) and technical folks (programmers).

3. Make sure your use cases are in the context of the object model and in the context of the GUI.

2. Make sure your robustness diagrams (and the corresponding use case text) don't attempt to show the same level of detail that will be shown on the sequence diagrams (i.e., don't try to do detailed design yet).

1. Follow our "six easy steps" to a better preliminary design (see Chapter 6).

With this review session complete, you can now be confident that the diagrams and the use case text match each other, and that both are complete and correctly represent the desired system behavior. It should now be a relatively straightforward matter to create the **detailed design**.

Detailed Design

Detailed design is about building the system right. We hope that by the time you get to this point, you have a pretty good understanding of what the "right system" is, because you've worked hard to develop that understanding. So now you're worrying about efficiency in terms of execution times, network loading, and memory footprint, and you're concerned with reusability of code where possible.

Figure 1-3 shows the steps involved in **detailed design**.

The steps shown in Figure 1-3 are covered in Chapters 8 and 9.

Milestone 2: Preliminary Design Review

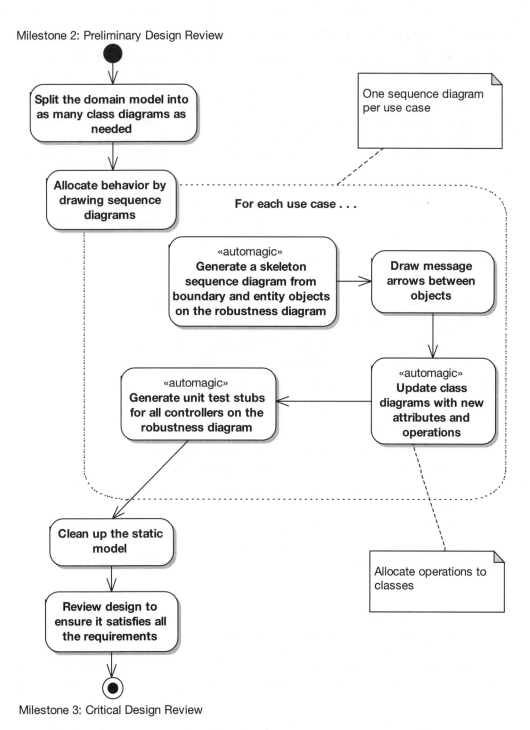

Milestone 3: Critical Design Review

Figure 1-3. *Detailed design*

Sequence Diagramming (Allocate Behavior to Classes)

ICONIX Process uses the **sequence diagram** as the main vehicle for exploring the detailed design of a system on a scenario-by-scenario basis.

In object-oriented design, a large part of building the system right is concerned with finding an optimal allocation of functions to classes (aka behavior allocation). The essence of this is drawing message arrows on sequence diagrams and allowing a modeling tool to automatically assign an operation to the class of the target object that receives the runtime message.

Here are our **top 10 sequence diagramming guidelines**. We describe these in more detail in Chapter 8.

10. Understand **why** you're drawing a sequence diagram, to get the most out of it.

9. Do a sequence diagram for every use case, with both basic and alternate courses on the same diagram.

8. Start your sequence diagram from the boundary classes, entity classes, actors, and use case text that result from robustness analysis.

7. Use the sequence diagram to show how the behavior of the use case (i.e., all the controllers from the robustness diagram) is accomplished by the objects.

6. Make sure your use case text maps to the messages being passed on the sequence diagram. Try to line up the text and message arrows.

5. Don't spend too much time worrying about focus of control.

4. Assign operations to classes while drawing messages. Most visual modeling tools support this capability.

3. Review your class diagrams frequently while you're assigning operations to classes, to make sure all the operations are on the appropriate classes.

2. **Prefactor** your design on sequence diagrams before coding.

1. Clean up the static model before proceeding to the CDR.

By now, you're almost ready to begin coding. You'll need to perform a Critical Design Review (CDR) first; but before that, it pays dividends to revisit the static model and clean it up.

Cleaning Up the Static Model

Take a long, hard look at your static model, with a view toward tidying up the design, resolving real-world design issues, identifying useful design patterns that can be factored in to improve the design, and so on. This should at least be done as a final step before proceeding to the CDR, but you can start thinking at this level in the design *before* drawing the sequence diagram.

By this stage, you should have an extremely well-factored design that works within the real-world constraints of your project's requirements, application framework design, deployment topology, and so forth. There's just one last stop before you begin coding: the CDR.

Milestone 3: Critical Design Review

The CDR helps you to achieve three important goals, before you begin coding for the current batch of use cases:

- Ensure that the "how" of detailed design matches up with the "what" specified in your requirements.

- Review the quality of your design.

- Check for continuity of messages on your sequence diagrams (iron out "leaps of logic" in the design).

Here are our **top 10 CDR guidelines**. We describe these in more detail in Chapter 9.

10. Make sure the sequence diagram matches the use case text.

9. Make sure (yes, again) that each sequence diagram accounts for both basic and alternate courses of action.

8. Make sure that operations have been allocated to classes appropriately.

7. Review the classes on your class diagrams to ensure they all have an appropriate set of attributes and operations.

6. If your design reflects the use of patterns or other detailed implementation constructs, check that these details are reflected on the sequence diagram.

5. Trace your functional (and nonfunctional) requirements to your use cases and classes to ensure you have covered them all.

4. Make sure your programmers "sanity check" the design and are confident that they can build it and that it will work as intended.

3. Make sure all your attributes are typed correctly, and that return values and parameter lists on your operations are complete and correct.

2. Generate the code headers for your classes, and inspect them closely.

1. Review the test plan for your release.

If you've gone through the detailed design for each use case and performed a CDR (as described in Chapter 9), then your design really should be fighting-fit now, and easily ready for coding.

Implementation

Figure 1-4 shows the steps involved in **coding and testing** (i.e., **implementation**).

Once you've made the effort to drive a model from use cases through detailed design, it would be lunacy to disregard the model and just start coding totally independent of the model you've produced.

Similarly, your modeling should provide a basis for knowing exactly what software functions will need to be unit tested, so you can drive the unit tests from the model in a similar manner to generating code from the detailed class diagrams.

Milestone 3: Critical Design Review

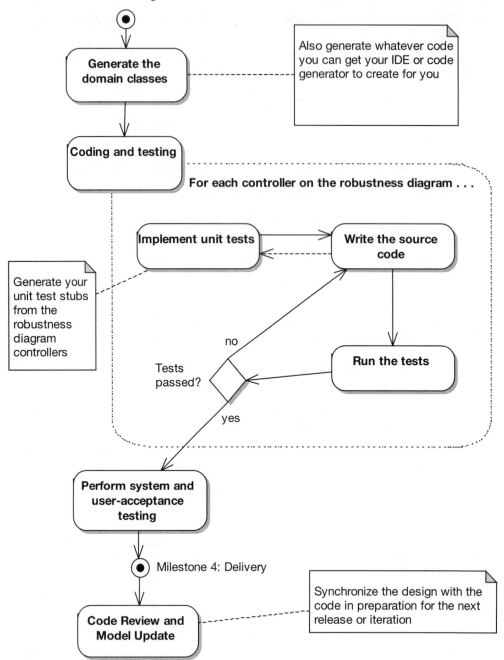

Figure 1-4. *Implementation*

Technology available in today's modeling tools (at least the ones we use) also provides for easy and convenient linkage between the UML model and the coding environment. We've extended ICONIX Process to leverage this exciting new technology.

The steps shown in Figure 1-4 are covered in Chapters 10, 11, and 12.

Implementation (Coding)

Here are our **top 10 implementation guidelines**. We describe these in more detail in Chapter 10.

10. Be sure to drive the code directly from the design.

9. If coding reveals the design to be wrong in some way, change it. But also review the process.

8. Hold regular code inspections.

7. Always question the framework's design choices.

6. Don't let framework issues take over from business issues.

5. If the code starts to get out of control, hit the brakes and revisit the design.

4. Keep the design and the code in sync.

3. Focus on unit testing while implementing the code.

2. Don't overcomment your code (it makes your code less maintainable and more difficult to read).

1. Remember to implement the alternate courses as well as the basic courses.

Unit testing is an important (and integral) part of implementation.

Unit Testing

While coding, you should also be writing unit tests that are tied into the use cases. These tests allow you to prove, in an automated and repeatable way, that the system behavior described in each use case has been implemented correctly. Essentially, you're testing all the software functions that you identified during robustness analysis.

Here are our **top 10 unit testing guidelines**. We describe these in more detail in Chapter 12.

10. Adopt a "testing mind-set" wherein every bug found is a victory and not a defeat. If you find (and fix) the bug in testing, the users won't find it in the released product.

9. Understand the different kinds of testing, and when and why you'd use each one.

8. When unit testing, create one or more unit tests for each controller on each robustness diagram.

7. For real-time systems, use the elements on state diagrams as the basis for test cases.

6. Do requirement-level verification (i.e., check that each requirement you have identified is accounted for).

5. Use a traceability matrix to assist in requirement verification.

4. Do scenario-level acceptance testing for each use case.

3. Expand threads in your test scenarios to cover a complete path through the appropriate part of the basic course plus each alternate course in your scenario testing.

2. Use a testing framework like JUnit to store and organize your unit tests.

1. Keep your unit tests fine-grained.

As we discuss in Chapter 12, other types of testing are performed on different project artifacts and at different stages in the project—in particular, **integration/scenario testing**.

Expand Threads for Integration and Scenario Testing

This activity involves expanding the sunny day/rainy day threads of the use cases. The integration tests come from the use cases, in the form of testing the following:

1. The entire sunny-day scenario (the basic course)

2. Part of the sunny-day scenario plus each individual rainy day scenario (the alternate courses)

For example, a use case with three alternate courses would need (at minimum) four integration test scenarios: one for the basic course and one for each alternate course (including whichever part of the basic course goes along with it).

With the code and tests written for a particular use case (and with the tests passing!), it's important to perform a **Code Review and Model Update**.

Code Review and Model Update

The main purpose of the Code Review and Model Update milestone is to synchronize the code and the model before the next iteration begins. This ongoing effort to keep the design tight prevents entropy, or **code rot**, from setting in as more and more functionality is added to a complex system. Once you've completed this milestone, the design and the code should be in a very good state, ready for development to begin on the next use case (or batch of use cases).

Here are our **top 10 Code Review and Model Update guidelines**. We describe these in more detail in Chapter 11.

10. Prepare for the review, and make sure all participants have read the relevant review material prior to the meeting.

9. Create a high-level list of items to review, based on the use cases.

8. If necessary, break down each item in the list into a smaller checklist.

7. Review code at several different levels.

6. Gather data during the review, and use it to accumulate boilerplate checklists for future reviews.

5. Follow up the review with a list of action points e-mailed to all people involved.

4. Try to focus on error detection during the review, not error correction.

3. Use an integrated code/model browser that hot-links your modeling tool to your code editor.

2. Keep it "just formal enough" with checklists and follow-up action lists, but don't overdo the bureaucracy.

1. Remember that it's also a Model Update session, not just a Code Review.

That about wraps up our overview of ICONIX Process. It probably seems as if there's a lot of information to absorb, but the process itself is actually very straightforward once you understand exactly why each step is performed.

Extensions to ICONIX Process

Although it's been used in hundreds of large-scale IT projects, the core ICONIX Process has stayed much the same in the last 10 to 15 years. However, in *Agile Development with ICONIX Process* (Apress, 2005), we published some extensions to the core process. These extensions include the following:

- Performing persona analysis
- Supplementing the process with Test-Driven Development (TDD)
- Driving test cases from the analysis model

Persona Analysis

Persona analysis as an interaction design technique makes actors and use cases more concrete and tangible for project stakeholders. Many people find actors and use cases too abstract, so this approach addresses the issue head-on.

A *persona* is a description of a fictional person: a prototypical target user. The person is given a name and a brief description of his or her job, goals and aspirations, level of ability—anything that might be relevant to how that person uses and perceives the product you're designing. You'd then write *interaction scenarios* (a form of use case that describes in more detail the user's motivations behind his or her interaction with the system), based around the persona you've defined. Using ICONIX Process, you would write a few detailed interaction scenarios to make sure the system is correctly focused on your target user, and then proceed to write the more minimal, ICONIX-style use cases for the system as a whole.

Test-Driven Development (TDD)

TDD is an increasingly popular method of designing software by writing unit tests. The design effectively "evolves" as you write the code. Teams have begun to realize that TDD by itself can be a long-winded design process (to say the least) and benefits greatly from some initial, up-front design modeling. ICONIX Process is a prime candidate for this, because its *robustness analysis* technique works well in collaborative design workshops with teams modeling on a whiteboard (or on a CASE tool hooked up to a projector).

Driving Test Cases from the Analysis Model

It makes sense to link your models as closely as possible to testing, and in fact to drive the testing effort from your use case–driven models. This extension to ICONIX Process drives the identification of test cases directly from the robustness diagram, in a parallel manner to the way we drive the creation of a skeleton sequence diagram from a robustness diagram. In short, the nouns (Entity and Boundary objects) from the robustness diagram become object instances on the sequence diagram, and the verbs (controllers) get test cases created for them. We discuss this process in depth in Chapter 12.

ICONIX Process in Practice: The Internet Bookstore Example

Starting in the next chapter, we're going to be following a running example, which we call the Internet Bookstore, through each phase of the process we've just outlined for you.

When we get to the sequence diagramming (detailed design) stage in Chapter 8, we'll begin to implement the Internet Bookstore using the Spring Framework, a popular Java enterprise application framework. This book isn't primarily about Spring, so we won't dwell on the technical details regarding Spring itself (although we will suggest further resources, both print and online). Instead we'll focus on the ways in which ICONIX Process is used to create well-designed source code for a realistic web-based application.

The techniques we describe in this book should still be more than relevant to users of other application frameworks and other object-oriented programming languages.

The use cases we'll be working through and the classes we'll discover exist to satisfy certain requirements that our customer (the fictional owner of the bookstore we're going to build) has specified. We'll cover these requirements in Chapter 2, where we show how to derive our first-pass version of the **domain model** from the requirements.

Summary

In this chapter we introduced ICONIX Process and described its background and the driving principles behind it. We also described its key features and walked through the process, from use cases to code.

In the next chapter, we describe in detail the first major stage of ICONIX Process: domain modeling.

PART 1

■ ■ ■

Requirements Definition

CHAPTER 2

■■■

Domain Modeling

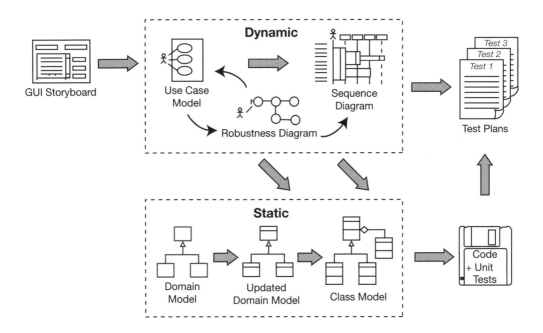

Imagine if everyone on your team was talking a different language. Let's say you're speaking German, your teammate is speaking French, and someone else is speaking Swahili. Every time someone speaks, people glean whatever slivers of meaning they can, and then nod as if they've understood perfectly. They then walk away with a completely wrong interpretation of what the speaker was really trying to say.

In virtually all IT projects, the problem of miscommunication is rampant, but it's rarely noticed because everybody *thinks* they're speaking the same language. They're not. One person says "book review" and some people interpret this as meaning "editorial review" (a review written by an editorial team), whereas others might interpret it as meaning "customer review" (a review written by a customer and posted to the site). The results can be—and often are— catastrophic, as the system gets developed with everyone interpreting the requirements and the design differently.

The domain model is a live, collaborative artifact. It is refined and updated throughout the project, so that it always reflects the current understanding of the problem space.

In this chapter we'll look at domain modeling, which aims to solve the problem of miscommunication on projects by establishing a common vocabulary that maps out the problem space.

The 10,000-Foot View

Domain modeling is the task of building a project glossary, or a dictionary of terms used in your project. The domain model for a project defines the scope and forms the foundation on which to build your use cases. A domain model also provides a common vocabulary to enable clear communication between members of a project team. So even though this book is about use case–driven development, we have to begin at the beginning with domain modeling.

What's a Domain Model?

As just mentioned, a domain model is, essentially, a project glossary: a "live" dictionary of all the terms used in your project. But a domain model is better than a project glossary, because it shows graphically how all these different terms relate to each other. In practice it's a simplified class diagram, with lines drawn between the different classes (*domain objects*) to show how they relate to each other. The domain model shows aggregation and generalization relationships (*has-a* and *is-a relationships*) between the domain classes.

Figure 2-1 shows an excerpt from a domain model. Don't worry about the details for now—our purpose in presenting this figure is just so you can visualize what it is we're going to be talking about the rest of the chapter.

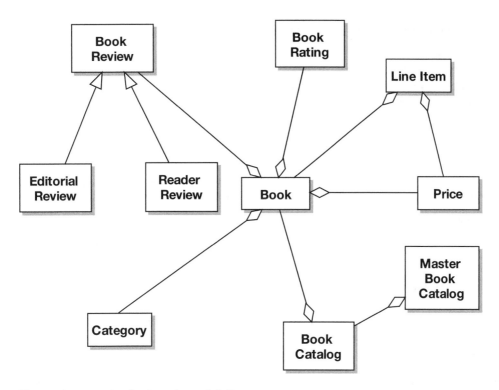

Figure 2-1. *Example of a domain model diagram*

Why Start with the Domain Model Instead of Use Cases?

You'll find that it really helps if you take a quick stab at a domain model right at the start of a project. When you write use cases, it's tempting to make them abstract, high-level, vague, and ambiguous. In fact, some gurus even recommend that you write your use cases this way (only they call it "abstract," "essential," "technology-free," etc.)—but more about that later. Our advice is pretty much the opposite: your use case text should be grounded in reality, and it should be very close to the system that you'll be designing. In other words, the use cases should be written in the context of the object model (i.e., the use case text needs to reference the domain objects by name). By doing this, you'll be able to tie together the static and dynamic parts of the model, which is crucial if you want your analysis and design effort to be driven forward by your use cases.

So before you write your use cases, you need to come up with a first-pass attempt at a domain model. The domain model forms the foundation of the static part of your model, while the use cases are the foundation of the dynamic part. The static part describes structure; the dynamic part describes behavior.

■**Note** At the analysis level, the terms "object" and "class" are sometimes used interchangeably (an object is a runtime instance of a class). However, when we get to the more grounded design level, the distinction between objects and classes becomes more important.

Domain Modeling in Theory

As you read this book, you'll see that each chapter follows a familiar pattern. We start by describing an aspect of modeling "in theory," using our Internet Bookstore example to illustrate the points we make. Then we cover it "in practice," showing typical modeling errors and how to correct them, and presenting a number of exercises. Finally, we round off each chapter with "more practice."

Top 10 Domain Modeling Guidelines

The principles discussed in this chapter can be summed up as a list of guidelines. Our top 10 list follows.

   10. Focus on real-world (problem domain) objects.

   9. Use generalization (is-a) and aggregation (has-a) relationships to show how the objects relate to each other.

   8. Limit your initial domain modeling efforts to a couple of hours.

   7. Organize your classes around key abstractions in the problem domain.

   6. Don't mistake your domain model for a data model.

   5. Don't confuse an object (which represents a single instance) with a database table (which contains a collection of things).

   4. Use the domain model as a project glossary.

   3. Do your initial domain model before you write your use cases, to avoid name ambiguity.

   2. Don't expect your final class diagrams to precisely match your domain model, but there should be some resemblance between them.

   1. Don't put screens and other GUI-specific classes on your domain model.

   Let's look at each of these in more detail.

10. Focus on Real-World Objects

When creating a domain model, be sure to focus on real-world objects within the problem domain. Try to organize your software architecture around what the real world looks like. The real world tends to change less frequently than software requirements.

CLASS NOTATION

Figure 2-2 shows two different types of class notation. On a full-blown detailed class diagram, you'd use the version on the left, with attributes and operations. However, during the initial domain modeling effort, it's too early to allocate these parts of a class. It's better to use the simpler notation shown on the right. This version only shows the domain class's name.

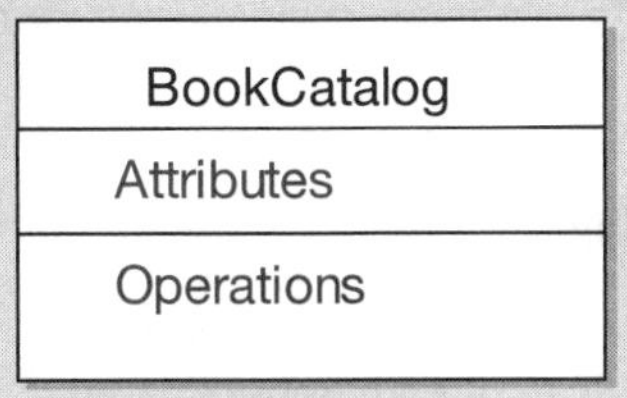

BookCatalog
Attributes
Operations

BookCatalog

Figure 2-2. *Class notations*

9. Use Generalization (Is-a) and Aggregation (Has-a) Relationships

Over time, you'll flesh out your domain model with new domain classes, as and when you identify them. You'll also notice relationships (or *associations*) between them—for example, a Book Review belongs to a Book, and a Purchase Order and Credit Card are two of a kind, as they're both Payment Types.

The first relationship (*Book Review belongs to a Book*) is called aggregation (has-a, because a Book has a Book Review). The second relationship (*Purchase Order and Credit Card are both Payment Types*) is called generalization (is-a, because a Purchase Order is a Payment Type). Figure 2-3 shows an illustration of these concepts.

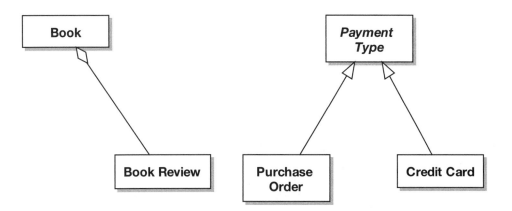

Figure 2-3. *Aggregation and generalization relationships*

These and regular (plain vanilla) associations are the most important relationships in your domain model. Ninety-five percent of your model's class relationships can be modeled using aggregation and generalization relationships.

■**Tip** Wherever possible, place your associations so that they read left to right and top to bottom, just like regular text. This will improve the readability of your diagrams.

---

8. Limit Your Initial Domain Modeling Efforts to a Couple of Hours

We recommend that you establish a time budget for building your initial domain model. A couple of hours is all you should need. You're not going to make it perfect anyway, so do it quickly and expect to fix it as you proceed. You should be vigilant about making necessary adjustments to your analysis-level class model in response to discoveries made during robustness analysis and throughout the project.

You'll discover missing objects as you work through use cases and robustness diagrams. The use case–driven process *assumes that the domain model is incomplete* and provides a mechanism for discovering what was missed.

The initial domain modeling session is probably the most important two hours you'll spend on the project! It's likely that you'll discover 80% of your domain classes during that two-hour brainstorming session. If you can get 80% of your domain vocabulary disambiguated, then that's two hours well spent.

7. Organize Your Classes Around Key Abstractions in the Problem Domain

It's generally good practice to organize your classes around key abstractions in the problem domain. Remember that the domain model is a first-cut class diagram that becomes the foundation of your software architecture. This makes the model more resilient in the face of change. Organizing the architecture around real-world abstractions makes the model more resilient in the face of changing requirements, as the requirements will usually change more frequently than the real world does.

6. Don't Mistake Your Domain Model for a Data Model

Even though the diagrams might look similar, remember that what's good practice on a data model is not likely to be good practice on a class diagram (and vice versa). Classes are small and tables are bigger. A table in a relational database often relates a number of things. Conversely, classes are better designed if they're relatively small packets of data and behavior.

In a class diagram, it's likely that you'll have a class that manages a database table, and you might show some sort of `TableManager` class aggregating a regular domain class. The purpose of these `TableManager`-type classes is to hide the details of the database management system (DBMS) from the rest of the code base.

5. Don't Confuse an Object with a Database Table

An object represents a single instance of something. A database table represents a collection of things. You don't have to be as literal-minded as in the Enterprise JavaBeans (EJB) world, where an entity bean generally represents a single row in a table. Domain classes are similar, though. If you call a domain class Book, then you don't mean a book table—you mean a single book.

Columns in a table generally map to attributes on a class. However, database tables typically contain a lot more columns than a class contains attributes (tables often have foreign keys, as one example), so there may not be a direct 1:1 mapping between table rows and objects.

4. Use the Domain Model As a Project Glossary

If ambiguous requirements are the enemy, the domain model is the first line of defense. Ambiguous usage of names by "subject matter experts" is very common and very harmful. The domain model should serve as a project glossary that helps to ensure consistent usage of terms when describing the problem space.

Using the domain model as a project glossary is the first step toward disambiguating your model. In every Jumpstart workshop that Doug teaches, he finds at least two or three domain classes where students are using ambiguous names (e.g., "shopping cart," "shopping basket," or "shopping trolley").

3. Do Your Domain Model Before You Write Your Use Cases

Since you're using the domain model to disambiguate your problem domain abstractions, it would be silly to have your use cases written using ambiguous terms to describe domain classes. So spend that two hours working on the domain model before writing your use cases. Writing the use cases without a domain model to bind everything together stores up lots of problems for later.

2. Don't Expect Your Final Class Diagrams to Precisely Match Your Domain Model

The class diagrams will become a lot more detailed than the domain model as the design progresses; the domain model is deliberately kept quite simple. As you're designing (using sequence diagrams), detailed design constructs such as GUI helpers, factory classes, and infrastructure classes get added to the class diagram, and the domain model diagram will almost certainly be split out into several detailed class diagrams. However, it should still be possible to trace most classes back to their equivalent domain class.

1. Don't Put Screens and Other GUI-Specific Classes on Your Domain Model

Doing so opens up Pandora's box and leads to an overcrowded domain model containing lots of implementation-specific detail. Performance optimization classes, helper classes, and so on should also be kept out of the domain model. The domain model should focus purely on the problem domain.

Internet Bookstore: Extracting the First-Pass Domain Model from High-Level Requirements

When you're creating your domain model, a good source of domain classes includes the high-level requirements—the ones that are usually (but not always) written in the form "The system *shall* do this; the system *shall not* do that." It's useful to scan these requirements, extracting the nouns and noun phrases. You can then refine these to create the initial domain model.

With that in mind, let's go through the high-level requirements for the Internet Bookstore and extract some **domain classes** from them.

1. The **bookstore** will be web based initially, but it must have a sufficiently flexible architecture that alternative front-ends may be developed (Swing/applets, web services, etc.).

2. The bookstore must be able to sell **books**, with **orders** accepted over the **Internet**.

3. The user must be able to add books into an online **shopping cart**, prior to **checkout**.

   a. Similarly, the user must be able to remove **items** from the shopping cart.

4. The user must be able to maintain **wish lists** of books that he or she wants to purchase later.

5. The user must be able to cancel orders before they've shipped.

6. The user must be able to pay by **credit card** or **purchase order**.

7. It must be possible for the user to return books.

8. The bookstore must be embeddable into **associate partners**' websites using **mini-catalogs**, which are derived from an overall **master catalog** stored in a central **database**.

   a. The mini-catalogs must be defined in XML, as they will be transferred between this and (later to be defined) external systems.

   b. The **shipping fulfillment system** shall be carried out via Amazon Web Services.

9. The user must be able to create a **customer account**, so that the system remembers the user's details (name, address, credit card details) at login.

   a. The system shall maintain a **list of accounts** in its central database.

   b. When a user logs in, his or her **password** must always be matched against the passwords in the **master account list**.

10. The user must be able to search for books by various **search methods**—**title**, **author**, **keyword**, or **category**—and then view the **books' details**.

11. It must be possible for the user to post reviews of favorite books; the **review comments** should appear on the book details screen. The review should include a **customer rating** (1–5), which is usually shown along with the book title in **book lists**.

a. **Book reviews** must be moderated—that is, checked and "OK'd" by a member of staff before they're published on the website.

b. Longer reviews should be truncated on the book details screen; the **customer** may click to view the full review on a separate page.

12. It must be possible for staff to post **editorial reviews** of books. These should also appear on the book details screen.

13. The bookstore shall allow third-party **sellers** (e.g., second-hand bookstores) to add their own individual **book catalogs**. These are added into the overall **master book catalog** so that sellers' books are included in search results.

14. The bookstore must be scalable, with the following specific requirements:

a. The bookstore must be capable of maintaining **user accounts** for up to 100,000 customers in its first six months, and then a further 1,000,000 after that.

b. The bookstore must be capable of serving up to 1,000 simultaneous users (10,000 after six months).

c. The bookstore must be able to accommodate up to 100 search requests per minute (1,000/minute after six months).

d. The bookstore must be able to accommodate up to 100 purchases per hour (1,000/hour after six months).

These requirements are a rich source of domain classes. Let's put all the highlighted nouns and noun phrases into a list (in the process, we'll turn all the plurals into singulars, and put them all in alphabetical order):

Associate Partner	Customer Account	Order
Author	Customer Rating	Password
Book	Database	Purchase Order
Book Catalog	Editorial Review	Review Comment
Book Details	Internet	Search Method
Book List	Item	Search Results
Book Review	Keyword	Seller
Bookstore	List of Accounts	Shipping Fulfillment System
Category	Master Account List	Shopping Cart
Checkout	Master Book Catalog	Title
Credit Card	Master Catalog	User Account
Customer	Mini-Catalog	Wish List

There's quite a bit of duplication in this list; similar terms are being used for basically the same thing. But that's really the main benefit of the domain modeling approach: you get to identify and eliminate these duplicate terms early on in the project.

■**Exercise** **Disambiguation via Grammatical Inspection**: We'll go through this list next, whipping it into shape and eliminating the duplicate terms. But first, try to identify the six duplicate pairs in the list. (Be careful: one pair *seems* like a duplicate but really isn't.)

Some of the items in the list are simply unnecessary because they fall outside the scope of the domain model, or they're actions sneakily masquerading as nouns.

Let's step through the list now and tune it up a bit:

- You'd *think* that the terms "Customer" and "Customer Account" are duplicates, but in fact they represent subtly different things: "Customer Account" is an entity stored in the database, whereas "Customer" is an actor (see the next item in this list).

- "Customer" and "Seller" are actors, and thus should be placed on use case diagrams. (See Chapter 3.)

- The terms "User Account" and "Customer Account" are duplicates. The choice of which one to keep is fairly arbitrary, so we'll go with "Customer Account."

- The terms "List of Accounts" and "Master Account List" are duplicates, so one of them should be removed. As we also have a "Master Book Catalog," the consistent thing would be to keep "Master Account List."

- The terms "Book Review" and "Review Comment" are duplicates, so we'll keep "Book Review."

- We have several different candidate terms for a catalog, or list of books: "Book Catalog," "Book List," "Mini-Catalog," and "Master Catalog." Catalogs and lists are probably different concepts. In fact, it seems that the requirements are trying to tell us something, which may just be implied in the text. When in doubt, *talk to the customer*. Ask questions until you get a clear, unambiguous answer.

  "Book Catalog" and "Master Catalog" are in fact the duplicates here, so we'll keep "Master Catalog," as it provides a good contrast with "Mini-Catalog." "Book List," meanwhile, is probably an umbrella term for different types of lists; we'll keep it in there for now and see how it fits in when we draw the domain model diagram.

- There's another duplicate in this area: "Master Catalog" and "Master Book Catalog." We'll delete "Master Catalog," as "Master Book Catalog" is the more descriptive term.

- The word "Internet" is too generic and doesn't add anything here.

- The word "Password" is a too small to be an object and would be shown as a UI element, so we should remove it from the domain model. If we start to include all the UI elements in the domain model, we're opening a serious can of worms and could be here all night backed into a corner, fighting them away with a large stick.

- Same goes for "Title" and "Keyword."

- Yet another duplicate is "Book" and "Book Details." We'll just keep "Book," as it's more concise than "Book Details," without losing any meaning.

- The word "Item" is just vague and fuzzy, but it does represent a valid concept: an item that's been added to the user's shopping cart. So we'll rename it "Line Item" and keep it in the list.

- The word "Bookstore" is a bit too broad and is unlikely to be referred to explicitly, so we can get rid of it.

Following is the updated list of candidate domain classes. Figure 2-4 shows those classes laid out in a class diagram.

Associate Partner	Customer Account	Order
Author	Customer Rating	Purchase Order
Book	Database	Search Method
Book List	Editorial Review	Search Results
Book Review	Line Item	Shipping Fulfillment System
Category	Master Account List	
Checkout	Master Book Catalog	Shopping Cart
Credit Card	Mini-Catalog	Wish List

As we mentioned earlier, although grammatical inspection techniques are useful to get a quick start, you shouldn't spend weeks or even days doing this. (As you'll see in Chapter 4, the rest of the objects for the Internet Bookstore were identified during robustness analysis.) A couple of hours is about the right amount of time to spend on the domain model before getting started writing the use cases.

■Caution Don't get bogged down in grammatical inspection.

Figure 2-4 shows one type of relationship, *aggregation* (aka has-a), which we described earlier. As this is a first-pass attempt, not all the relationships shown are correct.

A helpful technique is to read the diagram aloud and include the term "has-a." For example, a Shopping Cart "has" Line Items. But, does an Order "have" Checkouts? Perhaps not. Notice that a few of the domain objects currently don't match up with anything else (namely, Associate Partner, Shipping Fulfillment System, Database, and Search Method). We've grouped these together over on the right for now; during robustness analysis, these may get linked to other objects, warped into something different, or removed altogether.

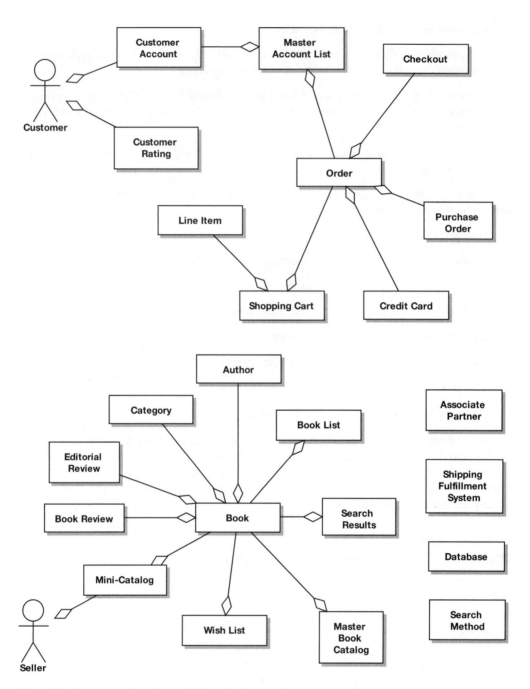

Figure 2-4. *First-pass domain model for the Internet Bookstore project*

There's still some work that needs to be done on this domain model before we're ready to move on to the next stage, so let's do some more tidying up work next. Hopefully, this will help to illustrate an important element of the ICONIX approach: ***continuous improvement via ongoing iteration and refinement***.

Internet Bookstore: Second Attempt at the Domain Model

When drawing up the domain model diagram, you're generally brainstorming as a team. Often the team will identify further domain objects that weren't in the requirements, but instead have been dredged from somebody's own understanding of the problem domain. To illustrate this, let's say we've discovered two additional domain objects: Order History and Order Dispatch. These weren't mentioned explicitly in the requirements, but they could still classify as minimum requirements for an Internet bookstore.

The updated diagram is shown in Figure 2-5, with the new domain classes shown in red.

In Figure 2-5, we've explored the concept of order fulfillment and dispatch. Shipping Fulfillment System still remains on the diagram, but we'll have to decide whether this is in scope for the current model or it's an external system that we need to interface with. **External systems are always modeled as actors**.

We've also removed Checkout, as on reflection this was really a verb in noun's clothing. And we've removed Author, as this is really just another field in the Book (i.e., it's too small to be a first-class object on the domain model[1]). Authors . . . who needs 'em?

There's some ambiguity around Master Book Catalog, which we've attempted to resolve. We've removed the link between Book and Master Book Catalog, and instead added a class called Book Catalog and linked Book to that instead. So we end up with a **tangle of relationships**: we're effectively saying that a Book belongs to a Book Catalog, and a Book Catalog belongs to a Master Book Catalog (i.e., a Master Book Catalog is really a catalog of catalogs). Ideally, a Mini-Catalog should also belong to the Master Book Catalog. But this tangle is getting complicated. What we really need is a simple way of saying that a Book can belong to Book Catalogs, and there can be various *types* of Book Catalogs. Luckily, a light sprinkling of ***generalization*** can work wonders on such relationship tangles, as you'll see in the next section.

---

1. Remember we're not creating a data model here. If this were a database design, we would almost certainly create a separate Authors table.

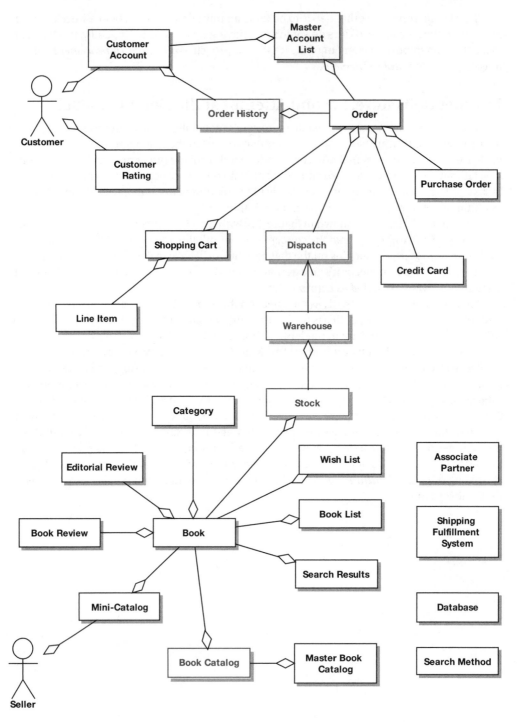

Figure 2-5. *Second snapshot of the evolving domain model for the Internet Bookstore project*

Internet Bookstore: Building Generalization Relationships

A *generalization relationship* is one in which one class is a "kind of" some other class—for example, a Cat is a kind of Animal. This is why generalization is often called an *is-a* relationship.

Cat is more specific than Animal (Cat is a "refinement" of the more general Animal class), hence the term "generalization." The more specific class is called the *subclass*, and the more general class is the *superclass*. Creating subclasses of more general classes is known as *subtyping*.

Within the Internet Bookstore, Book Catalog is a good candidate for subtyping, because doing so will help to "de-cloud" the relationship between Mini-Catalog and Master Book Catalog. Book List is also a good candidate for subtyping, because there may well be different types of accounts and different types of book lists.

As we delve more deeply into the user's needs for the Internet Bookstore system, we're beginning to identify different types of book lists: customer wish lists, recommendation lists, Related Books, Search Results, and so on. It's becoming clear that these are all simply lists of Books, so they could (conceptually, at least) have a common parent class. We've discovered that there are indeed aspects of Wish Lists, Related Books, and so on that are different enough to justify separate treatment, while they still have enough in common that they're all kinds of Book List. Figure 2-6 shows the notation for this generalization structure.

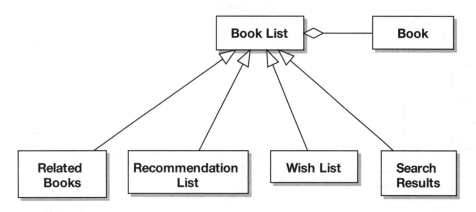

Figure 2-6. *Book Lists detail from the Internet Bookstore domain model*

The new classes (Related Books, Recommendation List, Wish List, and Search Results) inherit the attributes and operations that we define for Book List. Let's read this diagram out loud: A book list has books. Related Books is a book list. Recommendation List is a book list. Wish List is a book list. Search Results is a book list. All true statements that describe the problem space? Great, let's move on.

■Tip You could also add additional specialized attributes and operations for each of the new classes. In other words, if you were to add an operation to Related Books, it would only be available to Related Books. However, if you add it to Book List, the new operation would be available to all of its subclasses.

Figure 2-7 shows the updated Internet Bookstore domain model, which makes good use of generalization to clarify the relationships between the domain classes. The new classes are shown in red.

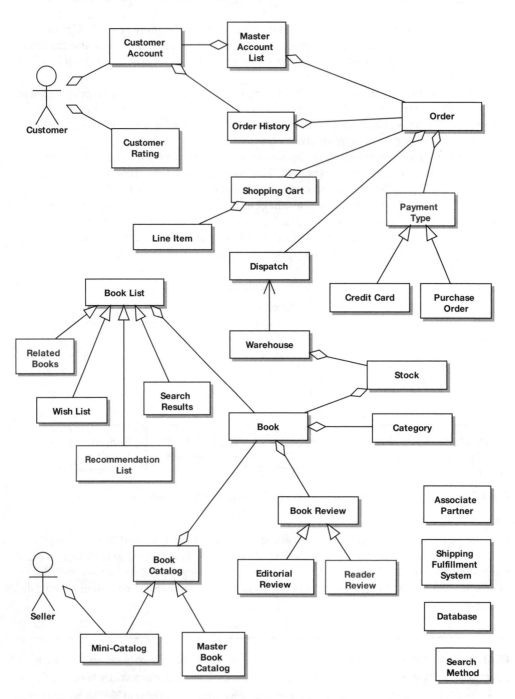

Figure 2-7. *Third snapshot of the evolving domain model for the Internet Bookstore project*

We've also changed the definition of Book Review, so that it's now the parent class for Editorial Review and the new class, Reader Review. And, finally, we've disentangled the relationships surrounding Order and its payment types (Credit Card and Purchase Order), by adding a new superclass, Payment Type.

■**Tip** If you need to, you can generalize to more than one level of subclass. Remember to look for is-a statements that are true in the real world.

Domain Modeling in Practice

The following exercises, taken from the domain model for the Internet Bookstore, are designed to test your ability to spot the most common mistakes that people make during domain modeling. After the exercises, you can find the diagrams with the errors highlighted on them, followed by the corrected diagrams.

Exercises

Each of the diagrams in Figures 2-8 to 2-11 contains one or more typical modeling errors. For each one, try to figure out the errors and then draw the corrected diagram. The answers are in the next section.

Exercise 2-1

Figure 2-8 shows a class diagram produced during the initial domain modeling effort. The UML syntax is correct, yet the diagram does point out a process-related error. Why is that? (Hint: The diagram is showing too much detail.)

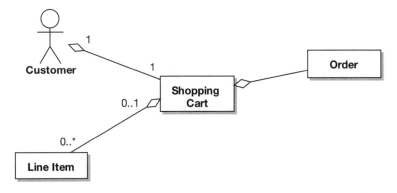

Figure 2-8. *Class diagram from the initial domain modeling effort*

Exercise 2-2

Figure 2-9 shows a domain model diagram with attributes on the Order class. What database-related problem does the diagram suggest?

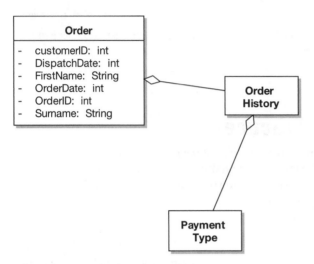

Figure 2-9. *Class diagram showing attributes*

Exercise 2-3

Figure 2-10 shows a domain model diagram in which the modeling team may have leapt ahead a little too soon. Which parts of the diagram were added too early in the process?

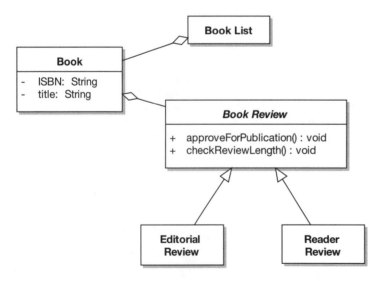

Figure 2-10. *Domain model diagram with details added too early*

Exercise 2-4

Figure 2-11 shows another domain model diagram in which the modeling team began thinking about certain details too early. What's gone wrong in this diagram?

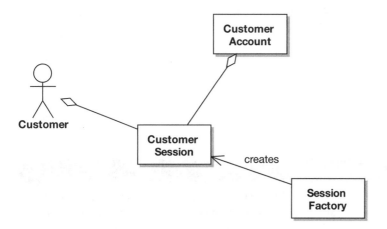

Figure 2-11. *Another domain model diagram with details added too early*

Exercise Solutions

Following are the solutions to the exercises.

Exercise 2-1 Solution: Multiplicity

Figure 2-12 highlights the errors in Figure 2-9. The initial domain modeling effort is way too early to start thinking about details like multiplicity. At this early stage, your main concern should be identifying domain objects and thinking at a broad level about how they relate to one another. Figure 2-13 shows the corrected diagram.

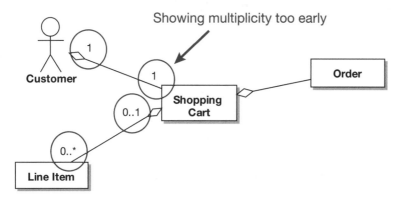

Figure 2-12. *Errors in Figure 2-9*

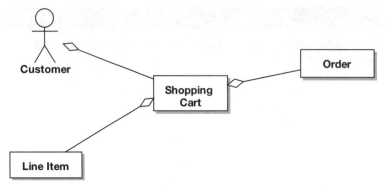

Figure 2-13. *Corrected version of Figure 2-9*

Exercise 2-2 Solution: Mapping Database Tables to Domain Classes

The Order domain class includes attributes that really don't seem like they belong in an Order class (see Figure 2-14). The most likely cause is that the modeler has mapped these domain classes directly from a relational database schema. Figure 2-15 gives the corrected diagram. The extra attributes have been separated out into their own domain classes (Customer Account and Dispatch). Note that we'd generally not show the attributes at all during domain modeling.

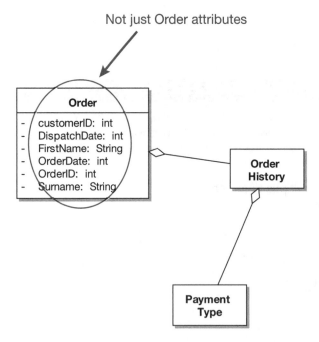

Figure 2-14. *Order class domain attributes erroneously influenced from database schema*

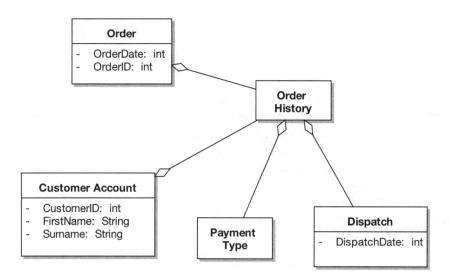

Figure 2-15. *Domain attributes from Figure 2-14, but this time in more appropriate classes*

Exercise 2-3 Solution: Operations and Abstract Classes

The domain model diagram shown in Figure 2-16 has a couple of problems. The first is that Book Review is an abstract class. While this isn't especially destructive, and the world probably won't end as a direct result, domain modeling is just a bit too early in the development process to be thinking about these sorts of design details.

Staying with Book Review, the other problem is that a couple of operations have been assigned: checkReviewLength() and approveForPublication(). Identifying and assigning operations to classes is very much a design thing—so again, domain modeling is just too early to be thinking about these sorts of details.

Figure 2-17 shows the corrected diagram.

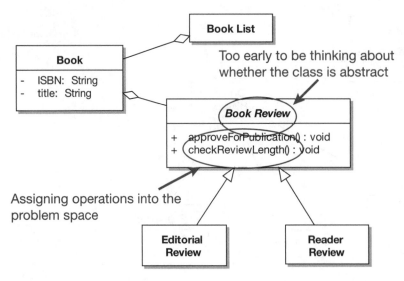

Figure 2-16. *Solution-space details (design) added into the problem space (domain model)*

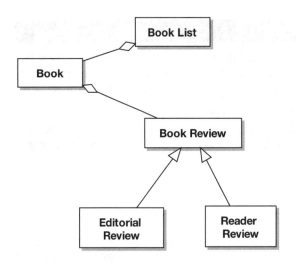

Figure 2-17. *Corrected version of Figure 2-16*

Exercise 2-4 Solution: Premature Patternization

In Figure 2-18, you can see the telltale beginnings of a Factory design pattern. Using this particular design pattern, the SessionFactory class will create new instances of CustomerSession. A SessionFactory is clearly part of the solution space, not the problem space, as are most design patterns. This sounds an awful lot like design, and the use cases haven't even been written yet, so again this is way too early to be thinking about implementation details.

Design patterns usually begin to emerge during robustness analysis (preliminary design), but domain modeling really isn't the time to be thinking about them.

Figure 2-19 shows the corrected diagram.

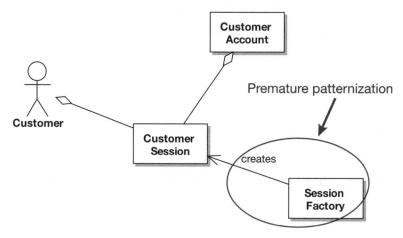

Figure 2-18. *Design details added too early in the project*

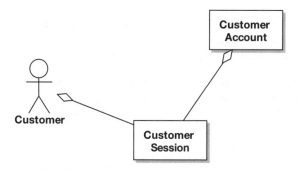

Figure 2-19. *Domain model diagram with the design details removed*

More Practice

This section provides a list of modeling questions that you can use to test your knowledge of domain modeling. The questions get progressively harder, but the answers can all be found by reading (and thinking about!) the domain modeling techniques described in this chapter.

  1. Which of the following is *not* one of the four types of association in a domain model?

   a) Has-a

   b) Creates

   c) Is-a

   d) Knows about

2. When creating a domain class list, how do you tell when you have an attribute?

    a) An attribute has cardinality in all cases.

    b) An attribute can only be contained in instances with no behavior.

    c) An attribute has a value that is typically not compound.

    d) An attribute has a value that is made up of lots of other values.

3. What technique(s) can you use to figure out domain classes in a system?

    a) Noun phrase analysis

    b) Reverse engineering

    c) Class verb category

    d) Extreme Programming

4. What term is used to describe when a child class is an extension of a parent class?

    a) Aggregation

    b) Inheritance

    c) Composition

    d) Encapsulation

5. Draw a domain model for an online music store, first by trying to imagine how it works in the abstract, without looking at any screens, and then after looking at an example website such as iTunes or Napster. Which of your domain models is better? Explain.

6. Assume you could reverse engineer the database schema from Amazon.com and import this into a visual modeling tool. Would this be a good starting point for a domain model? What changes would need to be made to a reverse-engineered database schema to make it a good domain model?

7. Assume someone hands you some Java code for a GUI prototype of a new Internet bookstore and you reverse engineer it into UML. Would this be a good starting point for a domain model? What changes would need to be made to a reverse-engineered GUI prototype to make it a good domain model?

8. Assume you are working on Release 3 of a project, and you have a detailed set of class diagrams showing the complete implementation of Release 2 that has been reverse engineered from C# code. Release 3 involves migrating the system to a new GUI framework and a different DMBS. What changes would need to be made to your detailed class diagrams from the previous release to make it a good domain model for the current release?

Summary

In this chapter we described in detail the first major stage of ICONIX Process. Domain modeling forms the basis for the whole object modeling activity. As you'll see in the next chapter, the use cases are written in the context of the domain model, and (as you'll see in Chapter 5) robustness analysis helps to tighten up both the domain model and the use case text, bringing them closer together.

The activity diagram in Figure 2-20 shows how domain modeling fits into the overall requirements analysis effort. The activities we covered in this chapter are shown in red.

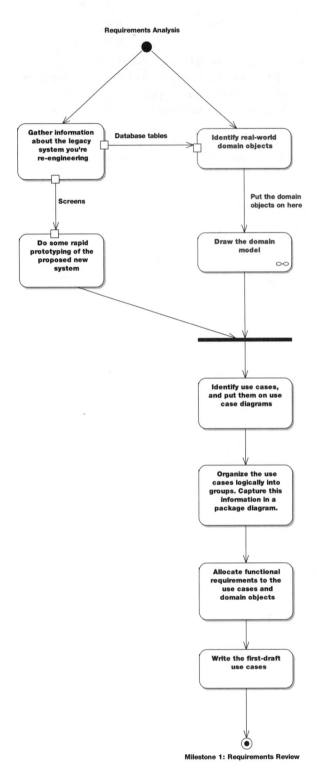

Figure 2-20. *Requirements Analysis Checkpoint 1*

CHAPTER 3

■ ■ ■

Use Case Modeling

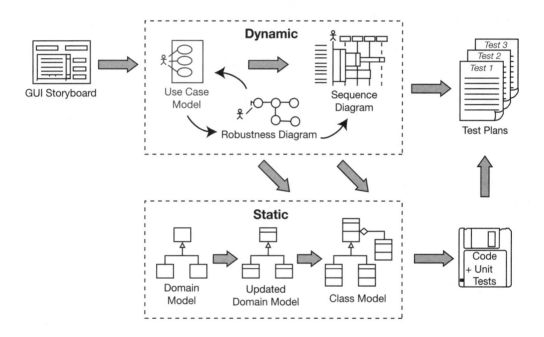

With an initial domain model in place, it's time to begin writing use cases. Use cases give you a structured way of capturing the behavioral requirements of a system, so that you can reasonably create a design from them. They help you to answer some fundamental questions: *What are the users of the system trying to do? What's the user experience?* A surprising amount of what your software does is dictated by the way in which users must interact with it.

The 10,000-Foot View

Use cases give you something that you can design from, and from which you can reliably estimate time and effort. While some use case books treat use cases as more of an abstract requirements specification technique, **this book teaches you how to write use cases as the first step toward doing a good object-oriented design and as a means to help you get quickly to high-quality code**.

■**Note** Look again at the process diagram at the start of this chapter. As you can see, you should create your use case model close to the start of the development process, just after creating an initial attempt at the domain model.

Why Do I Need Use Cases in Addition to Functional Requirements?

Functional requirements tend to be a mixture of high- and low-level requirements—virtually a stream of consciousness from managers, customers, and the marketing team captured in serial form and placed into a Word document. Not that there's anything wrong with that; it's just the first, early step along the path of getting a finalized, clear, unambiguous set of behavioral requirements that you can realistically create a design from.

Functional specifications are important, of course. But designing, coding, or estimating directly from a functional spec is like playing an enthralling game of "pick a random number." You need to do some exploratory work to even out the playing field. Use case modeling—and preliminary design after it—gets you there.

■**Note** Functional requirements aren't the only source of use cases. Further in-depth conversations with the customer and end users are also a very important source. Creating storyboards and prototypes (UI mock-ups, barely functional demos—those sorts of things) helps enormously when defining the use cases.

Don't Forget the Rainy-Day Scenarios

When you're writing your use cases, write them in such a way that your efforts are focused on capturing your users' actions and the associated system responses. As you'll see, use case modeling involves analyzing both the *basic course* (a user's typical "sunny-day" usage of the system; often thought of as 90% of the behavior) and the *alternate courses* (the other 90% of the system functionality, consisting of "rainy-day" scenarios of the way in which the user interacts with the system; in other words, what happens when things go wrong, or when the user tries some infrequently used feature of the program). If you capture all of this in your use cases, you have the vast majority of the system specced out.

Do an Initial Domain Model Before You Write the Use Cases

The use case is **written in the context of the domain model**—that is, all the terms (nouns and noun phrases) that went into the domain model should also be used directly in your use case text.

The ICONIX approach **assumes that the initial domain model is wrong** and provides for incrementally improving it as you analyze the use cases. That's why you should spend only a couple of hours at most on domain modeling before you begin use case modeling. As you write your use cases, you'll inevitably want to feed information and changes back into the domain model. Do so! Keep on updating the domain model, correcting it, and fleshing it out with details. That's how it evolves from the first-cut domain model into your detailed design-level static model.

During preliminary design, the domain model turns into an updated domain model, which in turn eventually (during detailed design) becomes your class model (i.e., the static model that defines the software classes). You should update the domain model not just when modeling use cases, but also when drawing robustness diagrams and sequence diagrams.

Driving Your Design (and Your Tests) from the Use Cases

Over the next few chapters, we'll show you how to write use cases that are directly tied into the classes that you design from. This gives you traceability from your code and your unit tests all the way back up to your behavioral requirements.

We've found in practice that if you write your use cases in the way we describe in this chapter and do robustness analysis (see Chapter 5), then it's also quite easy to identify a set of unit tests that verify your behavioral requirements. In other words, you're writing tests that prove that the use cases have been implemented.

Use Case Modeling in Theory

In this section, we describe the theory behind use case modeling, interspersed with examples from the Internet Bookstore project. Your primary concern is with writing use cases that you can drive the design from. In practical terms, this means that **there's a very close relationship between your use cases and your classes**. We'll begin with our top 10 list of things you should do when writing use cases.

Top 10 Use Case Modeling Guidelines

The principles discussed in this chapter can be summed up as a list of guidelines. These guidelines, in turn, can be summed up in a single sentence:

DESCRIBE SYSTEM USAGE IN THE CONTEXT OF THE OBJECT MODEL.

Items 10 through 5 of the following list relate to **describing system usage**, and items 4 through 1 relate to **putting the usage description in the context of the object model**.

10. Follow the two-paragraph rule.

9. Organize your use cases with actors and use case diagrams.

8. Write your use cases in active voice.

7. Write your use case using an event/response flow, describing both sides of the user/system dialogue.

6. Use GUI prototypes and screen mock-ups.

5. Remember that your use case is really a runtime behavior specification.

4. Write the use case in the context of the object model.

3. Write your use cases using a noun-verb-noun sentence structure.

2. Reference domain classes by name.

1. Reference boundary classes (e.g., screens) by name.

Let's look at each of these items in more detail.

10. Follow the Two-Paragraph Rule

Each use case should fit comfortably into two paragraphs, including both the basic course and alternate courses. Anything much longer than two paragraphs will result in some incomprehensible sequence diagrams. If your use case goes over two paragraphs, it probably needs to be divided into two or more separate use cases.

If someone gives you a long use case template, you can almost bet that that person is not expecting you to drive a software design from those use cases (at least not any time soon). **Long use case templates slow you down!** It's also a good bet that the template will be full of non-use-case information such as functional requirements. (See the sidebar titled "Disintermangling Dysfunctional Requirements from the Scenario Text" in Chapter 13.)

■**Tip** The use case writer *should not* include long lists of functional requirements in his or her scenario text. Instead, the writer should just write about how the users will be using the system and what the system will do in response.

HOW TO WRITE A USE CASE: THE THREE MAGIC QUESTIONS

Well, OK, this whole chapter describes how to write a use case. But when writing use cases, you need to keep asking the following three fundamental questions:[1]

1. What happens?

   (This gets your "sunny-day scenario" started.)

2. And then what happens?

   (Keep asking this question until your "sunny-day scenario" is complete.)

3. What else might happen?

   (Keep asking this one until you've identified all the "rainy-day scenarios" you can think of, and described the related behavior.)

---

1. For more about these "three magic questions," see p. 48 of *Use Case Driven Object Modeling with UML: A Practical Approach* by Doug Rosenberg and Kendall Scott (Addison-Wesley, 1999).

Questions 1 and 2 relate to the use case's **basic course** (also known as a *sunny-day scenario*, or the basic series of steps when it all goes right). Question 3 relates to the **alternate courses** (also known as *rainy-day scenarios*, or what happens when the user does something wrong or steps outside the basic course in some way). We'll return to these three questions later in the chapter, but it's worth stating them up front because, boiled down to the essence, they are really what writing use cases is all about.

9. Organize Your Use Cases with Actors and Use Case Diagrams

This seems like as good a time as any to stop for a moment and talk about use case diagrams and how they relate to use cases and actors.

A **use case diagram** shows multiple use cases on the one diagram. It's an overview of a related group of use cases. The text in each oval is the use case title. Figure 3-1 shows an example use case diagram.

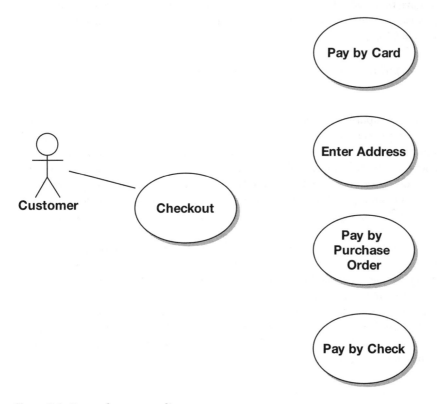

Figure 3-1. *Example use case diagram*

An **actor** is represented on the diagram as a stick figure and is analogous to a "role" that users can play. Sometimes the actor will just be called "User," but is often given a specific role name. For example, our Internet Bookstore system will have actors called Webmaster, Stock

Purchaser, Shipping Clerk, and Customer. The user **(actor) is external to the system**—he or she is on the "outside," whereas the system is on the "inside." Actors can represent nonhuman external systems as well as people. Sometimes people are confused by this notion; we've found that drawing a "robot stick figure" icon seems to clear this up.

An **association from the actor to a use case** means that the actor is the one who carries out that use case. The association can also signify responsibilities. For example, an Administrator pointing to a *Moderate Forum Messages* use case means "The administrator is responsible for moderating forum messages."

You can have more than one actor pointing to one use case, which simply means that the use case is associated with more than one role. Similarly, a user can serve as more than one type of actor; the same user might be both the Stock Purchaser and the Shipping Clerk.

8. Write Your Use Cases in Active Voice

If you weren't paying attention in your high-school English class (and you don't have a great copy editor like we do), then you may not be familiar with the terms *active voice* and *passive voice*. The terms have to do with the perspective from which you write a sentence. When you write in passive voice, you describe what is done without emphasizing—indeed, often without mentioning—who or what is performing the action. For example:

> *The capability is provided for users to log in, using a password-protected authorization scheme.*

Isn't this great? The capability is apparently already provided, so you don't have to worry about it. Unfortunately, that may or may not be the case (you might have to build that capability). The problem with passive sentences is that they hide the actor(s) and, more important, the software functions. The sentence just doesn't tell you. The example sentence also sounds remarkably like a **functional requirement**—the kind of thing that you tend to see in big, passively worded requirements specs (aka dusty tomes), and that it's your job to decipher for everyone by respecifying the requirements in use cases (i.e., by using active voice behavioral descriptions of the system).

To identify passive sentences, watch for forms of the verb "to be" ("is" in the preceding example) in front of another verb ("provided" in the example). The second verb is often in the past tense. A form of "to be" followed by a past-tense verb is a sure sign of a passive sentence that you should rewrite in active voice.

Passive sentences are often unclear and they lack energy; your readers will doze off. Active sentences make clear who does what, and they keep readers awake. Use active sentences and write from the user's perspective, and your use cases will be sharper and less likely to be misconstrued.

Here's an active voice rewrite of this use case:

> *The user enters her username and password, and then clicks the Login button. The system looks up the user profile using the username and checks the password. The system then logs in the user.*[2]

---

2. Remember this is the basic course—the sunny-day scenario that assumes everything goes correctly. There would also be an alternate course describing what happens if the username or password weren't found.

7. Write Your Use Case Using an Event/Response Flow

A use case is often triggered by a user-initiated event that the system has to respond to. However, it can also be triggered by a system-initiated event to which the user responds. But in either case, the use case follows the event/response flow (see Figure 3-2).

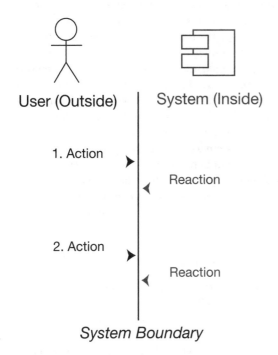

Figure 3-2. *Anatomy of a use case scenario*

■**Note** Quite often, the user is reacting to a system action, so the use case starts with "The system displays the XYZ screen (showing ZZZ information)," and then the user does something in response. The main benefit of starting your use case with "The system displays..." is that the system showing something on the screen involves initialization behavior (getting ZZZ information from somewhere) that is often forgotten otherwise.

We can refine our use case a bit further by starting with the system action, which has the beneficial effect of causing us to assign an unambiguous name to the screen, as follows (with the new sentence in red):

The system displays the Login screen. *The user enters her username and password, and then clicks the Login button. The system looks up the user profile using the username and checks the password. The system then logs in the user.*

Notice that in this version, we've identified more detail than the original passive-voice requirement contained. We now know that to log in, the user must click a Login button and that the system must then find the user profile using the username. This gets at the heart of what use cases are about: ***show, don't tell***. That is, instead of saying, "The system allows users to log in via a password-protected authorization scheme," you should actually ***describe the steps involved in logging in***: the user entering the username and password, the user clicking the Login button, and then the system checking the details and responding. Writing the use cases in this format encourages you to think through the finer details of the system's behavior.

It's also important to remember to ***write both sides of the user/system dialogue*** in your use case. Use case modeling can be thought of as an *outside-in* type of approach. When you write use case scenarios, you're describing the user's interaction with the system. But interaction is a two-way thing, so you also need to describe the system's behavior in addition to the user's behavior. A use case will typically consist of several steps. Each step involves an event and a response: the user's action and the system's reaction, or vice versa (see Figure 3-2).

So **a use case really describes a dialogue between a user and the system**. You need to write about the user side of the dialogue to keep your behavior requirements firmly user-focused, but it's not sufficient to just write down what the user does, because ultimately **you're trying to spec software, and software really consists of the system's behavior**. So it's vitally important to describe both sides of the dialogue between the user and the system in every use case.

6. Use Storyboards, GUI Prototypes, and Screen Mock-ups

Storyboards, GUI prototypes, and screen mock-ups are often very useful visual aids when writing a use case. If you're basing the use case on a GUI prototype, for example, it's important to include all the buttons and menus the user can touch to generate events within the use case.

Recently we've been gravitating toward the term "storyboard" instead of "prototype," because there's always the danger that GUI prototyping can escalate into extended GUI design. Then little bits of functionality get added into the supposedly "nonfunctional" prototype UI, and suddenly you've implemented the "complete" system, all cobbled together with string and sticky tape, before you've even begun to analyze the alternate courses (that other 90% of the system functionality).

If this scenario worries you, there are a few possible remedies:

- **Use something like the Napkin Look & Feel**[3] to give your prototype GUI that "sketched on the back of a napkin" appearance. This look sets management and customer expectations appropriately, so they don't think that your team has somehow miraculously reached the implementation stage yet.

- **Use line drawings** like the one in Figure 3-3. This keeps everyone focused on operational concepts, rather than being sidetracked with GUI minutiae ("That button should be 3 pixels to the right! Use spin buttons—no, a pop-up scrollbar!"). There will be plenty of time (although hopefully not *too* much time) for that tortuous experience later.

---

3. See http://napkinlaf.sourceforge.net.

- **Use your CASE tool to storyboard your screens** and attach them to your use cases. For example, in Enterprise Architect (EA), you can create a Custom (Extended Class) diagram as a subdiagram beneath your use case, and then place UI elements on the diagram.

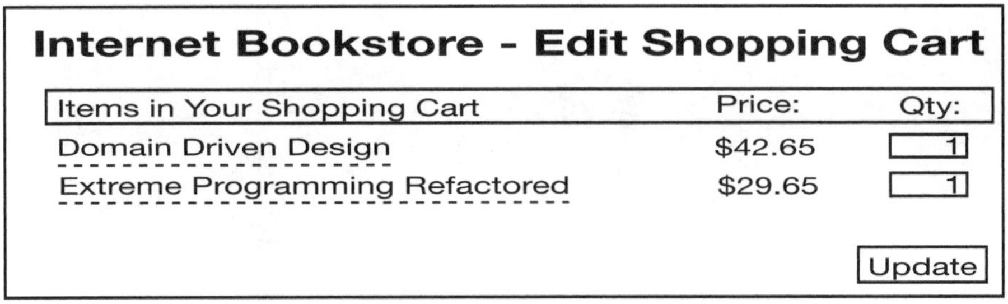

Internet Bookstore - Edit Shopping Cart

Items in Your Shopping Cart	Price:	Qty:
Domain Driven Design	$42.65	1
Extreme Programming Refactored	$29.65	1
		Update

Figure 3-3. *Example UI storyboard*

Here's an example use case derived from the storyboard in Figure 3-3:

The user clicks the Edit Shopping Cart button, and the system shows the Edit Shopping Cart page with a list of books in the user's shopping cart. The user selects one of the books, changes the quantity, and clicks the Update button. The system shows the page with the quantities and price totals updated.

The use case avoids making any references to specific element types. The hyperlinks for each book title could turn into buttons next to the book titles, for example, if you switched from an HTML front-end to a Flash rich-client front-end. But the use case text doesn't focus on these details, and instead focuses on event/response behavior.

If you created your UI files outside your CASE tool or have screenshots from a legacy system, then using Rational Rose or Enterprise Architect you can link the UI files to your use cases (see Figure 3-4).

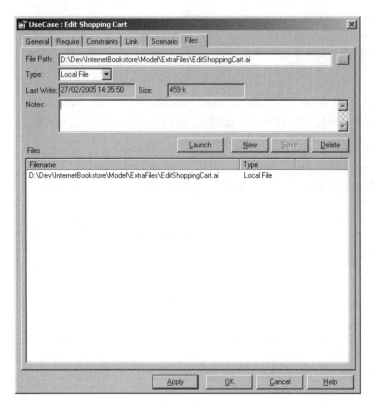

Figure 3-4. *Linking files to use cases within Enterprise Architect*

5. Remember That Your Use Case Is Really a Runtime Behavior Specification

With ICONIX Process, **you're driving the design from the use cases**. In practical terms, this means that you draw a sequence diagram for each and every use case in the current release. The sequence diagram shows in great detail how object instances collaborate together at runtime to accomplish the behavior of the use case. Therefore, the use case text will serve as a specification of the runtime behavior that you show on the sequence diagrams.

Q&A: USE CASE = USER DOCUMENTATION?

You can always think of the use case text as being a narrative describing the user's adventures when interacting with the system. So it goes, "First the user does this; next the user does that."

Q: But don't I also have to describe the system's response?
A: Yes. So the text should really go, "First the user does this; then the system responds with that. Next the user does something; then the system responds with . . ." and so on.

Q: Isn't that similar to writing a user guide?
A: You got it. In fact, being "use case driven" can be summed up like this: *First write the user guide and then write the code.*

Q: **Presumably this principle carries all the way through to the design?**
A: Yes, the goal is to build something that implements the behavior requirements, so the system you'll be designing will be strongly correlated with the viewpoint of the end users. In other words, first you're describing system usage from the user's perspective, and then you're designing and unit-testing from the user's perspective, too.

Q: **What if we're updating a legacy system?**
A: The same principle still applies. Simply *work backward from the user guide*. Analyze the existing functionality, and then make changes based on how those functions will be performed in the new system. You should find yourself breaking the legacy user guide down into its fundamental components, from which you can then derive your use case scenarios.

4. Write Your Use Case in the Context of the Object Model

Repeat this mantra at least a hundred times before breakfast:

> **You can't drive object-oriented designs from use cases unless you tie your use cases to objects.**

In practical terms, this means that you need to reference domain classes that participate in the use case, and you need to name your screens and other boundary objects explicitly in the use case text. Otherwise, your behavior requirements will be completely disconnected from your object model, and (surprise!) you won't be able to drive designs from the use cases.

3. Write Your Use Cases Using a Noun-Verb-Noun Sentence Structure

You'll be amazed how much easier it is to create an object-oriented design if your use case text follows the **noun-verb-noun** style. Your use case text will ultimately reside on the margin of your sequence diagram (see Chapter 8). And sequence diagrams are fundamentally geared around nouns and verbs:

- The nouns are the **object instances**. These usually either come from the domain model (entities) or are boundary/GUI objects.

- The verbs are the **messages between objects**. These represent the software functions (controllers) that need to be built.

So, by writing your use case in **noun-verb-noun** format, you're setting yourself up to make the sequence diagramming task considerably easier than it would be otherwise.

2. Reference Domain Classes by Name

Remember from Chapter 2 that **the domain model serves as a project glossary** that helps to ensure consistent usage of terms when describing the problem space. As we mentioned in item 4, when you try to drive an object-oriented design from use cases, **it's critically important that the use cases are linked to the objects.** While this may seem obvious after it's stated, it's a fact that's ignored in many books about use cases. But think about it: how can you drive an object model from use cases, if the use cases aren't linked to the objects? The short answer is you can't. At the same time, you don't have full knowledge of the eventual object model when you start writing use cases. What you *do* have knowledge of at that point in time is a preliminary version of the object model that describes the problem domain in unambiguous terms—that is, the domain model. So, link the use cases to the domain objects. In practice, this means **referencing the domain classes by name** in the use case text.

Let's say you have a domain model that contains domain classes such as Wish List, Book, Book List, and Shopping Cart. The following use case text is "sort of" using these domain classes, but it doesn't reference them by name (the errant text is shown in red):

> *The user selects a* title *and adds it to his* list of books to be saved for later. *The system displays a page with the updated list and also shows a* list of titles in the user's cart, ready for checkout.

Although this text seems clear, it's a hotbed of ambiguity. "List of books to be saved for later" might, in subsequent use case scenarios, be shortened to "list of books" or "saved books," both of which could be interpreted to mean something completely different.

Here's the corrected text (the corrected parts are shown in bold):

> *The user selects a **Book** and adds it to his **Wish List**. The system displays a page with the updated list and also displays the user's **Shopping Cart**.*

You've gone to the trouble of building a domain model so that you could unambiguously communicate about details of the system you're developing. Since keeping ambiguity out of your use cases is one of your primary goals, it would be silly not to use the terminology that your team collectively agreed upon in the domain model.

■**Exercise**   There's one other item in this section's use case text that is potentially ambiguous. We cover it in the next section ("Reference Boundary Classes by Name"), but see if you can spot it before moving on. Think about what you would replace it with.

---

1. Reference Boundary Classes by Name

Since you're on a mission to write unambiguous behavior requirements, and since behavior requirements nearly always involve the user interface, it's a good idea to not write vague and ambiguous phrases like "The system displays a web page" in your use cases. Rather, name your screens explicitly—for example, "The system displays the Checkout page."

In many cases, significant software behavior is related to initializing a page before display, and you need to write about this behavior as well: "The system displays the Checkout page showing the user's default billing and shipping addresses." Notice how the use case text is getting progressively less ambiguous!

Returning to the Wish List example, here's how the text would appear once the boundary class is referred to by name (the corrected text is shown in bold):

> The user selects a Book and adds it to his Wish List. The system displays the user's **Wish List Page** (which also shows the user's up-to-date Shopping Cart).

Note that we've progressively squeezed ambiguity out of the use case by putting it in the context of the object model and the GUI.

Organizing Use Cases into Packages: Internet Bookstore

Pretty soon we're going to start writing some of the use cases for the Internet Bookstore. But before we do that, we need some way of organizing all of these use cases. In a decent-sized system, you could have anywhere from 100 use cases upward.

Luckily, the UML provides us with the *package* mechanism, which is a way of grouping related elements (e.g., classes, diagrams, or use cases). Packages are basically hierarchical containers that can contain almost any UML constructs, including other packages. If you're a Java programmer, UML packages are not entirely dissimilar to Java packages, in that they allow you to divide your work broadly into different areas.

For the Internet Bookstore, Figure 3-5 shows a package diagram containing four packages. Each package contains lots of use cases. In addition, the shopping package contains an actor (Customer), and the admin package contains four actors (Customer Service, Seller, Shipping Clerk, and Webmaster).

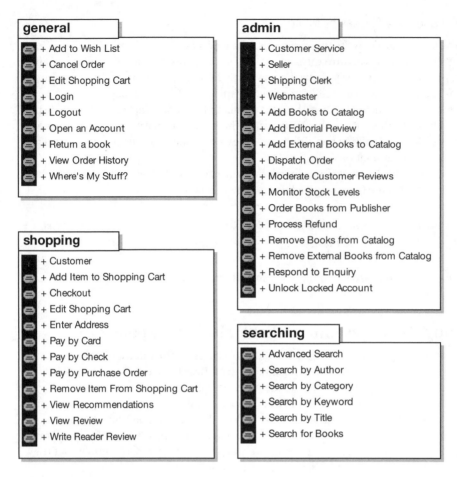

Figure 3-5. *Package diagram for the Internet Bookstore example*

Figures 3-6 through 3-9 show the individual use case diagrams for each of the four packages. You'll notice that we haven't bothered to pretty up the diagrams or even connect all the use case bubbles with arrows. That's because the more important part of the job is writing the use case text.

We do provide a brief discussion of the relationships that we've drawn in, but as you'll gather by the end of the discussion, we value **what goes into the use case text** much more than the relationships between the use cases.

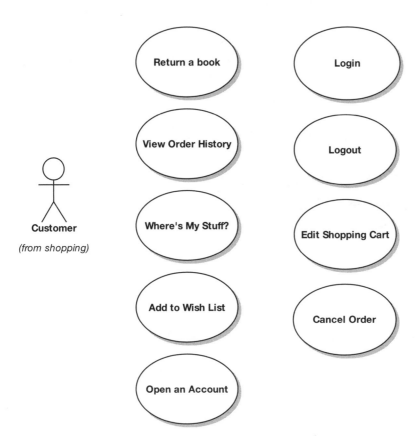

Figure 3-6. *Use case diagram for the "general" package*

FACTORING OUT COMMON BEHAVIOR

The last thing you want to do when writing use cases is to repeat the same behavior multiple times. This is a horrendous waste of effort, which you don't have time for, and one of the leading causes of analysis paralysis. So you need a mechanism for factoring this common behavior into its own use case. Our preference for this is an association called <<invokes>> and its partner-in-crime <<precedes>>.

Figure 3-7 has an arrow labeled "invokes" that points to Dispatch Order. You should read this in the direction of the arrow—in other words, "*Checkout* invokes *Dispatch Order.*" It simply means that in the course of stepping through the *Checkout* use case, the *Dispatch Order* use case can be invoked.

You should mention the use case being invoked in the use case text; otherwise, the invokes relationship won't make a lot of sense. So the use case description might say, "The user clicks the Confirm Order button; invoke *Dispatch Order.*"

The << and >>s are the UML notation for stereotypes. The *stereotype* is UML's extension mechanism, so you can extend its core notation with your own semantics by assigning a stereotype to a UML element.

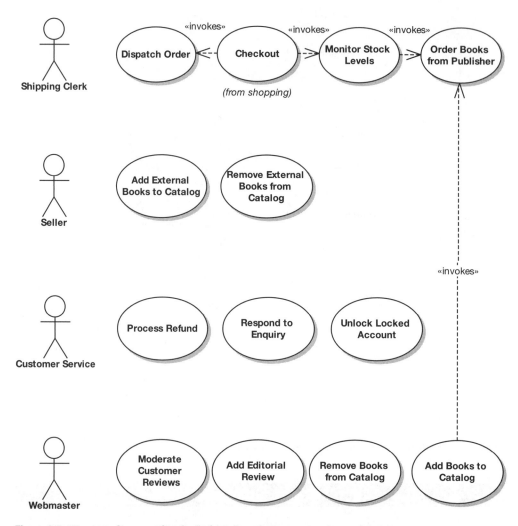

Figure 3-7. *Use case diagram for the "admin" package*

WHAT ABOUT <<INCLUDES>> AND <<EXTENDS>>?

UML defines some standard stereotypes for moving between use cases (notably, <<includes>> and <<extends>>; more about the subtle distinction between these shortly). You read <<includes>> associations in the direction of the arrow, while you read <<extends>> associations in the reverse direction.

It's good practice to have your use cases reviewed by "non-UML-experts" like end users and marketing people (because they're the ones who understand what the behavior should be). We've noticed that these folks sometimes get confused trying to read use case diagrams with some of the associations pointing forward and some pointing backward. And, after working with use cases for 15 years or so, we're convinced that the details inside the use cases are really the important bits, not the associations on the diagrams. You can think of <<invokes>> as a superset of <<includes>> and <<extends>>. If A invokes B, you can get to B from A, and the subtle details of inclusion and extension usually aren't all that important to getting the job done (see the sidebar titled "Use Cases and Aspects" later in this chapter for a case where those details are important).

Recall from Figure 3-7 that there is some sort of connection between *Checkout* and the use cases surrounding it. In Figure 3-8 (the complete version of that use case diagram) we've drawn in the relationships using <<invokes>> arrows.

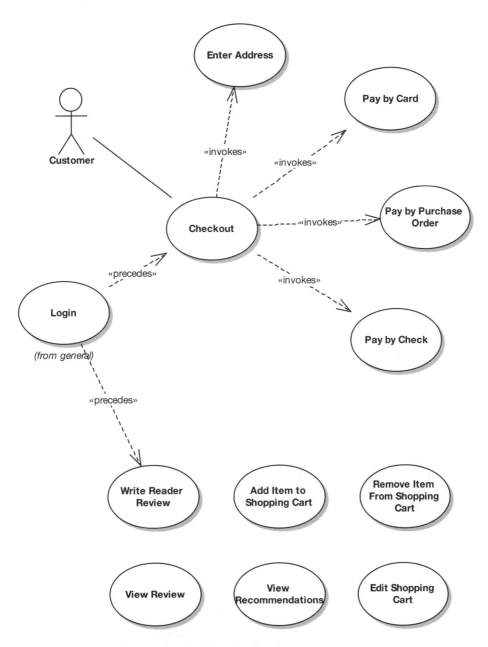

Figure 3-8. *Use case diagram for the "shopping" package*

There are also a couple of <<precedes>> stereotypes in Figure 3-8. A <<precedes>> rela-
tionship simply means that one use case **must be completed** before the next one is begun.
So in the diagram, the *Login* use case must be completed before *Checkout* is begun, and also
Login must be completed before *Write Reader Review* is begun.

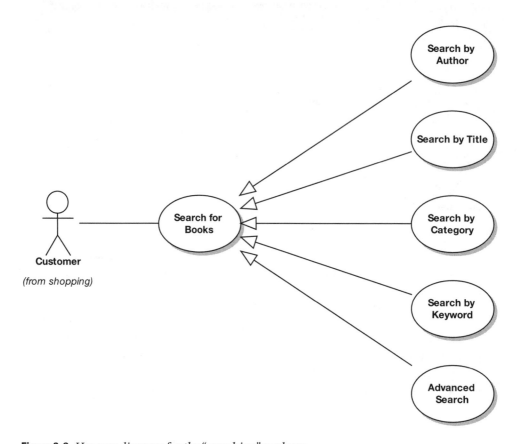

Figure 3-9. *Use case diagram for the "searching" package*

Figure 3-9 shows the "generalization" relationship, denoted by an arrow with a triangular
arrowhead. This relationship is similar to generalization with classes (we used this on the
Internet Bookstore domain model in Chapter 2). For example, in the diagram, *Search by
Author* "is-a" type of *Search for Books* use case.

Note that in addition to generalization, UML also defines an "extends" relationship,
modeled as a stereotype. Java developers might find this confusing at first, because in Java
"extends" is the mechanism used for implementing a generalization relationship between
classes. However, **with use cases, generalization and extends are different concepts**.

A concrete use case can "extend" an abstract parent use case. You denote it on a use case
diagram using the <<extends>> stereotype. The differences between extends and generalization are subtle but important:

- Extends defines a set of extension points in the parent use case; generalization doesn't.

- With extends, the parent must know that it's going to be extended (in order to define the extension points); this is not so with generalization.

- Extends adds to the parent's functionality; generalization **overrides** it (i.e., totally replaces it, albeit with something similar).

However, our experience with generalization has been that it's almost always **of no value whatsoever** in use case modeling. For example, in Figure 3-9, what do we gain from modeling the different search use cases as types of an abstract *Search for Books* use case? Absolutely nothing! The reason we don't gain anything from modeling this is because for our purposes, use cases are not classes, they're *fragments of a user guide*.

■**Tip** If you think you might need to show use case generalization on your diagram, think of what you intend to do as "user guide generalization," and hopefully (like us) you'll then think, "Huh?!"

With class design, generalization *is* useful, because you can use it to factor out commonality and eliminate duplicate code. However, with use cases, generalization doesn't give you this benefit. There are, however, *other* relationships that you can use to factor out commonality, to avoid writing duplicate use case text. (See Table 3-1 in the next section.)

Our advice is to really not dwell on these different relationship types for very long, if at all. Imagine you're doing some critical use case modeling with a roomful of expensive business consultants, and your main objective is to elicit all of the behavioral requirements from them. But the clock's ticking before they all stampede out for their three-hour liquid lunch break. What's more important: getting the notation exactly right, or extracting all the details that you can from the consultants, while you have them in the room with you?

■**Tip** Remember, it's what's inside the use cases that counts, not the way they've been drawn together on the use case diagram.

Use Case Relationship Roundup

Just as the deck chairs on the *Titanic* could be arranged in different configurations, use cases can be related many different ways, the most common of which are listed in Table 3-1. Note that it's perfectly acceptable to make hissing noises at the following table and to back carefully away shouting, "Back, evil stereotype spirits!" Use case relationships have been the cause of many lost hours of valuable use case modeling time, as analysts argue heatedly over which one would be best suited to put on their diagram next. Our own advice is simply to *pick one of these and stick with it, and to not worry too much about which ones to use*.

■**Tip** We've found that 97.3% of the time, the <<invokes>> and <<precedes>> relationships work just fine for linking up use cases; the other relationships shown in Table 3-1 mostly aren't needed.

For regular (non-aspect-oriented) OOAD, the important thing is that you're showing that the use cases are logically related in some way, and the *really* important thing is what goes inside the use case descriptions, because ***that's*** what you'll be designing, testing, and estimating from. You drive OOAD from class diagrams and sequence diagrams; the use cases drive the sequence diagrams. Therefore, the includes/extends construct is a distraction. It doesn't buy you anything, it slows you down, and it confuses readers of the use case model.

■**Note** There's a big exception to our point about includes/extends being a distraction. If you're going to structure your code along use case boundaries via **aspects**, then suddenly the distinction between includes and extends becomes important. See the sidebar "Use Cases and Aspects" later in this chapter.

Table 3-1. *Common Use Case Relationships*

Relationship	Description	Most Effective Remedy
Generalization (denoted by an arrow pointing from B to A, with a white triangle arrowhead)	Use case B is a type of use case A➤(Think of it as an "overrides" relationship, as the child use case inherits none of the steps of the parent use case.)	Garlic placed around the neck while sleeping
A <<includes>> B	Halfway through use case A, use case B is called. When B finishes, A carries on from where it left off. Most similar to a function call or a GOSUB in BASIC.➤A bit like saying "A *has-a* B."	Silver bullet
A <<extends>> B	All the steps from use case A are performed during the execution of use case B, at the extension point which is specified within B.➤For the most part, <<extends>> is <<includes>> with a backward arrow. (Both are subtypes of invokes.)	Stake through the heart
A <<precedes>> B	Use case A must take place in its entirety **before** use case B even begins.	Holy water
A <<invokes>> B	Use case B happens **during** the lifespan of use case A.	A nice cup of tea and a chocolate Easter egg

You might notice from Table 3-1 that all of these relationship types are remarkably similar; they're just subtly different enough to make them a real pain when people disagree about which one to use. In fact, we're hoping that the (quite factual) description in the sidebar "Use Case Diagram Stereotypes As a Treatment for Insomnia" should help to persuade you that 99% of the time, the distinction between these relationships just isn't important.

USE CASE DIAGRAM STEREOTYPES AS A TREATMENT FOR INSOMNIA

If you're worried about whether to use <<extends>>, <<includes>>, <<precedes>>, <<invokes>>, or generalization on your use case diagram, or if you've been having difficulty sleeping recently, this handy little sidebar should help you to decide and/or help you doze off. Feel free to print this out on a postcard and place it above your monitor:

The extending use case must define extension points where it may be extended, but the extended use cases must remain independent of the extending use cases, whereas including use cases do not define extension points even though their behavior is extended by the included use case, which is similar to use cases using generalization, which also do not define extension points but their behavior is not extended by the included use case per se—it's overridden, as opposed to preceding use cases, which must take place in their entirety before the child use case begins. The extends arrow MUST be drawn from the extended use case to the extending use case in an analogous fashion to a generalization arrow being drawn from the subclass toward its parent class, while an includes arrow is ALWAYS drawn from the including use case to the included use case in an analogous fashion to an aggregation arrow being drawn from the aggregate class to the classes being aggregated. You may consider both includes and extends to be subtypes of invokes (that is to say, invokes includes extends and invokes also includes includes, but includes does not include invokes, nor does extends include invokes), with the distinction being all that stuff about extension points and whether the extended use case knows about the use case that's extending it or not. If you think of a use case as a fragment of a user guide, as opposed to thinking of it as a classifier, which is, of course, how it is formally defined within the UML, you may discover that the difference between having extension points or simply including the use case into which you will be branching is not particularly significant, in which case a simple invokes may suffice and you don't have to worry about which way you should draw the arrow on the diagram since the extends arrow points in the opposite direction from the includes arrow, in a similar manner to how a generalization and an aggregation arrow are drawn in opposite directions, more specifically the extends arrow MUST be drawn from the extended use case to the extending use case in an analogous fashion to a generalization arrow being drawn from the subclass toward its parent class, while an includes arrow is drawn from the including use case to the included use case in an analogous fashion to an aggregation arrow being drawn from the aggregate class to the classes being aggregated. The bottom up-arrow convention for extends being analogous to generalization may cause confusion between generalization and extends, especially among Java programmers, to whom extends already means generalization. (Extends is a subtype of invokes, so you could say that extends extends invokes; but here we're using extends in the generalization sense, not in the UML extends sense, so it's an extension of the extended OO terminology; but to say that extends extends extends [but not a UML extends] would be extending the truth.) Additionally, when nontechnical personnel are asked to review the use cases, they occasionally experience consternation while attempting to follow the arrows on the use case diagrams, since some arrows point from the invoking use case to the invoked use case, while others point from the invoked use case back toward the invoking use case. This problem is generally indicative of a lack of UML training among nontechnical personnel and is readily solved by forcing all users and marketing folks to attend a three-day "UML for nontechnical personnel" workshop, which will educate them on these subtle yet critically important features of UML. Precedes, on the other hand, is a somewhat different stereotype than includes, invokes, or extends, in that it simply indicates a temporal precedence; that is to say it is *occasionally* useful to indicate on a use case diagram that use case A needs to happen BEFORE use case B (i.e., there is temporal precedence in which A MUST OCCUR before B). Neither of the standard UML use case diagram stereotypes (i.e., neither includes nor extends) provides a convenient mechanism for expressing this concept of temporal precedence (despite the fact that showing temporal precedence is often more useful than showing whether the invoked use case has knowledge of the invoking use case or not), and so in these cases you MAY find it useful to label the arrow with a stereotype of precedes. It is strongly recommended that in these cases the precedes arrow should originate from A (i.e., the preceding use case) and terminate with the arrowhead pointing at B (i.e., the use case that has been preceded), lest you cause massive confusion among readers of the use case diagram. Precedes does not necessarily imply that the preceded use case has intimate knowledge of the preceding use case, although in practice this is often the case, but the precedes stereotype simply indicates a temporal precedence. The case has been made that it is possible to draw an equally valid use case diagram by reversing the direction of the arrow and changing the stereotype from precedes to invokes, but IN FACT the meaning is changed subtly by this action, in that the invokes arrow would generally indicate that the invoking use case invokes the invoked use case during its execution, while the precedes arrow would indicate that the preceding use case actually temporally precedes (that is to say, happens earlier in time) than the preceded use case.

Conclusion (assuming you're still awake): Don't worry about it, just focus on what goes *inside* the use cases.

Internet Bookstore: Refining Use Cases

It's high time that we wrote the use case description for our first Internet Bookstore use case. We'll start with *Write Reader Review*, which over the course of the book we'll follow all the way to source code. (We'll also track the progress of the *Show Book Details* use case, beginning in Chapter 4.)

Checking the latest version of the domain model (see Figure 2-7), we have two types of book reviews: Reader Reviews (reviews submitted by Customers) and Editorial Reviews (reviews written by staff).

Here's the first cut of our use case:

The user types in a review of the selected item, gives it a score, and sends it. The review is sent to a moderator.

■**Exercise** The *Write Reader Review* use case scenario captures the basic points of the user's interaction with the system, but the text is rather terse. When it comes to writing text for use cases, a detailed description is preferable to a terse one. We improve on our current version in just a moment, but first, have a look at the reader review process on existing bookstore websites (e.g., Amazon.com or SpringerOnline.com), and try writing a more detailed version.

The text of your use case is important enough to take some care with. In particular, make sure that it's in active voice (present tense, describing user actions and system responses, or vice versa) and that you explicitly name the domain objects that participate. Your goals are to unambiguously describe the required behavior of the system and to identify which domain objects will be performing that required behavior.

■**Tip** Any ambiguity you leave in a use case will just result in more disambiguation work later, so try to be as precise as you can in your descriptions.

Let's now expand the use case text and put some meat on its bones:

The Customer selects the book. The system displays a book detail page. The Customer clicks the Write Review button, and the system shows the Write Review screen. The user types in a review of the book, gives it a rating out of five stars, and clicks the Send button. The system ensures that the review isn't too long or short, and that the rating is within one and five stars. The system then displays a confirmation screen, and the review is sent to a moderator, ready to be added.

With this new version, the narrative has begun slightly too early. By describing the events leading up to the Write Review page, we're actually describing part of a different use case. So let's remove the duplicate text:

The Customer clicks the Write Review button for the book currently being viewed, and the system shows the Write Review screen. The Customer types in a Book Review, gives it a Book Rating out of five stars, and clicks the Send button. The system ensures that the Book Review isn't too long or short, and that the Book Rating is within one and five stars. The system then displays a confirmation screen, and the review is sent to a Moderator, ready to be added.

Reading through the use case, you can see how it relates back to the domain model. Objects such as Book Review and Book Rating, which appear on the domain model, are referenced explicitly by name in the use case. There's a human actor named Customer, and we've also identified a new actor called Moderator (someone responsible for checking the reviews before they are added). And there will also be some kind of Write Reader Review screen.

The updated use case also describes the validation that the system performs on the submitted data (e.g., checking that the Book Rating is a legal value, within one and five stars). As you'll see when we move on to robustness analysis in Chapter 5, describing the validation right in the use case text is an important method of identifying controllers.

One last thing: The actual name of the use case also needs some work. It's called *Write Reader Review*, but in the domain model the name we have for the reader is Customer. So to keep the use case matched up with the domain model, we should change the title to *Write Customer Review*.

■**Exercise** One question that our use case hasn't yet answered is, ***What happens if the Customer does something wrong?*** This important question is covered by exploring the alternate courses, which we cover in the next section. But before that, have another look at the use case text and try to think about the different ways that the Customer might stray off the beaten track.

SUNNY-DAY/RAINY-DAY SCENARIOS

A use case describes a sequence of events—the "flow" of a user's interaction with the system. But users often don't use a system as if they're on rails. They do different or unexpected things, or the system might go wrong somehow (e.g., network error). But you have to ask yourself, "What happens if something goes wrong, or if the user does something out of the typical path?"

So, **a use case consists of an "on rails" scenario and various "gone off the rails" scenarios**.

There's one basic course (sometimes called the sunny-day scenario) and one or more alternate courses (rainy-day scenarios) Alternates can represent less typical usage paths as well as errors.

In their zeal to create a "use case guru" market by making the inherently simple task of modeling use cases incomprehensibly complex, some authors (you know who you are) have proposed long and complicated use case templates to follow when describing users interacting with the various scenarios of a system. Overly complicated use case templates usually just create unnecessary work; you end up trying to dream details up (i.e., guess) to go into an array of subheadings that probably aren't appropriate for your use case anyway. (See the section "A Couple of Thoughts on Use Case Templates" later in this chapter.) So, our use case "template" is really simple. It just consists of a "BASIC COURSE" heading and an "ALTERNATE COURSES" heading. Trust us, it's all you need!

The important thing (well, one of them) is not to skip any of the rainy-day scenarios. Remember the "three magic questions" from earlier in this chapter? The third one to keep asking is "What else might happen?" Each time you ask this question, the answer gets you a new alternate course for your use case. Write it down under the "ALTERNATE COURSES" heading.

Internet Bookstore: Basic and Alternate Courses

Within the *Write Reader Review* use case, all the text we have at this point is for the basic course, such as "The Customer types in a Book Review, gives it a Book Rating out of five stars, and clicks the Send button." There's an implicit assumption that the *Customer* has entered all the data for the given review correctly—the review isn't longer than *The Lord of the Rings* and *War and Peace* combined, the rating is in the range 1–5 (there may well be JavaScript validation in the browser, but the user could feasibly fiddle their local HTML page so that they can enter a 100-star rating, for example), and so forth. We should identify some alternate courses. Remember, keep asking yourself "What else happens?" Sort of like this:

We have our basic course. But, what else happens?

Uh . . . the user might not be logged in?

OK. And what else might happen?

The user might enter a review that is too long.

Cool. What else?

The review might be too short.

Too short?

Like, blank, or fewer than ten characters, say.

. . .and so on.

With these rainy-day scenarios typed up as alternate courses, our *Write Reader Review* use case should now look like this:

BASIC COURSE:

The Customer clicks the Write Review button for the book currently being viewed, and the system shows the Write Review screen. The Customer types in a Book Review, gives it a Book Rating out of five stars, and clicks the Send button. The system ensures that the Book Review isn't too long or short, and that the Book Rating is within one and five stars. The system then displays a confirmation screen, and the review is sent to a Moderator, ready to be added.

ALTERNATE COURSES:

User not logged in: *The user is first taken to the Login screen and then to the Write Review screen once he is logged in.*

The user enters a review that is too long (text > 1MB): *The system rejects the review and responds with a message explaining why the review was rejected.*

The review is too short (< 10 characters): *The system rejects the review.*

■**Exercise** See if you can uncover some more alternate courses for this use case (there are plenty more to be found!). If you're stuck, read each line of the basic course and ask yourself, "How might this go wrong?" and "What might the user do differently here?"

USE CASES AND ASPECTS

Synergy between use case modeling and aspect-oriented programming (AOP) is the topic of Ivar Jacobson's book, *Aspect-Oriented Software Development with Use Cases* (Addison-Wesley, 2004). We highly recommend you give this book a careful read-through, but we would like to present the following brief introduction to the material here. As it turns out, if you're doing AOP, the difference between extends and includes can be significant.

- Use cases help us to organize requirements around user concerns, while aspects help us to organize code around user concerns.

- A pervasive problem in software development is *cross-cutting concerns*, which generally affect multiple classes and components. Examples of cross-cutting concerns would be things like security, transaction management, persistence, and so forth.

- There are two main types of cross-cutting concerns, and they can be modeled as use cases: *peer use cases* (separate, independent use cases) and *extension use cases*. Extension use cases can extend one use case (e.g., enhancements) or multiple use cases (e.g., security, transaction management, persistence). The latter are called *infrastructure use cases*.

- In traditional (non-aspect) languages, implementation of peers can become tangled and/or scattered among components, and it's difficult to keep extension behavior separate from base behavior.

- Aspects help to organize peer code without scattering or tangling, and extensions can be kept separate using *pointcuts* and *advices*.

In short, if you partition your software into use cases and choose to program in an aspect-oriented language, you can basically organize your code along use case boundaries, something you can't readily do in traditional OO programming languages. Organizing code along use case boundaries has the potential for major cost savings over the lifetime of a program.

A Couple of Thoughts on Use Case Templates

Teams who adopt use cases usually do so because they are trying to "do the right thing." So the natural assumption would be that they therefore need to bury the project under reams of documentation, especially long and complex use case templates. Although well intentioned, this approach is—dare we say it—horribly misguided.

■**Caution** Don't waste time with long and involved use case templates.

Here's an example of a long and particularly ghastly (in our opinion) use case template from renowned guru Alistair Cockburn's book *Writing Effective Use Cases*:[4]

---

4. Alistair Cockburn, *Writing Effective Use Cases* (New York: Addison-Wesley, 2000), p. 119.

USE CASE 24: FULLY DRESSED USE CASE TEMPLATE <NAME>

<the name should be the goal as a short active verb phrase>

Context of use: *<a longer statement of the goal, if needed, its normal occurrence conditions>*

Scope: *<design scope, what system is being considered black-box under design>*

Level: *<one of: summary, user-goal, subfunction>*

Primary Actor: *<a role name for the primary actor, or description>*

Stakeholders & Interests: *<list of stakeholders and key interests in the use case>*

Precondition: *<what we expect is already the state of the world>*

Minimal Guarantees: *<how the interests are protected under all exits>*

Success Guarantees: *<the state of the world if goal succeeds>*

Trigger: *<what starts the use case, may be time event>*

Main Success Scenario:

<put here the steps of the scenario from trigger to goal delivery and any cleanup after>

<step #> <action description>

Extensions:

<put here there [sic] extensions, one at a time, each referring to the step of the main scenario>

<step altered> <condition>: <action or sub use case>

<step altered> <condition>: <action or sub use case>

Technology & Data Variations List:

<put here the variations that will cause eventual bifurcation in the scenario>

<step or variation #> <list of variations>

<step or variation #> <list of variations>

Related Information:

<whatever your project needs for additional information>

We regard this template as ghastly because, while it is theoretically elegant in that it comprehensively covers everything you might possibly want to discuss in conjunction with a use case, in practice, if you require your team to "fill out the long form" use case template, they will rapidly discover that

1. They are wasting time.

2. Wasting time will turn them off to the entire modeling process.

3. They can mindlessly fill out the form without focusing on the important parts (basic course and alternate courses) of the use case, and nobody will know the difference.

We've seen this happen in the real world on many occasions.

Consider the statements we just made as warnings about ways you might build up resistance to doing use cases, which offers an excuse to ditch modeling altogether—and we all know what happens then. (Hint: "The code's written, so I guess we're done!")

Use Case or Algorithm?

Many people get confused over the difference between use cases and algorithms, as both tend to be described with verb phrases and generally can be thought of as a sequence of steps. So here are some guidelines on how to differentiate between the two.

One of the main differences between a use case and an algorithm is that an algorithm, while it may contain a sequence of steps, **will not represent the dialogue between a user and the system**. From the use case perspective, even very complicated algorithms should just be considered a single step within the user/system dialogue. If you're faced with having to describe a complex algorithm when writing a use case (e.g., generating a list of recommended books, or sorting the list alphabetically), you should specify the algorithm elsewhere, but ***give the algorithm a name*** (e.g., "Generate Recommendations," "Sort List") so that it can be referred to in the use case text.

Table 3-2 sums up the differences between a use case and an algorithm.

Table 3-2. *Use Case vs. Algorithm*

Use Case	Algorithm
Dialogue between user and system	"Atomic" computation
Event/response sequence	Series of steps
Basic/alternate courses	One step of a use case
Multiple participating objects	Operation on a class
User and System	All System

Use Case Modeling in Practice

In this section, we illustrate the theory presented in the first part of this chapter by walking through a series of exercises that show the most commonly made use case modeling mistakes.

Exercises

For each of the following use cases, see how many errors you can spot, and try to rewrite the use case text. Then compare your rewritten version with the "fixed" version found near the end of this chapter. Good luck!

Exercise 3-1: Search by Author

BASIC COURSE:

The system displays the page with the search form; the user clicks the Author field and types in an author name (e.g., Fred Smith). The user clicks the Search button; the system reads the search form, looks up any books matching that author name, and displays them in a list.

ALTERNATE COURSES:

No matching books found: A page is displayed informing the user that no matching books were found.

Exercise 3-2: Edit Shopping Cart

PRECONDITIONS:

The user has logged in.

The user has navigated to the Edit Shopping Cart page.

BASIC COURSE:

The user adds or removes whatever items he wants to change, and then clicks the Update button. The system adds or removes the items, and then displays the page with the updated shopping cart.

ALTERNATE COURSES:

Shopping cart is empty: No items can be removed.

Exercise 3-3: Open an Account

BASIC COURSE:

The system displays the Create New Account page and enters the following fields: Username (must be unique), password, confirm password, first name, last name, address (first line), address (second line), city, state, country, zip/postal code, telephone number, and e-mail address. Then the user clicks the Submit button; the system checks that the Username is unique, creates the new user account, and displays the main Hub Page, along with a message indicating that the user account is now created and logged in.

ALTERNATE COURSES:

Password and Confirm Password don't match: The page is redisplayed with a validation message.

Username not unique: The page is redisplayed and the user is asked to choose a different username.

Exercise Solutions

Following are the solutions to the exercises.

Exercise 3-1 Solution: Explicit Boundary Object Names

The same problem can be found several times in this use case: the boundary objects haven't been given explicit names. The fixed version follows.

BASIC COURSE:

The system displays the Search Page; the user clicks the Author field and types in an author name (e.g., Fred Smith). The user clicks the Search button; the system reads the search form, looks up any books matching that author name, and displays the Search Results page showing the resulting Book List.

ALTERNATE COURSES:

No matching books found: The Search Not Found page is displayed.

Exercise 3-2 Solution: Vague and Ambiguous

There are at least three problems with this use case.

Problem 1: The use case includes a "Preconditions" clause. Although on very rare occasions, you might find that it's useful to include this clause, most of the time it serves no appreciable purpose. In this example, it actually throws the use case text off course, as the initial "display" action is missed. This would in turn be missed out on the robustness diagram, meaning it would likely be skipped on the design, not estimated for, and not tested.

Problem 2: The basic course text is a bit woolly. It doesn't describe a specific scenario, but instead tries to cover all bases ("The user adds or removes whatever item . . ."). As a result, an important behavioral aspect is missed: the user wouldn't necessarily want to add items from this page, just remove them (or change the quantity).

Problem 3: The alternate course doesn't tie into any particular action in the use case text. There are also several relatively obvious alternate courses that are missing.

The fixed version follows.

BASIC COURSE:

The system displays the Shopping Cart page. The user clicks the Remove button next to a Line Item. The system removes the item from the user's Shopping Cart, and then redisplays the page. The user then clicks the Quantity text field for another Line Item, changes its value from 1 to 2, and clicks the Update button. The system updates the Shopping Cart, recalculates the total amount, and redisplays the page.

ALTERNATE COURSES:

Item not found: The item that the user chose to remove wasn't found in the Shopping Cart (this could happen if the user had two browser tabs open and is viewing an older version of the page). The system refreshes the Shopping Cart page, along with a warning message that the user's action failed because the page was out of date.

Quantity changed to zero: This counts as removing the item, so the item is removed from the Shopping Cart.

Negative value or non-numeric "value" entered: The page is redisplayed with the original Quantity value, and a message next to it informs the user that he entered an invalid value.

Exercise 3-3 Solution: Too Many Presentation Details

This use case gets bogged down in presentation details; it spends too long listing the fields to be found on the Create New Account page. Instead, these fields should be added as attributes to the appropriate class in your domain model (most likely the Customer class). Then, when you need them later, they'll be right there. The fixed version follows.

BASIC COURSE:

The system displays the Create New Account page and enters the fields to define a new Customer account (username, password, address, etc.). Then the user clicks the Submit button; the system checks that the Username is unique, creates the new user account, and displays the main Hub Page, along with a message indicating that the user account is now created and logged in.

ALTERNATE COURSES:

Password and Confirm Password don't match: The page is redisplayed with a validation message.

Username not unique: The page is redisplayed and the user is asked to choose a different username.

More Practice

This section provides a list of questions that you can use to test your knowledge of use case modeling.

1. A use case captures

   a) Objects, classes, and their associations

   b) The flow of operations within a system

   c) A discrete, visible user function

   d) Collaborations between objects organized by time

2. A use case that is used to drive a software design must be

   a) Abstract, essential, technology-neutral, and implementation-independent

   b) Vague, incomplete, fuzzy, and ambiguous

   c) Specific and unambiguous, and must explicitly account for all user actions and system responses

   d) "Fully dressed"—in particular, specify preconditions, postconditions, and functional requirements

3. When writing a use case, a rainy-day scenario is referred to as

   a) An extension point

   b) A use case generalization

   c) An alternate course of action

   d) A precondition

4. Robustness diagramming a use case serves which of the following purposes:

   a) Makes sure you understand which objects participate in the use case

   b) Makes sure you understand how the users interact with the GUI

   c) Makes you double-check that you've covered all possible courses of action

   d) Disambiguates the use case text and puts it into proper noun-verb-noun form

   e) All of the above

5. List three things that are common between a use case and a section of a user's manual for a system. List three things that are different. (Hint: What things are missing from a user manual that are needed to develop an OO software design?)

6. Attack or defend the following statement:

   Long use case templates that include items like preconditions, postconditions, and functional requirements are a cause of analysis paralysis, and thus long templates should be avoided.

   Cite the pros and cons of this argument, and explain your conclusion.

7. List three major differences between use cases and Extreme Programming (XP) user stories. What are the advantages of each?

8. Explain the difference between <<includes>> and <<extends>> according to the UML specification. In particular, attack or defend the following statement:

   The difference between the <<includes>> and <<extends>> stereotypes on associations on use case diagrams is not generally significant unless the software is to be implemented using an aspect-oriented programming language that directly supports organizing code around extensions.

   How does the <<invokes>> stereotype relate to <<includes>> and <<extends>>? What is the primary purpose of all three of these stereotypes? Which do you feel are the more useful set of stereotypes: <<invokes>> and <<precedes>>, or <<includes>> and <<extends>>?

Summary

In this chapter, we covered in detail how to write the kinds of use cases that can be used to drive a software design. The activity diagram in Figure 3-10 shows how use case modeling fits into the overall requirements analysis effort; the tasks we discussed in this chapter are shown in red.

At Milestone 1, you'll have written the first-draft version of your use cases, having quizzed and grilled the customer, end users, and others to extract all the information you can from them about how the new system should behave. But the customer's role doesn't end there. In the next chapter, we cover the Requirements Review stage, in which you ensure that the domain model and the use cases work together to address the customer's requirements.

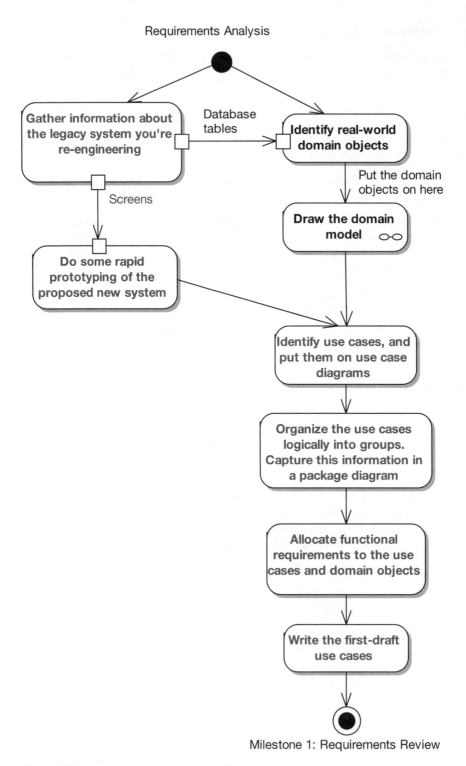

Figure 3-10. *Requirements Analysis Checkpoint 2*

CHAPTER 4
■ ■ ■
Requirements Review

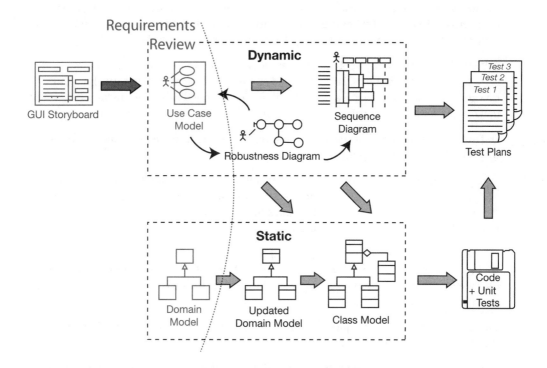

The requirements review session ensures that the system as described genuinely matches up with the requirements. It's a collaborative review session involving the customer representative(s), end users (i.e., the people who will actually be using the system, or who are using the current system being replaced), and marketing people—basically, all the project stakeholders who have a vested interest in ensuring the requirements fit their view of the system.

In this chapter, we provide an overview of the Requirements Review stage, and then show an example review for the Internet Bookstore.

Requirements Review in Theory

In this section, we look at the key elements of requirements review, including our top 10 requirements review guidelines.

Why Review Requirements?

Why bother reviewing requirements? Here's a hypothetical conversation that we hope will shed some light on the subject.

> **Q: My project looks like it's in pretty good shape already. I have a domain model that I've updated as I wrote the use case descriptions, and my use cases are, for the most part, written in the context of the domain model. It must be time to start coding, right? (After all, I've never done this much up-front work pre-coding before.)**

> A: Well, almost, but not quite. The customer was involved in the initial requirements-gathering effort and hopefully also involved in your use case modeling workshop. But, now that the first-draft use cases are all written up, you need to get the customer back and make sure that the system as described genuinely matches up with their requirements.

> **Q: That sounds like a tall order. My customer never even reads requirements specs—why should I waste time producing them?**

> A: If you e-mailed your customer a 200-page document and asked them to reply with a "Yes, please" or a set of required modifications, chances are that you'll just get a "Yes, please" a few minutes later. Then, in a year's time, the system you produce will be nothing like what the customer wanted.

> What's needed (aside from breaking down the development into smaller releases) is to **make the sign-off process collaborative**. You need to get the customer representatives into the room for a requirements review session, and go through all of the use cases with them.

> There's a whole set of techniques for doing these reviews that work pretty well in practice. We'll demonstrate those in this chapter.

> **Q: But what if I can't get the customer to visit me for the requirements review session?**

> A: Sure, all customers are infinitely busy. But if your customer won't offer you even a couple hours of their time before signing off on a costly IT project, then you're probably already looking at a "death march" project, whatever process you follow. But at least we don't require the customer to be in the same room as the programmers for the full duration of the project (like some "processes" we know)![1]

---

1. For a lyrical view of why this is a bad thing, see "The Customer's a Beast of Burden" on page 120 of our book *Extreme Programming Refactored: The Case Against XP* (Apress, 2003).

Top 10 Requirements Review Guidelines

The advice given in this chapter is summed up in our top 10 requirements review guidelines.

10. Make sure your domain model describes at least 80% of the most important abstractions from your problem domain (i.e., real-world objects), in nontechnical language that your end users can understand.

9. Make sure your domain model shows the is-a (generalization) and has-a (aggregation) relationships between the domain objects.

8. Make sure your use cases describe both basic and alternate courses of action, in active voice.

7. Make sure that passive voice, functional requirements (i.e., "shall" statements), are not absorbed into and "intermangled" with the active voice use case text.[2]

6. Make sure you've organized your use cases into packages and that each package has at least one use case diagram.

5. Make sure your use cases are written in the context of the object model.

4. Make sure your use cases are written in the context of the user interface.

3. Make sure you've supplemented your use case descriptions with some sort of storyboard, line drawing, screen mock-up, or GUI prototype.

2. Review the use cases, domain model, and screen mock-ups/GUI prototypes with end users, stakeholders, and marketing folks, in addition to more technical members of your staff.

1. Structure the review around our "eight easy steps to a better use case."

Let's walk through these top 10 items in more detail, and then we'll illustrate them in practice by following a requirements review for the Internet Bookstore.

10. Make Sure Your Domain Model Covers the Problem Domain

Sometimes "the best is the enemy of the good."[3] You don't want to spend endless weeks (and catch a case of analysis paralysis) fiddling around with the domain model, trying to make it perfect. Instead, you should be aiming for the following:

- A domain model diagram that has the most important abstractions from the problem domain

---

2. In Chapter 13, we introduce the term "intermangled" to describe use case text that has had functional requirements text mangled into it.

3. General George S. Patton, *War as I Knew It* (New York: Mariner Books, 1995), p. 335 (referring to battle planning).

- All the boxes on this diagram have unambiguous names that the users of the system can relate to

- Getting this diagram done quickly!

Further details will be uncovered as you analyze the use cases.

9. Show Generalization and Aggregation Relationships

These generalization (is-a) and aggregation (has-a) relationships go a long way toward making the diagram concrete and specific as opposed to vague and ambiguous.

Occasionally, you might need a "link class" (especially if you have underlying many-to-many relationships in the data model), but it's best not to overuse this construct. You can get most of the way just by using is-a and has-a.

Don't split hairs (yet) between aggregation and composition, either—it's too early to worry about this distinction.

8. Describe Both Basic and Alternate Courses of Action, in Active Voice

You already know this, but the use cases describe how the users are using the system, in present tense, active voice, and they must include both normal (sunny day) usage as well as less typical (rainy day) usage.

We know that you already know this, but we've also seen many of your peers who (in theory) already knew, but didn't do it correctly (in practice). So we're telling you again. We might tell you a couple more times, too.

7. Don't Mix Functional Requirements into Your Use Case Text

Functional requirements are passive voice "shall" requirements (e.g., "The system shall do this"). A common mistake is to include these in the use case descriptions. Instead, the functional requirements should be kept separately and "allocated" to the use cases. That is, the use cases satisfy the functional requirements, but the passive voice "shall" requirements don't compose the use cases. Keep the use cases focused on system usage (active voice).

In Chapter 13, we'll show you how easy it is to allocate requirements to use cases. It's just a single drag and drop if you do it correctly.

6. Organize Your Use Cases into Packages

You can organize your use case model by functionally related areas (subsystems), by release, or both. One useful strategy is to identify all the use cases within a functional area on the use case diagram, but write the narrative descriptions only for the use cases that will participate in the current release.

■**Tip** It's useful to use color-coding on the use case diagram to show which use cases will be implemented in the current release.

By all means don't get hung up on trying to perfect your use case diagram with a flawless use of stereotypes—here again, "the best is the enemy of the good" (i.e., you don't have time on your schedule for endless fiddling around). **The use case diagram really serves as a visual table of contents** for the package, and so it should be clear and easy to understand, but the real "meat" of the use case model is the text of the use cases and the corresponding robustness and sequence diagrams for each use case.

5. Write Your Use Cases in the Context of the Object Model

By far the most effective way to base your use cases on the domain model is to **do the domain model first**, and **write the use cases to explicitly reference the domain objects by name**.

Much of the ambiguity in use cases arises from the fact that they are often written entirely in "user terms" without explicitly and precisely referring to the particular "problem domain elements" that are affected by the scenario in question. So the first step in disambiguating your use case text is to make that text explicitly refer to the appropriate domain objects.

4. Put Your Use Cases in the Context of the User Interface

To base your use cases on the user interface, name the screens that will participate in the use case, and use those names in the use case text.

The use cases really need to link not only the object model but also the GUI model to the narrative behavior descriptions. In practical terms, this usually means that you should **name your screens explicitly and use those names in the use case text**.

While there is a theory that preaches keeping your use cases completely divorced from the user interface, our experience is that in practice, this inevitably leads to vagueness and ambiguity in the use cases. So name your screens. Trust us, you'll need to give them names anyway. You'll be happy that you've named them. Really.

■Tip Name your screens, and use those names in your use case descriptions.

---

3. Use Storyboards, Line Drawings, Screen Mock-ups, or GUI Prototypes

Make sure all of the user's behavior (e.g., buttons they can click, menus they can pick from) is accounted for in the use cases.

Once you've given your screen a name, you have no excuse for not creating some sort of storyboard or mock-up that helps you to walk through the actions that users can take when they interact with the system. It's amazing how much system behavior might be tied to, let's say, the Cancel button in, for example, a transaction-oriented system. You might have to roll back to the previously completed transaction. But if you don't draw some sort of visual aid that shows what's on the screen, you might forget to write the "On Click Cancel" behavior in your use case text. And you wouldn't want to forget that, would you?

Remember that these mock-ups don't need to be high-fidelity renderings with animated buttons ("the best is the enemy of the good," again). They need to be simple, clear illustrations that focus on what system behavior can be triggered by the user, and they need to be quick to create (otherwise you'll ignore our advice and skip drawing them—admit it!).

■**Tip** Don't be afraid to build some exploratory prototypes to help validate your requirements.

If you do have any exploratory prototypes, walk through them in conjunction with reviewing the use cases to gain insight into the required behavior. Sometimes a storyboard might not be enough, and you want to string a few screens together before a presentation to your users. If you need to do this, go right ahead.

2. Review the Behavioral Requirements with the Right People

Review the use cases, domain model, and screen mock-ups/GUI prototypes with end users, stakeholders, and marketing folks, in addition to more technical members of your staff. Make sure the requirements are well understood and agreed upon by all parties before proceeding toward design.

Your requirements review is a collaborative workshop that should be attended by the customer (or representatives of the customer), the business analyst (i.e., the senior analyst responsible for the use cases), and a senior member of your development team, plus any project managers who will be closely involved in the project. Ideally, an actual end user of the proposed (or current) system should also be there, to provide real-world feedback on whether the new system matches up with what is really needed.

The goal of your requirements review session is to achieve basic agreement among all parties that the use cases capture the behavioral requirements of the system.[4] And in order to achieve that goal, you must ensure that the required system behavior is unambiguously understood by all.[5]

In fact, you're not just reviewing the use cases; you also need to review the domain model and whatever prototype elements are in place. This works best when everyone is in a room together, with a facilitator/moderator who keeps the conversations on track and a scribe who records the results and the action items.

Call us old-fashioned, but we've found that "ready-aim-fire" works better than "ready-fire-aim." We've found over the years of doing Jumpstart training workshops that an amazing amount of understanding can be gained in a remarkably short period of time by getting everybody on the team to agree to a set of screens, a set of behavior descriptions that explain how users will use those screens, and a set of objects that support the behavior descriptions. We haven't met a project yet that didn't benefit from a common understanding of these things, reached early in the life cycle of the project.

1. Structure the Review Around Our "Eight Easy Steps to a Better Use Case"

Once you have everyone in the room, and they all understand why they're there and what they must achieve during the review session, then the following steps can be performed. As you'll see shortly, these steps form the bulk of the review session:

---

4. Doug Rosenberg and Kendall Scott, *Applying Use Case Driven Object Modeling With UML* (New York: Addison-Wesley, 2001), p. 53.

5. Ibid.

1. Remove everything that's out of scope.

2. Change passive voice to active voice.

3. Check that your use case text isn't too abstract.

4. Accurately reflect the GUI.

5. Name participating domain objects.

6. Make sure you have all the alternate courses.

7. Trace each requirement to its use cases.

8. Make each use case describe what the users are trying to do.

These eight steps will help you transmogrify your use case from a vague and ambiguous piece of mush to a razor-sharp, concise, and precise behavior specification. In the "Requirements Review in Practice" section, we walk through an example requirements review that illustrates most of these checks.

Allocating Functional Requirements to Use Cases

At some stage, you'll need to link up the functional requirements to the use cases, so that you can demonstrate that all the customer's requirements have been successfully implemented. It's good practice to do this just after you've written the use case descriptions, as the act of allocating requirements to use cases often shows up some areas of the requirements that might have been left out. But if you don't perform this activity at that stage, then you should definitely try to do this during the requirements review.

If you've used the functional requirements as the primary source of use cases, then there should already be a direct correlation between the requirements and the use cases. But for others (e.g., use cases that were discovered from UI prototypes or legacy user manuals), some backward-tracing (and possible updating of the functional requirements, in collaboration with the customer) may need to be done.

In Chapter 13, we show an example of modeling the linkages between functional requirements and use cases visually using the Enterprise Architect tool.

Requirements Review in Practice: Internet Bookstore

In this section, we illustrate the theory from the first part of this chapter, using an example from our Internet Bookstore project. We'll walk through an example review of the *Show Book Details* use case (we provided a "critique" of the *Write Customer Review* use case in Chapter 3).

For the Internet Bookstore requirements review, we'll follow the reviewer/use case analyst conversation as it unfolds in the following subsections.

■Note As described earlier, the requirements review should include at least one customer representative, the business analyst, a senior member of your development team, an end user, and any managers closely involved in the project. For the purposes of this example, and to keep the *dramatis personae* from running rampant, we're only following the conversation between the business analyst and a reviewer (who also doubles as a process mentor).

Removing Everything That's Out of Scope

A common affliction when specifying behavioral requirements is to begin or end each use case in the wrong place, or to include extra information that's way outside the scope of the simple use case being described. What follows is an extreme, but all too familiar, example.

Analyst: Here's the text for *Show Book Details*:

USE CASE: Show Book Details

LEVEL: User Goal

PRECONDITIONS:

 1. *The user MUST be viewing the website.*

 2. *The user MAY be logged in.*

BASIC COURSE:

If the user has an account, he MAY log in first (though this isn't essential for this use case). The user MAY navigate to the website's main area. This area MUST be easily accessible and SHOULD provide easy access to a search area and various book directories (e.g., top 10 bestsellers in different categories, editors' picks, etc.). Then the user browses the details for a book title. The system displays the screen showing the book information. If the user wishes to, he may proceed to purchase the book. Allowed payment options are as follows: Visa, American Express, and check (the check must be received by the billing department before the order is dispatched).

POSTCONDITIONS:

 1. *The Book Details screen is being shown.*

 2. *The details for the selected book have been retrieved.*

Reviewer: *(Silently, to self)* Oh, sweet mother of our great Lord Cthulhu. Where to begin?

Analyst: I'm actually quite proud of this use case, as I've packed in loads of extra detail around the subject matter.

Reviewer: Well, there are several ways this use case could be improved. We'll take them one at a time. To summarize, though, we can shorten the template and move those preconditions and postconditions out of the use case text. Remember the purpose of these use cases: we want to be able to link them to our classes, so that we can drive the design directly from the use case text. So things like preconditions and postconditions aren't needed.

Analyst: But hang on, the preconditions *are* important. They describe things that must be in place before the use case can proceed.

Reviewer: You're absolutely right that the information they contain is important, and it does need to be recorded somewhere. But the preconditions and postconditions describe stuff outside the scope of this use case. Most of the time, you can just delete them from the use case text, and you won't lose anything. If you must show them, it's better to show the ordering on the use case diagram with a <<precedes>> link between the two use cases.

Analyst: So you could have a *Login* use case that precedes *Show Book Details*.

Reviewer: Yep. You could also lose the Level field at the top of the use case template, as it doesn't achieve a huge amount. So that gives us the following:

BASIC COURSE:

If the user has an account, he MAY log in first (though this isn't essential for this use case). The user MAY navigate to the website's main area. This area MUST be easily accessible and SHOULD provide easy access to a search area and various book directories (e.g., top 10 bestsellers in different categories, editors' picks, etc.). Then the user browses the details for a book title. The system displays the screen showing the book information. If the user wishes to, he may proceed to purchase the book. Allowed payment options are as follows: Visa, American Express, and check (the check must be received by the billing department before the order is dispatched).

Reviewer: That's much more concise and, if you think about it, doesn't actually convey any less information. But it's still a long way from being the kind of use case we need. For one thing, the description still goes outside the use case's scope. Remember, we're only concerned with describing the steps involved to view a book's details. So all the stuff about proceeding to purchase the book is irrelevant. It all really belongs in a different use case.

Analyst: OK, so if we move that stuff out, then we're left with this:

BASIC COURSE:

The user MAY navigate to the website's main area. This area MUST be easily accessible and SHOULD provide easy access to a search area and various book directories (e.g., top 10 bestsellers in different categories, editors' picks, etc.). Then the user browses the details for a book title. The system displays the screen showing the book information.

Reviewer: Yes. Those other steps are important, of course, but they just belong in a different use case.

Naming Participating Domain Objects

When you try to drive an object-oriented design from use cases, it's vital that the use cases are linked to the objects. In the next review segment, our reviewer discovers a major disconnect between the use case text and the objects in the domain model.

Reviewer: This is a critical point. Most of this text doesn't match up with the domain model. That's just inviting trouble, because we'll end up talking at cross-purposes, the designers will add in duplicate classes, and so on.

Analyst: I didn't think it was that bad. Can you give me some examples?

Reviewer: Sure. Let's take a look at the first sentence: "The user may navigate to the website's main area." The domain model doesn't have a "user," but it does have a `Customer`. And instead of saying "website" you should really say `Bookstore`. Keep it consistent.

Analyst: OK . . .

Reviewer: Similarly, later on you have "book directories," but in the domain model we have "Book Lists" (see Figure 2-7). More precisely, we have an abstract `Book List` class, with concrete types called `Wish List`, `Recommendation List`, `Related Books`, and so on. It looks as if we could add another `Book List` type called, say, `Bestseller List`, or maybe `Home Page List`, to represent lists of books that appear on the `Bookstore`'s home page.

Analyst: OK, I see what you're getting at. We also have "book information" in the final sentence. Perhaps that should match up with a domain object as well?

Reviewer: Well, since the use case is called *Show Book Details*, we could have an object called `Book Details`. But really, that's what the `Book` domain object is. So, for consistency we could reword "showing the book information" to be "showing the `Book Details`." Anyway, here's the updated text:

BASIC COURSE:

The Customer MAY navigate to the Bookstore's main area. This area MUST be easily accessible and SHOULD provide easy access to a search area and various Bestseller Lists. Then the Customer browses the details for a book title. The system displays the screen showing the Book Details.

Making Sure You Have All the Alternate Courses

When you decompose a system along usage scenario boundaries, it's a good idea to consider not just sunny-day scenarios (the basic course) but also rainy-day scenarios (the alternate courses)—at least if you're planning to build a robust system. While some methodologies offer mantras such as Do The Simplest Thing That Could Possibly Work (DTSTTCPW) and You Aren't Gonna Need It (YAGNI), our experience has been that these philosophies, when taken literally, and especially when combined together, can often lead to disastrous results. The main reason for this is that **well over half of the complexity of a software project is usually caused by dealing with alternate courses of action**. Failure to build adequate infrastructure to account for the rainy-day behavior is simply unacceptable on many industrial-strength software projects. So, **make sure you've accounted for all the alternate courses of action**.

> **Reviewer**: I couldn't help noticing that this use case has no alternate courses. I guess that the main alternate course is just what happens if the book details aren't found. Let's add that at least:

> *ALTERNATE COURSES*:

> ***Book not found***: *The system displays a Book Details Not Found screen.*

> **Reviewer**: Notice that we've just identified a new screen, or page.

> **Analyst**: Handling a book not found is a fairly obvious one, I suppose. But now that you mention it, there are several other parts of the system where we could identify all sorts of "special cases." That adds up to a lot of missing functionality.

> **Reviewer**: And all that functionality would have been missed when you estimate how long it's all going to take to develop. Plus it would have been missed when you wrote the test cases, did the design, and so on . . .

■**Tip** If you see a use case without any alternate courses, alarm bells should start ringing. It's often a tell-tale sign that the user and system behavior for that use case haven't been explored in sufficient depth.

Checking That the Use Case Text Isn't Too Abstract

Many books about use cases, especially those that are focused strictly on use cases as a requirements definition technique, preach writing use cases that are "abstract, essential, technology-free, and implementation-independent." Our approach is a bit different, as you'll see in the following review segment, since we both come from a programming background (most programmers would call the aforementioned use cases "vague, ambiguous, incomplete, and incorrect").

Reviewer: The original text did get quite abstract in places, although we seem to have deleted most of it now. But there are a couple of things we could improve on, such as, what's a bookstore main area?

Analyst: The home page, I guess.

Reviewer: Actually, while we're at it, "browses the details for a book title" is a bit vague. In fact, the sentences around it seem rather strange:

> *Then the Customer browses the details for a book title. The system displays the screen showing the Book Details.*

Analyst: Should that change to "displays the `Book Details` screen"?

Reviewer: I think what we're missing here is the whole user action/system response thing. The use case isn't describing the user's action followed by the system's response to that action. So those two sentences should be

> *Then the Customer clicks a link to view a Book. The system retrieves the Book details and displays the Book Details screen.*

Reviewer: That's much more specific. It describes exactly how the customer interacts with the UI: clicking a link to view a book. And then it describes precisely what the system does in response. This is the kind of use case text that can be designed from. Let's go through the rest of the text and make it all follow the same user action/system response pattern.

> ***BASIC COURSE:***
>
> *The Customer MAY navigate to the Bookstore's main area, which the system displays. This area MUST be easily accessible, and SHOULD provide easy access to a search area and various Bestseller Lists). Then the Customer clicks a link to view a Book. The system retrieves the Book details and displays the Book Details screen.*

> ***ALTERNATE COURSES:***
>
> ***Book not found**: The system displays a Book Details Not Found screen.*

Analyst: So why is this version better?

Reviewer: Well, it still isn't perfect (we'll fix the remaining problems in a moment). But it's in a much better state, where we could hand this to the programmers and reasonably ask them to create a design from it. You want to avoid writing use cases that are abstract, essential, technology-free, or implementation-independent.

Analyst: Hey, but I just read a book on use cases that specifically told me to write use cases that are abstract, essential, technology-free, and implementation-independent.

Reviewer: Surprisingly, yes, it's depressingly common advice. But think about what happens when you hand that abstract, vaguely written use case to a programmer. Wouldn't it be better if the use case was coherent, specific, and unambiguous? *That's* the sort of use case that can be coded from!

Changing Passive Voice to Active Voice

Generally, passive voice statements describe requirements. Some people like to "intermangle" the passive voice requirements with the active voice usage descriptions (see the sidebar titled "Disintermangling Dysfunctional Requirements from the Scenario Text" in Chapter 13). We advocate linking the requirements to the use cases and keeping the active voice description (which becomes a runtime behavior specification) separate. As you'll see in the following review segment, activities are much more effectively described in active voice.

Reviewer: We're getting there. There's a lot of passive voice text in there, though: "The Customer MAY navigate . . . SHOULD provide easy access . . ." These sound like functional requirements to me. They definitely don't belong in a use case.

Analyst: But we can't just delete this stuff. I wrote those details in there because they're important!

Reviewer: Agreed. The goal here isn't to delete important requirements—it's just to make sure that they get recorded in the appropriate place. In this case, that will be the functional requirements spec, not the use case.

Analyst: I'm still not convinced that we can't just describe these details in the use case itself.

Reviewer: Think about it this way. "Use case" is a shorter way of saying "usage scenario"— that is, a scenario that describes how the user is interacting with the system. The key word here is "interacting." Describing user interactions and system responses is by its very nature a description of the user's activities. Can we describe activities in passive voice? Not really. "Shall" statements such as "the system shall support 300 concurrent transactions per minute" don't describe user actions or system responses.

Analyst: I see. So if we mix those "shall" statements into the use case, it's really defeating the purpose of the use case format.

Reviewer: You got it. OK, here's the reviewed and updated text for *Show Book Details*:

BASIC COURSE:

The Customer types in the URL for the bookstore's home page, which the system displays. Then the Customer clicks a link to view a Book. The system retrieves the Book details and displays the Book Details screen.

ALTERNATE COURSES:

Book not found: *The system displays a Book Details Not Found screen.*

Analyst: Actually, in retrospect, perhaps we should have made the active voice change right at the start of the review.

Reviewer: I think you're right. Out of all these steps, it's the one that helped clean up the use case text the most, so doing it at the start would have made a lot of other things fall right into place early on. That plus the "remove everything that's out of scope" step.

■**Note**   ICONIX Process is an intensely feedback-driven process. In the next chapter, we cover *robustness analysis*, in which the use case text gets even more of a going-over, to prepare it for the design stage.

Tracing Each Requirement to Its Use Cases

We once read a newsgroup posting by a famous and self-important "guru" that asked the question "Why would anybody want to trace requirements?" and then went on to profess that requirements traceability was all a matter of "fear" (see the inside front cover of *Extreme Programming Refactored: The Case Against XP* [Apress, 2003] if you'd like to find out who said it).

Our feeling about this is that it would be funny if it wasn't so sad. In the world we live in, project teams trace requirements (for example) to make sure that they are fulfilling their contractual obligations, which then allows them to get paid for delivering what the client ordered. If you're going to describe the functionality being delivered as a set of use cases, it would seem pretty obvious that those requirements would need to be traced back to the use cases. In our final requirements review segment, we show how this process could be started (see Chapter 13 for more about traceability).

Reviewer: OK, let's do a final check of the *Show Book Details* use case. Currently, we don't have a traceability matrix to show which requirements are satisfied by this use case, so we should sort that out.

■**Tip**   As we discuss in Chapter 13, the Enterprise Architect (EA) tool has a useful Relationship Matrix feature for tracing between requirements and use cases, among other model elements (see Figure 13-10).

Analyst: Well, we were meant to go through the use cases earlier on and allocate them to the functional requirements. (See Figure 3-10 and the section "Allocating Functional Requirements to Use Cases" in this chapter.) But as we didn't do that then, we should really do it now.

Reviewer: OK. So, looking at the requirements list (see Chapter 2), *Show Book Details* pretty clearly relates back to these requirements:

*11. It must be possible for the user to post reviews of their favorite books; the **review comments** should appear on the book details screen. The review should include a **customer rating** (1–5), which is usually shown along with the book title in **book lists**.*

    a. *Book reviews must be moderated—that is, checked and "OK'd" by a member of staff before they're published on the website.*

    b. *Longer reviews should be truncated on the book details screen; the **customer** may click to view the full review on a separate page.*

Analyst: What about requirement number 1?

*1. The **bookstore** will be web based initially, but it must have a sufficiently flexible architecture that alternative front-ends may be developed (Swing/applets, web services, etc.).*

Reviewer: Strictly speaking, all the use cases could be traced back to that one, although there isn't a very concrete connection there. We're really looking for functional links between the use cases and the requirements.

Analyst: Ah, OK.

Summary

In this chapter, we covered the Requirements Review milestone. It's a vital step because it ensures that the requirements are **sufficiently well understood** by both the development team and the customer/users/project stakeholders.

In the next chapter, we launch into preliminary design, a step that provides intensive feedback into the use cases and domain model, and an essential bridge between analysis and design.

Figure 4-1 shows where we are. (The item covered in this chapter is shown in red.)

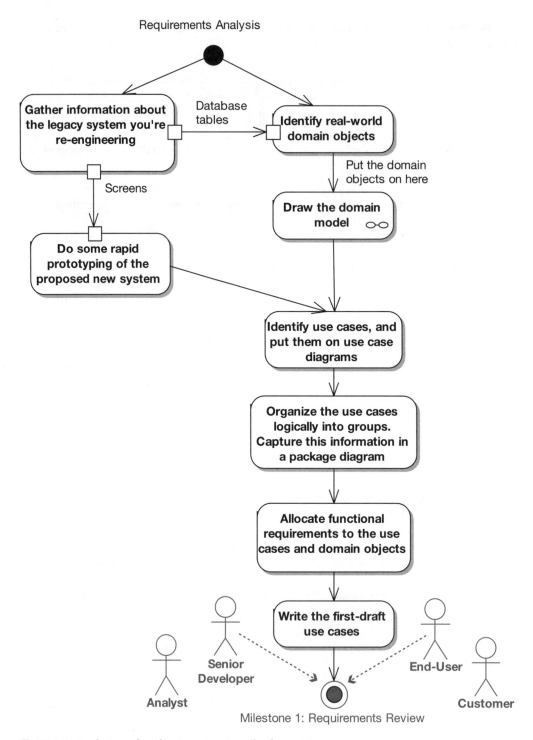

Figure 4-1. *Analysis and Preliminary Design Checkpoint 1*

PART 2

Analysis, Conceptual Design, and Technical Architecture

CHAPTER 5

■ ■ ■

Robustness Analysis

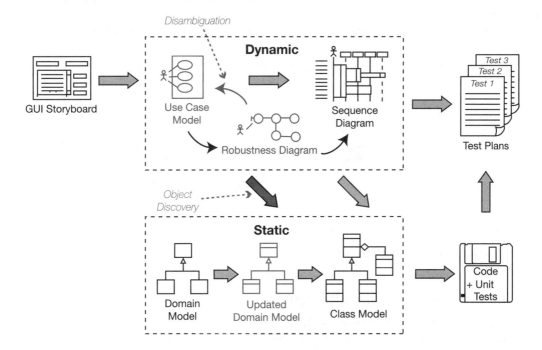

To get from use cases to detailed design (and then to code), you need to link your use cases to objects. The technique we describe in this chapter, robustness analysis, helps you to bridge the gap from analysis to design by doing exactly that. In a nutshell, it's a way of analyzing your use case text and identifying a first-guess set of objects for each use case. These are classified into boundary objects, entity objects, and controllers (which are often more like functions than objects).

The 10,000-Foot View

A robustness diagram is an object picture of a use case. The robustness diagram and the use case text have to match precisely, so the robustness diagram forces you to tie the use case text to the objects. This enables you to drive object-oriented designs forward from use cases, and this is really the "magic" of robustness analysis.

Drawing a robustness diagram ensures that the use case is **written in the context of the domain model**—that is, all the terms (nouns and noun phrases) that went into the domain model should also be used directly in your use case text.

Where Does Robustness Analysis Fit into the Process?

Looking at Figure 5-1, robustness analysis sort of takes place in the murky middle ground between analysis and design. If you think of analysis (i.e., the use cases) as the "what" and design as the "how," then robustness analysis is really preliminary design. During this phase, you start making some preliminary assumptions about your design, and you start to think about the technical architecture (also see Chapter 7) and to think through the various possible design strategies. So it's part analysis and part design.

It's also an important technique to remove ambiguity from (disambiguate) your use case text.

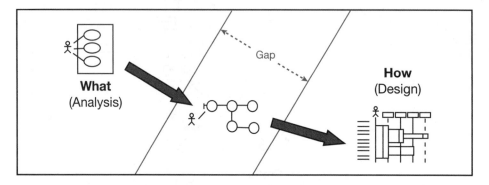

Figure 5-1. *Bridging the gap between "what" and "how"*

Like Learning to Ride a Bicycle

Learning this technique has a bit in common with learning to ride a bicycle. Until you "get it," robustness analysis can seem devilishly difficult, but once you do get it, it's really very simple. To jump-start your understanding, we'll walk through plenty of examples in this chapter. Experience has shown us that you usually need to draw six or so robustness diagrams before the penny drops and you suddenly get it. Just remember, **a robustness diagram is an object picture of a use case.**

Once you get the hang of it, you should be able to rattle off a robustness diagram in about ten minutes (or less) for each use case. Actually, as you'll see, **the trick is in writing your use case correctly.** If a robustness diagram takes more than ten minutes to draw, you can bet you're spending most of that time rewriting your use case text.

■Tip Using a CASE tool can make your life easier, but robustness diagrams are really quick and simple diagrams that you can scribble on a piece of paper or a whiteboard. It's often very helpful to sketch your diagram on paper before attempting to draw it on the computer (especially when you're first learning the technique).

Anatomy of a Robustness Diagram

A robustness diagram is somewhat of a hybrid between a class diagram and an activity diagram. It's a pictorial representation of the behavior described by a use case, showing both participating classes and software behavior, although it intentionally avoids showing which class is responsible for which bits of behavior. Each class is represented by a graphical stereotype icon (see Figure 5-2). However, a robustness diagram reads more like an **activity diagram** (or a flowchart), in the sense that one object "talks to" the next object. This flow of action is represented by a line between the two objects that are talking to each other.

There's a direct 1:1 correlation between the flow of action in the robustness diagram and the steps described in the use case text.

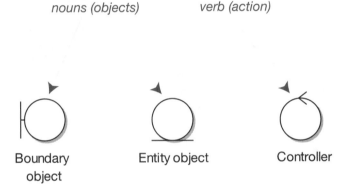

Figure 5-2. *Robustness diagram symbols*

The three class stereotypes shown in Figure 5-2 are as follows:

- **Boundary objects**: The "interface" between the system and the outside world (think back to Figure 3-2). Boundary objects are typically screens or web pages (i.e., the **presentation layer** that the actor interacts with).

- **Entity objects**: Classes from the domain model (see Chapter 2).

- **Controllers**: The "glue" between the boundary and entity objects.

It's useful to think of boundary objects and entity objects as being nouns, and controllers as being verbs. Keep the following rules in mind when drawing your robustness diagrams:

- Nouns can talk to verbs (and vice versa).

- Nouns can't talk to other nouns.

- Verbs can talk to other verbs.

We'll revisit these rules later in this chapter (see Figures 5-8 and 5-9).

■**Exercise** Two of the following are legal constructs, but which two?

a. Boundary ➤ Controller ➤ Entity

b. Entity ➤ Entity

c. Controller ➤ Controller

d. Boundary ➤ Boundary ➤ Controller

These rules **help to enforce a noun-verb-noun pattern in your use case text**. If your use case text follows this pattern, robustness diagrams are a snap to draw; if not, the diagrams can be really difficult to draw.

Think of this as an early warning signal: if you can't draw a simple ol' robustness diagram from a use case, how are you ever going to create a detailed design from it? **Sequence diagrams are completely noun-verb-noun in nature**: the objects are the nouns, and the messages that go between them are the verbs. So by getting your text in noun-verb-noun format now, you're making the detailed design task much easier than it would otherwise be.

Robustness analysis provides a sanity check for your use cases.

Robustness Analysis in Theory

In this section, we describe the theory behind robustness analysis, interspersed with examples from the Internet Bookstore project. We'll begin with our top 10 robustness analysis guidelines.

Top 10 Robustness Analysis Guidelines

The principles discussed in this chapter can be summed up as a list of guidelines. Our top 10 list follows.

10. Paste the use case text directly onto your robustness diagram.

9. Take your entity classes from the domain model, and add any that are missing.

8. Expect to rewrite (disambiguate) your use case while drawing the robustness diagram.

7. Make a boundary object for each screen, and name your screens unambiguously.

6. Remember that controllers are only occasionally **real control objects**; they are more typically **logical software functions**.

5. Don't worry about the direction of the arrows on a robustness diagram.

4. It's OK to drag a use case onto a robustness diagram if it's invoked from the parent use case.

3. The robustness diagram represents a preliminary conceptual design of a use case, not a literal detailed design.

2. Boundary and entity classes on a robustness diagram will generally become object instances on a sequence diagram, while controllers will become messages.

1. Remember that a robustness diagram is an "object picture" of a use case, whose purpose is to force refinement of both use case text and the object model.

Let's walk through the items in this list in more detail.

10. Paste the Use Case Text Directly onto Your Robustness Diagram

Doing this really helps to reinforce the fact that you're drawing an object picture of the events described in the use case. Plus, you'll **work through the use case a sentence at a time** as you draw the diagram, so it's handy to have the text nearby.

Figure 5-3 shows an example work-in-progress robustness diagram for the Internet Bookstore, for the *Login* use case. This is a snapshot of the diagram in its early stages. So far, only the first few sentences of the use case have been drawn onto the diagram.

In Figure 5-3, the use case text has been pasted directly into a note on the diagram. Because the robustness diagram is essentially a pictorial representation of the use case, it helps to have the text right there on the diagram: **they're two different views of the same thing**, so you should be able to walk through the text and trace it on the diagram (and vice versa).

■**Tip** Using a CASE tool such as EA, it's possible to create a live link between the use case and the note on the robustness diagram, so that if the use case is updated, the note on the diagram is updated automatically.

■**Exercise** We show the completed version of this diagram later, in Figure 5-5. But before you take a look, try completing the diagram, following the example of the controllers and message arrows that we've added so far in Figure 5-3. Simply follow the use case text, and draw the literal interpretation into the diagram (without trying to think about design details. Remember, you're not doing a real OO design yet—you're doing *just enough preliminary design to validate that you understand the use case*).

(Hint: It's early days yet, as we've only barely introduced the basic concepts, so expect to make some mistakes. But don't be discouraged; the intention here is simply to give it a try, and then think about the diagram that you drew while you read the next few pages.)

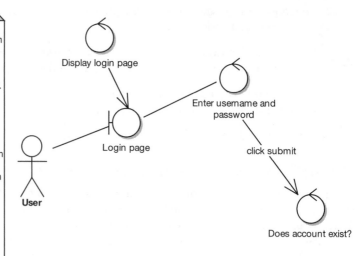

BASIC COURSE:
The user clicks the login link from any of a number of pages; the system displays the login page. The user enters their username and password and clicks Submit. The system checks the master account list to see if the user account exists. If it exists, the system then checks the password. The system retrieves the account information, starts an authenticated session, and redisplays the previous page with a welcome message.

ALTERNATE COURSES:
User forgot the password: The user clicks the What's my Password? link. The system prompts the user for their username if not already entered, retrieves the account info, and emails the user their password.

Invalid account: The system displays a message saying that the "username or password" was invalid, and prompts them to reenter it.

Invalid password: The system displays a message that the "username or password" was invalid, and prompts them to reenter it.

User cancels login: The system redisplays the previous page.

Third login failure: The system locks the user's account, so the user must contact Customer Support to reactivate it.

Figure 5-3. *Partially completed robustness diagram with the use case text pasted in*

9. Take Your Entity Classes from the Domain Model, and Add Any That Are Missing

Most of the entities on your robustness diagram will come from your domain model. However, since you time-boxed your initial domain modeling effort at a couple of hours, it's natural to expect that you might be missing some domain classes. When you're drawing robustness diagrams and this happens, make sure you **add the missing classes into the domain model**.

ICONIX Process **assumes that your initial domain model will be incomplete** and expects that missing objects will be discovered during robustness analysis. In this book, we refer to this process as *object discovery*.

TYING YOUR USE CASE TO THE DESIGN

The robustness diagram ties three elements to your use case: the GUI, the domain classes, and an intended list of software functions (see Figure 5-4).

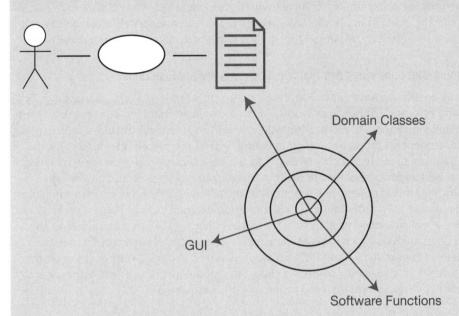

Figure 5-4. *Robustness diagrams tie three elements to your use case.*

As Figure 5-4 shows, the behavior requirements defined in your use case need to touch on several different aspects of the system, including how users interact with the GUI and manipulate the core objects from the problem domain. In between the GUI and the domain objects is the place where the software functions live.

On robustness diagrams, you describe GUI elements using boundary objects, software functions using controllers, and domain objects using entities. Note that this is substantially different from a collaboration diagram, which is sometimes confused with a robustness diagram. (Collaboration diagrams simply show object interactions.)

8. Expect to Rewrite Your Use Case While Drawing the Robustness Diagram

Experience has shown that **first-draft use cases** tend to exhibit the following characteristics: they **are typically vague, ambiguous, incomplete, and incorrect.** Small wonder that so many projects have struggled with use cases in the absence of a **disambiguation technique** like robustness analysis. Removing ambiguity from use cases is one of the primary purposes of this technique.

The "magic" of this technique is in reality hard work: **drawing a robustness diagram forces you to work through the use case one sentence at a time.** This simple act almost always brings to the surface errors in the first-draft use case text, so it's important to rewrite the use case in parallel with drawing the robustness diagram.

7. Make a Boundary Object for Each Screen

Drawing a robustness diagram can enforce unambiguous naming (or, as we like to say, *disambiguated nomenclature* of your boundary objects[1]). If you see boundary objects labeled "web page" on a robustness diagram, stop, figure out the name of the page, and use the real name.

6. Remember that Controllers Are Typically Logical Software Functions

It's certainly possible to have control-intensive classes in your design (e.g., manager classes), and you can definitely represent these as controllers. However, don't presume that every controller on a robustness diagram will represent an actual control class. In many cases, a controller on a robustness diagram is simply used as a placeholder for a software function. Overuse of controller classes (e.g., one use case controller per use case) in a design can lead us back to functional decomposition, so controller classes should be used sparingly.[2] Showing a mix of objects and functions is one of the other ways in which a robustness diagram is substantially different from a collaboration diagram.

If you see a cluster of controllers on a robustness diagram that are all communicating with each other, then that's a good candidate for a manager class (especially if the finite state behavior is nontrivial). If you feel like you might need to draw a state diagram for the use case, you might also need a controller class, but the majority of your use cases generally aren't likely to be state-intensive (even in some real-time systems).

5. Don't Worry About the Direction of the Arrows on a Robustness Diagram

Remember that your robustness diagram has two main missions in life:

- To force you to **disambiguate your use case text**

- To help you to **discover missing objects** in your domain model

Which direction the arrowheads point on the robustness diagram does nothing to further either of these goals. As a consequence, the direction of the arrows just . . . doesn't . . . *matter*. Seriously. Trust us. It really doesn't. Oh, and one other thing: it's not important.

Formally speaking, arrows on robustness diagrams represent *communication associations*. You can show either data flow or control flow and, in case we didn't mention it before, the direction of the arrows is **not** important.

---

1. For the benefit of any XPers who might be reading this book (!), that's "DisambiguatedNomenclatureOfYourBoundaryObjects."

2. As you'll see later, the current trend seems to be an even greater overuse of controller classes, where each software function actually has a controller class. It seems to us that the industry might have taken a giant step backward with this sort of thinking.

4. Show Invoked Use Cases on Your Robustness Diagram

It's OK to drag a use case onto a robustness diagram if it's invoked from the parent use case.

Not only is it OK to do this, but it's also the simplest way to show one case being invoked by another on a robustness diagram. In fact, it's the only reasonable way that we've found. Try it—it works really well.

3. The Robustness Diagram Represents a Preliminary Conceptual Design of a Use Case

Here are a couple of fundamental truths about system development:

- It's a good idea to fully understand the requirements before doing a design.

- It's often **impossible to fully understand the requirements without doing some exploratory design**.

These two statements may seem contradictory, but the solution is quite simple: you can do a conceptual design for the purpose of **validating the behavior requirements** *before doing the real design*, which you're going to code from. The robustness diagram represents the conceptual design, whereas the real design is shown on the sequence diagrams.

Programmers often have trouble with robustness diagrams because they're accustomed to thinking in terms of concrete detailed designs, and they need to take a step back from being literal-minded and learn to think at a slightly more abstract, conceptual level. This can be tricky, as programming tends to be a very literal-minded skill. However, once you've mastered the skill of **manipulating designs at the conceptual level** of abstraction, you'll find that a number of benefits result, especially the ability to write precise and unambiguous use cases.

The good news is, mastering this skill doesn't require you to retire to a Tibetan monastery to meditate and practice for several years; it only takes a few hours of drawing diagrams.

2. Objects on Your Robustness Diagram Will "Morph" into the Detailed Design

Boundary and entity classes on a robustness diagram will generally become object instances on a sequence diagram, while controllers will become messages. It's also advisable to create test cases for the controllers.

Keep in mind that both boundary objects and entity objects are nouns, and that controllers are verbs (i.e., an action performed on an object). As such, it makes sense that the controllers (the actions) will become methods on the boundary and entity classes.

1. Remember That a Robustness Diagram Is an "Object Picture" of a Use Case

A robustness diagram is an "object picture" of a use case, whose purpose is to force refinement of both use case text and the object model. *Robustness diagrams tie use cases to objects (and to the GUI).*

A robustness diagram isn't the same as a UML collaboration diagram. You show object-to-object communication on a collaboration diagram, but a robustness diagram is quite literally an object picture of a use case. Since the robustness diagram and the use case text have to match precisely, the robustness diagram forces you to tie the use case text to the objects, thus enabling you to drive object-oriented designs forward from use cases.

An important implication of all of this is that, because the robustness diagram must show all of the use case, *it must show not just the basic course, but all the alternate courses as well* (all on the same diagram). This is a good reason why your use cases should follow the two-paragraph rule (see Chapter 3).

Figure 5-5 shows the completed diagram for the *Login* use case (which we began earlier in this chapter), showing the basic course and the alternate courses.

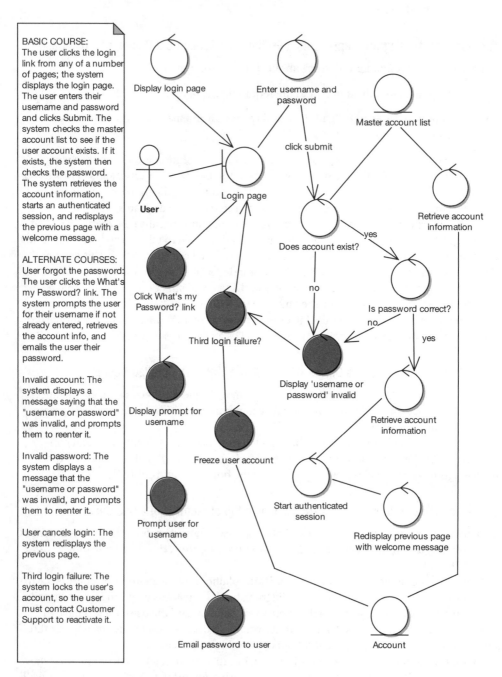

BASIC COURSE:
The user clicks the login link from any of a number of pages; the system displays the login page. The user enters their username and password and clicks Submit. The system checks the master account list to see if the user account exists. If it exists, the system then checks the password. The system retrieves the account information, starts an authenticated session, and redisplays the previous page with a welcome message.

ALTERNATE COURSES:
User forgot the password: The user clicks the What's my Password? link. The system prompts the user for their username if not already entered, retrieves the account info, and emails the user their password.

Invalid account: The system displays a message saying that the "username or password" was invalid, and prompts them to reenter it.

Invalid password: The system displays a message that the "username or password" was invalid, and prompts them to reenter it.

User cancels login: The system redisplays the previous page.

Third login failure: The system locks the user's account, so the user must contact Customer Support to reactivate it.

Figure 5-5. *Example robustness diagram*

Tip In Figure 5-5, some of the objects are shaded red. These are the objects (mainly controllers) for the alternate courses. Though it isn't essential, it's helpful to show the alternate courses in a different color from the basic course. The same effect can be achieved (and has an additional benefit as a form of review) by printing out the diagram and using different colored highlighter pens to trace the basic course and alternate courses.

DO I REALLY NEED ALL THOSE #$%^ DISPLAY CONTOLLERS?

A common issue that some people get concerned about when drawing robustness diagrams is that their diagram sometimes has a number of Display controllers.

Generally, if a controller is talking to a boundary object (as in Figure 5-6), then it wouldn't violate the diagram's noun-verb-noun rules to leave out the additional Display controller. The fact that the page is going to be displayed is already implied by the arrow from the Get Requested Addresses controller to the Delivery Address Page boundary object.

However, if you **think of Display as being "Initialize page,"** it makes sense to put the Display controller on the diagram wherever needed (see Figure 5-7). In fact, if it helps, call it "Initialize page" instead of "Display." In Figure 5-7, you can see that the system is getting the default delivery address and then initializing the page with the default settings (via the Display controller).

Display initialization code tends to be nontrivial, so it helps to place a Display controller explicitly on the robustness diagram. If you start leaving out the Display controllers, then you're **actually skipping a lot of initialization behavior in the use case.** For the most part, this is not stuff you want to forget about. When you draw a Display controller, ask yourself, "What gets displayed on this screen? Do I have to fetch it from the database?" (etc.)

In fact, when you begin drawing the sequence diagrams from the use case text (see Chapter 8), the Display controller usually becomes an operation on the boundary class, but that's a design decision (allocating operations to classes), and you shouldn't worry about design details while drawing the robustness diagrams.

As you'll see in Chapter 12, you can generate test cases directly from the controllers on your robustness diagrams, so this is another impetus to add that Display controller!

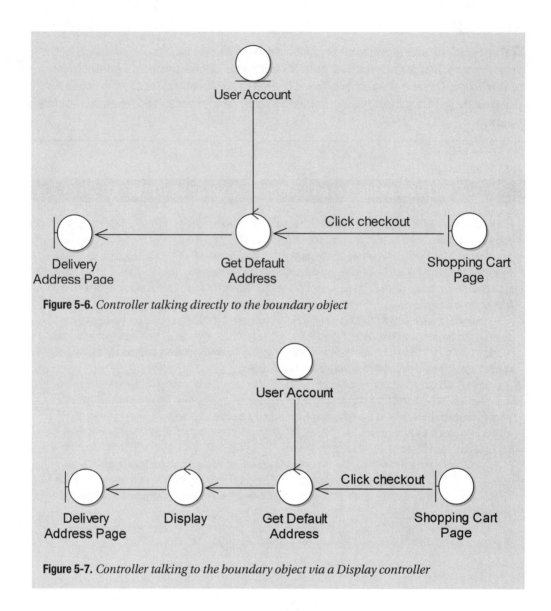

Figure 5-6. *Controller talking directly to the boundary object*

Figure 5-7. *Controller talking to the boundary object via a Display controller*

More About Robustness Diagram Rules

The robustness diagram noun-verb-noun rules may seem unnecessarily restrictive at first, but in reality they help you to prepare your use case text for the much more rigorous (if sometimes implicit) rules that you would need to apply when you create designs from your use cases. The robustness diagram rules are easy to learn, but there's now emerging tools support to catch rule violations. Figures 5-8 and 5-9 show our favorite modeling tool, EA, validating a couple of robustness diagrams for model errors. As far as we know, the folks at Sparx Systems (www.sparxsystems.com) are the only ones who have implemented rule checking for this diagram, as of the time of this writing.

In Figure 5-8, all of the possible valid relationships are shown (even though the diagram itself doesn't make a huge amount of sense), and in Figure 5-9, all of the possible *invalid* relationships are shown.

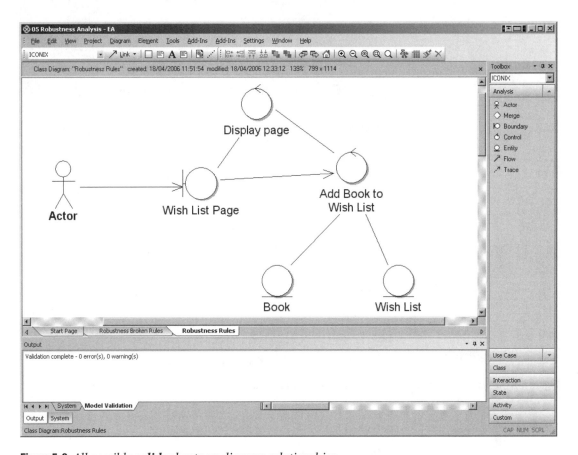

Figure 5-8. *All possible **valid** robustness diagram relationships*

The relationships shown in Figure 5-8 are allowed because

• An Actor can talk to a Boundary Object.

• Boundary Objects and Controllers can talk to each other (Noun <-> Verb).

• A Controller can talk to another Controller (Verb <-> Verb).

• Controllers and Entity Objects can talk to each other (Verb <-> Noun).

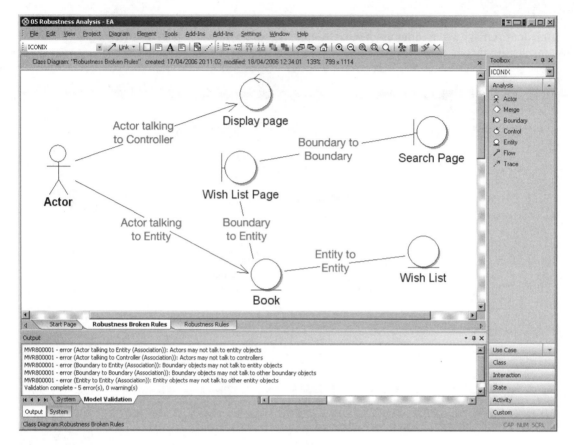

Figure 5-9. *Robustness diagram rule checker in EA showing all possible **invalid** relationships*

The relationships shown in Figure 5-9 are **not allowed** because

- An Actor can't talk directly to a Controller or an Entity (must talk to a Boundary Object).

- Boundary Objects and Entity Objects can't talk directly to each other (must go via a Controller).

- Entities can't talk directly to other Entities (must go via a Controller).

- Boundary Objects can't talk directly to other Boundary Objects (must go via a Controller).

How Do You Perform Robustness Analysis?

You perform robustness analysis for a use case by **working through the use case text, one sentence at a time**, and drawing the actor(s), the appropriate boundary and entity objects and controllers, and the connections among the various elements of the diagram. You should be able to fit the basic course and all of the alternate courses on one diagram.

Now for a couple of examples (both from the Internet Bookstore). We'll start with a completed robustness diagram, and then we'll walk through another diagram step by step.

Robustness Diagram for the "Show Book Details" Use Case

Figure 5-10 shows a first attempt at the robustness diagram for the *Show Book Details* use case, which we introduced in Chapter 4.

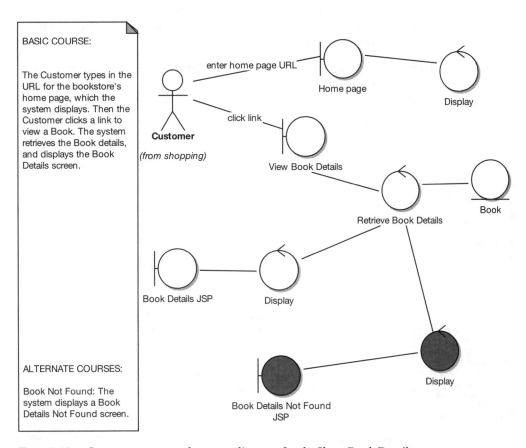

Figure 5-10. *A first attempt at a robustness diagram for the* Show Book Details *use case*

As you can see, it's possible to walk through the robustness diagram by reading the use case text and following along in the diagram itself. If you ever find that there's something in the use case text that isn't in the diagram, then the diagram is incomplete (and vice versa).

There are a few issues with this diagram that are worth clearing up:

- The "click link" should come from the home page boundary object and go to a controller that drives the display of the book details page (it's probably a "book details page" and not a "view book details page"). Always show the user actions coming *off* the boundary object and thus linking the previous screen/page to the next screen/page via a controller.

- Right now there are two boundary classes: "view book details page" and "book details JSP." Are there really two boundaries at the conceptual design level? Or do both of these represent the book details page? Is the "view book details page" boundary actually supposed to be a controller called "display book details page"?

- Don't call things JSPs (or ASPs, or whatever) on the robustness diagrams, as that's too technology specific for conceptual design. It's better to call them screens and pages (this is already done in the use case text).

- Try not to mix nouns and verbs as in "view book details page"—you will confuse yourself! **The name of the page should be a noun.**

Figure 5-11 shows the corrected version.

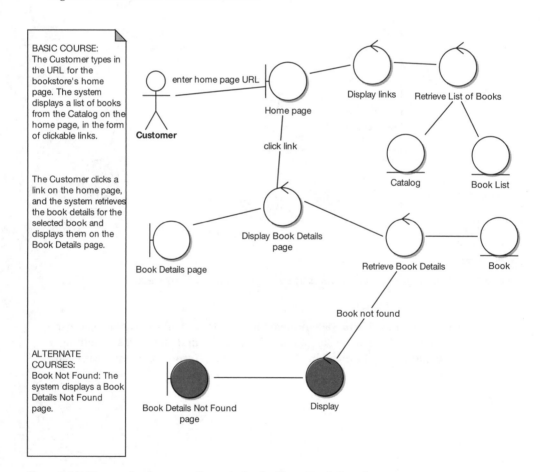

Figure 5-11. *Corrected robustness diagram for the* Show Book Details *use case*

We'll return to the *Show Book Details* use case periodically throughout the book, and we'll take it all the way to source code.

Of course, it's easy for us to simply show you a finished diagram and say, "There, that's how you do it!" So in the next section, we'll walk through the process of drawing a robustness diagram from the beginning.

Robustness Diagram for the "Write Customer Review" Use Case

We'll now walk through the robustness analysis process step by step for the *Write Customer Review* use case.

The first step is shown in Figure 5-12. We create a new, blank robustness diagram.

■**Tip** Make the robustness diagram a child diagram of the use case you're modeling. (The same goes for the sequence diagram, which you'll add later.) Nest these diagrams "inside" the use case in the project browser.

Next, paste the use case text directly onto the diagram.

The next stage is to read through the first sentence of the basic course in the use case text:

The Customer clicks the Write Review button for the book currently being viewed, and the system shows the Write Review screen.

The first thing referenced is the Customer, so we need to put a Customer actor onto the diagram.

■**Tip** You can drag the actor directly from the tree view (project browser).

■**Tip** If you're staring at the screen wondering how to begin . . . well, you aren't alone. When you're learning how to draw robustness diagrams, getting started on a new diagram is usually the trickiest part.

The easiest way to begin is simply to **start at the first sentence of the use case text and draw what you read**. If it just won't translate easily onto the diagram, then it's possible that the use case is starting at the wrong point (e.g., if it describes the actions leading up to the user's first action, then it's probably describing part of a different use case and should be rewritten).

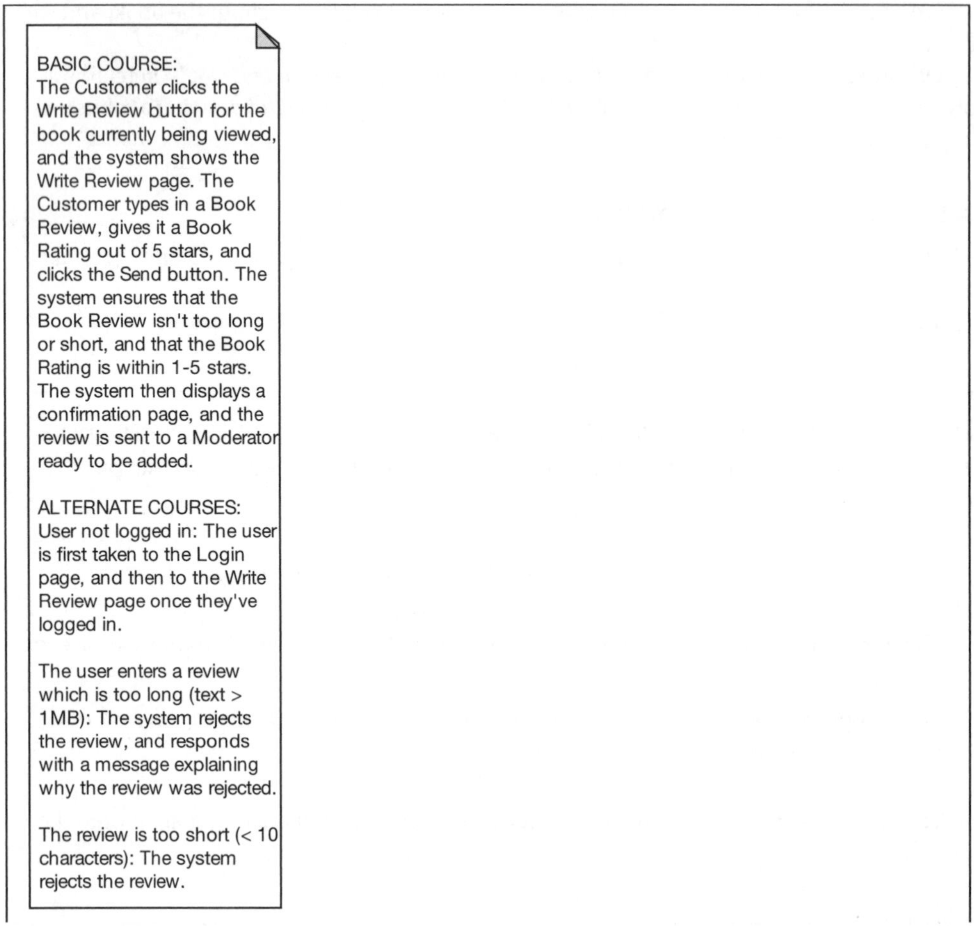

BASIC COURSE:
The Customer clicks the Write Review button for the book currently being viewed, and the system shows the Write Review page. The Customer types in a Book Review, gives it a Book Rating out of 5 stars, and clicks the Send button. The system ensures that the Book Review isn't too long or short, and that the Book Rating is within 1-5 stars. The system then displays a confirmation page, and the review is sent to a Moderator ready to be added.

ALTERNATE COURSES:
User not logged in: The user is first taken to the Login page, and then to the Write Review page once they've logged in.

The user enters a review which is too long (text > 1MB): The system rejects the review, and responds with a message explaining why the review was rejected.

The review is too short (< 10 characters): The system rejects the review.

Figure 5-12. *Step 1: Create a new, blank* Write Customer Review *robustness diagram*

Next, it *seems* like the obvious thing to do would be to show the Write Review button as a boundary object and show the Customer interacting with it (see Figure 5-13).

You might wonder whether it's OK to put GUI widgets such as buttons on our robustness diagrams. In practice, we find that doing so opens up Pandora's box. If you include one GUI widget, then you start to think that you should include them all, which means . . . you'll be there all night drawing controllers and boundary objects for all the text fields, list boxes, buttons, labels, and so on for every screen. Yikes. It's better to avoid falling into that trap, and ***avoid drawing individual GUI widgets (below the screen/page/frame level) on the robustness diagrams.***

As you can see in Figure 5-14, we've removed the Write Review Button boundary object and relegated it to a message between the Customer and the Write Review Screen object. If the UI element absolutely must be mentioned explicitly (e.g., if you feel it makes the diagram clearer), then it could be included as a message label, as we've done in Figure 5-15. It isn't essential, though—in fact, the diagram would probably even be slightly clearer without it.

BASIC COURSE:
The Customer clicks the Write Review button for the book currently being viewed, and the system shows the Write Review page. The Customer types in a Book Review, gives it a Book Rating out of 5 stars, and clicks the Send button. The system ensures that the Book Review isn't too long or short, and that the Book Rating is within 1-5 stars. The system then displays a confirmation page, and the review is sent to a Moderator ready to be added.

ALTERNATE COURSES:
User not logged in: The user is first taken to the Login page, and then to the Write Review page once they've logged in.

The user enters a review which is too long (text > 1MB): The system rejects the review, and responds with a message explaining why the review was rejected.

The review is too short (< 10 characters): The system rejects the review.

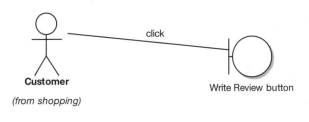

Figure 5-13. *Step 2: Spot the deliberate mistake.*

In Figure 5-14, we've also added a couple of controllers to represent the validation described in the use case text. The text represented in the diagram (so far) is as follows:

The Customer types in a Book Review, gives it a Book Rating out of five stars, and clicks the Send button. The system ensures that the Book Review isn't too long or short, and that the Book Rating is within one and five stars.

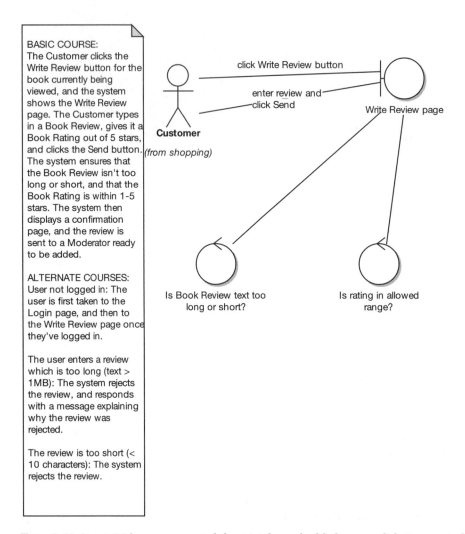

BASIC COURSE:
The Customer clicks the Write Review button for the book currently being viewed, and the system shows the Write Review page. The Customer types in a Book Review, gives it a Book Rating out of 5 stars, and clicks the Send button. The system ensures that the Book Review isn't too long or short, and that the Book Rating is within 1-5 stars. The system then displays a confirmation page, and the review is sent to a Moderator ready to be added.

ALTERNATE COURSES:
User not logged in: The user is first taken to the Login page, and then to the Write Review page once they've logged in.

The user enters a review which is too long (text > 1MB): The system rejects the review, and responds with a message explaining why the review was rejected.

The review is too short (< 10 characters): The system rejects the review.

click Write Review button

enter review and
click Send

Write Review page

Customer
(from shopping)

Is Book Review text too
long or short?

Is rating in allowed
range?

Figure 5-14. *Step 3: We've now corrected the mistake and added some validation controllers.*

There are a few issues with this diagram so far. The two messages between the Customer and the Write Review Screen boundary object are quite clumsy. In addition, this approach introduces some ambiguity into the diagram, as it isn't clear which controller is called when the user clicks the Write Review button versus when the user enters the review and clicks Send. As it turns out, the first sentence of the use case text ("The Customer clicks the Write Review button for the book currently being viewed") hints at a Book Detail screen, which isn't shown either in the text or on the diagram. If we add that screen, then we can have an arrow going from the Customer to the Book Detail screen, and we can also add a Display controller to show the Write Review screen being displayed.

Another issue is that the controller name "Is Book Review text too long or short?" is a tad long, so we could shorten this to "Is Book Review length OK?"

In Figure 5-15, we've corrected the diagram and also walked through the remainder of the basic course text. Notice that we've also corrected the use case text so that it doesn't just hint at a Book Detail screen, but instead refers to it explicitly.

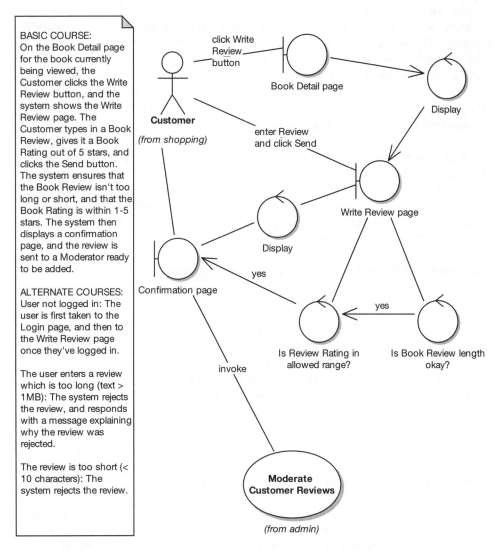

BASIC COURSE:
On the Book Detail page for the book currently being viewed, the Customer clicks the Write Review button, and the system shows the Write Review page. The Customer types in a Book Review, gives it a Book Rating out of 5 stars, and clicks the Send button. The system ensures that the Book Review isn't too long or short, and that the Book Rating is within 1-5 stars. The system then displays a confirmation page, and the review is sent to a Moderator ready to be added.

ALTERNATE COURSES:
User not logged in: The user is first taken to the Login page, and then to the Write Review page once they've logged in.

The user enters a review which is too long (text > 1MB): The system rejects the review, and responds with a message explaining why the review was rejected.

The review is too short (< 10 characters): The system rejects the review.

Figure 5-15. *Step 4: The remainder of the basic course text in graphic form*

The text shown in the new part of the diagram is

The system then displays a confirmation screen, and the review is sent to a Moderator, ready to be added.

(As you'll discover later, this text also needs work!)

We've included a controller called Display, which "controls" the display of the Confirmation Screen boundary. We don't attempt to draw the review being sent to the Moderator, because this is handled by a separate use case, *Moderate Customer Reviews* (from the admin package). Instead, we simply drag that use case onto the diagram as a link, and indicate that we'll invoke it directly.

You'd be forgiven for thinking that we've finished at this stage; the robustness diagram looks pretty complete. However, we still haven't modeled the alternate courses, and this is often where robustness diagrams provide the most value.

Let's take a look at the first alternate course:

> **User not logged in**: *The user is first taken to the Login screen and then to the Write Review screen once he is logged in.*

To model this course, we'll add a new controller: "Is user logged in?" If the user isn't logged in, we'll invoke the *Login* use case; otherwise, control passes to the Display controller as it did previously. Because the use case text specifies that the Write Review screen is displayed once the user has logged in, we also need to show this on the diagram, so there should be a line between the *Login* use case and the Display controller. As we do this on the diagram, we should also modify the use case to match:

> **User not logged in**: *Invoke* Login. *Then display the Write Review screen.*

■**Exercise**   Which object should the system ask whether the user is logged in? Currently there isn't a `Customer Session` class, but it looks as if we're going to need one. (If you're wondering what "object discovery" means, this is it. We just discovered that we're missing an object.) Looking at Figure 5-15, where should this go on the diagram? You'd also need to update the use case text to refer to `Customer Session`. Try doing this first, and then compare the result with the updated diagram in Figure 5-16.

The updated diagram and use case text are shown in Figure 5-16. Notice that we've shaded the arrow pointing to the *Login* use case in red, to indicate that it's part of an alternate course. While not essential, this is a useful visual aid. If you print out the diagrams, you can use highlighter pens to do this part.

In Figure 5-16, the new `Customer Session` object has been added to the robustness diagram (note that you'll also need to update the domain model anytime you identify a new domain object). The use case text shown to the left of the diagram has also been updated to refer to the `Customer Session`: "The system checks the Customer Session to make sure the Customer is logged in."

Finally, let's add the last two alternate courses:

> **The user enters a review that is too long (text > 1MB)**: *The system rejects the review and responds with a message explaining why the review was rejected.*

> **The review is too short (< 10 characters)**: *The system rejects the review and displays an error message.*

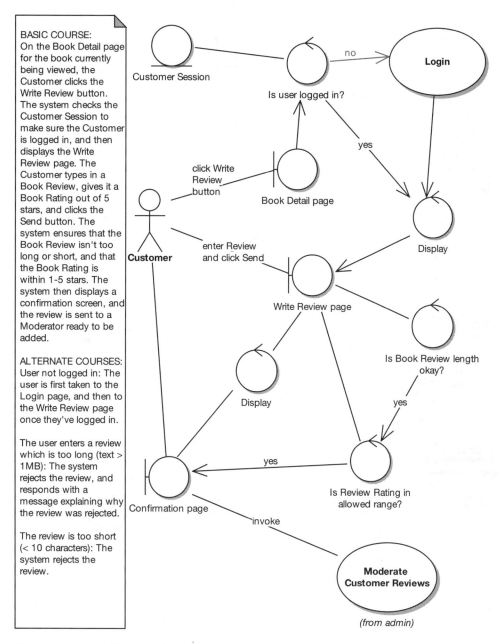

BASIC COURSE:
On the Book Detail page for the book currently being viewed, the Customer clicks the Write Review button. The system checks the Customer Session to make sure the Customer is logged in, and then displays the Write Review page. The Customer types in a Book Review, gives it a Book Rating out of 5 stars, and clicks the Send button. The system ensures that the Book Review isn't too long or short, and that the Book Rating is within 1-5 stars. The system then displays a confirmation screen, and the review is sent to a Moderator ready to be added.

ALTERNATE COURSES:
User not logged in: The user is first taken to the Login page, and then to the Write Review page once they've logged in.

The user enters a review which is too long (text > 1MB): The system rejects the review, and responds with a message explaining why the review was rejected.

The review is too short (< 10 characters): The system rejects the review.

Figure 5-16. *Step 5: The first alternate course has been added.*

Note the two implied requirements: the book review length shall not exceed 1MB, and the book review length shall not be fewer than ten characters.

The updated diagram is shown in Figure 5-17 (again, the objects for the alternate courses are shown in red).

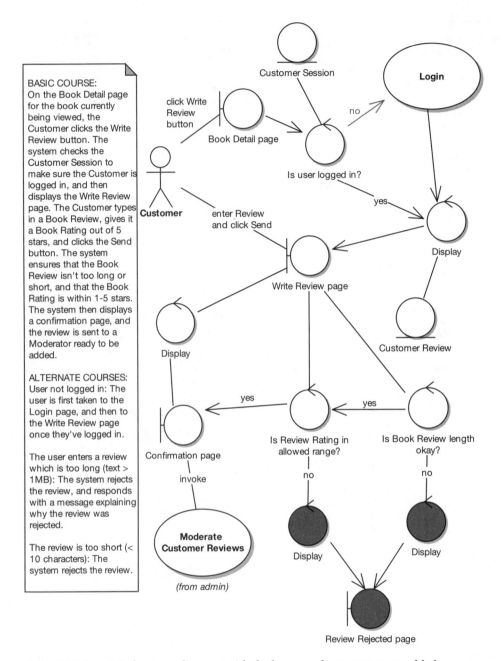

BASIC COURSE:
On the Book Detail page for the book currently being viewed, the Customer clicks the Write Review button. The system checks the Customer Session to make sure the Customer is logged in, and then displays the Write Review page. The Customer types in a Book Review, gives it a Book Rating out of 5 stars, and clicks the Send button. The system ensures that the Book Review isn't too long or short, and that the Book Rating is within 1-5 stars. The system then displays a confirmation page, and the review is sent to a Moderator ready to be added.

ALTERNATE COURSES:
User not logged in: The user is first taken to the Login page, and then to the Write Review page once they've logged in.

The user enters a review which is too long (text > 1MB): The system rejects the review, and responds with a message explaining why the review was rejected.

The review is too short (< 10 characters): The system rejects the review.

Figure 5-17. *Step 6: Robustness diagram with the last two alternate courses added*

■**Exercise** In Figure 5-17, following the "enter Review and click Send" arrow, it's difficult to say which controller we go to after Write Review page. How could the diagram be improved to make this clearer? We reveal the answer during the PDR in Chapter 6.

■**Exercise** In Figure 5-17, the diagram invokes the *Moderate Customer Reviews* use case, but this doesn't match up with the text on the left. What should be done to make the diagram and the text match up? (Again, check the PDR in Chapter 6 for the answer.)

This diagram is now "functionally" complete, and you could reasonably happily draw a sequence diagram from it. But there are still a few ambiguities that should be ironed out, a couple of which are mentioned in the Exercise elements here. Ironing out these ambiguities will make our lives that much easier when we draw the sequence diagram.

This fresh in from the Department of Cliffhanger Endings: We'll cover those issues (and improve this diagram some more) in the Preliminary Design Review (PDR) in Chapter 6.

Updating Your Domain (Static) Model

While you're drawing robustness diagrams, it's a good idea to also be updating the domain model incrementally, as you go along. You'll almost inevitably discover new domain classes. You'll also identify attributes to be added to classes. This all needs to go on the domain model (aka analysis-level static model), and it's best do it *now*, as soon as you identify these changes or new details, before they're forgotten about.

The new attributes may be discovered from the use case text, or from the UI prototypes, or even from the functional requirements.

■**Caution** Try not to get sidetracked by assigning **operations** to your classes just yet—that's a detailed design activity. If you spend time doing that now, you'll probably just need to redo it later.

The feedback cycle between the robustness model and the static model is shown in Figure 5-18.

CHECK:
Have you covered all of your alternate courses?
identified all of the methods/functions?
mapped all data flows between entities?

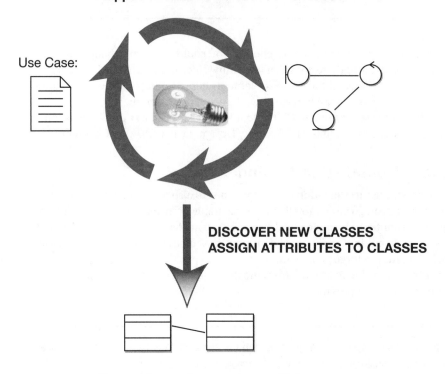

Use Case:

DISCOVER NEW CLASSES
ASSIGN ATTRIBUTES TO CLASSES

Repeat for each use case, until the
Domain model has evolved into a static model

Figure 5-18. *Robustness model/static model feedback loop*

Figure 5-19 shows the updated static model for the Internet Bookstore, following robustness analysis for the *Show Book Details* and *Write Customer Review* use cases. The added or updated classes are shown in red.

The changes that we've made to this diagram are as follows.

After doing robustness analysis for the *Show Book Details* use case (see Figure 5-11), we

- Added attributes to Book: title and synopsis (these details weren't in the use case text, but were found from looking at the screen UI mock-ups)

After doing robustness analysis for the *Write Customer Review* use case (see Figure 5-17), we

- Added CustomerSession, gave it an attribute called loggedIn (a Boolean), and linked it to CustomerAccount (which will later, in Chapter 8, become simply Customer)

- Deleted CustomerRating, because it turned into an attribute on BookReview

- Added new attributes to BookReview that were mentioned in the use case text

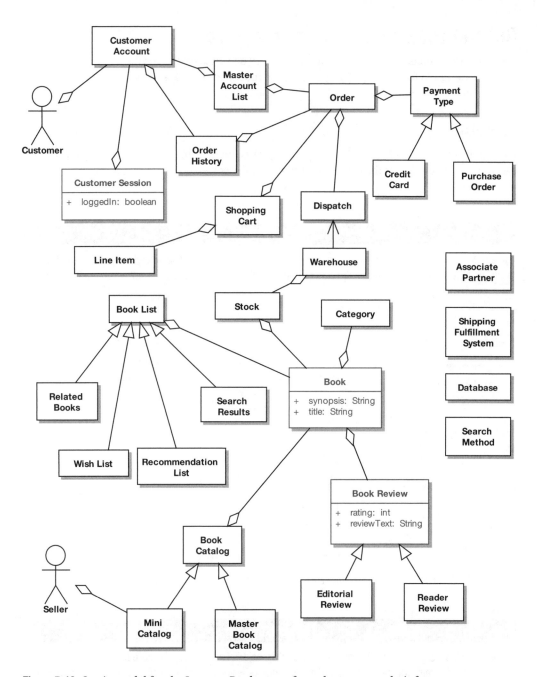

Figure 5-19. *Static model for the Internet Bookstore, after robustness analysis for two use cases*

There's one last step before you finish robustness analysis. Once all of your robustness diagrams are drawn, you must **finish updating the analysis-level class diagram**. Take a sweep through all of the robustness diagrams that you've drawn for this release, and make sure that all of the relevant details have been fed back into the static model.

Robustness Analysis in Practice

The following exercises, taken from the preliminary design activities for the Internet Bookstore, are designed to test your ability to spot the most common mistakes that people make during robustness analysis.

Exercises

Each of the diagrams in Figures 5-20 to 5-23 contains one or more typical modeling errors. For each one, try to figure out the errors and then draw the corrected diagram. The answers are in the next section.

Figure 5-20 shows an excerpt from a robustness diagram for the *Create New Customer Account* use case. It violates one of the rules of robustness analysis that we described earlier in this chapter—but which one?

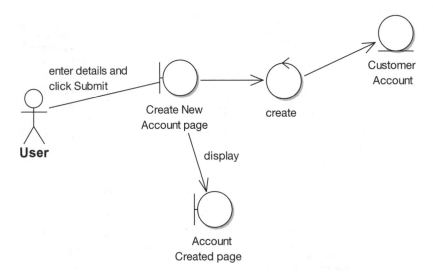

Figure 5-20. *Excerpt from a robustness diagram showing an invalid relationship*

Figure 5-21 shows a robustness diagram for the *Add External Books to Catalog* use case (in which bookseller partners may add their own titles to the Internet Bookstore website). It contains a couple of errors to do with the sort of detail you should put on a robustness diagram (Hint: Look at External Book) and an error where the alternate course doesn't have any relation to the events in the basic course. Speaking of alternate courses, there's also one other error related to alternate courses.

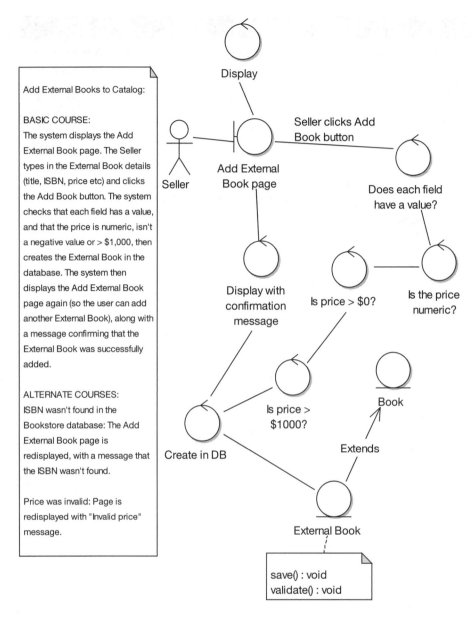

Add External Books to Catalog:

BASIC COURSE:
The system displays the Add External Book page. The Seller types in the External Book details (title, ISBN, price etc) and clicks the Add Book button. The system checks that each field has a value, and that the price is numeric, isn't a negative value or > $1,000, then creates the External Book in the database. The system then displays the Add External Book page again (so the user can add another External Book), along with a message confirming that the External Book was successfully added.

ALTERNATE COURSES:
ISBN wasn't found in the Bookstore database: The Add External Book page is redisplayed, with a message that the ISBN wasn't found.

Price was invalid: Page is redisplayed with "Invalid price" message.

Display

Seller clicks Add Book button

Seller

Add External Book page

Does each field have a value?

Display with confirmation message

Is price > $0?

Is the price numeric?

Book

Is price > $1000?

Extends

Create in DB

External Book

save() : void
validate() : void

Figure 5-21. *Robustness diagram for the* Add External Books to Catalog *use case, with four modeling errors*

Exercise 5-3

The robustness diagram excerpt in Figure 5-22 shows at least five modeling errors, including at least one in the use case text, in the last sentence of the basic course, and two where the text and the diagram don't match up. Have fun finding them all!

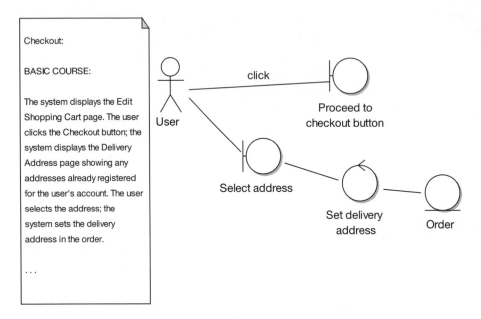

Checkout:

BASIC COURSE:

The system displays the Edit Shopping Cart page. The user clicks the Checkout button; the system displays the Delivery Address page showing any addresses already registered for the user's account. The user selects the address; the system sets the delivery address in the order.

. . .

Figure 5-22. *Excerpt from a robustness diagram containing five errors*

Exercise 5-4

The robustness diagram in Figure 5-23 is for the *Search for Books* use case. The diagram shows a total of eight modeling errors, including one in the first sentence of the use case text (Hint: Page name) and another in the fourth paragraph of the use case text. See how many errors you can find!

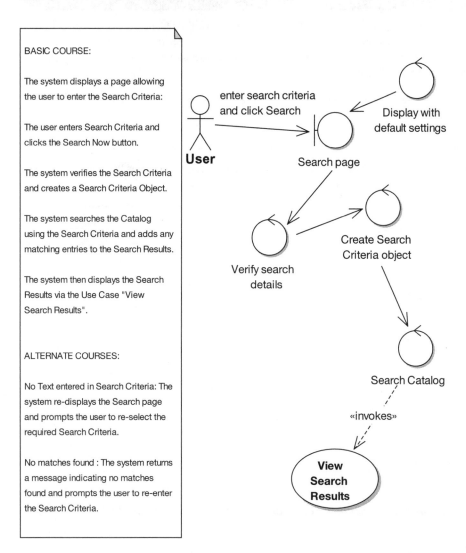

BASIC COURSE:

The system displays a page allowing the user to enter the Search Criteria:

The user enters Search Criteria and clicks the Search Now button.

The system verifies the Search Criteria and creates a Search Criteria Object.

The system searches the Catalog using the Search Criteria and adds any matching entries to the Search Results.

The system then displays the Search Results via the Use Case "View Search Results".

ALTERNATE COURSES:

No Text entered in Search Criteria: The system re-displays the Search page and prompts the user to re-select the required Search Criteria.

No matches found : The system returns a message indicating no matches found and prompts the user to re-enter the Search Criteria.

enter search criteria and click Search

Display with default settings

User

Search page

Verify search details

Create Search Criteria object

Search Catalog

«invokes»

View Search Results

Figure 5-23. *Robustness diagram for the* Search for Books *use case showing eight errors*

Exercise Solutions

Following are the solutions to the exercises.

Exercise 5-1 Solution: Noun-Noun Relationship

Figure 5-24 highlights the part of the diagram that violates a robustness diagramming relationship rule. The "Create New Account page" boundary object is talking to the "Account Created page" boundary object. These are both "nouns," and a noun-noun relationship isn't allowed. There must be a controller (a verb) between them, so that the relationship is noun-verb-noun.

Looking at Figure 5-24, the arrow is already labeled "display," so it makes sense simply to create a Display controller. Figure 5-25 shows the corrected diagram.

■**Note** See Figures 5-8 and 5-9 for all of the possible valid and invalid relationships that you can show on a robustness diagram.

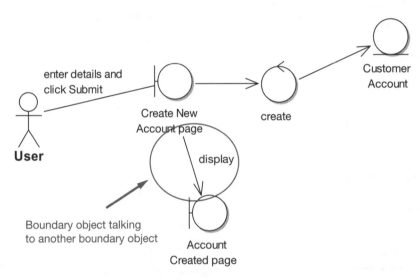

Figure 5-24. *The robustness diagram excerpt from Exercise 5-1, with the error highlighted*

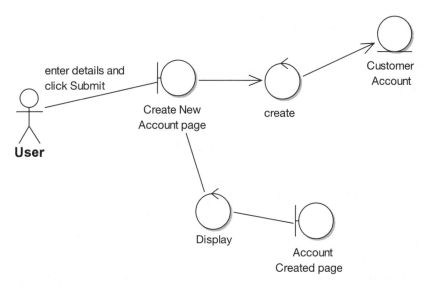

Figure 5-25. *The corrected robustness diagram excerpt for Exercise 5-1*

Exercise 5-2 Solution: Allocating Behavior

Figure 5-26 highlights the errors in Figure 5-21.

Let's start at the top of the diagram and work our way down. The diagram contains the validation controllers to check the incoming form values for the Add External Book page, but it doesn't show what happens if any of the validation checks fail. The solution is actually pretty straightforward—we just need a "Display with error message" controller pointing back to the Add External Book page—but it still needs to be shown on the diagram, so that the extra processing doesn't get forgotten about.

The next error, over on the left of Figure 5-26, is that there's an alternate course called "ISBN wasn't found in the Bookstore database," but there's no matching text in the basic course for this error condition to ever arise. The fact that it appeared in the alternate courses shows that the error condition was on the use case author's mind, but it needs to be stated explicitly so that the designers know that they're meant to deal with it.

Over to the right, Figure 5-26 shows an extends relationship between External Book and its parent Book. While this might be a valid relationship, the robustness diagram definitely isn't the right place to capture this sort of information. Extends relationships belong on the domain model diagram (and later, the class diagrams).

Finally, there's a note attached to External Book showing two methods (save() and validate()). Again, the robustness diagram just isn't the right place to allocate operations to classes; this information should go on the class diagrams and be captured during sequence diagramming (see Chapter 8).

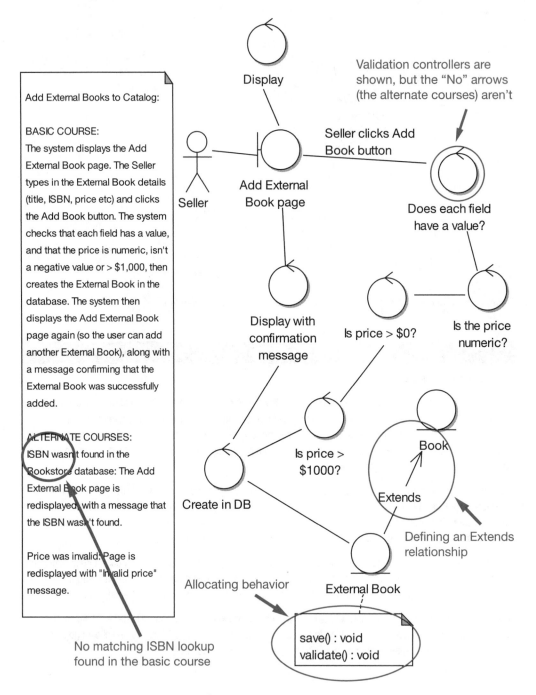

Figure 5-26. *The robustness diagram from Exercise 5-2, with errors highlighted*

Figure 5-27 shows the corrected diagram. In this version, we've also collapsed three controllers into one and called the new controller `Check legal price range`.

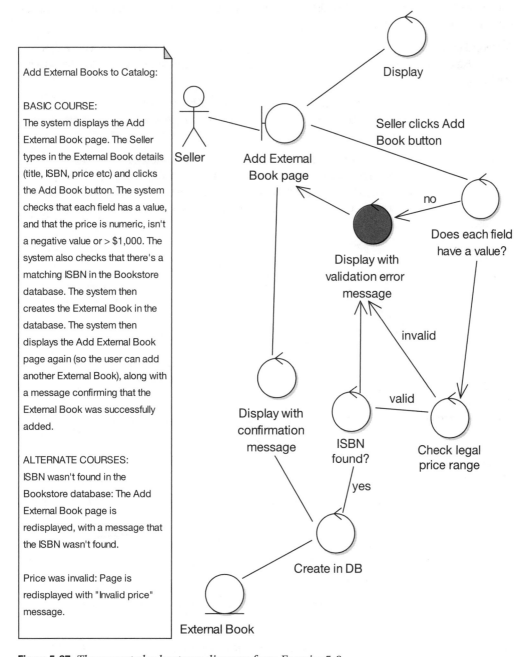

Figure 5-27. *The corrected robustness diagram from Exercise 5-2*

Exercise 5-3 Solution: Diagram Doesn't Match Up with the Description

Figure 5-28 highlights the errors in Figure 5-22. The first error in the example is that the text starts at an earlier point in time than the diagram (a common mistake). An easy way to spot this type of error is to use the "highlighter test" (see earlier in this chapter).

The second error—the GUI widget is shown as a boundary object—is another common mistake. A GUI widget such as a button is too fine-grained to be the boundary object; instead, the boundary object should be the screen or web page.

The third error is rather fundamental: an entire chunk of the use case text has been left off the diagram. It's surprising how often this happens. It's usually a sign that somebody isn't working through the use case one sentence at a time.

The fourth and final error is a direct consequence of ambiguous use case text: the text wasn't tied closely enough to the objects, so the modeler just sort of went off in a pseudo-random direction and, lacking the real boundary object to work with, used "Select address" as the boundary object, even though it's a verb and therefore is a controller masquerading as a boundary object. And as we're sure you know by now, actors can't talk directly to controllers.

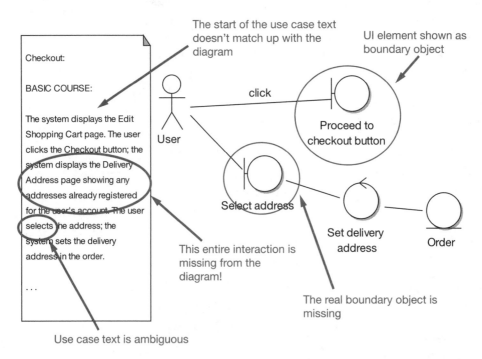

Figure 5-28. *The robustness diagram excerpt from Exercise 5-4, with errors highlighted*

Figure 5-29 shows the corrected diagram and use case text. In redrawing the diagram, we discovered another ambiguity in the text (funny how that happens!). The text "the system displays the Delivery Address page showing any addresses already registered for the user's account" implies some search and retrieval initialization behavior, which currently also doesn't appear anywhere on the diagram. So we rewrote this part of the use case and added it into the diagram, and in the process we discovered another domain class (Delivery Address List). This is exactly the kind of scenario where robustness analysis proves invaluable—discovering hidden functionality and missing domain classes, just in time to begin designing.

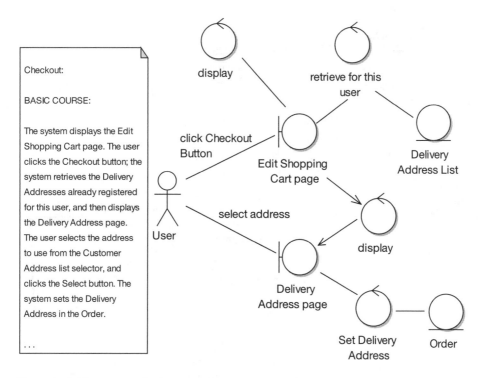

Checkout:

BASIC COURSE:

The system displays the Edit Shopping Cart page. The user clicks the Checkout button; the system retrieves the Delivery Addresses already registered for this user, and then displays the Delivery Address page. The user selects the address to use from the Customer Address list selector, and clicks the Select button. The system sets the Delivery Address in the Order.

. . .

Figure 5-29. *The corrected robustness diagram excerpt for Exercise 5-4*

Exercise 5-4 Solution: Alternate Courses Not Shown

Figure 5-30 highlights the errors in Figure 5-23.

To kick off, the text "a page allowing the user to enter the Search Criteria" sounds like a roundabout way of saying "the Search Page," and it's always better to give your pages explicit names.

On the arrow between User and Search Page, the text "click Search" should be "click the Search Now button" to match it up with the use case text.

On the controller at the top right, some extra detail has been added to the diagram—"Display with default settings"—that doesn't appear in the use case text. Remember, the text and the diagram should be virtual carbon copies of each other. As "Display with default settings" is a bit like saying, "The system displays what it displays" (i.e., it doesn't add anything meaningful in this case since the screen doesn't have to fetch any data when it initializes), it can safely be removed.

Back in the use case description, the text "adds any matching entries to the Search Results" is rather vague. It doesn't describe exactly what the "entries" are. "Entries" is vague and ambiguous. This is another example of use case text that isn't tied closely enough to the domain model. Simply replacing "matching entries" with "matching Books" fixes this.

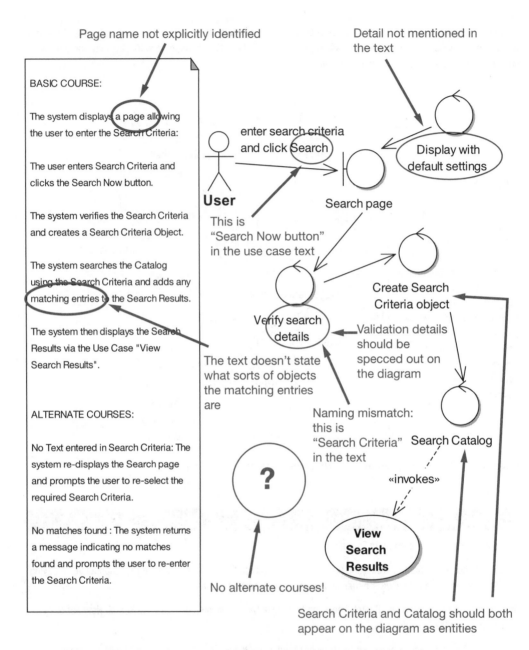

Figure 5-30. *The robustness diagram from Exercise 5-3, with errors highlighted*

There's another naming mismatch on the "Verify search details" controller: it should be called "Verify Search Criteria." And while we're at it, this is really *validating* the search form, but the diagram doesn't walk through the validation checks, which it should.

■**Note** The robustness diagram doesn't need to specify the validation checks in detail, as that would be quite cumbersome, but it should at least name the function, with a controller per function (or group of closely related functions).

These validation checks have been left off because of the next (and biggest) error, which is that the diagram doesn't show *any* of the alternate courses! (This happens surprisingly often, but the alternate courses represent a huge proportion of the system functionality, so they must be given the same amount of attention as the basic course.)

Finally, the diagram is missing entity objects. Two should be on there: Search Criteria and Catalog.

Figure 5-31 shows the corrected robustness diagram. We've also done a small amount of additional tidying-up in the corrected version: see if you can spot what else we've fixed.

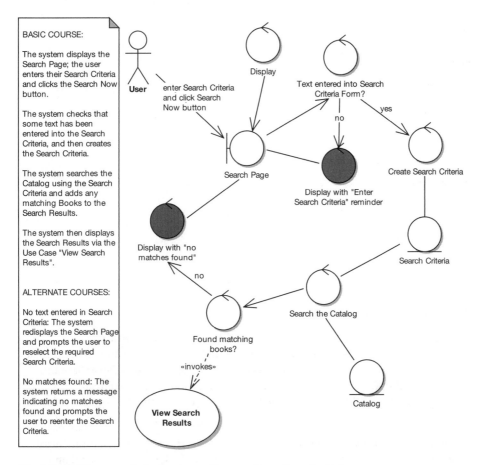

Figure 5-31. *The corrected robustness diagram from Exercise 5-4*

More Practice

This section provides a list of modeling questions that you can use to test your knowledge of robustness analysis.

1. Which of the following is *not* accomplished during robustness analysis?

   a) Object discovery

   b) Disambiguation of use case text

   c) Modeling the problem domain

   d) Validation of requirements by doing conceptual design

2. Which of the following is probably *not* a boundary class?

   a) Login screen

   b) Account table

   c) Mailbox

   d) Error dialog

3. Arrows on a robustness diagram can represent

   a) Data flow

   b) Control flow

   c) Communication associations

   d) All of the above

4. Which of the following is probably *not* a controller?

   a) Validate password

   b) Transaction manager

   c) Line item

   d) Display error message

5. Performing robustness analysis as an intermediate step between writing use cases and drawing sequence diagrams adds an additional modeling step and an additional required diagram to a software process, as opposed to drawing sequence diagrams immediately after writing use cases. Does adding this additional step make the process more or less efficient? Give at least three reasons to support your answer.

6. Robustness diagrams and collaboration diagrams (also called *communication diagrams* in UML2) both show objects collaborating. Does this mean that a robustness diagram and a collaboration diagram are the same, or are they different? Explain.

7. List four things accomplished during robustness analysis that help to close the gap between "what" (requirements analysis) and "how" (detailed design). Explain the benefits of each.

8. Attack or defend the following statement:

> It's impossible to completely understand your requirements without doing some exploratory design.

If you agree with the statement, list three benefits of doing this exploratory design as a "conceptual design" modeling step, as opposed to doing all exploratory design in code.

Summary

In this chapter, we moved from analysis to design, using one of the industry's most useful and yet best-kept secrets: robustness analysis.

The activity diagram in Figure 5-32 shows where we are (the tasks we discussed in this chapter are shown in red). This brings us to Milestone 2 (Preliminary Design Review), which we cover in the next chapter.

Milestone 1: Requirements Review

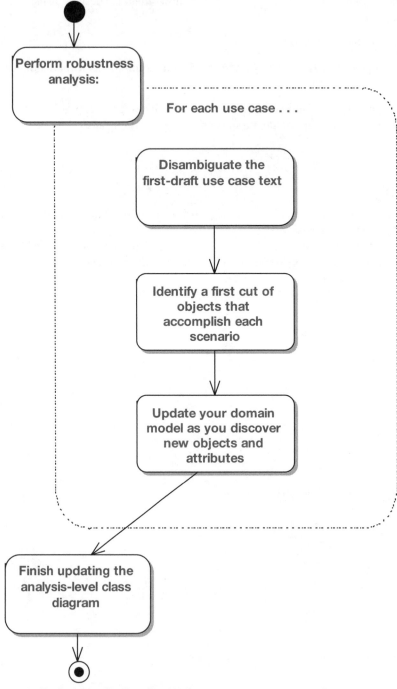

Figure 5-32. *Analysis and Preliminary Design Checkpoint 2*

CHAPTER 6

■■■

Preliminary Design Review

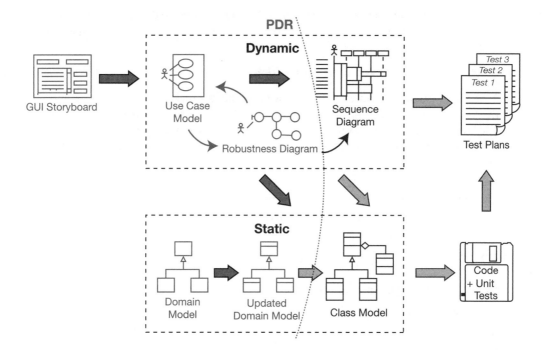

The Preliminary Design Review (PDR) session helps you to make sure that the robustness diagrams, the domain model, and the use case text all match each other. This review is the "gateway" between the preliminary design and detailed design stages, for each package of use cases.

In this chapter, we provide an overview of the PDR, and then we show an example review for the Internet Bookstore.

Preliminary Design Review in Theory

In this section, we look at the key elements of the PDR, including our top 10 PDR guidelines.

Why Do a PDR At All?

Why bother reviewing your model after robustness analysis? Here's a hypothetical conversation that we hope will shed some light on the subject.

Q: I've drawn a robustness diagram for each use case, and as a result I think the use cases are in pretty good shape. Can I start designing now?

A: There's just one quick review step first: the Preliminary Design Review (PDR). This review session helps you to make sure that the robustness diagrams, the domain model, and the use case text all match each other.

Q: Who should be involved in the PDR session?

A: The same group of people you had at the requirements review: customer representatives, the development team, and any managers who are closely involved in the project. The customer is quite closely involved in the proceedings, but this review is the last stage in the process where the customer has direct input. After this, it's detailed design—the job of the senior developers.

■Note Of course, the customer may still comment on work in progress, screenshots, and so forth, but you wouldn't want a nontechnical (or worse, semitechnical) customer to be commenting on or driving the design.

Q: But what if the customer wants to add new requirements later on?

A: That's a different issue. All we're saying is that the customer doesn't have input into the design and coding (i.e., the remaining steps following the PDR and leading up to delivery).

Q: If the customer *does* want to add new requirements, how does this affect the process?

A: Then you're back to step 1 of the process (modifying use cases and the domain model, as needed), at least for the new requirements. Handling the analysis and design effort in a sea of changing requirements is a complex subject with many pitfalls, so we've written a separate book about that.[1]

---

1. Doug Rosenberg, Matt Stephens, and Mark Collins-Cope, *Agile Development with ICONIX Process* (Berkeley, CA: Apress, 2005).

Q: So what else needs to be achieved during the PDR?

A: It's a good opportunity to make sure your entity classes have been populated with attributes, that the screens in your system all have names, and that you can trace the data flow between the screens and the entity classes.

Q: If we're on the verge of doing a detailed design, shouldn't we also be thinking about the technical architecture (TA)?

A: Yes, the TA should also be reviewed during this session. You need to make sure that the burgeoning new design is going to work with your chosen architecture.

Top 10 PDR Guidelines

The principles discussed in this chapter can be summed up as a list of guidelines. Our top 10 list follows.

10. For each use case, **make sure the use case text matches the robustness diagram**, using the highlighter test.

9. Make sure that all the entities on all robustness diagrams appear within the updated domain model.

8. Make sure that you can trace data flow between entity classes and screens.

7. **Don't forget the alternate courses,** and don't forget to write behavior for each of them when you find them.

6. Make sure each use case covers **both sides of the dialogue between user and system.**

5. Make sure you haven't violated the syntax rules for robustness analysis.

4. Make sure that this review **includes both nontechnical** (customer, marketing team, etc.) **and technical folks** (programmers).

3. Make sure your **use cases are in the context of the object model and in the context of the GUI.**

2. Make sure your robustness diagrams (and the corresponding use case text) don't attempt to show the same level of detail that will be shown on the sequence diagrams (i.e., **don't try to do detailed design yet**).

1. Follow our "six easy steps" to a better preliminary design (see Chapter 6).

Let's look at each of these top 10 items in more detail.

10. Use the Highlighter Test to Match the Use Case Text with the Diagram

Sometimes people think they should show only the basic course of action on a robustness diagram, or that they should do a separate diagram for each alternate course. But it's best to show the entire use case (basic and all alternates) on a single robustness diagram.

If the diagram becomes too big (or if you find that the alternates have their own subalternates), consider splitting up the use case.

■Tip Many people like to use a different color for the alternates to make the diagram easier to follow.

A 59-cent highlighter proves to be an invaluable tool for verifying that your use case text matches your diagram. Simply highlight a sentence of your use case, highlight the corresponding section of your robustness diagram, and continue until all the text is highlighted. You should also see the entire robustness diagram highlighted.

If you find a mismatch between the text and the diagram (and trust us, you will), then you have more work to do.

9. Make Sure That All the Entities Appear Within the Updated Domain Model

Since *object discovery* is one of the primary purposes of robustness analysis, it makes little sense to discover new objects on our robustness diagrams and not add them back into the class model (which is evolving from the domain model).

The safest way to avoid forgetting to add them to the class model is to actually add the new classes on the class model, stereotype them as entities, and then drag them onto the robustness diagram.

8. Make Sure That You Can Trace Data Flow Between Entity Classes and Screens

Your use case very likely involves users specifying information by using the screens of the system. This data needs to find its way into the entity classes, which hold the values entered as attributes. Of course, this also works the other way: values from the entity classes will be displayed on the screens.

One of your tasks before coding is to determine the set of attributes that each of your classes needs. So, as you're tracing data flow between screens and entity classes, populate the class model with any missing attributes that are needed.

7. Don't Forget the Alternate Courses, and Don't Forget to Specify Their Behavior

You're probably tired of hearing us say this by now, but we wouldn't keep repeating it if it wasn't important. Forgetting about alternate courses (aka "Whoops, it crashed!") is one of the main failure modes in software development.

■Note Alternate courses are not necessarily error paths but can include infrequent/atypical usage paths.

For each alternate course, make sure that the system behavior in response to the condition that triggers it is fully detailed. Identifying that an alternate course can happen is necessary, but not sufficient to complete your use case. In addition to simply listing the alternate courses, it's critical that you detail the exact behavior (of the user and system) of how the alternate course is handled.

Since **alternate courses generally account for more than half the complexity** of a piece of software, it should be obvious why you need to specify the behavior for the alternates. If you don't, your classes will be missing all the operations that handle the alternate courses.

6. Make Sure Each Use Case Covers Both Sides of the User/System Dialogue

One of the most common errors we've seen among people learning to write use cases for the first time is that they simply **write down all the steps that the user follows** and then announce that they've completed their use cases (inevitably faster than anyone else in the training class).

This flawed process ignores a fundamentally important point: in most cases, **the goal is to fully understand and specify the software behavior of the system**. If you write only the user actions and ignore the system behavior, you're just not going to make very much progress toward the goal of specifying the software behavior.

■Tip Always keep in mind that a use case is a dialogue between the user(s) and system, and you need to write about both sides of that dialogue.

---

5. Make Sure You Haven't Violated the Syntax Rules for Robustness Analysis

Refer back to Figures 5-8 and 5-9 for the full rules of robustness analysis. In particular, during the review make sure that

- Actors are only linked to boundary objects.

- There's no noun-noun communication between boundary/entity, boundary/boundary, or entity/entity objects without controllers in between. **The controllers represent the system behavior**, so it would be a very bad thing to leave them out.

The robustness analysis syntax rules might seem a little bit irksome at times, but bashing your use case's preliminary design into shape so that it fits these rules *seriously* prepares your use case for detailed design. Coding should be a breeze if you get this stage right.

Think about it: if a use case is proving troublesome to turn it into a valid robustness diagram, then **turning it into a valid working design (and valid working, maintainable code) will be ten times as troublesome!** **The robustness diagram provides a handy early warning system that the use case text needs more work (i.e., is vague, ambiguous, incomplete, etc.).**

As you saw in Chapter 5, automated tools support for ICONIX Process is continuing to improve. Validating the robustness diagram syntax rules is now as easy as pulling down a menu.

■Tip As you'll see later, you can automatically generate unit test stubs for each controller as well.

---

4. Include Both Nontechnical and Technical People in the Review

Your use cases after robustness analysis should be treated as "mini-contracts" between the clients and the programmers. As such, they need to be understandable by the end users and clients, but unambiguous enough to be clearly understood by the programmers. It's during PDR that you finalize those contracts.

To put it another way, each use case must reach the *magic abstraction level*—**not vague and ambiguous, but not geek-speak**—where **everybody understands what the use case means**, very clearly. (What a concept!)

3. Make Sure Your Use Cases Are in the Context of Both the Object Model and the GUI

The magic abstraction level we just described is readily achieved by putting the use case in the context of the object model and of the GUI. In practical terms, this means that you've named your screens and your domain classes. Resolving name ambiguity in usage of domain objects and screens solves a great many problems.

The use cases at this level also need to be in the context of the (evolving) technical architecture of the system, but they shouldn't cross the line into detailed design, because you'll quickly lose the attention of the nontechnical clients if they do. (Hint: If you notice all of the nontechnical folks looking glassy-eyed in the review meeting, consider whether they might have entered the state of hypnotic stupor while trying to follow a use case that discusses the details of object instantiation via the factory pattern. Also check to see if somebody spiked the coffee.)

2. Don't Drift into Detailed Design Territory

Remember that the robustness diagram represents an idealized, conceptual design, not the "real software design." In practical terms, this means that decisions related to allocating behavior among classes should not be made on robustness diagrams. These decisions are best deferred until you draw the sequence diagrams.

ICONIX Process takes a two-pass approach to get to detailed design. In the first pass, you intentionally ignore "who's doing what" and focus on identifying objects, naming screens, and unambiguously describing behavior. Once you've done this correctly (and you've verified it during the PDR), you're ready to take on the behavior allocation problem (i.e., how the methods are distributed among the classes) during detailed design.

1. Follow Our "Six Easy Steps" to a Better Preliminary Design

To achieve the purpose of the PDR (as described at the start of this chapter), it helps to carry out some key checks on the preliminary design diagrams and the use case text. For each robustness diagram that you're reviewing[2]

- Make sure the diagram matches the use case text.

- Make sure the diagram follows the rules of robustness analysis.

- Check that the diagram focuses on the logical flow of the use case.

- Make sure the diagram shows all alternate courses of action for the use case.

- Watch out for "design-pattern-itis" in the diagram.

- Check that the diagram isn't trying to be a detailed design.

We'll illustrate these steps in the review conversation in the next section.

---

2. These steps are described in more detail in Chapter 6 of *Applying Use Case Driven Object Modeling with UML* by Doug Rosenberg and Kendall Scott (Addison-Wesley, 2001).

Preliminary Design Review in Practice: Internet Bookstore

In this section, we illustrate the theory from the first part of this chapter, using an example from our Internet Bookstore project. The result is actually a continuation of the robustness diagram we developed step by step in Chapter 5.

PDR for the "Write Customer Review" Robustness Diagram

For this example PDR session, we'll follow the reviewer/analyst conversation as it unfolds. We left the robustness diagram in Figure 5-15, so it's worth flipping back to that version of the diagram as you walk through this example session.

The Customer Review Object Isn't a Container for the "Enter Review" Text

A common theme for the topics in this review is that the diagram didn't go into sufficient detail, or it skipped over vital details that were mentioned in the use case text.

> **Reviewer**: Looking at the robustness diagram *(see excerpt in Figure 6-1)*, I'd expect the `Customer Review` object to be the container for the "enter Review" text that's entered on the screen, but it's not connected.

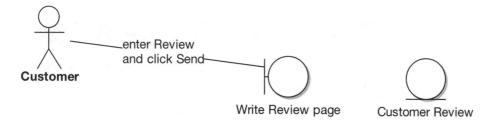

Figure 6-1. *"enter Review" should be a controller*

> **Analyst**: We could draw a line between the "`Write Review page`" boundary and the `Customer Review` entity . . .

> **Reviewer**: It's tempting, but it would violate the rules of robustness analysis. Remember, noun-noun communication is a major no-no.

■Note Such a strict and seemingly restrictive rule exists for a very good reason: if you're drawing a line between two nouns on the diagram, then there's almost certainly some behavior (aka verbs) not being accounted for.

> **Analyst**: Come to think of it, I don't think we're showing the behavior for *two* user actions: assigning a rating and typing in the review text.

Reviewer: We should add controllers to handle both of these behaviors and use them to link "Write Review page" with the Customer Review entity. Problem solved! *(The "click Send" label also needs to move, but we'll cover that in the next segment; Figure 6-2 shows the updated excerpt.)*

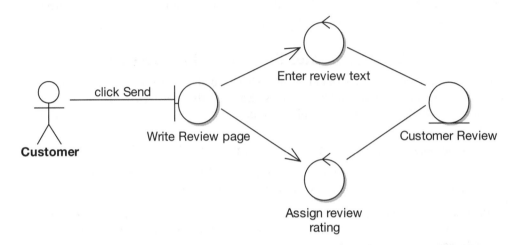

Figure 6-2. *Label text is "promoted" to be a controller, and a second controller is identified.*

"BUT WE'RE MODELING WEB PAGE INTERACTIONS . . ."

A common reaction to this advice (showing the user inputting text or other data into the UI as a controller) is that if it's implemented in the form of a web page, then you'll never actually write code to handle these events—it's all done in the browser.

The simple answer to this is that you're not actually designing at this stage. What you're primarily interested in with this diagram is showing everything from the use case text in picture form. Going to this level of detail might seem like a drag at first, but it's amazing how much hidden functionality gets uncovered this way. These details would have otherwise been left uncovered until *after* the software had been designed and coding had begun.

In extreme cases, the details might not have been discovered until after the software shipped, the user did something unexpected, and the program crashed because the excruciating details hadn't been properly analyzed during robustness analysis. So, the lesson to learn from this is, *if it's in the use case text, put it on the diagram!*

Label Positioning Makes for Ambiguous Paths

Fixing one problem sometimes leads to the identification of another. After taking a thoughtful look at the two new controllers added in Figure 6-2, our reviewer spots another potential source of trouble.

Reviewer: In the robustness diagram *(see excerpt in Figure 6-3)*, you've labeled the message between the actor (Customer) and the "Write Review page" boundary object.

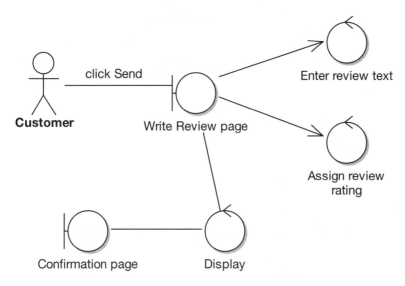

Figure 6-3. *The Customer clicked Send . . . but which way next?*

Analyst: Seems harmless to me. You need to know what action the Customer performed on the boundary object.

Reviewer: Sure, but this is more to do with *where* the label goes. The problem is that if you have multiple actions going into one boundary object, then it quickly becomes ambiguous as to where each action goes after the boundary object.

Analyst: So because we've got three controllers coming out of "Write Review page," we don't know which one is for the "click Send" action?

Reviewer: Exactly. It makes the diagram much clearer if, instead, **you label the message between the boundary object and the controller.** If you put the user's action ("click Send") there instead, then there's no confusion about which controller handles which user action. *(Figure 6-4 shows the updated excerpt from the robustness diagram.)*

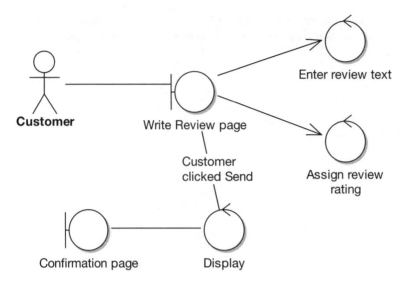

Figure 6-4. *Improved label positioning eliminates ambiguity in the diagram.*

Display Controllers Need More Detailed Names

Sometimes when you're adding controllers left, right, and center, it's tempting to leave detail out of the diagram. But this can result in ambiguity that comes back to bite you later, during the detailed design. In the next example, the reviewer discovers that some detail has been subtly left out of the diagram.

> **Reviewer**: You've used a single boundary object ("Review Rejected page") to show the results of the two alternate-course validation controllers ("Is Review Rating in allowed range?" and "Is Book Review length OK?"). However, each one has its own Display controller. *(See excerpt in Figure 6-5.)*

> **Analyst**: But I thought we're meant to show separate Display controllers like that?

> **Reviewer**: Absolutely. But they're just a tad ambiguous. The problem is that a specific message would be constructed to tell the user why the review was rejected, such as "The review needs to be at least ten characters long, but yours contained only five characters."

> **Analyst**: Let me guess, we're not stating explicitly what gets displayed differently on the "Review Rejected page" for each controller.

> **Reviewer**: You've got it. To correct this, let's rename each Display controller to something more specific. *(See Figure 6-6.)*

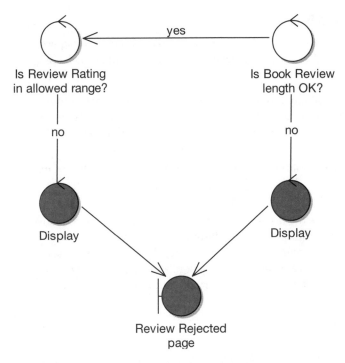

Figure 6-5. *Insufficient detail on what gets displayed to the user*

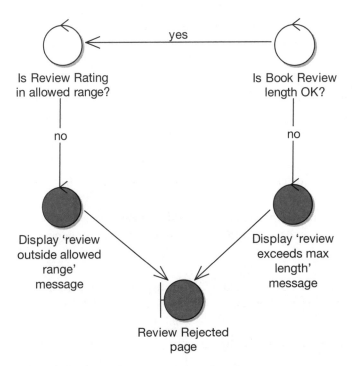

Figure 6-6. *Disambiguated Display controllers*

The Use Case Text Is Missing Some Detail

During the PDR, **you should be equally focused on the use case text** as on the robustness diagrams. In the final example from this review, the reviewer notices some missing detail in the use case description.

> **Reviewer**: OK, this is really starting to look like a diagram that you could easily produce a detailed design from. Just one last thing, though. The diagram invokes another use case called *Moderate Customer Reviews*. In the use case, it matches up with this text:

> > *The system then displays a confirmation screen, and the review is sent to a Moderator, ready to be added.*

> But the text is missing some of the details of what actually happens. At the moment, we're taking it as read that the newly submitted review will somehow find its way to the Moderator, who will then check the Customer's `Review` before it's published on the site. As I mentioned, the Moderator's actions are handled by a separate use case, *Moderate Customer Reviews*. But what we haven't modeled (or described) is how the `Review` makes its way to the second use case.

> **Analyst**: We could update the use case text like this:

> > *The system then displays a confirmation screen, and the Customer Review is queued for moderation (this will be handled by the* Moderate Customer Reviews *use case).*

> **Reviewer**: It's better, but don't forget that we need to tie the use cases to the objects. Simply saying that "the review is queued for moderation" doesn't quite do that, as it doesn't provide any sort of link to the object that will track the incoming `Customer Reviews`.

> **Analyst**: *(Pondering)* "The object that will track the incoming `Customer Reviews`"? Hmm, it sounds as if we've just identified a new domain object—an object that queues up the incoming `Customer Reviews`.

> **Reviewer**: Let's call it "`Pending Reviews Queue`."

> **Analyst**: OK, so here's the updated use case text *(the updated text is shown in red)*:

> > *The system then displays a confirmation screen and the Customer Review is* **added to the Pending Reviews Queue** *for moderation (this will be handled by the* Moderate Customer Reviews *use case).*

> **Reviewer**: This also suggests that the Book ID needs to be an attribute of the `Customer Review`, which in turn suggests that `Book` should probably also be on the diagram somewhere. Now we can add our new `Pending Reviews Queue` object to the diagram.

> **Analyst**: Wow, all that new detail discovered, just by tying the use case text more closely with the model!

■**Tip** **If you leave the behavior implied** on the robustness diagram and in the use case, **it never gets done on the sequence diagram**, and (if you're allocating operations to classes by working through the use cases) it just sort of **falls through the cracks to be dealt with in coding-land**. The more stuff that falls through those cracks, the less useful the models are, and the less the team will "model like they mean it."

The Finished "Write Customer Review" Robustness Diagram

Figure 6-7 shows the finished version of the robustness diagram. As you can see, it's now possible to read the use case on the left of the diagram and walk your way through the diagram at the same time. (A common convention is to start the use case at the top-left of the diagram and finish at the bottom-right, although this is by no means essential.) Nothing in the use case has been assumed or left to chance, and the text is nicely tied to the domain object model. We've done the groundwork, so this diagram is now something that we can design from very easily.

Astute readers will have noticed that this diagram has now become what we commonly call "very big." In fact, it's pretty much at the upper limit of use case size (remember the two-paragraph rule from Chapter 3). If the use case was any longer, or the diagram any more complex, we'd seriously think about splitting it into two or more smaller use cases (and hence, two or more smaller robustness diagrams).

In Chapter 8, we'll return to the *Write Customer Review* use case and show the next step: drawing the sequence diagram.

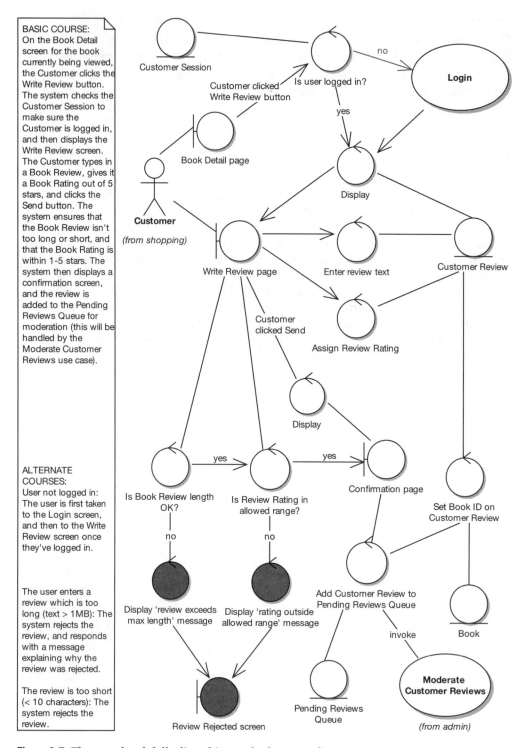

BASIC COURSE:
On the Book Detail screen for the book currently being viewed, the Customer clicks the Write Review button. The system checks the Customer Session to make sure the Customer is logged in, and then displays the Write Review screen. The Customer types in a Book Review, gives it a Book Rating out of 5 stars, and clicks the Send button. The system ensures that the Book Review isn't too long or short, and that the Book Rating is within 1-5 stars. The system then displays a confirmation screen, and the review is added to the Pending Reviews Queue for moderation (this will be handled by the Moderate Customer Reviews use case).

ALTERNATE COURSES:
User not logged in: The user is first taken to the Login screen, and then to the Write Review screen once they've logged in.

The user enters a review which is too long (text > 1MB): The system rejects the review, and responds with a message explaining why the review was rejected.

The review is too short (< 10 characters): The system rejects the review.

Figure 6-7. *The completed, fully disambiguated robustness diagram*

Summary

In this chapter, we covered the Preliminary Design Review (PDR) milestone. This step involves making sure that the diagrams and the use case text match each other and that both are complete and correctly represent the desired system behavior.

Once the PDR is complete, you're ready to move on to the detailed design, which we cover in Chapter 8. The technical architecture (TA) is also a vital step. The formulation of the TA begins during robustness analysis, but it really kicks into high gear just prior to the detailed design. We cover the TA in Chapter 7.

Figure 6-8 shows where we are (the milestone covered in this chapter is shown in red).

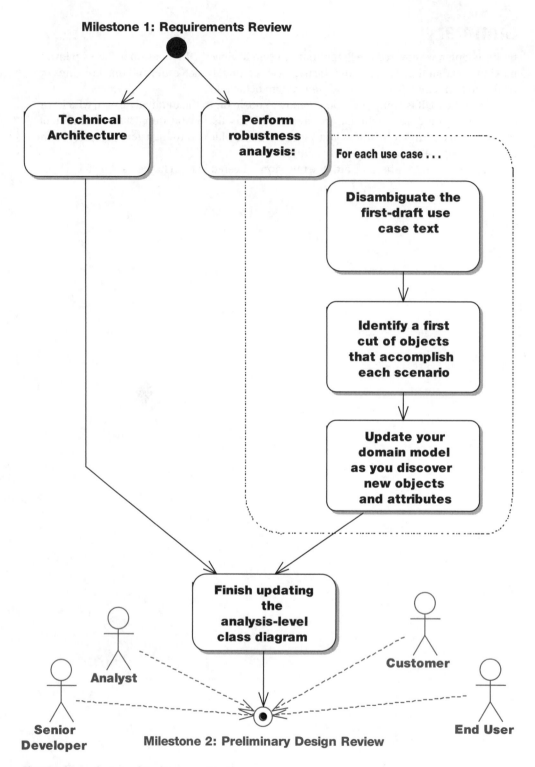

Figure 6-8. *Analysis and Preliminary Design*

CHAPTER 7

■ ■ ■

Technical Architecture

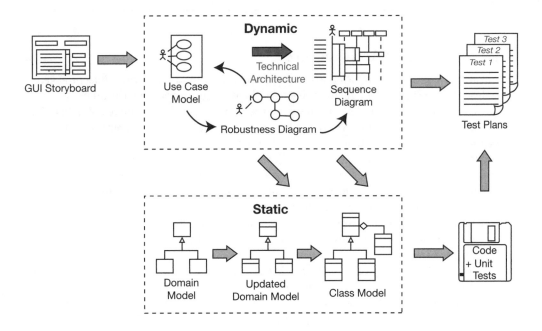

GUI Storyboard

Dynamic

Use Case Model

Technical Architecture

Robustness Diagram

Sequence Diagram

Test Plans

Static

Domain Model

Updated Domain Model

Class Model

Code + Unit Tests

The purpose of technical architecture (TA) is to get an overall feel for the system that you're going to be developing. Will it be a web-based system? Or a rich-client system in VB .NET or Java Swing? Does it need to use a specific application framework (e.g., a company-standard framework)?

There's no standard notation or format for documenting the TA; the depth and format of the technical architecture—and the conventions for creating it—vary widely from company to company, so we don't dwell in this area for too long. In this chapter, we follow a practical example of TA in action, for the Internet Bookstore.

■Note What we describe in this chapter isn't by any means a "standard ICONIX method" for creating an architecture, but it provides us with an opportunity to discuss the server-side framework (Spring Framework) that we'll use to design and build the Internet Bookstore example.

The 10,000-Foot View

You should start thinking seriously about TA during robustness analysis (see Chapter 5). TA should be reflected to a degree on the robustness diagrams, but it must be finalized once you've finished robustness analysis, and it *really* needs to be nailed down before you begin the detailed design (see Chapter 8).

■**Note**   Although TA precedes robustness analysis in the process, we've left the discussion of TA until now so as not to introduce too many different topics all at once.

What Is Technical Architecture?

Technical architecture (also referred to as *system architecture* and *software architecture*) generally describes the system you're intending to build in terms of *structure*. The architecture is built to satisfy the *business* and *service-level* requirements of the system you're going to build. The architecture includes (but isn't limited to) the system topology (the server nodes, physical location on the network, choice of application server[s], etc.).

A good TA will be based on some thorough analysis of the "numbers" involved—that is, the number of people who will be using the system at any time, whether there are peak usage hours (and what those peaks are likely to be), the number of transactions per minute, failover criteria, and so on. These numbers will play a huge role in deciding such factors as what sort of application server (or web server) should be used, how many licenses to buy, and which server- and client-side technologies the project should use. These are not decisions for the fainthearted!

Documented architectures range in depth and formality from several volumes of detailed specs (with every "i" dotted and "t" crossed) to a bunch of e-mails and Visio diagrams. The ideal level lies somewhere between the two extremes, though of course the needs will vary depending on the nature and size of the project.

What Are the Duties of a Technical Architect?

In addition to simply creating the right architecture to solve the problem posed by the requirements, the architect must also document the architecture in an expressive and unambiguous written format, and **make sure the latest version is available to everyone on the project**. The technical architect must also truly believe in the TA he or she has created, and be prepared to evangelize it and communicate its intent to all the project stakeholders. This is an important point, because an architect who doesn't follow the courage of his or her convictions will end up with a disjointed system, where individual teams or team members head off in different directions and do slightly different things. For example, one team will use WebWork for their presentation tier, another team will use Velocity, another JSP, and so on. Nothing will quite fit together properly, and it will never quite be clear whether the requirements have been fully met. If one part of the system meets the failover requirements, but another part has been designed slightly differently, has the requirement been met?

This means that the architect needs leadership skills. The architect must be prepared to resolve disputes and help the team to reach a compromise if needed. There may also be team leaders involved, and a project manager, and so on, but ultimately it's the architect who binds the whole thing together and sees the project through to completion. (And don't get us started on nontechnical architects who write a big, quasi-academic architecture document and then swan off onto a different project!)

■**Tip** A list of the duties of a chief software architect can be found at the Carnegie Mellon Software Engineering Institute website: `www.sei.cmu.edu/activities/architecture/arch_duties.html`.

Technical Architecture in Theory

In this section, we take a brief look at what TA is. After that, we'll dive into the TA for the Internet Bookstore project.

Top 10 Technical Architecture Guidelines

The principles discussed in this chapter can be summed up as a list of guidelines. Our top 10 list follows.

10. Separate functional, data, and system architecture.

Architectures generally cover three broad areas:

- The deployment model (network and application servers, and how they fit together; system topology; web browsers supported; etc.)

- The package/component model (separation of concerns to different strata/components)

- The data model

9. Understand why you're creating an architecture.

Before you even think about the system's architecture, it's important to understand precisely why an architecture is even needed.

8. Base the architecture objectively on the requirements.

It's tempting to base the architecture on the latest technology or whatever happens to be the "flavor of the month," rather than listening to what the requirements are trying to tell you and making an objective decision based on what's needed. Budget considerations are also important. If you decide that, technically speaking, the best application server for the project is "BankBreaker 8.0 Service Pack 12," is the budget available to handle this? Are there cheaper (and more robust) alternatives that match the requirements just as well?

7. Consider factors such as scalability, security, and availability.

6. Consider internationalization and localization.

5. Pose hard questions to all the people involved.

Questions regarding such issues as security, auditing, portability, and scalability need to be answered now, not six months into the project.

4. If you don't get the answers you need, ask again—and keep on asking!

3. Consider testability.

Our co-author on *Agile Development with ICONIX Process* (Apress, 2005), Mark Collins-Cope, described a trading system he'd been working on. According to the spec, orders should time out after between 1 and 30 days. To test this, the team couldn't really wait around (a tad boring), so they built functionality to enable the UI to set the date and time, specifically for testing. This is just one example of how testing must be considered even in the early stages when you're thinking about the architecture.

2. Explore which external systems you'll need to interface with.

Scour the requirements for anything relating to synchronous or asynchronous external system interaction. For synchronous systems, think about external system availability. Is it a requirement that your system be able to operate without the other system?

1. Have the courage to believe that your architecture is right and the strength to push its adoption throughout the project.

Building software is a complex process. It's all too easy to end up with a big plate of spaghetti, tangled and amorphous, rather than an elegant haute cuisine plate of pristine perfection (see the next section on layering for the "lasagna model"). You would think that those involved would pull together to achieve the latter instead of the former. But people are people, and if they're simply left to it, each individual or group will form its own "micro-project" with its own direction, set of goals, and set of standards—even its own "mini-architecture." The technical architect (actually, the chief architect) must communicate his or her documented architecture and make sure everyone understands it, not just at the beginning of the project but throughout.

Architectural Layering

■Note Our thanks to Mark Collins-Cope, our co-author on *Agile Development with ICONIX Process* (Apress, 2005), for providing most of this section's content.

Architectural layering is a visual metaphor whereby the software that makes up a system is divided into bands (layers) in an architectural diagram. Many such diagrams have been used, and by way of introduction we show two of these.

Figure 7-1 presents a view of a strictly layered architecture.

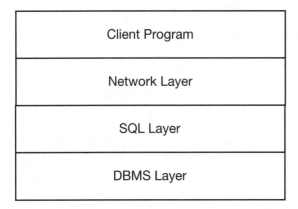

Figure 7-1. *Layered architecture example*

Figure 7-2 shows a type of ad hoc architecture diagram that is not uncommon in modern technical documentation.

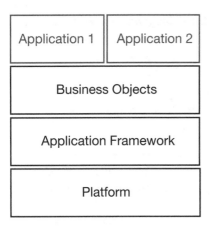

Figure 7-2. *Typical ad hoc architectural layering diagram*

Some common themes run through these diagrams:

- It's possible to identify a number of layers in the construction of pieces of software.

- Some layers sit on top of others (although there may be some question as to what one layer being above another actually means).

- We may broadly categorize layers as being either horizontal (applicable across many, if not all, business domains) or vertical (applicable across a subset or only one domain).

Turning to UML class diagrams (a younger notation), we notice that common convention usually places subclasses, which are more specialized, below their parents, which are more general purpose (see Figure 7-3). This convention is the exact opposite of the architectural convention "highest is most specific" and the cause of an undoubtedly confusing visual metaphor mismatch. This mismatch is discussed further in the article "The Topsy Turvy World of UML."[1]

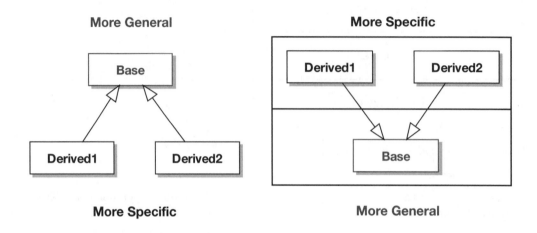

Figure 7-3. *Class diagrams and architectural views*

Technical Architecture in Practice: Internet Bookstore

In this section, we show an example of a TA for the Internet Bookstore. This project uses Spring Framework, so we'll also use this opportunity to introduce the basic concepts behind Spring. We describe these concepts in more detail during detailed design (Chapter 8), during CDR (Chapter 9), and when we begin coding (Chapter 10).

About Spring Framework

During TA, one of the really big design decisions is (for web-based systems) which web framework to use, if any, and of course which programming language to code the solution in. Even the basic assumption that this is to be a web-based system shouldn't be taken for granted. Of course, in many projects, this decision will already have been made at a sales or management level before the software designers get involved, but (in theory at least) it should be an entirely design-driven decision, led by the technical needs as uncovered by the requirements. (Oh, for an ideal world . . .)

---

1. Hubert Matthews and Mark Collins-Cope, "The Topsy Turvy World of UML," *ObjectiveView* Issue 4, available at www.softwarereality.com/ObjectiveView.jsp, 2000.

So, we know that we need to design a web-based system from our use cases. For this example, we'll implement the Internet Bookstore using Java, and we'll use Spring Framework,[2] a popular *lightweight* J2EE container. More specifically, we'll use the part of Spring Framework called Spring Web MVC. As the name suggests, this part of Spring allows you to create a web application using a Model-View-Controller (MVC) architecture. For the front-end (the "View" part of the MVC), we'll use JavaServer Pages (JSP),[3] augmented with Sun's standard JSP Tag Library (JSTL).[4] For the back-end data store connected to our model, we'll use Spring's JDBC support to implement our Data Access Objects (DAOs).

Because this is a "quick 'n easy" demo application, we'll use HSQL[5] for the database. HSQL is a "personal" database, not suited for large-scale multiuser web applications, but it's certainly well suited for quick and painless prototype development work.

■**Tip** HSQL includes an in-memory persistence mode, which (because it doesn't access the hard disk) is very fast and ideal for unit testing.

We'll also show how to use EA to generate Spring-ready Java code from the domain objects and controllers in our UML model.

Although some familiarity with Spring Framework will help you to follow the Internet Bookstore example, it isn't essential. In fact, one of the qualities of Spring is that it allows you to program using so-called Plain Old Java Objects (or POJOs), which have absolutely no dependency on the container framework. POJOs are just straightforward JavaBeans with the usual "getters and setters." In Chapter 9, we show how to generate these directly from your static model. Using Spring, dependencies between JavaBeans can be set up by wiring the beans together using simple XML files.

We'll describe more about Spring Framework (or at least the parts of it that we need) as we go along. We'll also return to it when we create the detailed design in Chapter 9 and when we begin programming from the detailed design in Chapter 10. The next section introduces the basic concepts underlying Spring.

Anatomy of Spring Framework

To follow along with the Internet Bookstore example, it isn't essential for you to know how Spring works. However, this section should help to explain why we're designing and coding things in the way that we are. Although this book isn't really about Spring, you'll gain a good understanding of Spring and the way it's used for building web applications using JSP, JSTL, and JDBC.

---

2. See www.springframework.org.

3. See http://java.sun.com/products/jsp.

4. See http://java.sun.com/products/jsp/jstl.

5. See http://hsqldb.sourceforge.net.

What Exactly *Is* Spring Framework?

Spring Framework is many things. It's generally viewed as a lightweight J2EE application framework, although it isn't necessarily limited to J2EE. In fact it also has a rich-client sub-project (Spring Rich Client), which makes use of its elegant design to create Java Swing client-side applications. However, Spring is mostly used on the server.

The definition is further complicated because Spring allows different frameworks to be "plugged in" to handle object-relational mapping (ORM), views/templating, and so forth. On the ORM side of things, Spring has support for JDBC, Hibernate, Java Data Objects (JDO), and iBATIS. On the view side, Spring has support for a number of templating/web content solutions including JSP, Velocity, and Struts.

Spring's JDBC support is particularly nice because it provides you with "ultimate" control over how your objects are persisted to (and read from) the database, while eliminating the swathes of repetitive boilerplate code that JDBC-based programs normally suffer from.

To make use of Spring's J2EE features, you need to run it inside a J2EE server. At the very least, to use its web MVC features, you need to run it in a Java servlet/JSP container such as Tomcat or Resin. For the Internet Bookstore we'll use Tomcat.[6]

In the next few sections, we take a quick look at some of what Spring Framework has to offer, with particular emphasis on how we'll use it for the Internet Bookstore.

Inversion of Control/Dependency Injection

The most compelling aspect of Spring is its use of the ***Inversion of Control*** (IoC) design pattern. In short, IoC allows a class to be written as a "pure" JavaBean with its own properties, but without any dependencies on the framework that it's running in.

Compare this with EJB, for example, where an entity bean must implement the EntityBean interface, and therefore must include methods such as ejbActivate() and ejbRemove(), and must have a matching remote interface which extends EJBObject, and so on. As a result, EJBs are tightly coupled with the server technology. An EJB can be nothing but an EJB—that's no life for a young Java class to look forward to. To top it all, if the entity bean needs to access a resource (such as a database connection or another entity bean), it must take it upon itself to go looking for the resource. This often results in repetitive, brittle code in which semantics leak between classes, and (as the program increases in size) it's increasingly difficult to make changes or test individual functions in isolation.

Using the IoC design pattern, objects (or "beans") don't actively go looking for data. Instead, dependent objects are handed to the bean via the framework. It's best to illustrate this idea with a quick example, so here goes.

■**Note** You should find it useful to get an idea of how we'll be using Spring's IoC mechanism in our design to bind the classes together. See the section "A (Very) Brief Example of IoC" in Appendix B.

---

6. See http://jakarta.apache.org/tomcat.

Spring Web MVC

Spring's web framework centers around a Java servlet called `DispatcherServlet`. As the name suggests, this servlet dispatches requests to controllers and provides some additional functionality that web applications can make good use of.

So as you might expect, the Internet Bookstore's design will be based around Spring's `DispatcherServlet`. When a request is received from the customer's web browser, it is first "picked up" by the web server (in our case, Tomcat). Tomcat passes the request to `DispatcherServlet`, which then hands the request on to one of the Internet Bookstore's controller classes.

The "MVC" part of Spring Web MVC refers to the Model-View-Controller design pattern. This is a well-known design pattern that fits in very nicely with the boundary, entity, and controller classes used by ICONIX Process, and it is almost a ubiquitous design pattern for both rich-client and web-based thin client GUI applications (i.e., it isn't limited to Spring). The premise behind MVC is that the application is divided into three distinct areas:

- **Model**: This is an object representation of the data, usually read in from a database. Sitting "behind" the model is all the detailed plumbing code for mapping objects to tables, rows, columns, and relationships in the database.

- **View**: This is the boundary between the computer and the user. In a web application, the view typically refers to both the web page and the template (e.g., JSP or Velocity file) that creates the web page.

- **Controller**: Controllers are the "glue" between the view and the model. When a request is received, the controller fetches (or updates) the data from the model, decides which view to show the user, and hands the requisite data to the view. Typically an MVC application has lots of fine-grained controllers (using ICONIX Process, these are mapped directly from the controllers on the robustness diagrams). The controllers might actually contain both application logic and business logic; in a highly structured design, these may be separated into different layers.

■Note If you design your domain logic into separate layers, be careful not to fall into the trap of turning your domain classes into "data-only" containers without any behavior of their own. During the development of the Internet Bookstore example over the next few chapters, we demonstrate what can happen if your domain classes become data-only containers, and we discuss ways of avoiding this trap.

One of Spring's great strengths is the way in which it separates the view from the rest of the MVC framework. Essentially, this means that you can choose which view technology you want to use (e.g., Tiles, Velocity, XSLT, and even Acrobat or Excel files).

For the Internet Bookstore, the view will be handled by JSP coupled with JSTL. In the next section, we look at Spring's support for JSP.

Controllers

A controller is an intrinsic part of the MVC design pattern. Controllers are where the application processing logic goes. In Spring, a `Controller` object interprets user input and transforms the result into a model that will be shown to the user in the view.

■**Note**   **Controllers and controllers**: As Spring makes use of `Controller` classes, this might cause confusion when we're also talking about the controllers on our robustness diagrams. As luck would have it, Spring `Controller` classes are almost always mapped directly from controllers on the robustness diagrams. Where we need to distinguish between the two, we'll refer to them as *Spring* `Controllers` (capital "C") and *UML controllers* (lowercase "c").

To carry data between the view and the controller, Spring uses `Command` objects, so we'll introduce those next. See Appendix B for more details about Spring `Controllers`.

Command Objects

You'll see much discussion in the next few chapters about `Command` objects, especially when we get to the design review stage.

In a web application, a `Command` object contains data that has been read in from the browser's request parameters. For example, a page that handles a user login form might have a `Command` object called `UserLoginCommand` with two properties, `username` and `password`. The HTML login form would, in turn, have two matching field names called, as you might expect, `username` and `password`. The `UserLoginCommand` would be passed into a `UserLoginFormController` to process the form login and to determine which page the user should be presented with next.

In Spring, `Command` objects don't have to implement a special interface or extend a "Spring-only" superclass. Instead, any old POJO will do, as long as its property names match up with the names used in the request parameters.

■**Tip**   Though you may not find this tip in the Spring literature, we've found that after putting all the work into creating a domain model, creating additional, separate `Command` classes is quite counterintuitive. The `Command` classes often end up being thin wrappers around your domain classes, which seems like rather a waste to us. Instead, try to use your domain classes where you would normally create an additional `Command` class. We show an example of this in the next chapter, with the `CustomerReview` domain class.

Views

The ***view*** is the JSP page that will generate the HTML that the user sees. Controllers in Spring generally return a `ModelAndView` object, which tells Spring what view to send back to the browser and what model data to populate it with.

> **■Note** We'll explain this mechanism in more detail when we start coding the Internet Bookstore in Chapter 10. Also see Appendix B for more about creating and configuring JSP views using Spring. For now, we're just introducing what you'll need in order to draw the sequence diagrams in the next chapter.

DAO and JDBC Support

One of the reasons we chose Spring for the Internet Bookstore example is that it allows you to create a persistent object model using straightforward JavaBeans, with simple get and set methods for each property. These JavaBeans are our domain classes; there is (for the most part) a direct mapping between these and the classes in the domain model.

Spring also provides excellent DAO support. It allows you to define DAOs as simple interfaces (with methods such as findBooksByTitle()). At runtime, these DAOs are mapped onto concrete classes that utilize the object persistence technology of your choice (e.g., JDBC, JDO, or Hibernate).

> **■Note** See Appendix B for more details about Spring's JDBC support and how we've used it for the Internet Bookstore example.

Is a DAO a Collection?

When you're domain modeling, it's useful to include a Collection object to represent many instances of the same domain class. For example, a Book domain class might be associated with a BookCollection. The BookCollection is analogous to a database table, whereas the Book is analogous to a row in the table.

Often this representation carries over perfectly well into the detailed static model. However, on other occasions, the analogy might not quite fit the implementation and design details. For example, with DAOs, a DAO class is really a source of Collections (where a Collection in this case is actually derived from the java.util.Collection interface, meaning that it's a cluster of objects). In other words, the DAO isn't a Collection itself, but it's a source of Collections. The DAO will return different Collection objects (collections of Books) of different sizes and containing different subsets of Books depending on the DAO method called.

Even in this case, it's useful when at the domain modeling stage to think in terms of Book and BookCollection. Figure 7-5 shows the transition from the initial, analysis-level domain model to the implementation-focused static model.

ALL IN A DAO'S WORK

A Data Access Object (DAO) provides an abstraction from the underlying database. A DAO class includes "finder" methods that access the database and return instances of domain classes.

DAOs aren't specific to Spring; they're found in many other frameworks and languages. For example, they're common in the Visual Basic and VB .NET worlds.

It's useful to think of a DAO as being the database table and a domain object as being a row in the table (see Figure 7-4). Note that the mapping between the DAO and the table isn't necessarily 1:1 (although it often is). For example, if DAO A uses Table A, which in turn contains a reference to Table B, but no other DAOs use Table B, then it might make sense simply to access Table B from DAO A. However, most of the time it's useful to think of a DAO as being directly analogous to a database table. See Figure 7-5 for an example of a group of related domain objects transitioning into a set of classes in the detailed design.

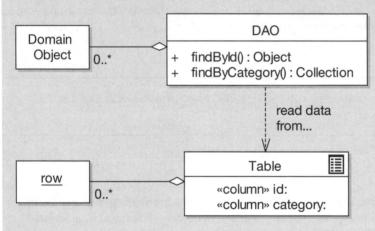

Figure 7-4. *A domain object is to a DAO as a row is to a table.*

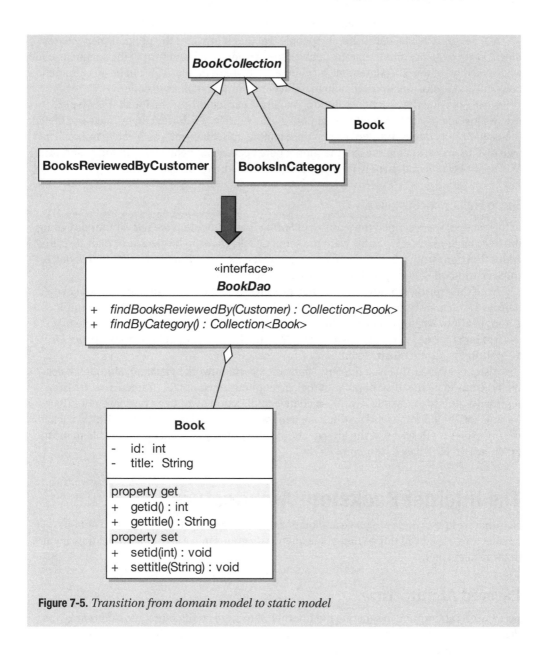

Figure 7-5. *Transition from domain model to static model*

Spring AOP

Aspect-oriented programming (AOP) is turning out to be an interesting (if controversial) extension to object-oriented programming (OOP). AOP allows you to define ***cross-cutting concerns*** through your code (e.g., to precede all methods starting with "write" with some code that first authenticates the user). AOP is typically used for logging, user authorization and authentication, and transactions.

AOP is controversial because some people feel that it provides the programmer with too much power to create impossible-to-debug code; it's potentially a return to the spaghetti-code wild-west days of the `GOTO` statement. Of course, in the right hands, AOP can be an extremely powerful and useful tool that can help to reduce the number of lines of code.

Spring provides its own AOP solution, making it particularly useful for all three typical uses we just mentioned. In our Internet Bookstore example, we don't actually make use of AOP (it was tempting, but we wanted to keep the example under control!), so if you're unfamiliar with AOP then don't panic. We just mention it here because we believe that in the near future, AOP might become much more important for use case–driven development.

Spring Framework Summary

In this section, we described the features of Spring Framework that are relevant for designing the Internet Bookstore. We didn't want the sequence diagrams to be generic or high-level diagrams that don't truly reflect the implementation details. For this reason, we've had to delve some way into the underlying framework that we'll be building on.

Note that Spring Framework is a huge product. It includes lots of features not covered here, as we've mainly just covered the areas relevant to the Internet Bookstore example. For more about Spring, check out their `spring-reference.pdf` document (available from `www.springframework.org/documentation`). We can also recommend the book *Spring Live* by Matt Raible (SourceBeat, 2005).[7]

Also note that Spring isn't the only "lightweight" framework of its kind, although it certainly seems to be the most popular of the current new breed of J2EE frameworks. It also represents a trend in the J2EE world—a change in direction away from heavyweight EJBs towards IoC-based frameworks, which are generally much easier to develop with. As such, the principles we describe in the Internet Bookstore example should be applicable to most other Java or .NET-based web frameworks.

The Internet Bookstore Architecture

Now that we know which language and platform we're targeting, let's briefly map out our architecture. We'll need this so that our sequence diagrams make sense when we draw them in the next chapter.

Layered Architecture

Let's start by attempting to separate the Internet Bookstore architecture into different layers. Figure 7-6 shows the first attempt. Note that it's an ad hoc "lines and boxes" diagram, not following an official notation.

---

7. Available in traditional pulped-tree format or as an e-book subscription from `www.sourcebeat.com`.

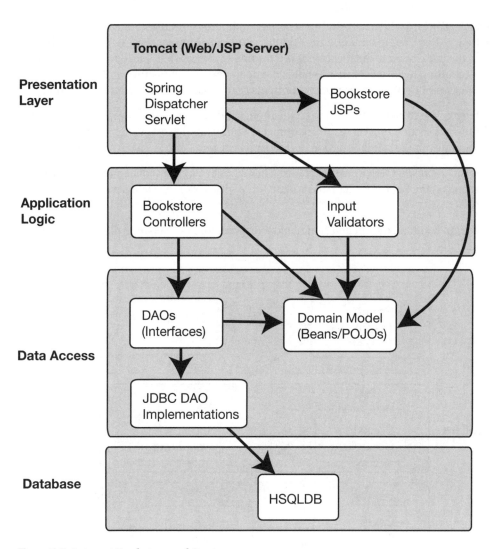

Figure 7-6. *Internet Bookstore architecture*

It's a start, but Figure 7-6 raises a few issues:

- The diagram appears to be mixing two aspects of architecture: the *deployment* model and the *package/component* model. We should separate these out into two diagrams.

- Tomcat runs on the application server (middle tier), not the presentation layer. However, what the diagram is attempting to show is that, as this is an MVC architecture, we're using JSP to create the presentation layer (the "view"). The reason for the mix-up is again because we're attempting to show two separate things in the same diagram.

- Spring's DispatcherServlet almost certainly should be on the application server middle tier; the presentation tier should be the web browser. Again, this comes back to the issue of what the diagram is attempting to show. What question is the diagram attempting to answer? Is it a) What is the deployment architecture of the Internet Bookstore? or b) What are the components that make up the Internet Bookstore?

- It isn't clear from the diagram what the input validators are doing. You'll know from the previous section that these are an artifact of Spring Framework, which requires us to separate out the validation code into separate classes.

- It isn't clear what the arrows represent. They actually represent dependencies so, for example, the Bookstore Controllers use (or "depend on") the Data Access Objects (DAOs).

Let's take another attempt and separate the diagram into two separate diagrams (see Figures 7-7 and 7-8).

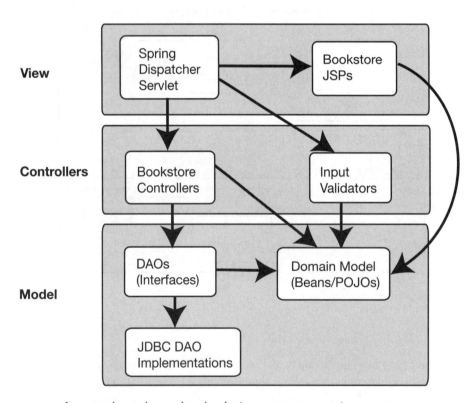

Arrows show dependencies between components.

Figure 7-7. *Internet Bookstore package/component architecture*

In Figure 7-7, we've removed the data layer entirely, as this is more relevant to the deployment diagram. We've also renamed each of the layers, to make it more obvious that this is a classically mapped-out MVC architecture. While this move wasn't essential, it always helps to utilize well-known terminology to make the architecture more expressive. The people who need to refer to this diagram will (we would hope) already know what MVC is all about, so we can use that to our advantage.

■**Exercise** Later in this book, during the review stages, you'll find that we have issues with domain classes that contain no behavior, just data. The root of the problem can be seen in Figure 7-7. What should have changed here, at the architectural level, to encourage a more "behavior-rich" set of domain classes? (Check the code review for the *Write Customer Review* use case in Chapter 11 for the answer.)

It was debatable whether Spring's `DispatcherServlet` should remain in the view layer. It isn't strictly speaking the view, because it handles incoming requests from the web browser and then delegates to the JSP to create the actual view. It's more of a request/response router, or go-between. From that perspective, it probably doesn't even need to be on this diagram at all, except that it does help to show visually where in the component/layer hierarchy the Spring Web component is involved.

■**Caution** If you're unsure whether something belongs on one diagram or another, don't dwell on it, just put it *somewhere* and move on. Teams often get stuck for days on these sorts of fine details. But trust us, 99% of the time, it just doesn't matter. Will it affect the eventual design? Probably not. Getting stuck on such issues typifies *analysis paralysis*, which we introduced in the Introduction and which we spend a large part of this book describing how to avoid. For more about making your models *minimal yet sufficient*, see this book's companion volume, *Agile Development with ICONIX Process* (Apress, 2005).

The controller layer contains the "guts" of the Internet Bookstore application. It's responsible for validating and processing the user's input (via browser requests and form submissions) and deciding which page should be sent back to the user next.

The data access layer provides a façade over the database (or whatever the persistence mechanism may be). The DAOs are "clean" interfaces, designed to hide away the details of the code behind them. A DAO is roughly equivalent to an EJB Home, in that it's used to find beans (domain objects) and persist changes.

Figure 7-8 shows the deployment model, using a nonstandard notation so as to model the layered architecture.

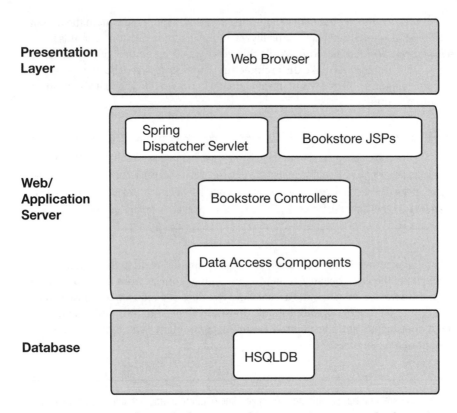

Figure 7-8. *Internet Bookstore deployment architecture using nonstandard notation*

We could also show this using a "proper" UML deployment diagram—see Figure 7-9.[8]

The result of this layered approach is that the domain classes have absolutely no dependencies on the database being used. Even the DAO interfaces can remain unchanged if we swap in a different database. In fact, each layer is only dependent on the layer directly beneath it.

The interaction with the user's web browser is handled by the web server (Tomcat), which contains the DispatcherServlet and the JSPs for the Internet Bookstore. (As you'll see later, the Internet Bookstore page URLs don't end in .jsp, though, because the user doesn't request the JSP pages directly. Instead, a suitable JSP is resolved by the Internet Bookstore Controllers and handed back to the DispatcherServlet, which then invokes the JSP and sends the resultant HTML page back to the browser.)

This is, of course, a very simple architecture, because we have only one application server (Tomcat), which is also our web server. For persistence, our database is HSQLDB (often referred to for historical reasons as HSQL).

---

8. We show another example of a deployment diagram in Appendix B, in Figure B-13.

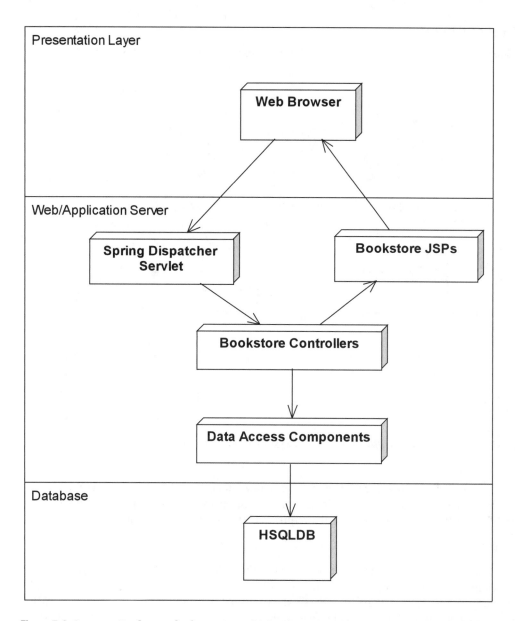

Figure 7-9. *Internet Bookstore deployment architecture using a UML deployment diagram*

Flow of Events

Figure 7-10 shows, at a broad level, what happens to a browser request when it "hits" the web server.

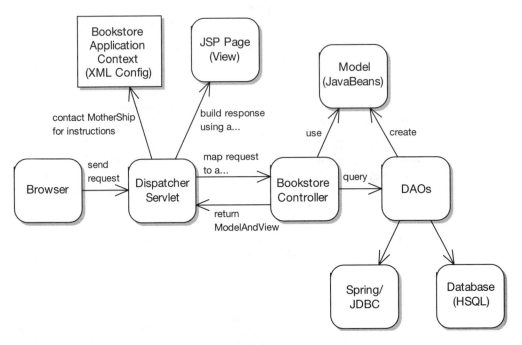

Figure 7-10. *Life cycle of a typical Internet Bookstore browser request*

Let's walk through the sequence of events shown in Figure 7-10. First, the user requests a page from the web server (in our development example this is Tomcat, but it could be any JSP-compliant web server). Assume the request's URL is something like this:

```
http://localhost/bookstore/bookDetails.jsp?bookid=101
```

The "bookstore" part of the URL tells Tomcat that this is the Bookstore web application, so without further ado, the incoming request is handed to the Bookstore, which is configured to use Spring's DispatcherServlet. This servlet uses the Internet Bookstore application's XML config to determine which controller to map the request to. Spring also dissects the request and creates "command" objects to represent any parameters that were part of the request (in our example, "bookid" would go into a property in a Command object). The Command object is also handed to the controller.

The Controller that receives the request hands the book ID value to the appropriate DAO, which finds the book in the database and returns a Book domain object (a simple Java-Bean). The Controller returns a ModelAndView object, which—as the name suggests—gives Spring two things: the view (JSP page) to use and the objects (model) to populate the JSP page with. This JSP page is then processed, and the resultant HTML page is handed back to the browser.

If that seems like a lot of stuff to remember, don't worry. To follow along with the sequence diagrams, the key parts that you'll need to know are as follows:

1. When a browser request is received, Spring dissects the request, populates `Command` objects (similar to Struts actions) to hold the request parameters, and hands the request to a `Controller` object.

2. The `Controller` object does whatever it wants to process the request and returns a `ModelAndView` object that tells Spring which JSP page to process and send back to the browser.

3. The domain objects are stored in JavaBeans (or POJOs).

4. The `Controller` objects use DAOs to fetch and save domain objects to and from the database.

Testability

One of the advantages of the IoC architecture is that individual classes are very easy to test. Each class can be instantiated individually and tested outside of the application server. For example, you could write some JUnit tests that run inside your IDE or that are executed by an automated Ant build script. Being able to test your application logic without deploying to an application server and restarting the whole framework is a major time-saver.

Because we're keeping all of the application logic code out of the view, the JSPs themselves should be very straightforward. So testing of the JSPs should mostly be a case of "visual testing"—stepping manually through the use cases' basic and alternate courses. As long as we've done our job well, once created, the JSPs shouldn't need to change very much. If you desperately want to unit-test the view components, though, web testing frameworks such as HttpUnit are available.

Note, however, that testability isn't just about unit testing; it's also about testing for nonfunctional requirements such as scalability and failover.

Web Security

To keep the example under control, we're just going to use "pretend" user authentication/authorization. We'll use a class called `CustomerSession` that gets stored in the servlet's `HttpSession` attributes (i.e., each customer/user gets his or her own `CustomerSession` object). `CustomerSession` consists simply of a "get" method to get the customer's name and a static factory method to get new `CustomerSession`s.

Spring Framework doesn't actually offer its own security framework. However, a number of open-source security frameworks exist. One that's particularly worth a look is *Acegi Security* (`www.acegisecurity.org`), which is designed specifically for Spring applications.

Security frameworks like Acegi handle a lot of the user security details for you. The decision of how security is handled should be made as early as possible in the project (ideally before the sequence diagrams are drawn), as it's one of those fundamental details that affects everything. You definitely don't want security to be "bolted on" to a project late in the day.

Top 10 Technical Architecture Errors (the "Don'ts")

The following list could be thought of as the flip side of the top 10 "do's" that we described at the start of this chapter. These are some common errors that we've seen in real projects.

10. Picking an architecture without considering the cost of the hardware or new hardware.

9. Using the old legacy architecture because "that's the way it's always been done."

8. Not considering scalability.

   Think about the numbers. How many users will typically be using the system at any time? Are there periods of peak usage? How many transactions per minute must the system handle? These are all questions that affect the TA (and therefore pretty much the whole project), so they need to be thought through and answered up-front.

7. Not considering security.

   By "security," we mean authentication and authorization of the people using the system (the users). All too often, security is bolted on to a system near the end of its life cycle. This typically results in a system riddled with security flaws.

   AOP is promising to make it a little easier to apply security to projects where it wasn't initially a first-rate concern. But getting it right first time is still the best way. The security should run through a system like the writing in a stick of Brighton rock.[9] It's the only way to make sure your product is watertight.

6. Picking a new technology (language, platform, framework) because that's the way the market is heading, and not really knowing about the technology.

   "We must use this technology because everyone in the papers is talking about it!" In particular, XML-HELL comes to mind. Commonly, this TA error means picking an architecture that uses a platform you and your team have no prior experience with. By definition, the fashionable new technology is new. As we discussed earlier, however, an effective architect really needs to have an in-depth knowledge and prior experience with the technology he or she is evaluating and mixing into the design.[10]

5. Failing to formulate the TA objectively based on the project's requirements.

4. Spending too long on the architecture before delving into design.

   Architectural paralysis can be as dangerous and project-stopping as analysis paralysis. Because the architecture is so important, it's tempting to spend six or more months thinking about it and debating it with your colleagues. Eventually someone might remember that there's also a system to be written.

---

9. See `http://en.wikipedia.org/wiki/Rock_(confectionery)`.

10. The article "Software Fashion" equates designers who automatically buy into the latest technology with "fashion victims": `www.softwarereality.com/soapbox/softwarefashion.jsp`

3. Forgetting to think about how the system will be tested.

2. Defining the TA before understanding what the users need to do.

1. Failing to do an architecture at all.

Summary

In this chapter, we took a brief look at technical architecture (TA). We dug deeper than what might be considered "architecture-level", in order to introduce Spring Framework, and to walk through the way in which we'll use it for the Internet Bookstore.

TA varies immensely from project to project (and from organization to organization), and it isn't the core focus of ICONIX Process, so we've touched on the subject only briefly in this chapter.

Figure 7-11 shows where TA sits in the preliminary design stage of the process.

In the next chapter, we look at detailed design and flesh out the Internet Bookstore using sequence diagrams.

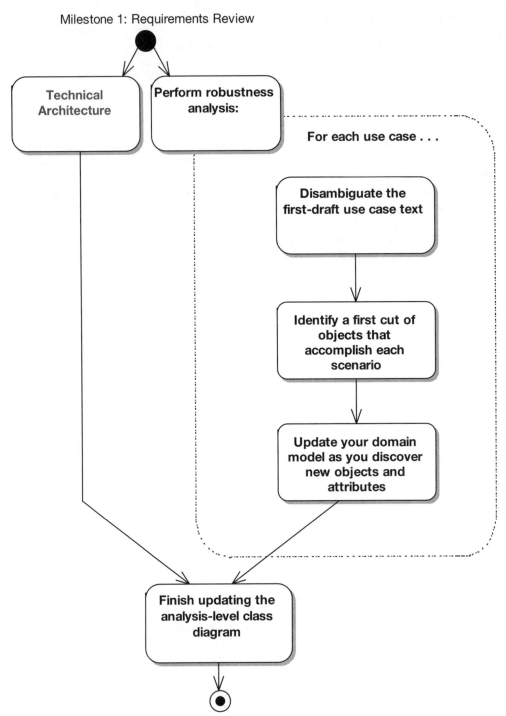

Figure 7-11. *Technical architecture and the preliminary design stage*

PART 3

Design and Coding

CHAPTER 8

Sequence Diagrams

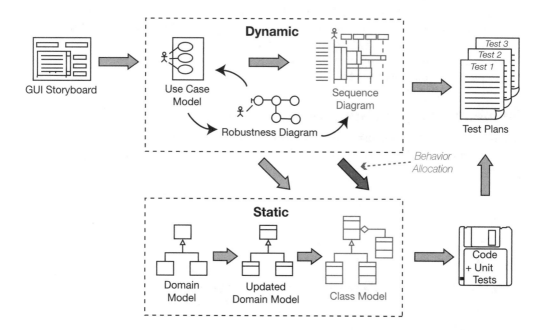

Once you've finished robustness analysis, and you've held a preliminary design review, it's time to begin the detailed design effort. By this time, your use case text should be complete, correct, detailed, and explicit. In short, your use cases should be in a state where you can create a detailed design from them.

All the steps in the process so far have been preparing the use cases for the detailed design activity. Having completed robustness analysis and the PDR, you should now have discovered pretty much all of the domain classes that you're going to need. You also need to have the technical architecture (TA) nailed down by this stage.

The 10,000-Foot View

Before we leap into the details of sequence diagramming, let's take a step back (or up) and look at the bigger picture of object-oriented design (OOD).

Sequence Diagrams and Detailed OOD

If you figure that preliminary design is all about discovery of classes (aka **object discovery**), then detailed design is, by contrast, about allocating behavior (aka **behavior allocation**)—that is, allocating the software functions you've identified into the set of classes you discovered during preliminary design.

When you draw sequence diagrams, you're taking another sweep through the preliminary design, adding in detail.

With preliminary design, you made some informal first guesses at how the classes will interact with each other. Now it's time to make those statements very precise, to turn them into a detailed design that works within the TA that you've defined.

You use sequence diagrams to drive the detailed design. But note that we advocate drawing your sequence diagrams in a minimal, quite specific format (which we describe fully in this chapter). There's a direct link between each use case, its robustness diagram, and the sequence diagrams. Just as you drew one robustness diagram per use case, you'll also draw one sequence diagram per use case.

Sequence Diagram Notation

Before we dive into the best practices for drawing sequence diagrams from your use cases, it helps to understand the stuff that a sequence diagram is composed of (see Figure 8-1).

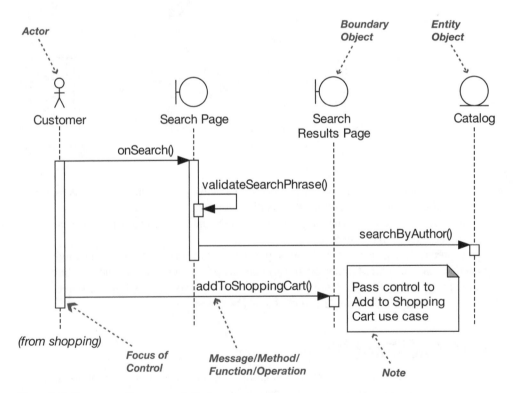

Figure 8-1. *Sequence diagram notation*

The objects across the top of the diagram (Customer, Search Page, etc.) are interacting with each other by passing **messages** back and forth. The vertical dotted lines (or *object life- lines*) represent time, so the process shown in the diagram begins with the topmost message (Customer calling onSearch() on Search Page).

An **actor** (the Customer in Figure 8-1) is the user whose interaction with the system you've described in each of the use cases. (See the "system boundary" diagram in Figure 3-2.) You should recognize the **boundary object** and **entity object** icons from robustness diagram- ming in Chapter 5. (In Figure 8-1, the boundary objects are Search Page and Search Results Page; the entity object is Catalog.)

However, notice that **there are no controller objects on the sequence diagram** (although there could be). This is because when you draw the sequence diagrams, the controllers (the verbs) are turned into messages on the boundary and entity objects (the nouns). Sometimes you'll find real controller classes, such as a "manager" or a "dispatcher" class, and sometimes a framework might tempt you to litter your design with dozens of tiny "controller classes," but as a general rule of thumb, 80% or so of the controllers from the robustness diagrams can be implemented as one or more operations on the entity and boundary classes. (More about this important aspect of sequence diagramming later.)

The **focus of control** represents the time that a particular method/function has control. It starts with the arrow going *into* the function and finishes when the function returns.

■**Note** You normally don't need to draw a return arrow, except in special circumstances (e.g., to show an asynchronous return value). That's because parameters can be passed back as arguments to the operation.

As you'll see in item 5 in the next section, the focus of control is best switched off, as it tends to be something of a distraction from what you're trying to achieve at this stage in the process.

Sequence Diagramming in Theory

In this section, we demonstrate how to use sequence diagrams as a mechanism for exploring and filling in the detailed OO design for each use case. We illustrate this theory with examples from the Internet Bookstore project. And we begin, as usual, with our top 10 guidelines list.

Top 10 Sequence Diagramming Guidelines

10. Understand **why** you're drawing a sequence diagram, to get the most out of it.

9. Draw a sequence diagram for every use case, with both basic and alternate courses on the same diagram.

8. Start your sequence diagram from the boundary classes, entity classes, actors, and use case text that result from robustness analysis.

7. Use the sequence diagram to show how the behavior of the use case (i.e., all the controllers from the robustness diagram) is accomplished by the objects.

6. Make sure your use case text maps to the messages being passed on the sequence diagram. Try to line up the text and message arrows.

5. Don't spend too much time worrying about focus of control.

4. Assign operations to classes while drawing messages. Most visual modeling tools support this capability.

3. Review your class diagrams frequently while you're assigning operations to classes, to make sure all the operations are on the appropriate classes.

2. **Prefactor** your design on sequence diagrams before coding.

1. Clean up the static model before proceeding to the CDR.

Let's look at each of these top 10 guidelines in more detail.

10. Understand Why You're Drawing a Sequence Diagram

When drawing sequence diagrams, you're meticulously exploring the ins and outs of the **detailed design** for each use case, in microscopic detail. This means exploring not just the basic course, but also **all the alternate courses of action in each use case**. (We can't stress this point strongly enough!)

It's surprising how many design issues can be caught at this stage, saving time on refactoring your design later, so it pays to design and explore every facet of each use case, not just the sunny-day scenario.

Sequence diagramming has three primary goals in ICONIX Process:

- **Allocate behavior to your classes**: You identified these classes during robustness analysis. During sequence diagramming, the controllers (also discovered during robustness analysis) are turned into operations on the classes. However, you don't necessarily end up with a 1:1 correlation between the controllers and the operations. Often, a controller turns into two or more operations. (Check the examples later in this chapter to see how this happens.) And as we mentioned earlier, occasionally a controller may also be turned into a **controller class**.

- **Show in detail how your classes interact with each other over the lifetime of the use case**: When sequence diagramming, you should be exploring **how** the system will accomplish the behavior described in your use cases. You do this by thinking about and then depicting how your **objects** (runtime instances of a class) will interact with each other at runtime.

- **Finalize the distribution of operations among classes**: Having performed robustness analysis, you should by now have identified at least three-quarters of the attributes (the **data**) on your classes, but very few, if any, of the operations (the **behavior**). By now you've probably gathered that we advocate a two-pass approach to the design. The first pass (preliminary design) is driven by thinking about attributes while deliberately ignoring "who's doing what to whom." Then the second pass (the subject of this chapter) focuses all your attention on that exact question. That's because during pre-liminary design, the information just wasn't there to allocate operations without guessing. However, now that you're at the detailed design stage, you should have everything in place to correctly allocate the behavior among your classes.

■**Note** Objects interact by sending messages to each other. In the Ruby programming language, the *message* paradigm is used literally, and all object interactions are considered to be messages. However, in other languages such as Java or C++, the messages you draw on sequence diagrams equate to method or function calls. To complicate things a little, in UML each message is also called an **operation** once it's assigned to a class.

■**Note** Messages, methods, functions, operations, verbs, and controllers—these are all basically different versions of the same thing: the behavior that you allocate to a class (via sequence diagramming) and eventually implement and test.

DON'T TRY TO DRAW FLOWCHARTS ON SEQUENCE DIAGRAMS (FOCUS ON BEHAVIOR ALLOCATION INSTEAD)

UML 2.0 allows you to draw full-blown flowcharts on your sequence diagrams. However, even though the notation supports it, we consider the practice of drawing flowcharts on sequence diagrams to be inadvisable, because it puts emphasis on the wrong part of the problem.

In large part this is because *drawing flowcharts simply misses the point of what you should be thinking about when you draw a sequence diagram*. If you're trying to drive a software design from use cases, it's vitally important to get the allocation of operations to classes correct. This allocation of operations to classes tends to be a make-or-break design issue.

In ICONIX Process, the primary purpose of the sequence diagram is to make this behavior allocation visible so that you get it right. If your mind is on drawing a flowchart, it's not going to be focused on this critically important set of behavior allocation decisions.

9. Do a Sequence Diagram for Every Use Case

It's pretty simple to make sure you've covered everything in your design, if you stick to these two simple rules:

- Write a use case for every scenario you're going to build in your current release (include basic and alternate courses in each use case).

- Draw a sequence diagram for each use case and use the sequence diagram to put the operations on the classes.

Simple but effective. You've then allocated all the software behavior you need, and presumably nothing you don't need, into your classes.

■**Tip** When you're starting a sequence diagram, the very first thing you should do is paste the text of the use case into a Note on the left margin.

One question that we often get asked is, "Should I have a separate sequence diagram for each alternative course of action?" This question is frequently posed by people who have enormous use case templates and ten-page use cases.

Our preference is to keep the use case short (see the two-paragraph rule in Chapter 3), and thus be able to show the entire use case (sunny- and rainy-day scenarios) on a single sequence diagram. It's too easy to lose track of one or two alternate courses of action if you split up the use case and sequence diagrams. And losing track of alternate courses of action tends to be problematic.

8. Start from Where You Left Off with Robustness Analysis

You identified which objects will be collaborating together on the sequence diagram when you drew your robustness diagram. If your use case has a GUI, the boundary objects will represent screens and other UI elements. Entity classes from the domain model will collaborate with the GUI objects.

In many cases, controllers from the robustness diagram will not actually be "real controller objects" on a sequence diagram, although in some cases they will be. In the remaining cases, controllers will map to messages between objects on the sequence diagram.

Keep in mind that your sequence diagram shows the design at a much more concrete and detailed view than the idealized conceptual design shown on a robustness diagram. So your sequence diagram may show additional helper infrastructure objects, details of persistence storage mechanisms, and so forth.

7. Show How the Use Case's Behavior Is Accomplished by the Objects

Controllers on a robustness diagram generally map to "logical" software functions. Each logical function may be realized by one or more messages between objects that will be shown on the sequence diagram. As you draw messages, you are actually allocating operations to classes, so the sequence diagram is "about" allocating behavior among collaborating objects.

EXAMPLE SEQUENCE DIAGRAM: DISPLAYING THE BOOK DETAILS PAGE

Our *Write Customer Review* use case example (which we'll return to shortly) gets quite involved at the design stage, as it uses lots of different parts of Spring Framework, JSP, and our own controller logic. So it makes sense to ease you into sequence diagramming (and Spring Framework) with a simple example first.

We'll start out with a very small use case, *Show Book Details*. The use case text is as follows:

BASIC COURSE:

The Customer types in the URL for the bookstore's home page, which the system displays. Then the Customer clicks a link to view a Book. The system retrieves the Book details and displays the Book Details screen.

ALTERNATE COURSES:

 Book not found: The system displays a Book Details Not Found screen.

We weren't kidding when we said this is a simple use case! Really, this barely qualifies as a use case (remember the two-paragraph rule from Chapter 3). However, it suffices for our purpose, which is to illustrate how we get from the use case to a finished sequence diagram.

We showed the robustness diagram for this use case back in Figure 5-11. The accompanying sequence diagram is shown in Figure 8-2 (the part of the diagram that handles the alternate course is shown in red).

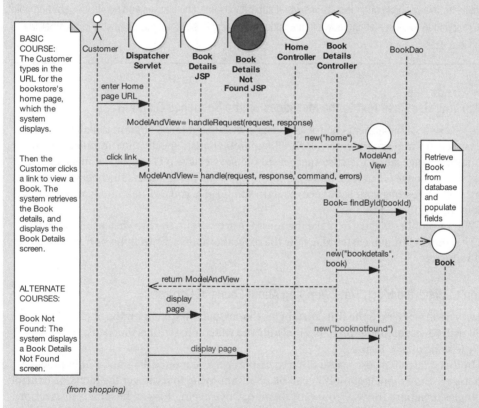

Figure 8-2. *Sequence diagram for the* Show Book Details *use case*

The processing in this diagram is quite detail-rich, so we've lumped it into Appendix B (in the section titled "'Show Book Details' Use Case"). If you're interested in the Spring plumbing, please do take a look there before moving on.

Later in this chapter, we walk through a step-by-step example of drawing a sequence diagram directly from its matching robustness diagram. As you'll see, when done properly, it's really a mechanical process allowing us to focus on the design details.

■**Exercise** The Book class in Figure 8-2 doesn't appear to do a huge amount, except exist. This doesn't seem especially domain-oriented, as domain classes are meant to contain both data and behavior. Looking at Figure 8-2, how could the design be improved to give Book a more prominent role?

■**Note** Although the design shown in Figure 8-2 seems fine on the surface—and (we regret to say) a *lot* of web-based applications are created this way—it actually violates a key principle of the ICONIX approach, namely that **the domain class should be the central point of responsibility for operations relating to that domain class**. For example, all of the responsibilities related to a Book Review ought to be located in the Book Review domain class, even if that class delegates some of those responsibilities to helper classes.

Violating this principle often results in several superfluous one-line classes and no obvious starting point if you're trying to track something down in the code. We review this diagram in Chapter 9 to hammer the design into shape.

6. Map Your Use Case Text to the Messages on the Sequence Diagram

The use case text that appears on the left margin of the sequence diagram is really a contract between clients and programmers. It should unambiguously specify the runtime behavior requirements that satisfy the customer's needs. Since we have this contract, it makes sense to use the sequence diagram to show graphically how the design meets the behavior requirements. In fact, reading your sequence diagram should give you a visual trace from the design back to the requirements.

Whenever possible, try to make the message arrows and the use case text line up visually. This makes it much easier to review the diagrams and verify that the design meets the requirements.

5. Don't Spend Too Much Time Worrying About Focus of Control

Focus of control refers to the little rectangles that magically appear on the object lifelines when using a visual modeling tool. They indicate which object "has the focus," or is currently in control (see Figure 8-1).

In theory, this is a very useful thing to display on a sequence diagram. But in practice, with many visual modeling tools, it can be really annoying to try to get the focus-of-control rectangles to behave the way you want them to. Once again, this can become a distraction from the real purpose of the sequence diagram, which is (repeat after us) *allocation of behavior among collaborating objects*.

If focus of control starts to become a distraction, the easiest thing to do is just switch it off. You might find that your diagrams are cleaner and more readable without this extra detail anyway.

■**Tip** Using EA, simply right-click the diagram and choose Suppress Focus of Control.

ARE SEQUENCE DIAGRAMS DIFFICULT TO DRAW?

Many people find sequence diagrams rather tortuous to draw for the following reasons:

- Sequence diagrams can be difficult to draw and edit in some CASE tools (especially if the **focus of control** is visible).

- The diagrams are densely packed with information, which can make them as difficult to read as to draw, unless they're carefully organized.

- The people who draw sequence diagrams often don't really know *why* they're drawing them or what they're supposed to be getting out of the diagram.

To make matters worse, this is the time when you're also making the really hard design decisions—when you are presented with a bunch of analysis documents and are expected to somehow magically transform them into a detailed design that captures every last nuance of the business analyst's (often abstractly worded) requirements.

One issue we have with many approaches to UML is that there's generally a lack of emphasis on pre-liminary design, so developers must take a giant leap of faith between analysis and design, assuming (or praying) that the resultant design will somehow match up with the use cases. This is why many people find sequence diagrams so difficult to draw: they're trying to answer too many questions (i.e., juggle too many dust-bunnies) all at once.

ICONIX Process, however, is specifically geared toward laying the groundwork for sequence diagram-ming, so **if you've performed robustness analysis properly, drawing the sequence diagrams should be significantly easier**.

To answer the three issues we just listed:

- **Sequence diagrams are difficult to draw using a CASE tool**: This tends to be the case when someone doesn't really understand what it is he is trying to draw, so he spends most of his time struggling with the sequence diagram notation, wondering why the sequence diagram editor won't allow him to just draw whatever he wants. We've observed in practice that this frustration happens most often when *the use case the person is trying to nail down with a sequence diagram is vague and ambiguous*, and he has to keep changing it around as he's in the middle of drawing the sequence diagram. The CASE tool often takes the blame for this frustration. At any rate, as you already know, we're strong advocates of completely and thoroughly disambiguating the behavior requirements (see Chapter 5) before starting detailed design.

- **Sequence diagrams are densely packed with information**: You do need to show lots of detail on each sequence diagram, because it's describing in detail *how* the use case behavior is going to be implemented. If necessary, you can split the diagram onto more than one page, if it makes it easier to draw; but even better, learn to keep your use cases short by factoring them on the use case diagrams using invokes and precedes.

- **Sequence diagram authors are unclear on their purpose and goals**: Having a clear idea of what you're trying to achieve when you draw a diagram definitely makes life easier. See "Understand Why You're Drawing a Sequence Diagram" earlier in this chapter.

Separating the "what" from the "how" (see Figure 5-1) is an essential task in software development, as is having a clear transition between them.

4. Assign Operations to Classes While Drawing Messages

Generally speaking, there are two ways to label messages on a sequence diagram:

- By simply typing a label on the arrow

- By using an explicit command such as a right-click or button-press near the arrowhead

The second option directly adds an operation to the class of the target. It's important to use the sequence diagram to drive the allocation of operations to classes. So, if that's your intent when drawing a message, make sure to use the second option.

3. Review Your Class Diagrams Frequently While You're Assigning Operations to Classes

Since you're now actively assigning operations to classes, and since it's very easy to make mistakes while drawing sequence diagrams, you should continually cross-check your sequence diagram and your class diagram to make sure that when you assign an operation to a class, you've done it in a way that makes sense.

An excellent reference that can help you to make good design decisions is Rebecca Wirfs-Brock's book *Object Design: Roles, Responsibilities, and Collaborations* (Addison-Wesley, 2002). This book teaches a very useful technique called *Responsibility-Driven Design* (we describe this technique in a little more detail later in this book).

2. Prefactor Your Design on Sequence Diagrams

Prefactoring your design on sequence diagrams saves massive amounts of refactoring after code. Many times, the need for code-level refactoring is the result of the programmer making suboptimal behavior allocation decisions. Refactoring techniques such as "Move Method," "Replace Method with Method Object," and (deep breath) "Consolidate Duplicate Conditional Fragments"[1] involve moving methods around among classes. The sequence diagram should be used as a tool to help you to *prefactor* your design and make these behavior allocation decisions correctly, **before** going to all the trouble of coding and unit testing.

If you use a sequence diagram for this purpose, you'll find that you spend a lot less time using refactoring techniques to fix the mistakes that you avoided making in the first place. The lost art of getting the design right the first time can still be practiced (and quite successfully) using sequence diagrams. And you don't even have to be a Druid to do it.[2]

1. Clean Up the Static Model Before Proceeding to the CDR

Take a long, hard look at your static model, with a view toward tidying up the design, resolving real-world design issues, identifying useful design patterns that can be factored in to improve the design, and so on. This should at least be done as a final step before proceeding to the CDR, but you can get started thinking at this level in the design even *before* drawing your sequence diagrams.

After you complete *preliminary* design, the class model should have fewer holes in it than it did before robustness analysis. Chances are that some additional classes have been discovered that were missing from the original domain model, and many of the classes

---

1. See *Refactoring: Improving the Design of Existing Code* by Martin Fowler (Addison-Wesley, 2000).
2. See our next book, *Prefactoring the Druid Way*. No goats required.

should be populated with attributes. However, even when you consider that the system behavior will be allocated to the classes as message arrows are drawn on the sequence diagrams, in most cases the class model will require additional work to complete it to the point that it's ready to code from.

Here are a few examples of the sorts of things that you may still need to deal with:

- Using infrastructure/scaffolding classes

- Using design patterns

- Meshing the design with application frameworks

- Completing parameter lists on operations

- Etc.

So, **plan on finalizing your class model during detailed design** along with doing your sequence diagrams. It's often a good idea to do a lot of this finalizing *before* the sequence diagram is drawn, so that the sequence diagram simply represents the way the code is going to work. An alternative strategy is to draw the sequence diagram at a slightly simplified level and then finalize the class model in the coding environment.

■**Tip** New tools, such as MDG Integration from Sparx Systems (`www.sparxsystems.com`), make the synchronization task between model and code orders of magnitude easier than it used to be.

Now that we've described the **notation** you use to draw sequence diagrams, and we've examined the top 10 guidelines of sequence diagramming, we'll walk through the steps involved in drawing a sequence diagram effectively.

How to Draw a Sequence Diagram: Four Essential Steps

We've distilled the process of drawing a sequence diagram to four essential steps, which we describe in this section. We illustrate these steps by drawing the sequence diagram for the *Write Customer Review* use case.

The first three steps are completely mechanical in nature. This means they can be automated, which can be very useful in achieving momentum as you get serious about your design. The fourth step, **deciding which methods go on which classes**, is really what sequence diagramming is all about.

Figure 8-3 shows the four steps you perform when drawing sequence diagrams the ICONIX way. Next, we describe the four steps in more detail. To illustrate the steps, we return to the *Write Customer Review* use case we disambiguated using robustness analysis in Chapter 5.

■**Note** In Chapter 12, we extend these steps to show how to systematically build a suite of test cases at the same time as your sequence diagrams (see Figure 12-2).

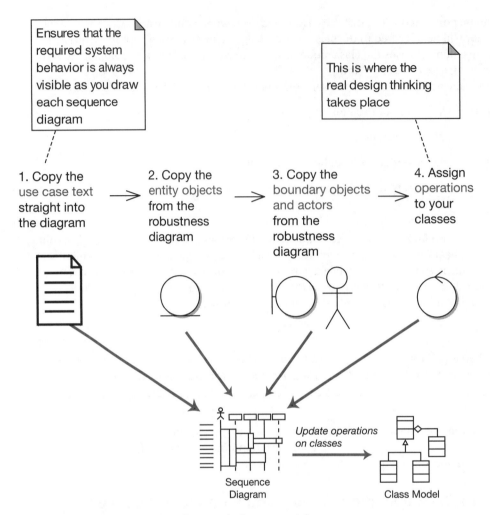

Ensures that the required system behavior is always visible as you draw each sequence diagram

This is where the real design thinking takes place

1. Copy the use case text straight into the diagram

2. Copy the entity objects from the robustness diagram

3. Copy the boundary objects and actors from the robustness diagram

4. Assign operations to your classes

Update operations on classes

Sequence Diagram

Class Model

Figure 8-3. *Building a sequence diagram in four essential steps*

IF THE STEPS ARE MECHANICAL, WHY NOT AUTOMATE THEM?

In fact, we've turned the first three steps of our process for drawing a sequence diagram into an executable script that automatically generates a skeleton of a sequence diagram. We originally did this some years ago for Rational Rose, and if you use Rose, you can download a copy of this script here: www.iconixsw.com/ RoseScripts.html. More recently, we've created an upgraded version for the EA tool from Sparx Systems. The upgraded version also generates test cases for each controller on the robustness diagram (see Figure 12-7) and is available as an add-in on Doug's CD "Enterprise Architect for Power Users." (More information can be found at www.iconixsw.com/EA/PowerUsers.html.)

Scripts and add-ins such as this have proven to be very useful in achieving momentum as you get serious about your design. You get an immediate payback in time savings from the work you invested in your robustness diagrams, which can help to get some buy-in to the process from your team.

Step 1: Copy the Use Case Text Straight into the Diagram

After all the preparatory steps that you've gone through so far, the use case text should be remarkably fit and healthy. Having put all that effort into writing disambiguated use cases that you can design from, it makes sense to place the use case text directly on the design diagram so that, as you're doing the design, *the required system behavior is right there on the diagram too*. The initial version of the *Write Customer Review* sequence diagram, with just this first step completed, is shown in Figure 8-4.

Remember that each use case is, essentially, a mini-contract that should have gotten sign-off from the project stakeholders. And because each use case is quite fine-grained (two paragraphs at most), it's a small capsule of discrete, self-contained functionality. Having the text there on the screen helps you to keep the sequence diagram focused on **just the steps described in those two paragraphs**.

Also remember that the robustness diagram you drew was an object picture of the given use case, and the process of drawing the robustness diagram caused you to rewrite the use case so that it uses the domain object names literally in the text. As a result, when you're designing, you should be able to look at the use case text and (when you get really good at it) visualize the named objects interacting with each other. For example, the text "The system places the Book Review on the Reviews Pending Queue" strongly suggests that there will be a BookReview class, a ReviewsPendingQueue class, and a message between the two probably called addToQueue(bookReview).

■Note Because you're designing directly from the use case text, then it follows that if you didn't analyze the use case in detail and write down all its alternate courses, you shouldn't be doing detailed design yet. Designing from an incomplete use case means that you won't discover all of the necessary methods for your objects.

BASIC COURSE:
On the Book Detail page for the book currently being viewed, the Customer clicks the Write Review button. The system checks the Customer Session to make sure the Customer is logged in, and then displays the Write Review page. The Customer types in a Book Review, gives it a Book Rating out of 5 stars, and clicks the Send button. The system ensures that the Book Review isn't too long or short, and that the Book Rating is within 1-5 stars. The system then displays a confirmation page, and the review is added to the Pending Reviews Queue for moderation (this will be handled by the Moderate Customer Reviews use case).

ALTERNATE COURSES:
User not logged in: The user is first taken to the Login page, and then to the Write Review page once they've logged in.

The user enters a review which is too long (text > 1MB): The system rejects the review, and responds with a message explaining why the review was rejected.

The review is too short (< 10 characters): The system rejects the review.

Figure 8-4. *Building a sequence diagram, step 1*

Step 2: Copy the Entity Objects from the Robustness Diagram

Assuming you updated your static model during robustness analysis, the entity objects should now each have an equivalent class on one of the class diagrams (see Figure 8-5). (And if you *haven't* updated your static model yet, **be sure to do it now**.) The updated *Write Customer Review* sequence diagram is shown in Figure 8-6.

Until now, the entity objects have been little more than simple bags of data with lots of attributes but no behavior (read: no personality). This will change during sequence diagramming. Now that they're on the diagram, you'll soon start to allocate operations to them—in effect, assigning their classes with behavior. But first you need to get the remaining "nouns" (the boundary objects and actors) onto the diagram.

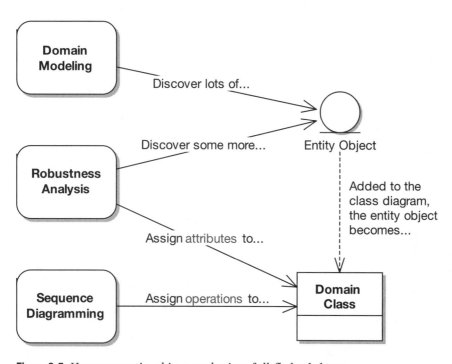

Figure 8-5. *How your entity objects evolve into full-fledged classes*

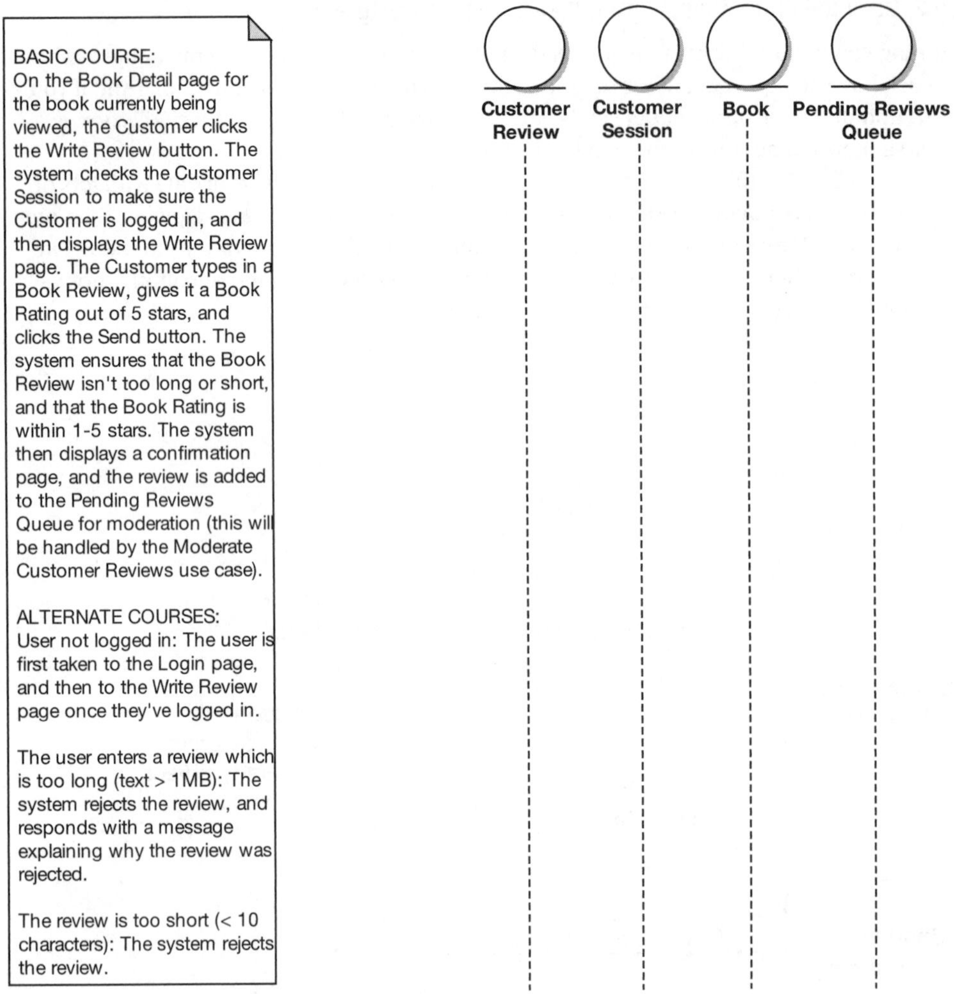

BASIC COURSE:
On the Book Detail page for the book currently being viewed, the Customer clicks the Write Review button. The system checks the Customer Session to make sure the Customer is logged in, and then displays the Write Review page. The Customer types in a Book Review, gives it a Book Rating out of 5 stars, and clicks the Send button. The system ensures that the Book Review isn't too long or short, and that the Book Rating is within 1-5 stars. The system then displays a confirmation page, and the review is added to the Pending Reviews Queue for moderation (this will be handled by the Moderate Customer Reviews use case).

ALTERNATE COURSES:
User not logged in: The user is first taken to the Login page, and then to the Write Review page once they've logged in.

The user enters a review which is too long (text > 1MB): The system rejects the review, and responds with a message explaining why the review was rejected.

The review is too short (< 10 characters): The system rejects the review.

Customer Review   Customer Session   Book   Pending Reviews Queue

Figure 8-6. *Building a sequence diagram, step 2*

Step 3: Copy the Boundary Objects and Actors from the Robustness Diagram

See Figure 8-7. The boundary objects and actors are the remaining "nouns" (see Chapter 5). There can be more than one actor on the sequence diagram, although typically there's only one, and it usually goes on the left of the diagram. The updated *Write Customer Review* sequence diagram is shown in Figure 8-8.

You win the ripest piece of fruit in the fruit bowl if you wondered why we're adding the boundary objects and actors from the robustness diagram and not from the domain model. In fact, the boundary objects and actors were never added to the domain model, as they're part of the solution space (the "how"). By contrast, **the entity objects that we've added *were* on the domain model**, as they're part of the problem space (the "what").

Depending on the type of GUI you're creating, the boundary classes usually turn into JSP or ASP pages. So you have the option to treat the boundary classes as "not real classes," and not allocate behavior to them. How GUIs are treated varies widely if you're doing JSP, ASP.NET, HTML, or a desktop application (for example). So during sequence diagramming, it's better to focus on allocating behavior into the domain/entity classes (see step 4).

■**Note** We're not saying that you should *never* add attributes or operations to your view/boundary classes, but as a general rule, these classes (or pages) tend not to do any of their own processing. Your own experiences may vary depending on the GUI or web-application toolkit that you're using.

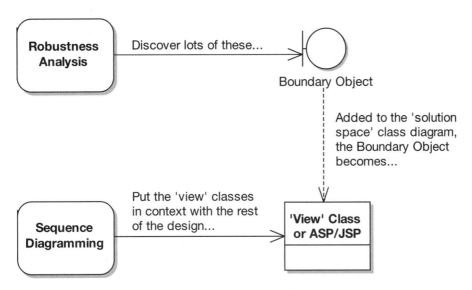

Figure 8-7. *How your boundary objects evolve into view classes or view pages (e.g., JSP pages)*

■**Tip** It helps to maintain a pure domain model diagram, containing only the entity classes (but not showing any attributes or operations). But at some point (right about now, in fact, during detailed design), you'll need to draw some more detailed class diagrams that show both *solution space* classes and *problem space* classes. As you'll end up with some very large detailed class diagrams, you should split them up—for example, have one diagram per use case package. (Refer to Chapter 3 for a discussion of use case packages.)

■**Tip** And another thing: These detailed class diagrams should use the same elements as on the sequence diagrams, so when you assign a message on the sequence diagram (the dynamic model), an operation is automatically added to the appropriate class in the static model.

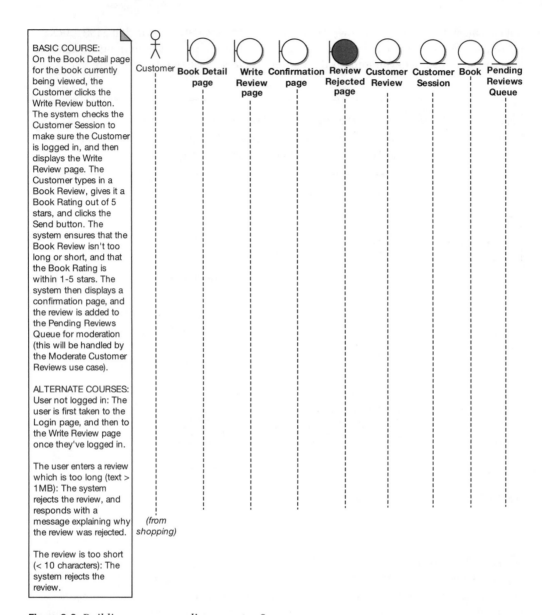

Figure 8-8. *Building a sequence diagram, step 3*

Once you've finished these steps, you're over the hump of getting your design started, and it's time to move on to the real work.

Step 4: Assign Operations to Your Classes

This step is where the real decision-making takes place (see Figure 8-9). Up until now, everything has been rather mechanical and aimed at prepping the sequence diagram so that the highly skilled surgeon (that's you) can come in and amaze everyone with his or her precise and scrupulous design work. A surgeon must make some high-pressure decisions during an operation (we should know, we've seen reruns of *Dr. Kildare*), and similarly, when you're designing software, you're faced with difficult decisions that mostly shouldn't be put off until later. You've done all the preparatory work leading up to this point, and this next step is the crux, the essence of detailed design.

Unfortunately, as you may have gathered, this step is also pretty hard (at least until you get the hang of it). Every decision, large and small, really counts. **Experience and talent are required to do a good job at detailed design.**

What you've done with this process so far is to clear the way so that, during detailed design, there are no distractions—all you need to think about is the design itself. But you still need to do the actual thinking, of course. On the bright side, the more you do it, the better you'll become. As your experience grows, you'll find it becomes easier to make good design decisions.

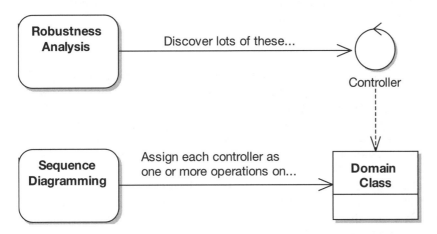

Figure 8-9. *How your controllers evolve into operations on your domain classes*

The best place to get started with behavior allocation is to convert the controllers from the robustness diagram.

Converting the Controllers from Your Robustness Diagram

To allocate operations/methods to your classes, you need to convert the controllers from the robustness diagram into messages on your sequence diagram. It's possible to do this systematically. Step through each controller on the robustness diagram. For each one, draw the corresponding message(s) on the sequence diagram, and then check the controller off (rather like a checklist) and move on to the next controller.

■**Tip** Remember that when you step through each controller on the robustness diagram, each message should automatically be turned into an operation (or several operations) on the appropriate class(es). on the appropriate class. Make your CASE tool work harder, so that you can work smarter!

Remember that you've already checked the robustness diagram against the use case text. So by using the robustness diagram as a checklist for your sequence diagram, you're providing a level of assurance that you are designing precisely what the user needs—in other words, *you're ensuring that your design matches up with the requirements*.

Although we recommend turning each controller into an operation, every now and then it makes sense to turn a controller into a full-fledged control class. How often this happens depends on whether you're building a real-time embedded system and whether the framework you're using more-or-less demands that you have lots of itty-bitty controller classes all over the place.

■**Tip** Have both the sequence diagram and any relevant class diagrams at hand. You should be flipping between the sequence and class diagrams frequently while you assign operations and think about the design. It's a two-way process: sometimes you make a change to the class diagram and then feed the change back into the sequence diagram, and vice versa.

During this stage in the design, it pays to have a catalog of well-established design patterns to fall back on. The "classic set" of patterns can be found in the book *Design Patterns: Elements of Reusable Object-Oriented Software* by Erich Gamma, Richard Helm, Ralph Johnson, and John Vlissides (Addison-Wesley, 1995). If you're developing enterprise software, we can also recommend *Patterns of Enterprise Application Architecture* by Martin Fowler (Addison-Wesley, 2002). Although the book's title suggests that it's about architecture, the patterns it describes are really design patterns for the enterprise.

However, it's also important to not become too obsessed with design patterns. Always try to remember that they're there for guidance—a starting point for when doing your own detailed designs. We've seen the unfortunate results of many projects that have become too complex for their own good, because of a tendency to overapply design patterns. As Groucho Marx once said, "I like my cigar, too, but I take it out of my mouth once in a while!"

Deciding Which Controllers to Assign to Which Classes

This is the big one, of course. To decide which controllers go on which classes, you must answer two questions:

- What are the classes?

- Which classes are *responsible* for which operations?

The second question has as its roots Rebecca Wirfs-Brock's Responsibility-Driven Design (RDD). A **responsibility** is a combination of things: knowledge or data (the attributes), behavior (the operations), and the major decisions made at runtime that affect others.

Usually, you'll find that the decision of which responsibilities to put in which classes is clear-cut. For example, it should be obvious that a BookReview will be responsible for validating its own data. Sometimes, however, the decision isn't quite so clear-cut. Responsibilities can be hazy or too complex to be comfortably managed by a single class. In *Object Design:*

Roles, Responsibilities and Collaborations, Wirfs-Brock describes how complex responsibilities should be allocated:[3]

> *An object has three options for fulfilling any responsibility. It can either:*
>
> ** Do all the work itself*
>
> ** Ask others for help doing portions of the work (collaborate with others)*
>
> ** Delegate the entire request to a helper object*
>
> *When you're faced with a complex job, ask whether an object is up to this responsibility or whether it is taking on too much. A responsibility that is too complex to be implemented by a single object essentially introduces a new sub design problem. You need to design a set of objects that will collaborate to implement this complex responsibility. These objects will have roles and responsibilities that contribute to the implementation of the larger responsibility.*

As we described earlier, assigning responsibilities to each class involves giving your class some *personality*, but it's also possible for a class to become overallocated and end up with perhaps a little too *much* personality. Dan Rawsthorne (a former ICONIX instructor) once summarized the responsibility-driven thought process to Doug as follows:

> *If you think of your objects (or classes) as people, then the set of behaviors (operations) that they are responsible for gives them a sort of personality. We want to* watch out for schizophrenic objects *(that is, objects with split or multiple personalities) because an object should be focused on a cohesive, related set of behaviors.*

A class with a split personality—or multiple personalities—is a class that has more than one responsibility. A clear sign of such a troubled class is if it contains *discordant* attributes—that is, attributes that don't seem to fit in with their peers. If you discover discordant attributes, use **aggregation** (see Chapter 2) to move them into separate, more appropriate classes. Most likely, these new classes will need to collaborate with each other.

Four Criteria of a Good Class

While you are making behavior allocation decisions, you are making decisions that affect the quality of the classes in your design. Grady Booch's *Object-Oriented Analysis and Design with Applications* (Addison-Wesley, 1994) introduces the *Halbert/O'Brien criteria* of reusability, applicability, complexity, and implementation knowledge.

If you follow the RDD thought process, you'll generally wind up with a set of behaviors that are all applicable (i.e., not schizoid), don't depend on implementation details of another

---

3. Rebecca Wirfs-Brock and Alan McKean, *Object Design: Roles, Responsibilities and Collaborations* (New York: Addison-Wesley, 2003), p. 132

class, aren't overly complex for any single class, and result in a reusable piece of code that maps nicely to a problem-domain abstraction.

Following a responsibility-driven thought process (done correctly) results in classes that meet the Halbert/O'Brien quality criteria. Or, to go back another 15 years or so: maximize cohesion, minimize coupling.

Continuing the Internet Bookstore Example

To illustrate the theory step by step, let's return to our Internet Bookstore example and the *Write Customer Review* use case. So far we've added the entities, actor, and boundary objects to our sequence diagram (see Figure 8-8). The next step, as described in the previous section, is to walk systematically through the controllers on the robustness diagram and apply them to the sequence diagram.

Referring back to the robustness diagram in Figure 6-7, you can see that the Customer clicks the Write Review button on the Book Detail page. The system then performs a check to see if the Customer is logged in. On the robustness diagram, this is represented as the "Is user logged in?" controller. This controller checks the Customer Session entity. On the sequence diagram, then, we'd have an isUserLoggedIn() method on a class called CustomerSession.

As we now need to be thinking in terms of the implementation details, we need to establish where the CustomerSession instance is found. In our Spring/JSP example, the CustomerSession would be an object contained in the HTTP Session layer (i.e., naturally associated with the current user session). When the user browses to the bookstore website, a new CustomerSession object is created and added as an attribute to HttpSession. This is then used to track the user's state (currently just whether the user is logged in). To make this explicit, we should show HttpSession on the sequence diagram, so that we can see exactly where CustomerSession is found.

Figure 8-10 shows the (nearly) completed sequence diagram. Notice that it's possible to read through the use case text on the left and simultaneously walk through the sequence diagram, tracing the text to the messages on the diagram.

■**Exercise** In Figure 8-10, the "User not logged in" alternate course describes (at a high level) the process of logging in before proceeding with the current use case. Should the sequence diagram invoke a separate *Login* use case, and if so, how would this be represented on the sequence diagram? We discuss the answer in the CDR in Chapter 9.

As it turns out, a couple of objects weren't used at all. Review Rejected Screen wasn't used, although we originally (in the use case text) described the system taking the user to a separate screen to show that the review was rejected. However, on drawing the sequence diagram, it seemed like it would be much nicer to take the user back to the Write Review Screen and show the validation errors there, so that the user can simply correct the errors and resubmit the review. We should update the use case text ***at the earliest opportunity*** (this means right now) to reflect this, so that the use case doesn't fall out of sync with the design (and thus lose its usefulness).

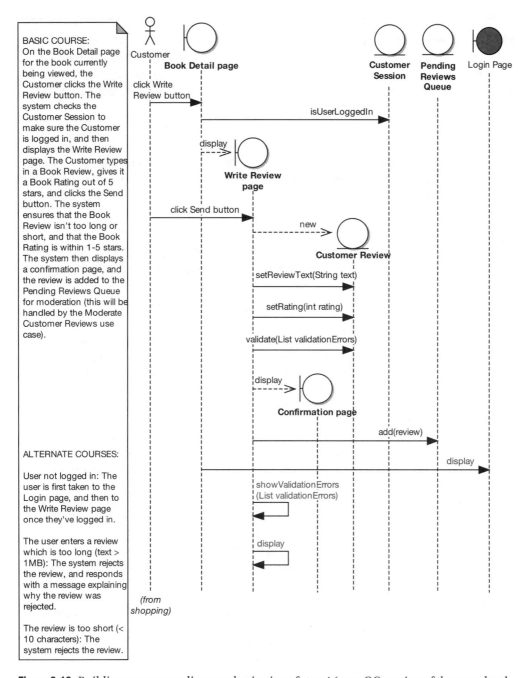

BASIC COURSE:
On the Book Detail page for the book currently being viewed, the Customer clicks the Write Review button. The system checks the Customer Session to make sure the Customer is logged in, and then displays the Write Review page. The Customer types in a Book Review, gives it a Book Rating out of 5 stars, and clicks the Send button. The system ensures that the Book Review isn't too long or short, and that the Book Rating is within 1-5 stars. The system then displays a confirmation page, and the review is added to the Pending Reviews Queue for moderation (this will be handled by the Moderate Customer Reviews use case).

ALTERNATE COURSES:

User not logged in: The user is first taken to the Login page, and then to the Write Review page once they've logged in.

The user enters a review which is too long (text > 1MB): The system rejects the review, and responds with a message explaining why the review was rejected.

The review is too short (< 10 characters): The system rejects the review.

Customer

Book Detail page

click Write Review button

isUserLoggedIn

Customer Session

Pending Reviews Queue

Login Page

display

Write Review page

click Send button

new

Customer Review

setReviewText(String text)

setRating(int rating)

validate(List validationErrors)

display

Confirmation page

add(review)

display

showValidationErrors (List validationErrors)

display

(from shopping)

Figure 8-10. *Building a sequence diagram, beginning of step 4 (pure OO version of the completed sequence diagram)*

■**Caution** You don't need to go back and redraw the robustness diagram 17 more times once you're in the middle of sequence diagramming. You know the robustness diagrams aren't going to be perfect, and that's OK—it isn't important to make your preliminary design diagrams look like you clairvoyantly knew what the detailed design would look like (doing this would, in fact, cause analysis paralysis). It's only important that the preliminary design gets you properly started with detailed design.

Additionally, Book wasn't used at all so, after double, triple-checking to make sure we hadn't missed a critical detail, we removed it. We discuss the reasons why Book fell off the diagram when we get to the CDR (see Chapter 9).

■**Note** Figure 8-10 raises some other issues, which we'll also address during the CDR. In fact, most of these issues would have been caught using a *__design-driven testing (DDT)__* approach, which we describe in Chapter 12.

This version of the diagram follows a pure OO design. It's a "wouldn't it be great if . . ." diagram reflecting the OO design principles we've discussed. As it's quite high level, it could be transferred to a target platform other than Spring Framework without much (or indeed any) modification. In other words, so far we haven't tied the design in very closely with the nitty-gritty implementation details of our target framework—and we'll need to do that before we begin coding.

Because we're reusing a third-party web framework rather than designing our own, the design is dictated to an extent by the framework's creators. For example, in Figure 8-10 we show the validation taking place as a method on the entity class being validated. However, the approach in Spring Framework is to separate validation into a separate class. This isn't pure OO, as it breaks encapsulation and we potentially end up with lots of tiny "controller classes," each of which implements a single function. Having said that, there are practical, ground-based reasons why Spring does it this way.[4]

So, we need to explore the implementation details and fill in these details on the sequence diagram before we can really code from it. To complete the final step in our four essential steps, we need to add in more detail taking into account the framework and the technology being targeted.

Figure 8-11 shows the finished diagram. This is now something that we can code from directly (after the CDR, of course!).

The processing in this diagram is quite detail-rich, so we've moved the description into Appendix B (in the section titled "'Write Customer Review' Use Case"). If you're interested in the Spring details, please do take a look there before moving on.

---

4. Spring is actually one of the better frameworks for not imposing too many design constraints. For example, Struts (a popular MVC web framework) contains a much more rigid design, in which your classes must extend specific Struts classes. Because Java doesn't allow multiple inheritance, this can be a limiting factor.

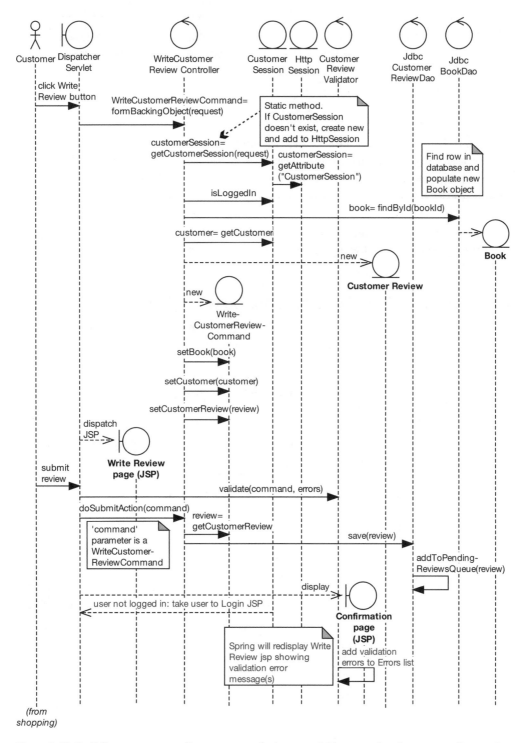

Figure 8-11. *Building a sequence diagram, completing step 4 (the completed sequence diagram)*

■**Exercise** `WriteCustomerReviewCommand` seems quite redundant, as it's simply there to hold data that gets set in the `CustomerReview` domain class anyway. What could be done to improve this part of the design? We reveal the answer during the CDR in the next chapter.

■**Exercise** The `Book` class in Figure 8-11 doesn't seem to do a huge amount. How could this design be improved to give `Book` a more prominent role? (Remember, we had the same problem with the *Show Book Details* sequence diagram in Figure 8-2.) Again, we reveal the answer during the CDR in the next chapter.

Now that we've completed the sequence diagram, it's time to bring the static model up to date. After walking through the theory, we show the updated static model for the Internet Bookstore.

Updating Your Class Diagrams As You Go Along

As you've probably gathered by now, you need to keep updating and refining your static model (the class diagrams) as you go along (see Figure 8-12).

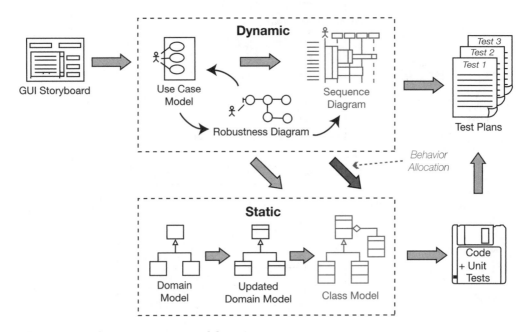

Figure 8-12. *Updating your static model, again*

Synchronizing the Static and Dynamic Parts of the Model

CASE tools take much of the burden out of keeping the static and dynamic models in sync by putting operations on classes as you draw message arrows on sequence diagrams. But we do recommend that, with each message arrow you draw on the sequence diagram, you take a peek at the class diagram to make sure it's updated correctly.

It's a good habit to check that the operations are added to the correct class each time you draw a message, and if you spot any missing attributes, add them as soon as you notice they're missing. Seeing each class evolve should also cause you to think about the class structure, and evolve the class design. You might spot an opportunity for generalization, for example; you may see a possible use of a design pattern; or you could find that a class has gained too many responsibilities and needs to be split in two using aggregation.

As you're adding implementation details to the sequence diagrams, don't be surprised if you start to see lots of new classes appear on the static model that were never there on the domain model during analysis. That's because you're now identifying the *solution space* classes. By contrast, the domain model shows classes only from the problem space.

The two spaces are now converging during detailed design. By updating the static model as you work through the sequence diagrams, you're now converging the problem space with the solution space.

So, as you add in more functionality from the use cases, you'll also come up with scaffolding and other types of infrastructure (e.g., "helper" classes).

Adding getters and setters to your class diagrams can be time-consuming and doesn't give you much in return, except a busy-looking class diagram. Our advice is to avoid adding them to your model. For now, just add the attributes as private fields and utilize encapsulation. As you only ever allow access to attributes via getters and setters, adding them is kind of redundant. When you generate code, you should be able to generate get and set methods from attributes anyhow. Pretty much all modern IDEs and diagramming tools are scriptable or have this sort of automation built in.

Although we suggested that you avoid adding too much design detail during domain modeling (since there just wasn't enough supporting information available at that time), now that you're at the detailed design stage, this really is the time to go wild (so to speak) and think the design through in fine detail. You and your team are shaping up the design—collaboratively, we hope—and getting it ready for coding.

In the next section, we illustrate how to synchronize the static and dynamic parts of the model for the Internet Bookstore.

Internet Bookstore: Updating the Static Model

In this section, we show three different versions of the static model updated from the sequence diagrams (review the previous version in Figure 5-19 to see how the static model has evolved so far). Figure 8-13 shows the static model updated from the pure OO sequence diagram shown in Figure 8-10.

Book and BookCollection are on the static model because they also appeared on the domain model; however, neither class has operations yet because we haven't drawn any sequence diagrams that allocate behavior to them.

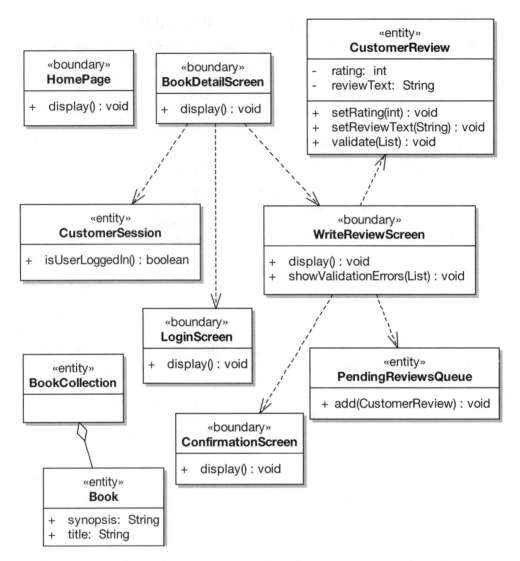

Figure 8-13. *Internet Bookstore static model based on the pure OO sequence diagram in Figure 8-10*

CustomerSession used to have a loggedIn attribute (see the domain model diagram in Figure 5-19), but after sequence diagramming, this has turned into a method, isUserLoggedIn(), without an attribute to back it (i.e., it's a "live" or calculated value that is rechecked each time the method is called).

Figure 8-13 reveals some commonality between some of the classes. Each of the boundary classes has its own display() method. So it would make sense to move this up to a new parent class. Figure 8-14 shows the result of this prefactoring (it's much quicker to do this sort of thing now, while we're looking at the bigger picture, before we have source code dependent on the class we're prefactoring).

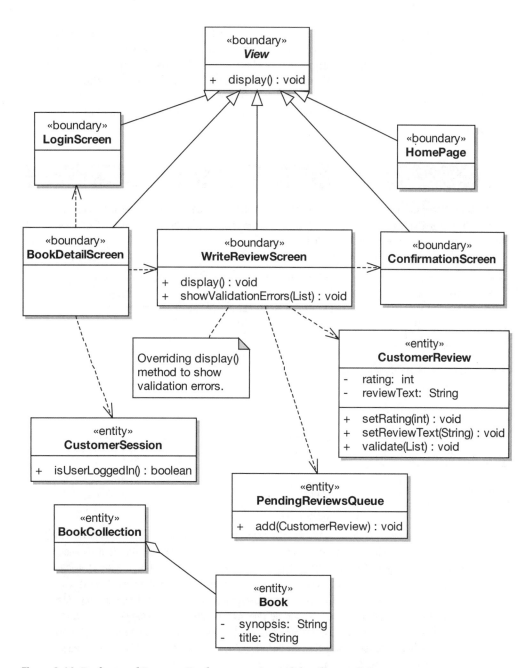

Figure 8-14. *Prefactored Internet Bookstore static model, still pure OO*

In Figure 8-14, we created a new abstract class called View, which contains the common display() method. The boundary classes only need to override this method if they're doing something special. In this case, WriteReviewScreen overrides it because it needs to display the validation errors set via showValidationErrors().

We don't want to go any further without grounding the design in the reality of the target platform. What we especially want to avoid is designing our own framework (which we're starting to risk doing by creating a common View class), instead of just wrapping the design around the predesigned target framework. So let's correct that now: Figure 8-17 shows a much more detailed version of the static model, derived from the detailed, nitty-gritty version of the sequence diagram, taking into account the real-world constraints (and benefits!) of Spring Framework.

MULTIPLICITY

Multiplicity refers to the numbers that you often see on the lines between classes on class diagrams. For example, Figure 8-15 shows an excerpt from a class diagram showing multiplicity, and Figure 8-16 shows how the same diagram might be described in text form.

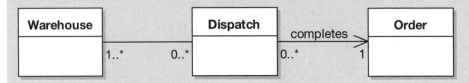

Figure 8-15. *Example class diagram notation for associations*

A Warehouse has zero to many Dispatch items

Each Dispatch belongs to one to many Warehouses

Dispatch completes an Order

Figure 8-16. *The same diagram in text form*

The level of detail shown in Figure 8-15 would probably be more appropriate for a relational data model than a class diagram. On relational data models (usually shown using entity-relationship [ER] diagrams), showing the precise multiplicity for each relationship is of paramount importance. However, for class diagrams it's much less important—optional, even. One possible exception to this is if you want to use multiplicity to indicate validation rules (e.g., a Dispatch *must* have at least one Order before it completes).

You might also want to use multiplicity to indicate whether a variable will be a **single** object reference or a **list** of object references, in which case, just showing **1** or ***** (respectively) would be sufficient. For example, in Figure 8-15, the Warehouse class can have many Dispatch items, so this would be represented in Java with a List (or some other Collection class):

```
private List<Dispatch> dispatches = new ArrayList<Dispatch>();
```

On the other hand, a Dispatch references only one Order, so this would be represented by a single object reference:

```
private Order order;
```

Figure 8-17 has been updated to show the details from the sequence diagrams for both the *Show Book Details* and *Write Customer Review* use cases.

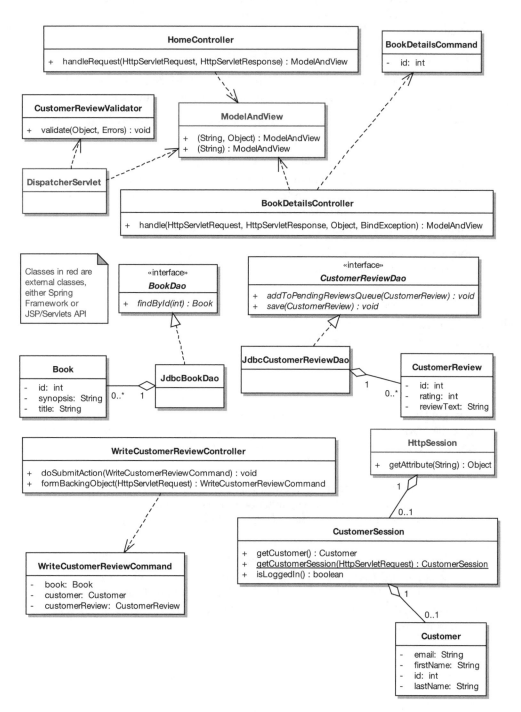

Figure 8-17. *Internet Bookstore static model after drawing sequence diagrams for two use cases*

What's changed in Figure 8-17?

- We've introduced a couple of Spring classes (`DispatcherServlet` and `ModelAndView`) and a class from the Java Servlet API (`HttpSession`), and we've shown which of our own classes relate to them.

- The aggregation relationships now show their **multiplicity** (see the previous sidebar).

- We've filled in the properties that were identified in the use case, plus any supplementary specs (screen mock-ups, passive-voice functional specifications, etc.).

- Our Screen classes have been replaced with (mostly) Spring `Controller` classes. Which brings us to the next point . . .

- Some of the methods that originated from controllers on the robustness diagrams have escaped and turned into their own `Controller` classes. While we wouldn't normally recommend this, Spring requires that each form has its own `Controller` class. This class handles the details of extracting postvalidated data, processing it, and then telling the framework which JSP page to send back to the user.

- We've introduced a `Command` class (`WriteCustomerReviewCommand`), which represents the data extracted from the user's form post.

■Note In the next chapter, we revisit this part of the design and look at how to make it more "domain oriented" while lessening our reliance on separate `Command` and `Controller` classes *and* still fitting into the Spring design mold.

- We've got DAOs. `BookDao`, `CustomerReviewDao`—you name it, we've got it. Remember that a DAO (e.g., `BookDao`) is analogous to a database table, whereas a domain class (e.g., `Book`) is analogous to a row in a database table. A `BookDao` is a source of `Books`, so it's similar to an EJB Home object.

- `BookCollection` has disappeared. Instead we have `BookDao`, as mentioned in the previous point. In fact, `BookDao` will actually return collections of `Books`—though we haven't shown this yet, as we haven't drawn these `Collection` operations on any of the sequence diagrams.

- Because Spring has its own validation framework that we want to take advantage of, we've separated the `CustomerReview` validation into its own separate class, `CustomerReviewValidator`. (Note that although this separation of concerns seems like a good idea on the surface, it turns out to be not that good an idea after all. We discuss the reasons why in Chapter 11.)

Although it contains a lot of detail, Figure 8-17 contains purely the detail we've uncovered during domain modeling, robustness analysis, and sequence diagramming, and nothing more. There are no leaps of logic, leaps of faith, or leaps of any kind. The operations on each class are taken directly from the messages we drew on the sequence diagrams. The relationships between each class are also derived from the relationships in the domain model and from the operations. The attributes on each class are derived from the detail in the use cases and any supplementary specs that the use cases reference (e.g., screen mock-ups, data models, etc.).

It's tempting to add detail to the class diagram because you think it might be needed, but (as we hope we've demonstrated) it's better fill in the detail while drawing the sequence diagrams. If, after you've fleshed out the static model using the sequence diagrams, the static model still appears to be missing some detail, then you should revisit the sequence diagrams (and possibly even the robustness diagrams and use cases), as it's likely that something has been missed. Always trust your gut instinct, but use it as an indication that you need to revisit your previous diagrams, not that you need to second-guess yourself and add detail arbitrarily to the static model.

We've now finished the detailed design for the two use cases we're implementing. The next stage before coding will be the CDR, a "sanity check" involving senior technical staff to make sure the design is shipshape before the use cases are implemented.

Sequence Diagramming in Practice

The following exercises, taken from the detailed design activities for the Internet Bookstore, are designed to test your ability to spot the most common mistakes that people make during sequence diagramming.

Exercises

Each of the diagrams in Figures 8-18 to 8-20 contains one or more typical modeling errors. For each diagram, try to figure out the errors and then draw the corrected diagram. The answers are in the next section.

Figure 8-18 shows an excerpt from a sequence diagram for the *Add External Books to Catalog* use case (which you also encountered in the exercises in Chapter 5). It shows quite a few examples of a common behavior allocation error. (Hint: Which objects are the messages pointing to?) Try to explain why the behavior allocation in the diagram is wrong, and then draw the corrected diagram.

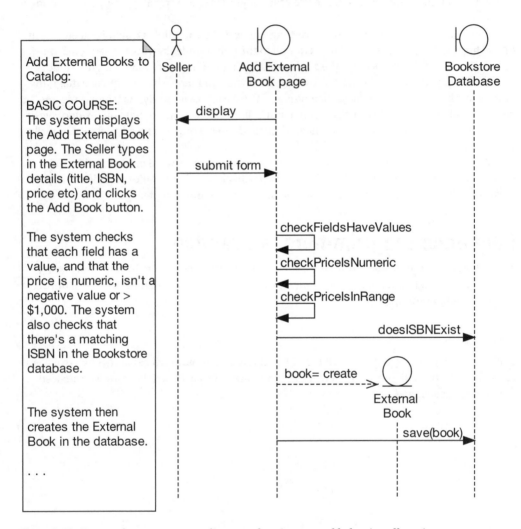

Figure 8-18. *Excerpt from a sequence diagram showing several behavior allocation errors*

Exercise 8-2

Figure 8-19 shows an excerpt from a sequence diagram for the *Create New Book* use case (this use case is intended for Bookstore staff, so that they can add new Book titles to their online Catalog). There are a couple of problems with this diagram excerpt (one of which is repeated many times in the diagram). See if you can find them both.

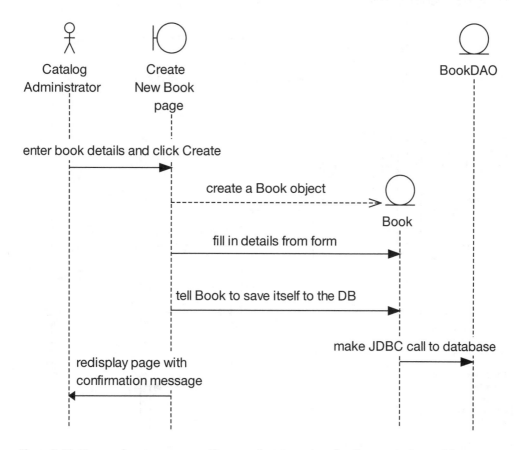

Figure 8-19. *Excerpt from a sequence diagram showing a couple of pretty major problems*

Exercise 8-3

Figure 8-20 shows an excerpt from a sequence diagram for the *Edit Shopping Cart* use case. The problems with this diagram are partly related to the diagram showing too much detail in some aspects, but also (ironically perhaps) the diagram displays too little detail where it should be showing more of the design's "plumbing." There are also a couple of issues to do with the use case's scope (i.e., where it starts and finishes). In total, you should find six errors on this diagram. Good luck!

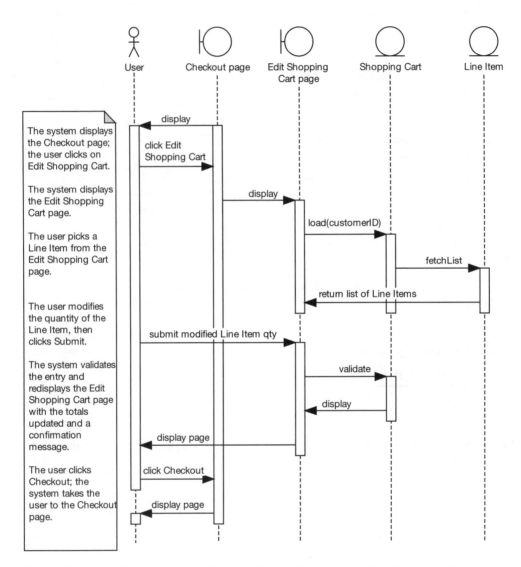

Figure 8-20. *Excerpt from a sequence diagram showing both too much and too little detail*

Exercise Solutions

Following are the solutions to the exercises.

Exercise 8-1 Solution: Non-OO Behavior Allocation

Figure 8-21 highlights the parts of the sequence diagram where the messages were allocated incorrectly. The highlighted messages are really the responsibility of ExternalBook. In the current design, the validation checking goes on in the boundary object, and only after that's all done is the ExternalBook object created. Its only purpose in life is to be passed into BookstoreDatabase for saving.

Note that two of the methods haven't been highlighted: checkFieldsHaveValues and checkPriceIsNumeric. These are legitimately a part of the boundary object, as they're checking that the incoming data is both present and in the correct format. checkPriceIsInRange, on the other hand, is "genuine" data validation, so it belongs on ExternalBook.

On BookstoreDatabase (over on the right of Figure 8-21), two more methods have been highlighted: doesISBNExist and save(book). In this case, it's the *caller* that's wrong—both methods should be called by ExternalBook.

Figure 8-22 shows the corrected diagram.

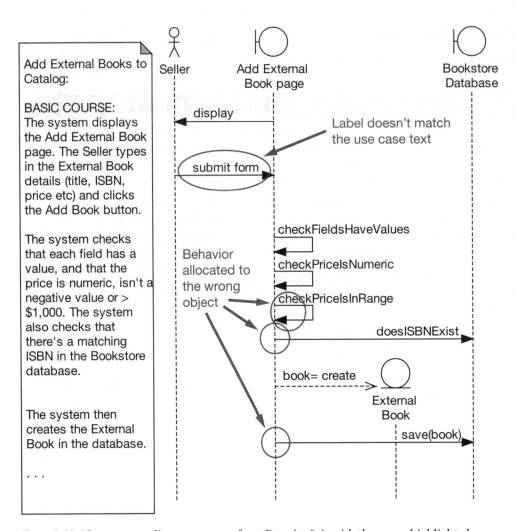

Figure 8-21. *The sequence diagram excerpt from Exercise 8-1, with the errors highlighted*

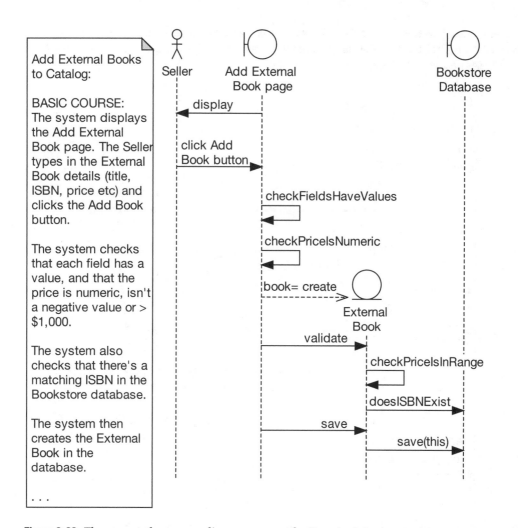

Figure 8-22. *The corrected sequence diagram excerpt for Exercise 8-1*

Exercise 8-2 Solution: Flowcharting

Figure 8-23 highlights the parts of the sequence diagram that have gone wrong. The main issue is that the sequence diagram is being used as a flowchart, instead of for its primary purpose in life: to allocate behavior to classes.

Flowcharting on sequence diagrams isn't necessarily an evil thing in and of itself, and it is almost certainly better than not doing the sequence diagram at all. But we consider it to be (at best) a weak usage of a sequence diagram because it doesn't leverage the ability to assign operations to classes while drawing message arrows. Since, in our opinion, this activity is pretty much the fundamental place where "real OOD" happens, we've flagged it as an error. We think you can (and should) do better than just using the sequence diagram as a flowchart.

The second issue is that there's no validation performed on the incoming form data—and therefore no error handling code for rejecting bad data. Either the validation steps were left out of the use case or the designer didn't draw the sequence diagram directly from the use case text.

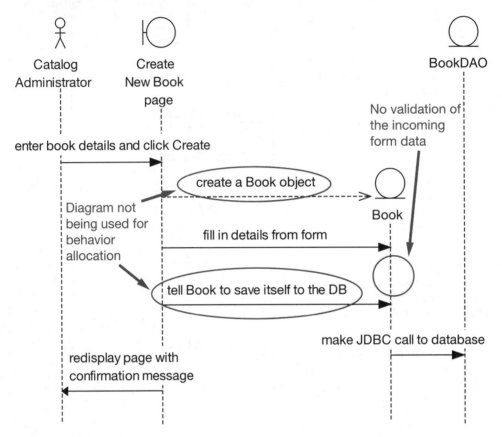

Figure 8-23. *The sequence diagram excerpt from Exercise 8-2, with the errors highlighted*

Figure 8-24 shows the corrected diagram. The corrected version includes the alternate course (shown in red) for when the form validation fails.

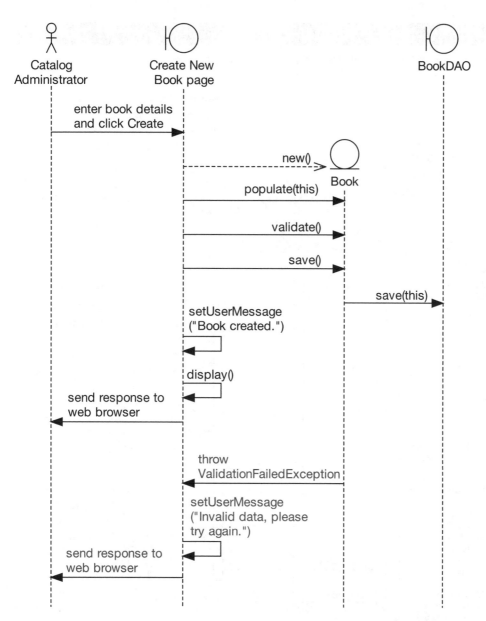

Figure 8-24. *The corrected sequence diagram excerpt for Exercise 8-2*

Exercise 8-3 Solution: Plumbing

Figure 8-25 highlights the parts of the sequence diagram that have gone wrong.

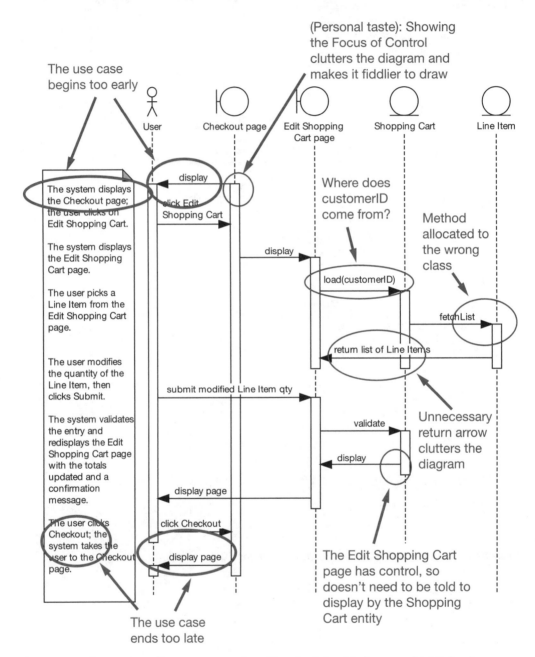

Figure 8-25. *The sequence diagram excerpt from Exercise 8-3, with the errors highlighted*

The use case starts and finishes at the wrong stages, suggesting a problem with the overall scope of the use case. It's a use case about editing the Shopping Cart, but it contains details about interacting with the Checkout page (i.e., the use case lacks focus). Luckily in this example, the problem is easy to fix, but normally you'd expect to catch this kind of scope issue during robustness analysis or the PDR at the latest. If you encounter a sequence diagram where the use case's scope is still wrong, you should take a look at the process and work out what's gone wrong.

The next issue is more a matter of personal taste than an egregious error. The sequence diagram is showing the focus of control (the rectangles that indicate the "lifetime" of each message). Note that this isn't necessarily an error, as some people do prefer to show these, but for the purposes of **behavior allocation**, our preference is to not show them, as they clutter the diagram and make it more difficult to draw, without giving a whole lot back in return.

On to the next issue, which is definitely a modeling error. In the `load(customerID)` message, you'd be forgiven for wondering where the `customerID` sprang from. Any time you see a leap of logic on a sequence diagram, where it isn't clear where something came from, then it's probable that a part of the design has been missed. In this case, the diagram is missing the `CustomerAccount` object, which should have been populated when the session began. This can then be retrieved from `CustomerSession`. These design details all need to be shown on the diagram, as it's essential "plumbing" work. (In this example, it would be reasonable to put a note on the diagram stating that `CustomerSession` and `CustomerAccount` are set up during the *Login* use case, so that the diagram remains focused on the use case that we're currently designing.) In fact, it would also make sense to retrieve the `ShoppingCart` from the `CustomerAccount`, instead of telling the `ShoppingCart` to "go find itself" based on the customer's ID.

Next up is the `fetchList` method, which `ShoppingCart` calls on `LineItem`. A quick check of the class diagram (assuming this is being automatically updated as you allocate messages on the sequence diagram) quickly reveals that `fetchList()` just doesn't belong on the `LineItem` class, as it returns a *list* of `LineItems`. Instead, it would make more sense for this method to be on `ShoppingCart` itself, but to be called from the `EditShoppingCart` boundary object.

Still on `LineItem`, the "return list of Line Items" arrow isn't needed. Normally, you don't need to draw an arrow to show return values, as the method returning is implied by the arrow that initially calls the method.

Finally, there shouldn't be a display method going from the `ShoppingCart` entity, as the boundary object is already in control, and the very next thing it does is display the page anyway.

Figure 8-26 shows the corrected diagram.

■Exercise   Figure 8-26 still lacks some detail around populating the LineItems list component—for example, where does the Edit Shopping Cart page get the names and quantities from for each Line Item in the list? Try redrawing the diagram with this additional detail added.

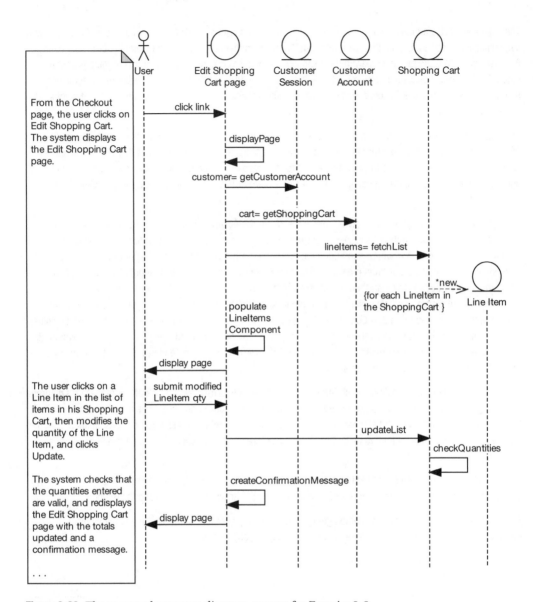

Figure 8-26. *The corrected sequence diagram excerpt for Exercise 8-3*

More Practice

This section provides a list of modeling questions that you can use to test your knowledge of sequence diagramming. If you can't answer a question, review the relevant sections in this chapter until you *can* answer it.

1. The primary purpose of a sequence diagram should be

    a) To show detailed flow of control for a use case

    b) To specify real-time, finite-state behavior

    c) To help make an optimal allocation of functions to classes within the context of a use case

    d) To separate out alternate courses of action

2. A sequence diagram should always be

    a) Cross-checked against a class diagram with operations shown on the classes

    b) Reviewed to make sure all behavior specified in the use case is accounted for by messages between objects

    c) Reviewed against a GUI prototype or storyboard to make sure all possible user actions are accounted for

    d) All of the above

3. Readability of a sequence diagram is best accomplished by

    a) Using detailed use case templates showing pre- and postconditions

    b) Drawing it to the same level of detail as a robustness diagram

    c) Following the two-paragraph rule and keeping the use cases short

    d) Showing branching and conditional logic on the diagram

4. Which of the following statements is *not* true?

    a) It's preferable to show all alternate course of actions on a single diagram rather than produce a separate diagram for each alternate.

    b) It's OK to turn off "focus of control" if it gets in your way.

    c) Sequence diagrams show essentially the same information as collaboration diagrams, in a different format.

    d) You should always rewrite your use case text when drawing a sequence diagram.

5. What things should you consider when drawing a message between objects on a sequence diagram? List at least four criteria, and explain why you should consider each of them.

6. The allocation of behavior can be effectively accomplished by following a responsibility-driven thought process. Explain the premise of Responsibility-Driven Design (RDD). (Hint: A good book on RDD was written by Rebecca Wirfs-Brock.)

7. Is it a good idea to draw flowchart-level sequence diagrams that focus on branching and conditional logic? Why or why not?

8. How should the level of abstraction of the use case text that appears on the margin of the sequence diagram compare to the abstraction level of the diagram? (Hint: The diagram should show an object/message detailed design view.)

Discuss the pros and cons of each of the following possibilities:

a) Use case text should match the diagram's abstraction level.

b) Use case text should remain at the abstract, technology-free, implementation-independent requirements level as in the first-draft use cases.

c) Use case text should remain at the robustness diagram abstraction level (conceptual design), while the sequence diagram should show additional design detail.

Summary

In this chapter we covered **detailed design**, the second step in the two-step design process (the first step was preliminary design). Figure 8-27 shows where we are; the items covered in this chapter are shown in red.

Once you've drawn all the sequence diagrams for the use cases you're working on in the current release and updated your static model, then you can safely say that you've finished this stage in the process.

By now, you're almost ready to begin coding. There's just one last stop before code: the Critical Design Review (CDR), which we cover in the next chapter. It's an essential step, as it forms something of a reality check for your design.

Milestone 2: Preliminary Design Review

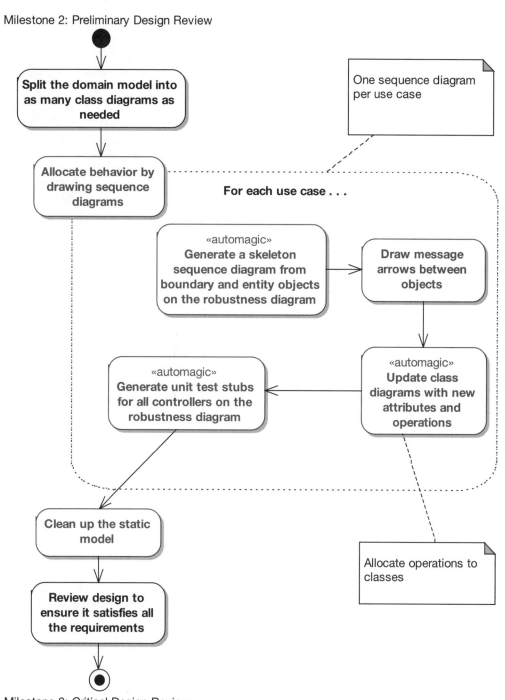

Figure 8-27. *Activities during the detailed design stage*

CHAPTER 9

■ ■ ■

Critical Design Review

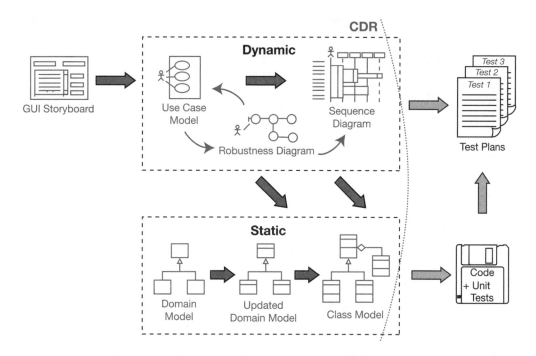

Your project should now be in much better shape than many other projects normally are by this stage. By now, you've used robustness analysis to disambiguate the use case text and discover any missing domain classes, you've held a Preliminary Design Review (PDR) to make sure the use cases match up with what the customer really wants, and you've carefully crafted a detailed design for the use cases you're implementing in this release.

So, you're nearly ready to begin coding—there's just one quick (but vital) milestone to check off the list first: the Critical Design Review (CDR).

The 10,000-Foot View

Why bother reviewing the design again? Here's a hypothetical conversation that we hope will shed some light on the subject.

Q: What's a CDR and why am I spending time on it when I could be writing code?

A: The CDR helps you to achieve three important goals, before you begin coding:

- Ensure that the "how" of detailed design matches up with the "what" specified in your requirements. In other words, for each use case, you need to match up the use case with its sequence diagram.

- Review the quality of your design. So you'll want to have at least one design expert in the room.

- Check for continuity of messages. You need to check the direction of the message arrows on your sequence diagrams, and make sure you can always tell which object is in control. Sometimes you'll see leaps between objects that don't involve a message between them. These leaps of logic need to be ironed out.

■**Note** See the section "Using the Class Diagrams to Find Errors on the Sequence Diagrams" later in this chapter for an example problem caused by leaps of logic.

Q: Who should be involved in the CDR?

A: This might surprise you, but the customer should not be involved in the CDR—just the designers and developers. It's a technical review session, so it should be populated by technically minded people.

The customer (plus key users, etc.) has a lot to contribute to the functional requirements, use cases and so forth, but unless the customer really is a technically minded design expert who can contribute to a design review, it's preferable that he or she not attend the CDR. Picture yourself having to explain to a nontechnical customer, for the fiftieth time, what a Façade pattern is and why you're not using it in this particular design!

Q: But isn't it supposed to be better if the customer is closely involved in the project?

A: Absolutely—just not to the point of silliness. Remember that by this stage, the customer has signed off on the use cases twice. And—assuming you're following an agile process with small, frequent releases—the customer will get to give lots of feedback on the evolving feature set and on the UI during development. Also, keep in mind that it is possible for a customer to micromanage a software project. Your programmers might not actually enjoy this too much, unless of course you've negotiated an "optional-scope contract"[1] whereupon the scope of what you deliver is optional, and customers are promised they can change their mind about the requirements during coding "for free."

---

1. See "Optional-Scope Contracts" on page 260 of *Extreme Programming Refactored: The Case Against XP* (Apress, 2003).

Q: When is the right time to begin the CDR?

A: You need to have completed all of the sequence diagrams for the use cases that you're planning to implement in the current release. You should also have updated the class diagrams so that all of the operations that you assigned during sequence diagramming are reflected in the static model. Having to update the diagrams during the review would be too much of a distraction, so it's important to make sure all of that work is finished before the review begins.

Critical Design Review in Theory

In this section, we cover the key elements of CDR, structured as usual around our top 10 guidelines.

Top 10 Critical Design Review Guidelines

The principles discussed in this chapter can be summed up as a list of guidelines. Our top 10 list follows.

10. Make sure the sequence diagram matches the use case text.

9. Make sure (yes, again) that each sequence diagram accounts for both basic and alternate courses of action.

8. Make sure that operations have been allocated to classes appropriately.

7. Review the classes on your class diagrams to make sure they all have an appropriate set of attributes and operations.

6. If your design reflects the use of patterns or other detailed implementation constructs, make sure that these details are reflected on the sequence diagram.

5. Trace your functional (and nonfunctional) requirements to your use cases and classes to ensure you have covered them all.

4. Make sure your programmers "sanity check" the design and are confident they can build it and that it will work as intended.

3. Make sure all your attributes are typed correctly, and that return values and parameter lists on your operations are complete and correct.

2. Generate the code headers for your classes, and inspect them closely.

1. Review the test plan for your release.

Let's walk through these top 10 CDR practices in more detail.

10. Make Sure the Sequence Diagram Matches the Use Case Text

You need to be able to trace from the behavior requirements (on the left margin) across to see how those requirements will be implemented by messages being sent between objects.

The sequence diagram should provide a visual requirements trace at a glance. That is, the disambiguated behavior requirements should be clearly visible on the left margin of the diagram, and directly to the right of each sentence should be the objects/messages that will implement those behavior requirements. So it should be trivially simple to see back to the requirements while looking at the detailed design.

During reviews, the "highlighter test" works exceptionally well (again). Highlight a sentence of use case text on the margin, and then highlight the messages that show the design for that bit of required behavior. Then just "lather, rinse, repeat" the process until the whole use case has been checked.

9. Cover Both Basic and Alternate Courses of Action

Don't make the mistake of saying YAGNI[2] about those pesky rainy-day scenarios. They're too important.

8. Make Sure That Operations Have Been Allocated to Classes Appropriately

Follow the principles of Responsibility-Driven Design (RDD; see Chapter 8), and make sure each of your classes has a cohesive, focused set of operations. With automated tools, you can usually distinguish between operations on classes and messages that have just been labeled on the sequence diagram by looking for parentheses "()" following the operation name on the message arrow.

7. Review the Attributes and Operations on Your Classes

You need to review the classes on your class diagrams to ensure they all have an appropriate set of attributes and operations. The easiest way to do this is to continuously bounce back and forth between the sequence diagram and a detailed class diagram that shows all the attributes and operations for the classes. It's easy to make mistakes on sequence diagrams, so after you draw each arrow, take a peek at the class diagram and make sure you've put the operation where you intended it to go.

■Tip Look for classes without attributes and for classes with "schizophrenic personalities" (i.e., unrelated sets of operations).

Sometimes you'll find that you've overloaded a class with too many responsibilities, or you may find that, once all the behavior allocation is done, some classes end up rather impoverished, with *no* responsibilities (as in the Book example later in this chapter).

---

2. YAGNI stands for *You Aren't Gonna Need It*, a much-loved saying among Extreme Programmers.

You'll notice a responsibility-driven theme in the Internet Bookstore review later on. The thought process behind assigning responsibilities to classes is summed up nicely by Rebecca Wirfs-Brock in her book *Designing Object-Oriented Software:*[3]

> *Responsibilities are meant to convey a sense of the purpose of an object and its place in the system. The responsibilities of an object are all the services it provides for all the contracts it supports. When we assign responsibilities to a class we are stating that each and every instance of that class will have those responsibilities, whether there is just one instance or many.*

6. Make Sure the Chosen Design Patterns (Etc.) Are in Your Sequence Diagrams

While there are some exceptions, the general guideline here is that the sequence diagram should show the "real design" as you intend to code it. Magic is not permissible on sequence diagrams.

5. Trace Your Requirements to Your Use Cases and Classes

Trace your functional (and nonfunctional) requirements to your use cases and classes to make sure you have covered them all. Adjust your formality level to what's appropriate for your project and organization, but if you're going to trace requirements to the design, this is the best time to do it. Tools like EA make it easy with the built-in traceability matrix.

4. Make Sure Your Programmers "Sanity Check" the Design

It doesn't do anybody any good to have your analysts attempt to dictate a design that's inefficient or otherwise problematic to build. **Programmers need to be involved in detailed design.**

3. Check for Correctness (Return Values, Typos, Etc.)

Make sure all your attributes are typed correctly, and that return values and parameter lists on your operations are complete and correct. You're going to hit the Generate Code button real soon now, so you'd best have all your ducks lined up before you do.

2. Generate the Code Headers for Your Classes, and Inspect Them Closely

See, we told you that you were about to generate code. Once you've done so, inspect the code headers carefully.

1. Review the Test Plan for Your Release

The key here is that you're generating a list of unit tests at the logical software function level—that is, as defined by the controllers on your robustness diagrams. Each of these logical functions might explode to more than one message on a sequence diagram, and you'll probably

---

3. Rebecca Wirfs-Brock, Brian Wilkerson, and Laura Wiener, *Designing Object-Oriented Software* (Upper Saddle River, NJ: Prentice-Hall, 1990), p. 62.

want to unit test each of these as well, but generating skeleton tests from the robustness diagram will make sure you test the logical result of each of these functions as well.

■Tip Remember that you can generate (stub) test cases for the controllers on your robustness diagrams automatically using EA with the ICONIX Process add-in. You can then collect these into a test plan, and also generate the class/method skeletons for your unit tests.

In the second part of this chapter, we illustrate some of these points by following a CDR session for the Internet Bookstore.

Using the Class Diagrams to Find Errors on the Sequence Diagrams

A technique that works really well during the CDR is, as the title of this section suggests, using the class diagrams to find errors on the sequence diagrams. Basically, this involves the reviewer zooming in on various classes in the class diagram and looking for methods on the wrong classes, or other anomalies, and then finding the guilty sequence diagrams.

In a recent training workshop, Doug found a Queue class that had only an Add method. Nobody was removing anything from the queue, ever! Doug found the sequence diagram that was supposed to use the items from the queue and discovered that the message arrows were drawn backward—the Pull Item from Queue method had been put on the wrong class. The Queue was on the sequence diagram (as it should have been) because the diagramming tool put it there automatically, but somehow they still managed to draw the arrow backward.

You can find most sequence diagram errors by looking at the class diagram.

Critical Design Review in Practice: Internet Bookstore

In this section, we walk through an example CDR for the *Show Book Details* and *Write Customer Review* use cases. To make things a bit more interesting, we've structured the review as a typical conversation between the reviewer and one of the designers.

CDR for the "Show Book Details" Use Case

The sequence diagram for the *Show Book Details* use case raises some important questions about the role of encapsulation and RDD in designing modern web applications. For the original sequence diagram, refer back to Figure 8-2, and for the class diagram, refer to Figure 8-17.

Book Is Devoid of All Responsibilities

In the following conversation, our astute reviewer uncovers a flaw in the design. The flaw is indicated by a class that does no work. Listen in as the details unfold.

Reviewer: I've had this nagging feeling at the back of my mind about this design. I couldn't put my finger on it for a while, but then it struck me while I was gargling Beethoven's `Fifth` during my shower this morning. In short, the use case is all about finding a book and displaying its details—but the `Book` class isn't at the center of the design. It's just kinda hanging off the right edge of the diagram on its own.

Designer: Well, the `Book` is a domain class, so it contains all the data you'd associate with a book: title, description, and so on.

Reviewer: But it has no behavior. It will end up with lots of getters and setters, but no actual responsibilities.

Designer: It's a flexible, loosely coupled design, though. We have all these other classes to handle individual aspects of `Book`'s behavior. We have a validator class, `BookDetailsController`, `BookDetailsCommand`...

Reviewer: That's exactly the thing that's been nagging away at the back of my mind! All the behavior that should be in `Book` will be spread about in other classes, making for a rather amorphous design with no obvious starting point. What you're talking about amounts to functional decomposition. Distribution of responsibilities among classes has been taken so far that you now have lots of tiny, single-method classes. In effect, each class is being used just like a function.

■**Note** Back in the days of the Roman Empire, the old "OO-decomposition vs. functional decomposition" debates used to rage fast and furious on the object design forums. The matter has long since been settled: RDD good, functional decomposition bad.

Designer: But it's more maintainable this way . . .

Reviewer: You'd think so, but it often turns out to be *less* maintainable, because there's no single point in the design to go to if you want to find out, say, what a `Book` does. It makes it time-consuming and problematic to track things down. If you make a change that affects `Book`, you have to change five or six (or more) classes instead of just one, and sometimes it isn't entirely clear whether you've tracked down all the classes that need to change.

Designer: So, what you're saying is, `Book` should be the main focal element in the design for all `Book`-related behaviors and responsibilities?

Reviewer: You've got it. Obviously, you have to take into account the design limitations imposed on you by the framework that you're using. Will Spring allow you to make such a profound change in the design?

Designer: It's a change in design *philosophy*. So yes, it's quite profound as changes go. Luckily Spring is quite flexible, so you can do whatever you want with it, up to a point.

Reviewer: That's good to hear. What this design is missing is good, old-fashioned OO encapsulation (coupled with RDD).

■Note Centralization of responsibility for books in the Book class means that if something changes about books (and over time you have to assume it will), you ought to be able to find it pretty quickly by looking at the Book class, instead of searching through dozens of itty-bitty one-method classes. In other words, all the responsibilities of doing things related to books ought to be encapsulated in the Book class.

Reviewer: Let's take a look at which responsibilities have "leaked out" of Book, and try to stuff them back in.

Designer: Well, there's BookDetailsCommand. This shows up only in the sequence diagram as an argument in the handle(..) method on BookDetailsController *(see Figure 8-2)* and in the class diagram *(see Figure 8-17)*. It's simply there as a placeholder for the book ID handed in via a URL, like this:

http://pretendbookstore.com/bookdetails.jsp?id=123

Designer: BookDetailsCommand gets populated with the ID (123) and handed into the controller. But when we code it, it will look like this (peeking ahead to the source code for a second):

```
public class BookDetailsCommand {

    private int id;

    public BookDetailsCommand() {
    }

    public void setId(int id) {
        this.id = id;
    }

    public int getId() {
        return id;
    }

}
```

Reviewer: That's the entire class?

Designer: Uh, yep.

Reviewer: OK, so the way to fix this is to start with Book. It already has an ID attribute, so we can put that to good use. The Command class would be Book itself, initially populated only with an ID (read in from the URL). Then you call a method on Book that tells it to go find itself in the database and populate all its other attributes. load() would be a good name for the new method. Then we can get rid of BookDetailsCommand altogether! *(The relevant section from the updated sequence diagram is shown in Figure 9-1.)*

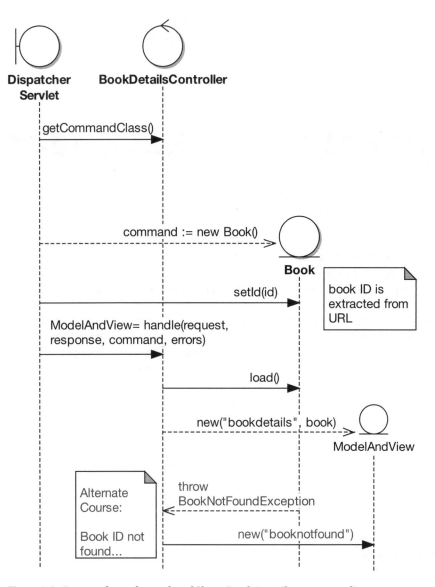

Figure 9-1. *Excerpt from the updated* Show Book Details *sequence diagram*

■**Note** The first operation, getCommandClass(), is how Spring "knows" to create a Book for the Command class. Because the incoming URL has a parameter called id, Spring will look for a property on the Command class (i.e., Book) called setId.

Designer: I see what you're getting at. So Book is now much more at the center of the design, logically speaking. If you want to do something with a book, you go to the Book class.

Reviewer: That's right. Of course, Book can still delegate to other classes, but it's safe to regard it as the start of the journey.

SWARMS OF TINY CLASSES

In the Java and C# universes, one (particularly prevalent) school of design encourages you to separate the "real" functionality (the operations) out of the domain classes and put them in separate support classes (validators, DAOs, Controllers, etc.). There has, however, been much discussion on the Spring message forum about this particular approach.

The problem is that it's possible to "overnormalize" the design and end up with hundreds of tiny classes flying around. Also, as we hope we've reinforced over the last few chapters, just because the official design blueprints for a language or framework recommend that you follow a particular design, that doesn't mean you *have to* follow that design. It's important to look at how the design will work for your application—how maintainable it will be.

Remember the rules of OO design and encapsulation: a class consists of both data (the attributes/properties) *and* behavior (the operations/methods). It's a noticeable modern design trend to separate these out so that you get separate classes to handle different aspects of a domain class's behavior. While it does make the design more flexible, it isn't necessarily a good thing because (for example) a book is no longer a cohesive, self-contained Book class; it's splintered out into a BookDetailsValidator, a BookDao, a JdbcBookDao, a BookDetailsController, and so on, with each class often containing just one short method.

This type of design is typified by an *anemic domain model*—that is, a design where the domain classes are all data and no behavior.

The following quote from object guru Martin Fowler sums up the situation extremely well: [4]

> *The basic symptom of an Anemic Domain Model is that at first blush it looks like the real thing. There are objects, many named after the nouns in the domain space, and these objects are connected with the rich relationships and structure that true domain models have. The catch comes when you look at the behavior, and you realize that there is very little behavior on these objects. Indeed often these models come with design rules that say that you are not to put any domain logic in the domain objects. Instead there are a set of service objects which capture all the domain logic. These services live on top of the domain model and use the domain model for data.*

---

4. See www.martinfowler.com/bliki/AnemicDomainModel.html.

The fundamental horror of this anti-pattern is that it's so contrary to the basic idea of object-oriented design; which is to combine data and process together. The anemic domain model is really just a procedural style design, exactly the kind of thing that object bigots like me (and Eric[5]) have been fighting since our early days in Smalltalk. What's worse, many people think that anemic objects are real objects, and thus completely miss the point of what object-oriented design is all about.

For the Internet Bookstore, we've tried to reach a compromise: using aggregation to link all the itty-bitty classes that Spring wants to see to the Book domain class, and having Book delegate behavior into these helper classes. We can thus still easily understand our design (all the "bookish" behavior is in the Book class), while following the "Spring rules" of using validators, DAOs, and so forth.

While some separation can be useful in order to satisfy certain design patterns, a balance needs to be achieved between monolithic, thousand-line classes at one extreme and swarms of tiny classes at the other.

The Updated Diagram Doesn't Go into Enough Detail

Sequence diagrams need to be detailed. You're well past the point at which you can gloss over poorly thought-out functionality. It's time to spell out the hard details.

> **Reviewer**: I feel like we're making some progress here now. But the sequence diagram we just updated *(see Figure 9-1)* still tells only half the story. What happens when the load() method is called on Book? Presumably the book's DAO is called? That seems like a whole lot of stuff that's just left to the reader's imagination, so to speak.

> **Designer**: Yeah, I just thought I'd summarize that on the diagram, as it's a lot of detail to draw in.

> **Reviewer**: Well, let's try drawing it in anyway, and see where it takes us.

> **Designer**: OK, so when load() is called, Book needs to call the equivalent load() method on BookDao. Hang on, that means that Book needs to be handed an instance of BookDao.

> **Reviewer**: So we'll need to draw a setBookDao() line from BookDetailsController to Book, before the load(). Anything else?

> **Designer**: The next thing is . . . wait a minute. At the moment, BookDao has only a findById() method, which returns a new Book. That's no good—we want it to populate our own Book object. So we'll need to change the way that the DAO operates.

> **Reviewer**: For example, instead of doing this . . . *(See Figure 9-2.)*

> **Reviewer**: . . . we're doing this. *(See Figure 9-3.)*

> **Designer**: If you want to load a Book, it's implicit that you have to first set its ID. So we could make that explicit by combining the setId() and load() methods.

---

5. Eric Evans is the author of *Domain-Driven Design: Tackling Complexity in the Heart of Software* (Addison-Wesley, 2003).

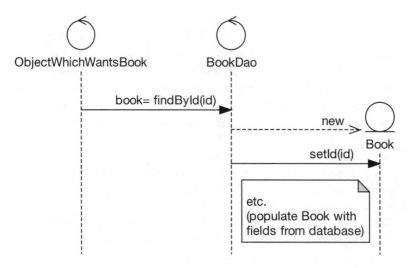

Figure 9-2. *Not very domain-oriented or responsibility-driven*

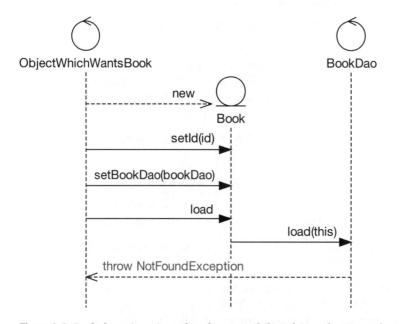

Figure 9-3. *Both domain-oriented and responsibility-driven, but it needs tightening up*

Reviewer: You're right. That would also make it impossible for the calling code to acciden-tally call load() without first setting the ID. Same goes for setting the Book DAO.

Designer: Yep. So the method call would now be this *(see Figure 9-4)*:

```
book.load(id, bookDao);
```

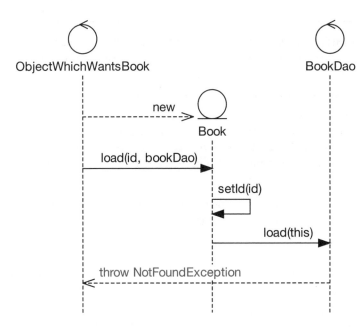

Figure 9-4. *Narrowing the number of possible defects*

Designer: If we're taking this approach throughout the design, we could get rid of the findByID() method altogether, which means we don't have to test for it, and so on.

Reviewer: It's a good thing we decided to design the system in detail before we began coding, then! *(The finished, updated sequence diagram is shown in Figure 9-7.)*

CDR for the "Write Customer Review" Use Case

As it turns out, several questions are raised by the sequence diagram for the *Write Customer Review* use case. These questions lead to some further issues that need to be tightened up before we move to code. We cover these questions in the next few sections, and then we show the updated diagrams.

For the sequence diagram that's being reviewed here, refer back to Figure 8-11, and for the class diagram, refer back to Figure 8-17.

Should the Sequence Diagram Be Invoking a Login Use Case?

In the next part of the review, a question arises about whether it's OK to invoke a use case from a sequence diagram—and what that actually even means, in practice.

Reviewer: Let's look at the first alternate course, "User not logged in." Rather than saying "take user to Login JSP" and drawing a message arrow to the Dispatcher servlet (at the bottom of Figure 8-11), it would make more sense to invoke a separate *Login* use case.

Tip   To show a use case being invoked, simply add a note to the sequence diagram with text such as "Invoke *Login* use case and then restart sequence diagram." Or if your modeling tool supports it, drag the use case directly onto the sequence diagram.

Designer: I guess that would make more sense. It might be a bit unclear what's invoking the use case, so the note could read "`CustomerSession` invokes the *Login* use case . . ." I think the diagram should still show the login check, but then invoke a separate use case to handle the case where the user needs to log in.

Reviewer: Actually, invoking a use case isn't the same thing as making a software function call at all. It just means you jump from one scenario into another.

Designer: Uh-huh.

Reviewer: Hey, while we're at it, we could even separate out the login check as well as the actual login.

Designer: Well, remember that the user doesn't have to be logged in for *all* the use cases in the Internet Bookstore. You can search for books, view book details, that sort of thing. It's only when you want to update stuff—write a review, buy a book, or whatever—that you need to be logged in.

Reviewer: So you're saying we should keep the login check in each diagram where it's performed, but separate the actual login part into a separate use case? OK, let's run with that.

Why Is "Book" Unused on the Sequence Diagram?

If you find an object sitting all on its own on the sequence diagram, without any messages being passed to it, it's likely that you've discovered a part of the design that hasn't been thought through in sufficient detail. Questioning the object's existence can uncover all manner of design questions, as our reviewer and designer now find out.

Reviewer: Over on the right of the sequence diagram (see Figure 8-11), you create a new `Book` instance, and then (near the center of the diagram) you pass the new instance into `WriteCustomerReviewCommand`. However, `Book` itself isn't used at all. You can determine this by the simple observation that no message arrows point at `Book`.

Designer: Yikes, you're right. So, we could fix it by simply removing `Book` from the diagram. But it makes me wonder why `Book` appeared on there at all if it isn't even used.

Reviewer: This has happened because the use case text and the robustness diagram don't match. The use case doesn't mention that "the system sets the book ID on the review" . . . therefore, the sequence diagram doesn't have a `setBookId()` method on it. This would have been caught if we'd done the "highlighter test" on the robustness diagram.

Designer: Here's the thing, though: I'm still not sure if we even need Book at all here. From an implementation standpoint, the book ID would be passed in via the URL, something like this: *(Jumps up and starts scribbling on the whiteboard)*

```
www.pretendbookstore.com/review.jsp?bookID=1234
```

Reviewer: So you're saying that you would never have to actually get Book to retrieve its ID, because you've already got it?

Designer: Exactly.

Reviewer: Except that now we're missing a validation step: checking that the ID really exists in the database. But perhaps more important, the fact that we're talking about removing Book raises an alarm bell, kind of. It suggests to me that we're not following a responsibility-driven approach to the design—that is, designing around the domain classes.

Designer: *(Thinks for a minute)* How about this? We could use Book to validate whether the ID exists in the database. We'd do something like create a Book instance, set its ID from the incoming request, and then call a method on it called doesBookIDExist() to make sure it's in the database.

Reviewer: That's the sort of thing. Or we could call a load() method, which throws a NotFoundException if the book ID doesn't exist.

Designer: OK, that would also make it more consistent with the *Show Book Details* use case, I guess.

Reviewer: In fact, you're right, we already solved this problem. We can reuse the design from the previous use case. *(See Figure 9-4.)*

WriteCustomerReviewCommand Seems Redundant

It's easy to simply accept design decisions that are pushed on you by your application framework. But holding a CDR, in which reviewers question the design from different angles, can often result in an improved design.

Reviewer: Looking at the class diagram *(see excerpt in Figure 9-5)*, it seems like WriteCustomerReviewCommand is just a wrapper class around the CustomerReview entity. Is the Command class really needed?

Designer: It's part of the Spring design. When you get an input from a form, the form data must be encapsulated in a command object, hence WriteCustomerReviewCommand. The command object gets populated from the form fields, then validated, and then passed into the controller. The controller then transfers the data from the command class to the domain object, which we then save to the database.

Reviewer: So we need to keep a command class of some sort; fair enough. But could you use CustomerReview itself as the command class?

Designer: Let me take a look at the design. Actually, yes, that could simplify things and still fit within the Spring "design way."

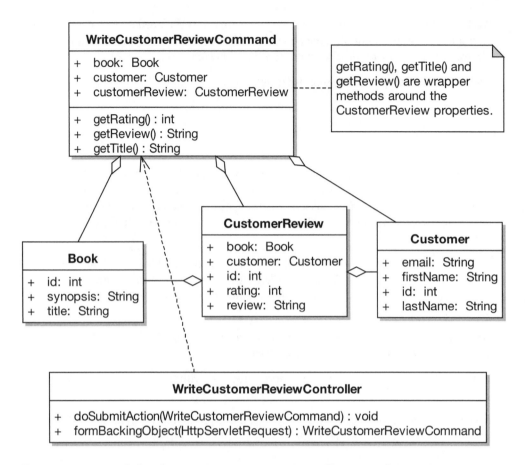

Figure 9-5. *Command class for WriteCustomerReviewController, pre-prefactoring*

Reviewer: One other thing while we're looking at this particular diagram: At this stage of the design process, we really should have identified the multiplicity for all these kinds of relationships and added them onto the diagram.

The updated class diagram excerpt is shown in Figure 9-6. As you can see, simply eliminating that strange "wrapper" class makes the design much cleaner, reducing the number of dependencies between classes.

■Exercise If you compare Figure 9-6 with the domain model shown back in Figure 2-7, there's an error to do with aggregation. Can you spot what it is? (We revisit the error during the Code Review and Model Update in Chapter 11; see the fixed diagram in Figure 11-9.)

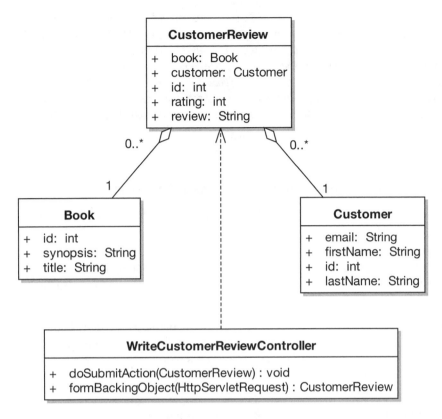

Figure 9-6. *Command class for WriteCustomerReviewController, after prefactoring and with multiplicity added in for good measure*

SEARCHING FOR A STABLE SET OF ABSTRACTIONS

In the old days, before refactoring replaced up-front design, it used to be a goal of a development team to minimize the amount of code breakage and rewriting that happened over time, as these activities were deemed quite costly. This perception of costliness has changed (hey, change is free!), but perhaps not the reality.

If you're trying to minimize code breakage and resultant refactoring, you want to try really hard to identify the most stable set of abstractions you can find, and then organize your code around those abstractions that will change the least as your system evolves over time. This leads to a resilient architecture that doesn't break when small changes happen.

Which abstractions should you choose? The use cases? The requirements? The feature set of the program? The feature set of the framework? The data model? The answer is . . . none of the above. You really want to **base the key abstractions in the code on true statements about the problem domain, because the problem domain winds up being the most stable.**

Consider the Internet Bookstore example. You want to sell books on the Internet and give people the ability to view details of the books, and to read and write reviews of the books. Visitors need to be able to search a book catalog to find the book they want. So a catalog has books, and the books have details, which include reviews.

You can add a new use case to your design, you can change the database from SQL Server to Oracle, a new release of Spring Framework can come out that changes how the MVC paradigm works, and the requirement to rate books between one and five stars can expand to six stars. *But you're still selling books on the Internet, and users are still searching catalogs, viewing book details, and writing reviews.*

So if you organize the behavior of the software around these abstractions, your architecture will prove resilient to change. How do you accomplish this? Follow a responsibility-driven approach and allocate behavior into the domain classes.

Is the Save Method on CustomerReviewDao or JdbcCustomerReviewDao?

A CDR can also help to ensure that the team truly understands the design that they're proposing.

Reviewer: Hmm, I'm not sure if your sequence diagram matches the class diagram. The sequence diagram shows WriteCustomerReviewController calling the "save" method on JdbcCustomerReviewDao. But on the class diagram, the method is actually on CustomerReviewDao.

Designer: Yep, CustomerReviewDao is the interface, but the method is actually implemented in JdbcCustomerReviewDao. It seemed sort of redundant to show the same method twice on the class diagram. You can infer from looking at the diagram that if it's defined in the interface, then the nonabstract implementing class *must* also have it. A bit too subtle, perhaps?

Reviewer: Depends on your audience. Think about it: if you have to take the time to explain the method's absence, then would its inclusion have really been redundant?

Designer: I guess I had been wondering if the sequence diagram should have CustomerReviewDao on it instead of the concrete JDBC class. Do we want the sequence diagram to be showing the JDBC implementation, or a slightly more generic version that would work if we switched to some other persistence/ORM toolkit (which is where the DAO approach with all its interfaces and abstractions finally comes in handy)?

Reviewer: Well, we're designing a solution here, not an abstract framework. So let's keep the concrete class, JdbcCustomerReviewDao, on the sequence diagram.

The Entity Classes Don't Have Any Attributes

Finally, the CDR is an effective technique for discovering areas in the **analysis space** that haven't been fully explored.

Reviewer: Looking at the class diagram *(see Figure 8-17)*, we have Book, Customer, and CustomerReview, but all three classes are totally empty. What gives?

Designer: I was driving the methods and fields from the actions on the sequence diagram and from the use case text. The situation didn't come up where I "identified" that they needed any attributes (or operations for that matter), so I left them off.

Reviewer: If you know that a class needs an attribute, add it to the class diagram! It's your last chance to do so before coding. You identified the attributes—book ID, title, and so on—partly in the use case text, and also (if there were any) in the page specs and prototypes. These are all added to the domain model as it gets fleshed out and transforms into the detailed static model.

■**Tip** You should identify attributes and add them to their classes during robustness analysis. You then *put the functions where the data lives* (one of the essential thought processes of OOD) as you draw the sequence diagrams. You'll also find that your understanding of the domain model is increased greatly by going through the exercise of putting attributes on the classes.

You can also identify attributes from functional requirements. If the project is using an existing data model, you should use this to identify which fields go in your entity classes. Another good source is your GUI prototype/storyboard. Fields on screens often imply attributes on entity classes.

The Updated Bookstore Diagrams

Figure 9-7 shows the sequence diagram for the *Show Book Details* use case, and Figure 9-8 shows the sequence diagram for the *Write Customer Review* use case, which have both been updated following the CDR.

Exercise If you've been paying close attention to the details of the Spring "command" mechanism, you'll notice a flaw in the sequence diagram in Figure 9-7. (Fairly major hint: Look at Book its ID.) See if you can spot the flaw. We'll let slip another hint when we look at the source code for BookDetailsController in Chapter 10, and then we'll revisit and fix the error during the Code Review and Model Update in Chapter 11.

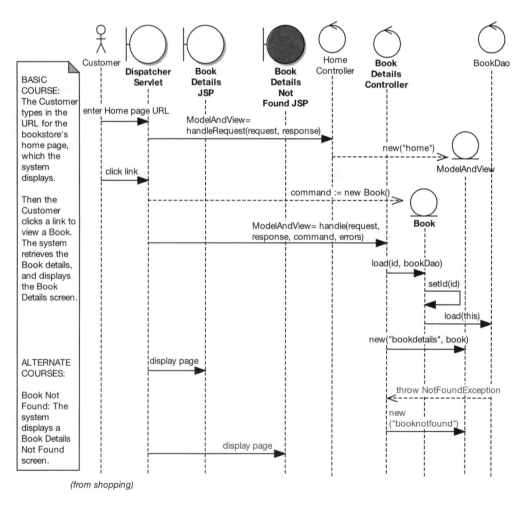

Figure 9-7. *Updated sequence diagram for the* Show Book Details *use case*

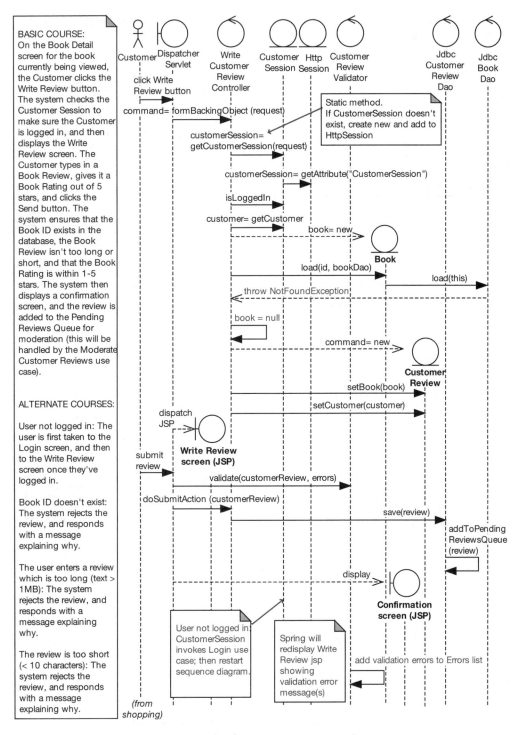

Figure 9-8. *Updated sequence diagram for the* Write Customer Review *use case*

While you update the sequence diagram, you should also update the static model. The finished class diagram is shown in Figure 9-9.

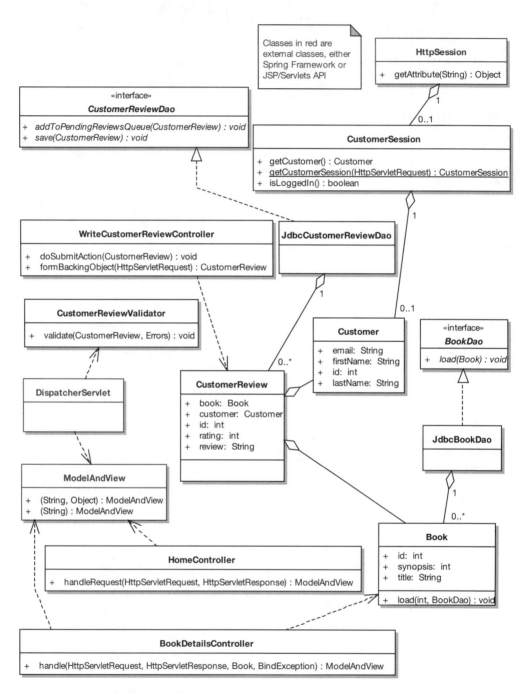

Figure 9-9. *Updated static model following the CDR*

█Exercise As we mentioned earlier in this chapter (for Figure 9-6), Figure 9-9 shows an aggregation error if you compare it with the domain model diagram (see Figure 2-7). If you couldn't find the error earlier on, try again here. (We revisit the error during the Code Review and Model Update in Chapter 11.)

The changes to this diagram aren't as severe as the changes to the sequence diagrams. However, a couple of things have changed (see the original in Figure 8-17). `WriteCustomerReviewCommand`, of course, has disappeared; instead, `CustomerReview` itself is being used as the command class. The `Book`, `Customer`, and `CustomerReview` entities now have attributes (meaning that when you're coding, you won't need to guess what they are). `BookDao` has a new method, `doesBookIdExist(int)`, which came straight from the sequence diagram. And following the *Show Book Details* CDR, `BookDetailsCommand` has disappeared altogether. We've also moved some of the classes around to tidy up the layout.

█Caution It's useful to tidy up class diagrams so that the layout is clearer. But try not to spend hours tinkering with the layout until it's so tidy and symmetrical it could be mistaken for a map of midtown Manhattan. Class diagrams just aren't meant to be about that—they're about showing a structural overview of the code you're about to write.

Notice how the `Customer` entity doesn't have a `CustomerDao`. This is because we're skimping somewhat on the security concerns for this example, but in a real-world project you'd expect to see a `CustomerDao`, which `CustomerSession` uses to lookup the "real" customer IDs.

Summary

In this chapter, we looked at the Critical Design Review (CDR), an important milestone that takes place between detailed design and implementation. As we discussed at the start of this chapter, the CDR involves three main goals:

- Matching the use case text with its sequence diagram
- Checking for continuity of messages
- Reviewing for good design

If you've gone through the detailed design for each use case and reviewed it for these three criteria, then your design really should be fighting-fit now and easily ready for coding.

In the next chapter, we delve into implementation. If you have your detailed design right (as verified by the CDR milestone), then implementation should be a relatively short and straightforward process. For this reason, we focus mainly on coding the Internet Bookstore example, so that you can see how the code is driven directly from the sequence diagrams and detailed class diagrams.

Figure 9-10 shows where we are (the areas covered in this chapter are shown in red).

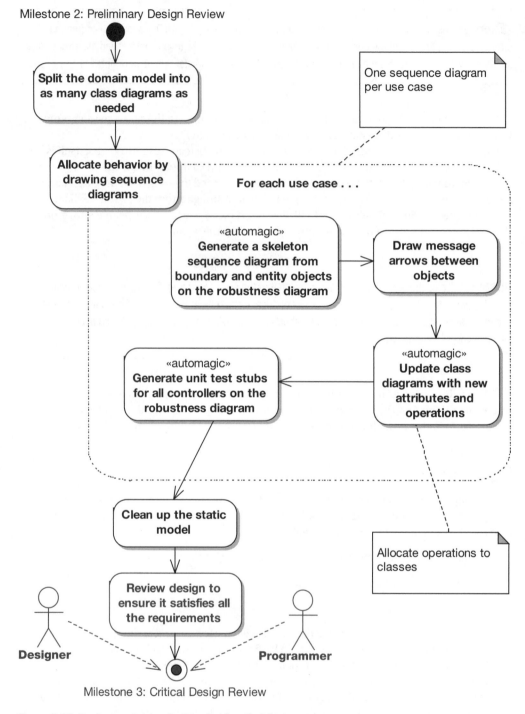

Figure 9-10. *Review activities during the detailed design stage*

CHAPTER 10

■ ■ ■

Implementation: Getting from Detailed Design to Code

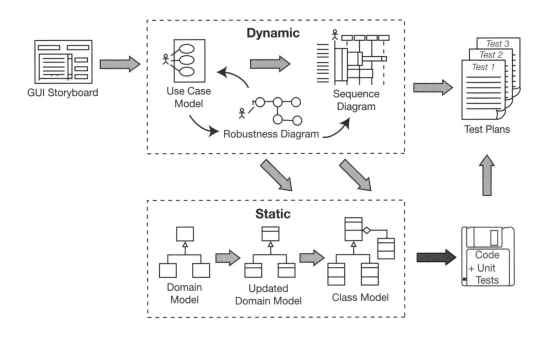

If you've gone through all the effort to create a nice, detailed design, it pays to have a good idea about how to translate that detailed design into source code (and unit tests, of course; see Chapter 12). In this chapter, we walk through two of the use cases for the Internet Bookstore and show a systematic method of taking them from sequence diagrams to source code.

The 10,000-Foot View

Assuming you've done a good job with your analysis and design, you can expect coding to be a nice, straightforward process. But you must continue to keep a close eye on your users' requirements and, of course, on the design itself. However, if any part of the design turns out to be wrong once you've begun coding, don't hesitate to correct it.

The effort you've put into the design should make your life a lot easier, but it isn't sacrosanct.

Programmer-Driven Design

Hopefully the design wasn't handed down to the programmers like an ironclad contract. That sort of arrangement is highly dysfunctional and should be avoided if at all possible. The programmers should have been heavily involved in the design process (better still, they should be driving the design). The programmers will have the greatest insight into the implementation details and the issues that they're likely to face.

Spring Framework

We're targeting Spring Framework for the Internet Bookstore. In this chapter, we show how to implement the Internet Bookstore use cases that we've been following from their inception.

Remember that the process we've described so far can be applied equally well to any object-oriented language. The purpose of this chapter is to provide an example of how to make that last little leap from the detailed design to the source code, to show how it all fits together. Specifically, we'll use Spring Web MVC using JSP for the HTML templating and Spring's JDBC support for data access.

■Note To keep the example from getting too bogged down in Spring-specific details, we've moved some of the heavier explanations into Appendix B.

Implementation in Theory: Getting from Design to Code

Before you begin coding from your design, you need to make sure that you have a sequence diagram for each use case for which you're going to deliver code in the current release, and you need to make sure you've completed the Critical Design Review (CDR; see Chapter 9).

Top 10 Implementation Guidelines

The principles discussed in this chapter can be summed up as a list of guidelines. Our top 10 guidelines list follows.

10. Be sure to drive the code directly from the design.

9. If coding reveals the design to be wrong in some way, change it. But also review the process.

8. Hold regular code inspections.

7. Always question the framework's design choices.

6. Don't let framework issues take over from business issues.

5. If the code starts to get out of control, hit the brakes and revisit the design.

4. Keep the design and the code in sync.

3. Focus on unit testing while implementing the code.

2. Don't overcomment your code (it makes your code less maintainable and more difficult to read).

1. Remember to implement the alternate courses as well as the basic courses.

Let's look at each guideline in turn.

10. Be Sure to Drive the Code Directly from the Design

You've spent the time producing a highly focused, unambiguous, clean, crisp design. Make sure you use it! (However, see the next guideline.)

■**Tip** Try to automate the process, and generate source code, SQL, XML, and so forth directly from the design diagrams whenever possible.

■**Note** You shouldn't attempt to generate SQL from the domain model, which is not a data model. But you can draw out the database schema on a separate diagram and then generate SQL, Data Definition Language (DDL), and so forth from it.

INTERNET BOOKSTORE: GENERATING THE ENTITY CLASSES

All of the entity classes that we need are now nicely filled out with details (attributes and operations) in our Enterprise Architect (EA)[1] model. As luck would have it, EA has some useful code generation features, so it's possible to generate quite a bit of the source code directly from the model. Note that other CASE tools such as Together,[2] Rational XDE,[3] and so on also offer code generation features. It's also possible to use a "dedicated" code generator such as the open-source XDoclet[4] or the commercial JGenerator[5] to do a lot of the grunt work for you.

For each entity class, we need to generate several classes to be used by Spring: the "plain" entity class itself (a very simple JavaBean consisting mainly of getters and setters; although recall from the review chapters that this was something of a bone of contention between the reviewer and the designer!), a Data Access Object (DAO, actually an interface), and an implementation of the DAO. The implementation class will use a specific persistence framework (e.g., JDO or Hibernate), which will "plug into" the Spring framework. You can also model your database schema in UML (using classes with a stereotype of `<<table>>`) and generate the SQL that creates the database tables.

This is all fairly mechanical stuff—exactly the sort of thing that computers are designed to be good at—so the more of this that can be automated, the better.

9. If Coding Reveals the Design to Be Wrong in Some Way, Change It

As soon as you realize that something has gone wrong, there's no point continuing on the basis that it might get better once you bury the problem under several thousand more lines of code. Instead, fix the design immediately and bring the code and the design back in sync.

But it's also important to **review the design process that led up to the error**. Check the milestones listed at the end of each chapter in this book. Were the use cases fully disambiguated? Is there a tight enough link between the use case text and the object model? And so on.

8. Hold Regular Code Inspections

Give each programmer the space needed to concentrate and write error-free code. But do make sure that everyone in the team is keeping to the design and following the same coding conventions. The code inspection can be a part of the Code Review and Model Update that we illustrate in Chapter 11.

1. See www.sparxsystems.com.au and also www.iconixsw.com.
2. See www.borland.com/together.
3. See www-306.ibm.com/software/awdtools/developer/rosexde.
4. XDoclet is a code generation engine that operates by placing tags in your Java code. Visit http://xdoclet.sourceforge.net/xdoclet for more information.
5. JGenerator is an enterprise software automation tool from Javelin Software. Visit www.javelinsoft.com/jgenerator for more information.

7. Always Question the Framework's Design Choices

If people didn't question the design choices made by the creators of their target platform, we would all still be writing horribly slow, fine-grained entity beans that cause expensive network traffic for every single method call. If a particular design decision that the framework forces upon you is questionable, look for better ways of approaching the problem, and if necessary choose a different framework.

Speaking of frameworks . . .

6. Don't Let Framework Issues Take Over from Business Issues

The moment that framework design issues start to drive the shape of the finished product instead of the customer's business requirements, something has gone wrong. It gives a whole different meaning to the term "inversion of control."

In fact, we often question the wisdom of using a framework at all. The framework is ultimately there to save you from having to write the same "plumbing" code over and over—in other words, it's there to save time and effort. If the framework you've chosen for your project demands that you jump through crazy design-pattern hoops, fill out reams of XML forms in triplicate, and sacrifice a stray cat on the second Tuesday of every month, it's time to hit the panic button and think about alternatives.

5. If the Code Starts to Get out of Control, Hit the Brakes and Revisit the Design

Actually, if you've followed all the steps we've suggested up until now, and the code is still getting out of control, you probably have some serious issues to address. Like, for example, are the programmers ignoring the design completely?

Once you've done detailed sequence and class diagrams, programming should mostly involve filling in the algorithmic details for relatively small methods that reside within highly cohesive classes. Pretty much the whole point of everything you've done up to this point is to prevent the code from getting out of control, so if you find that it is, pause, take a giant step backward, take a couple of deep breaths, and address the underlying issues on your project. Try to answer this question: *What went wrong?*

a) Your team didn't do a good design (and you didn't correct it in the design review).

b) Your programmers ignored the good design and "went cowboy."

c) Your programmers didn't participate in the design process.

d) b + c.

e) All of the above.

4. Keep the Design and the Code in Sync

Some development processes actually advise you to let the code "escape" from the design and take its own course, and only to update the design when its obsolescence starts to "hurt."[6] Presumably this means when you discover that half your team has written to completely the wrong set of interfaces because the design model was out of date . . .

---

6. Scott W. Ambler, *Agile Modeling: Effective Practices for eXtreme Programming and the Unified Process* (Hoboken, NJ: John Wiley & Sons, 2002), p. 66.

We much prefer to keep the design and the code in sync. If you've kept the design lean and concentrated on keeping it grounded in reality, then keeping the design model in sync with the developing code really shouldn't take very long—and it shouldn't need to be done all that often.

MDG INTEGRATION FOR ECLIPSE AND FOR VISUAL STUDIO 2005

If you're using Eclipse or Microsoft Visual Studio 2005, an amazing way of keeping the design model and the code in sync is to use Sparx Systems' MDG Integration plug-in.[7] The plug-in allows you to edit and navigate your UML model from inside the IDE, and generate code from your detailed design.

The plug-in will also reverse-engineer your code to synchronize it with the design. You can change your UML model and push those changes into the IDE, or you can edit the code in the IDE and push the changes back into your model. You can also use the UML model to browse instantly to an operation on a class by double-clicking the operation in the UML browser.

As you can probably imagine, we see tools like this as being key components in the implementation and Code Review and Model Update stages of your project, because it's now possible to right-click a class to synchronize model and code. The tool syncs up one class/method at a time, incrementally. There just isn't any excuse for letting the model and code get out of sync anymore!

3. Focus on Unit Testing While Implementing the Code

It's a good idea to write the unit tests as you write the code. That way, you can verify that your code works as expected and fix any bugs as they're introduced, instead of having to try and track them down later.

■**Tip** The tests can also be used to ensure that all of the use case scenarios have been implemented. We demonstrate a technique for doing this in Chapter 12.

2. Don't Overcomment Your Code

Overcommenting your code makes it less maintainable and more difficult to read. If the code is well designed and you follow a decent naming convention, it should be possible to see what the code is doing just by reading it (now there's a concept!).

---

7. See www.iconixsw.com/EA/MDGLinkIntegration.html. At the time of this writing, Sparx Systems is about to release an Eclipse version of this plug-in for Java developers. It will be released before this book goes to press.

For example, a block of code with a comment above it like this:

```
// Wait for the request data to become available:
. . .
```

could be moved out to a separate method called waitForRequestData(), and the comment could be deleted.

You shouldn't need comments that narrate what the code is doing step by step; the most useful comments generally explain the intent behind the code. But even then, often the very fact that you need to add a comment may be a warning sign that the design itself needs to be less obtuse.

Tip Where comments in code are needed to describe the intent behind the code, consider that as long as you've followed the process described in this book, it should be very easy to determine which use case scenario is being implemented by comparing the code with the static model and the use case text, so quite often, no comment is required.

---

1. Remember to Implement the Alternate Courses As Well As the Basic Courses

This point carries over from the detailed design. Recall from Chapter 8 that it's vital to include the alternate courses on your sequence diagrams, so that all the bases are covered. Once you begin coding from the design, you'll quickly thank yourself for having done this work, as there shouldn't now be any nasty surprises lurking in the design—no "Oh my gosh, we didn't take into account what happens if the user cancels at this point!" leading to additional (unscheduled and undesigned) development work.

Similarly, having spent the time identifying and then designing the alternate courses, you do need to make sure you remember to implement them all. The use case scenarios form a handy checklist for making sure that none of the alternate courses have been missed.

Implementation in Practice: Internet Bookstore

Without further ado, let's leap into the Internet Bookstore implementation, starting with the database tables that we'll be using.

Creating the Database

We've created a very straightforward database to develop and test against. Figure 10-1 shows the database tables and the relationships between them.

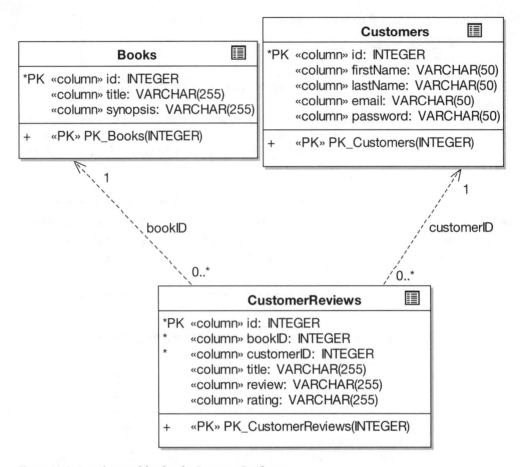

Figure 10-1. *Database tables for the Internet Bookstore*

And then to create the database, we use some SQL along the lines of the following:

```
CREATE TABLE Books (
  id INTEGER NOT NULL IDENTITY PRIMARY KEY,
  title VARCHAR(255),
  synopsis VARCHAR(255)
);
CREATE INDEX books_title ON Books(title);

-- and so on . . .
```

It's also useful to create some test data, which we'll put in another SQL script. As you can see, our bookstore has something for everyone, as long as everyone is a Harry Potter fan:[8]

---

8. Avid Harry Potter fans will instantly notice that this is "Philosopher's Stone" in the UK and "Sorcerer's Stone" in the United States.

```
// Insert bookstore data:

INSERT INTO Books (id, title, synopsis)
  VALUES
(101, 'Harry Potter and the Philosopher's Stone',
  'Harry discovers that he is a wizard.'
);

INSERT INTO Books (id, title, synopsis)
  VALUES
(102, 'Harry Potter and the Chamber of Secrets',
  'Harry and chums attempt to solve the mystery of the Chamber of Secrets.'
);

-- etc . . .
```

■Note If you're following along with the Spring technical details, at this juncture you might want to refer to the "Folder Structure" section in Appendix B, and then the "Java Package Hierarchy" section, also in Appendix B.

Preparing the Style Sheet

The Internet Bookstore project uses one style sheet, bookstore.css, which looks like this:

```
body {
  font-family : Verdana, Arial, Geneva, Helvetica, sans-serif;
  background-color : white;
  font-size : 10pt;
}

.navbar {
  background-color : #CCCCFF;
  border : 1px solid;
  padding : 5px;
}

.error {
  color: #FF0000;
  font-size: 12pt;
}
```

We're sure you've seen a style sheet before, but we're showing you this particular one because of the .error style. It's been said that in any good movie, if the director is going to show a murder, then he or she must introduce the murder weapon at least two scenes earlier. So we're kind of doing that here: you'll see the .error style get used shortly.

Mapping Domain (Entity) Classes to Real Classes

As the domain model evolved and turned into the more detailed static model, the entity classes (i.e., the classes from the domain model) were padded out with attributes (mostly during robustness analysis) and operations (mostly during detailed design). Depending on your target platform, you may or may not be able to map entity classes directly to implementation classes. However, Spring Framework positively thrives on the concept of "pure" domain classes.

■**Note** We discussed this issue in the sidebar "Swarms of Tiny Classes" in Chapter 9.

We'll look at three of the completed entity classes here: Book, Customer, and CustomerReview.

Figure 10-2 shows part of the static model that contains these three entity classes (the full static model is in Figure 9-10). Note that each of these classes corresponds well to a row in the database tables shown earlier—***not*** to the entire table.

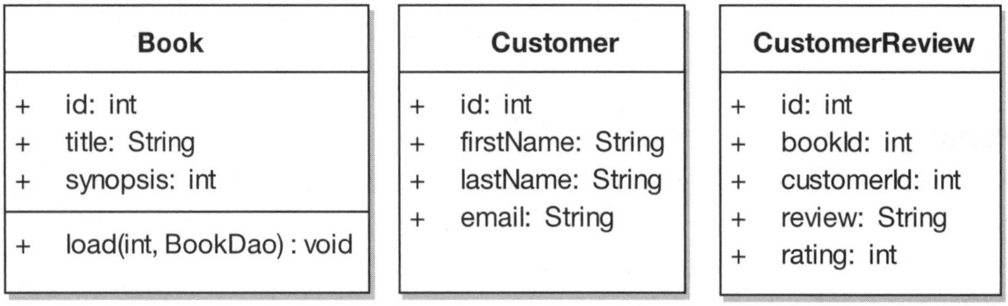

Book
+   id: int   +   title: String   +   synopsis: int
+   load(int, BookDao) : void

Customer
+   id: int   +   firstName: String   +   lastName: String   +   email: String

CustomerReview
+   id: int   +   bookId: int   +   customerId: int   +   review: String   +   rating: int

Figure 10-2. *The three entity classes from the static model*

■**Note** Considering that it represents incoming book reviews, CustomerReview is still somewhat lacking in personality—that is to say, it exhibits no behavior whatsoever. As we've discussed, moving the validation logic into CustomerReview (where it really does belong) would go a long way toward fixing this problem. We'll revisit this part of the design in Chapter 11.

In Figure 10-2, we've suppressed the getters and setters for each of the properties, but when we generate the Java code from these classes, the get and set methods will be generated for us.

Here's Book.java, generated directly from the static model:

```
package com.iconixsw.bookstore.domain;

import java.io.*;

public class Book implements Serializable {

    private int id;
    private String title;
    private String synopsis;

    public Book() {
    }

    public int getId() { return id; }
    public void setId(int id) { this.id = id; }

    public String getTitle() { return title; }
    public void setTitle(String title) { this.title = title; }

    public String getSynopsis() { return synopsis; }
    public void setSynopsis(String synopsis) {
        this.synopsis = synopsis;
    }

    public void load(int id, BookDao bookDao) {
    }
}
```

There are several points to keep in mind with this code:

- The load method has been generated as an empty method, leaving us to fill in the gap, which we'll do shortly.

- Book doesn't extend any particular class, because (unlike other enterprise application frameworks), Spring doesn't force us to use its own class hierarchy—at least not for entity classes. This is the essence of Spring's "lightweight framework" approach: your entity classes are very simple "beans" that can be instantiated independently of Spring if needed (e.g., for unit testing).

Customer and CustomerReview are, at this stage at least, a similarly not-too-interesting sea of getters and setters, so we'll spare you those and press on to the more interesting stuff.

As the project builds up a head of steam and additional use cases are implemented, we would also add new properties and operations to these entity classes; for example, Book might also get an author (or authorCollection) property and some "business-level" book handling behavior. However, we only add these properties and methods as and when we encounter them in the use cases. It's important not to add code prospectively, just in case it will be needed later. Luckily, you'll be able to see exactly what needs to be added because you'll have mapped out the use cases and the design beforehand.

Now that we have the preliminaries out of the way, let's take a look at the first of our two use cases and turn it into working source code.

Implementing the "Show Book Details" Use Case

We'll start with the simpler of the two use cases, *Show Book Details*. To refresh your memory, here's the basic course:

> *The Customer types in the URL for the bookstore's home page, which the system displays. Then the Customer clicks a link to view a Book. The system retrieves the Book details, and displays them on the Book Details page.*

The completed sequence diagram for this use case is shown in Figure 9-7.

So, the first page we need to implement is the bookstore's home page. According to the class diagram in Figure 9-9, we need a HomeController class that tells Spring to display home.jsp.

HomeController

HomeController is about as simple a controller as it's possible to get. It's simply there to return the main ("home") view page, so it doesn't do a huge amount. Figure 10-3 shows HomeController from the static model (ModelAndView is shown in red because it's an "external" class—part of the Spring framework).

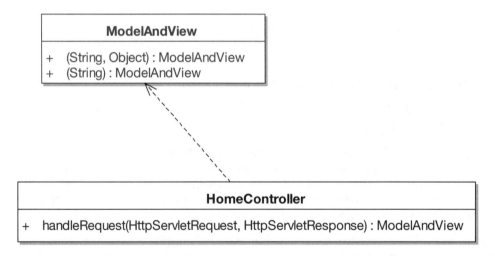

Figure 10-3. *HomeController from the static model*

We need to define homeController in bookstore-servlet.xml, like this:

```
<bean id="homeController"
     class="com.iconixsw.bookstore.web.HomeController"/>
```

This declaration is saying that we want a single instance of the class HomeController, and if it's to be referred to by other beans in the XML configuration, it shall be referred to using the ID homeController.

Next, here's the class in its entirety:

```
package com.iconixsw.bookstore.web;

// import statements omitted . . .

public class HomeController implements Controller {

    public ModelAndView handleRequest(
                        HttpServletRequest request,
                        HttpServletResponse response)
    throws ServletException, IOException
    {
        return new ModelAndView("home");
    }

}
```

It really is about as simple as the archetypal "Hello World" Java program. All it does is return a new `ModelAndView` object, primed with the word "home." This tells Spring's `DispatcherServlet`, in effect, to forward the request to `home.jsp`, which will then be displayed to the user.

The Home Page: home.jsp

Here's `home.jsp`, which will be the first page that the user sees when visiting the website:

```
<%@ include file="include/IncludeTop.jsp" %>

<h2>Welcome to our streamlined Internet Bookstore.</h2>

<p>
  We offer a comprehensive range of books, from Harry Potter to Harry Potter.
</p>
<p>
  You can <a href="search.jsp">search for books</a>; or alternatively browse
  using our bestseller list below, or 'drill down' through our
  list of categories.
</p>

<lu>
  <li>
    <a href="bookdetails.htm?id=101">
      Harry Potter and the Philosopher's Stone
    </a>
  </li>
```

```
<li>
  <a href="bookdetails.htm?id=102">
    Harry Potter and the Chamber of Secrets
  </a>
</li>

<!-- etc . . . -->
</lu>

</body>
</html>
```

The first line of home.jsp invokes the IncludeTop.jsp file, which gives us the consistent top section of the page. Then there's some introductory blurb and a link to a search page (search.jsp, which we haven't implemented for this example).

The bulk of the page consists of a list of links to "book details" pages for each of the books in our catalog. Each link points to bookdetails.htm (a "virtual" page that will map to BookDetailsController) and includes an ID parameter that will map to the command object (Book). (Quick reminder: During the CDR in Chapter 9, we dropped the BookDetailsCommand class altogether, deciding instead to use Book itself as the command object.)

■**Note** The book list shown in home.jsp is hard-wired, partly because that was what we specified in the *Show Book Details* use case, but also because (given the use cases that we're implementing) it isn't yet time to implement the dynamic functionality we'd need to create an automatically updated selection of books (e.g., a list of top 10 bestsellers).

Later, when it's time to implement the *Search for Books* use case, for example, we could return to this page and turn it into a dynamic list retrieved from the database—something more like what you'd see on the front page of Amazon.com or BarnesAndNoble.com.

We have enough in place to try building the project (what there is of it so far) and deploying the resultant Web Archive (WAR) file to Tomcat. We won't go into the details of the build, as you can get this information from a multitude of Spring books,[9] as well as the Spring website itself.

Figure 10-4 shows the screenshot for the working home page.

---

9. See www.springframework.com/books for a good list of Spring books. We can also highly recommend Matt Raible's book *Spring Live* (SourceBeat, 2005). See www.sourcebeat.com for more information.

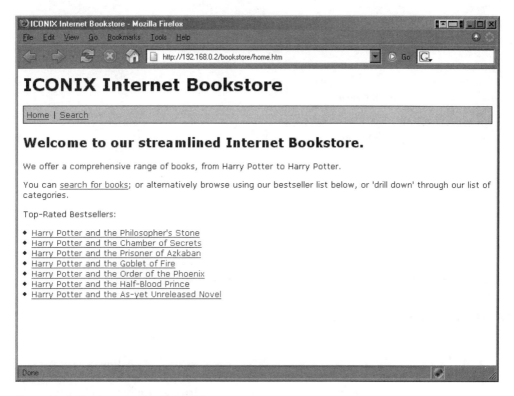

Figure 10-4. *The Internet Bookstore's home page*

Here's the sequence of events that led to the home page being displayed (see Appendix B for the details of how all this is configured in Spring):

1. The browser request `http://<domain>/bookstore/` went to the bookstore web application's default page, `index.jsp`.

2. `index.jsp` forwarded the request to the home page, a virtual page called `home.htm`.

3. This request was picked up by `DispatcherServlet`, which handed the request to `HomeController`.

4. `HomeController` (the equivalent of a "Hello World" Controller) simply returned a `ModelAndView` object pointing to `home.jsp`, and `home.jsp` was then invoked and the result was displayed in the browser (see Figure 10-4).

Clicking one of the book links in `home.jsp` will take the user to the Book Details page for that book. Of course, we still don't have a Book Details page, so our first use case isn't yet complete. Let's fix that next.

Checking the sequence diagram for *Show Book Details* (excerpt shown in Figure 10-6), and the static model (excerpt shown in Figure 10-5), after the user has clicked a Book Details link, `DispatcherServlet` (via various helper classes which it calls behind the scenes) creates a new `Book` object and then passes the request and the new `Book` to `BookDetailsController`, via `BookDetailsController`'s `handle(..)` method.

BookDetailsController

Figure 10-5 shows BookDetailsController from the static model.

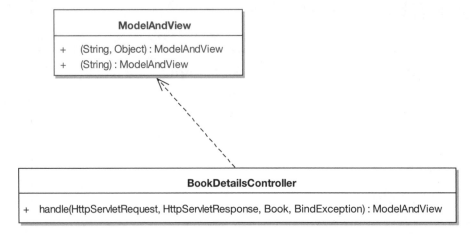

Figure 10-5. *BookDetailsController from the static model*

Figure 10-5 shows that BookDetailsController has a handle() method that returns a ModelAndView. So in our code, we'll need to construct a ModelAndView object. In fact, checking the sequence diagram (detail shown in Figure 10-6), we need to create a ModelAndView pointing to the "bookdetails" view, and—for the alternate course—an alternative ModelAndView pointing to the "booknotfound" view.

Figure 10-6 shows us pretty much exactly what we need to implement in the handle() method, so coding it is almost entirely a mechanical process.

PROGRAMMER == DESIGNER == PROGRAMMER

Of course, we're not trying to push programmers out of a job here—the point is really that detailed design involves thinking like a programmer, just as programming involves thinking like a designer. So detailed design is as much a part of the programmer's job as cutting code is.

However, the big benefit when following this approach is that you'll have separated out the "designing" issues from the "coding" issues to a large extent, and reviewed the design before coding. So, coding itself becomes, in effect, a design review stage: you're validating the design one last time by actually coding it. (As you'll see in Chapter 12, you can also write unit tests following a Design-Driven Testing approach as another form of design validation.)

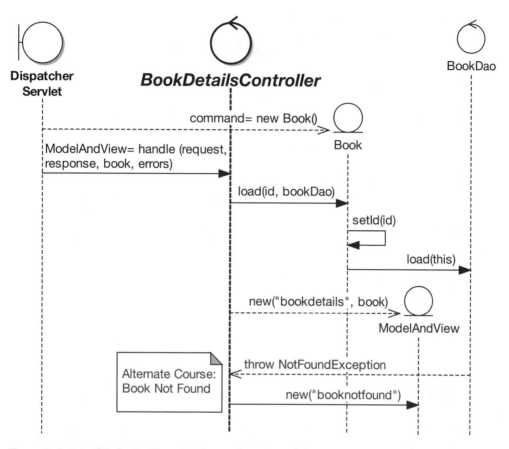

Figure 10-6. *Detail from the* Show Book Details *sequence diagram focused on BookDetailsController*

So, coding from the sequence diagram, here's `BookDetailsController` (the code for the alternate course is shown in red):

```
package com.iconixsw.bookstore.web;

// import all and sundry . . .

public class BookDetailsController extends AbstractCommandController {

    public BookDetailsController() {
        setCommandClass(Book.class);
    }
```

```
protected ModelAndView handle(
            HttpServletRequest request,
            HttpServletResponse response,
            Object command,
            BindException errors) throws Exception {

    Book book = (Book) command;
    try {
        book.load(book.getId(), bookDao);
    }
    catch (NotFoundException e) {
        return new ModelAndView("booknotfound");
    }
    return new ModelAndView("bookdetails", "book", book);
}

public void setBookDao(BookDao bookDao) {
    this.bookDao = bookDao;
}
private BookDao bookDao;


}
```

This extends the Spring class `AbstractCommandController`, indicating that we want to read command objects from the HTTP request (in this case, the book ID parameter). In the constructor, we set the bean class (`Book`) that will be populated.

In the `handle(..)` method, we cast the incoming `command` to a `Book` (which it's safe to do because the command type was set in the constructor). Next, we tell `Book` to go find itself in the database and load its data.

■**Exercise** In the `book.load(..)` line, the fact that we have to tell the `Book` its ID by getting it via `book.getId()` is a warning sign: the code is trying to tell us that something isn't quite right. There's a fairly major clue in the sequence diagram in Figure 10-6 that points to the root cause of the problem—see if you can deduce what it is. The answer will be unveiled during the Code Review and Model Update in Chapter 11.

`handle(..)` finishes by returning a new `ModelAndView` object, which it populates as follows:

- The *view* is "bookdetails," indicating that the view page will be `bookdetails.jsp`.

- The *model* is called "book," indicating that the JSP page will be able to refer to an object called "book," and its value will be the `Book` that we retrieved.

In BookDetailsController, there's a property called bookDao. Notice that there's no getter for this property, as it's used only internally by this class. Also notice that we don't go off and find the value of bookDao anywhere. Instead, we make use of Spring's bean wiring feature to set this automatically for us. (Of course nothing's ever *completely* free, as we still need to tell Spring to do this for us, as you'll see in a moment.)

To add BookDetailsController into the Spring framework and wire it up with the other beans, we need to define it as a bean in bookstore-servlet.xml:

```
<bean id="bookDetailsController"
 class="com.iconixsw.bookstore.web.BookDetailsController">
    <property name="bookDao">
        <ref bean="bookDao" />
    </property>
</bean>
```

In this XML fragment, we've given the bean an ID, bookDetailsController (following the Java object naming convention of lowercase first letter followed by "name case" or "camel case" for the remaining bunched-up words), and we've given it a class, BookDetailsController, in the package com.iconixsw.bookstore.web.

Because we want the controller's bookDao property to be "autopopulated" by Spring, we define it in the XML. bookDao refers to another bean (also called bookDao), which we define in bookstore-servlet.xml as follows:

```
<bean id="bookDao"
class="com.iconixsw.bookstore.dao.jdbc.JdbcBookDao"
lazy-init="true">
    <property name="dataSource">
        <ref local="dataSource"/>
    </property>
</bean>
```

This in turn has a dataSource property that refers to a bean, also called dataSource, which configures the JDBC database connection.

Earlier, we showed the empty Book.load() method, which was generated for us. We can now populate this method (compare this code with the sequence diagram excerpt in Figure 10-6):

```
public void load(int id, BookDao bookDao) throws NotFoundException {
    setId(id);
    bookDao.load(this);
}
```

What else needs to be implemented for this use case? Checking the sequence diagram excerpt in Figure 10-6, we also need BookDao (the interface) and JdbcBookDao (the concrete class). Figure 10-7 shows an excerpt from the static model focused on BookDao.

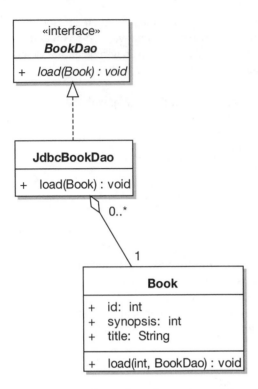

Figure 10-7. *BookDao from the static model*

JdbcBookDao is used in both the *Show Book Details* and *Write Customer Review* sequence diagrams. The Java code for the DAO interface is pretty straightforward, as it currently defines only one method:

```
package com.iconixsw.bookstore.dao;

import com.iconixsw.bookstore.domain.Book;
import org.springframework.dao.DataAccessException;

public interface BookDao {
    public void load(Book book) throws DataAccessException;
}
```

We won't go into the details of the JDBC implementation as it's code-heavy and doesn't add a huge amount to the discussion, but if you're interested, the complete example can be downloaded from the book's web page.

So, that's basically it for this use case. There's more explanation than code here, so it might seem more complex than it really is. All that's left is bookdetails.jsp (the view), which is the fun part.

The View: bookdetails.jsp

Here's bookdetails.jsp in all its brevity:

```
<%@ include file="include/IncludeTop.jsp" %>

<h2><c:out value="${book.title}"/></h2>
<p><c:out value="${book.synopsis}"/></p>

<p>
  <a href="writecustomerreview.htm?bookid=<c:out value="${book.id}"/>">
    Write a review of this book
  </a>
</p>

</body>
</html>
```

Let's look at the first three lines in bookdetails.jsp:

- The first line invokes IncludeTop.jsp, which gives us the top half of the page.

- The second line displays a heading with the book's title. The c:out tag is part of JSTL; c:out allows us to output the value of bean properties. The "book" bean (referred to in ${book.title}) was returned by BookDetailsController in the ModelAndView object, effectively making it available in the JSP page.

- The third line displays a synopsis of the book. Then we see a link to the page for writing a review of the book, which we cover in the next use case.

Figure 10-8 shows the screenshot for the Book Details page.

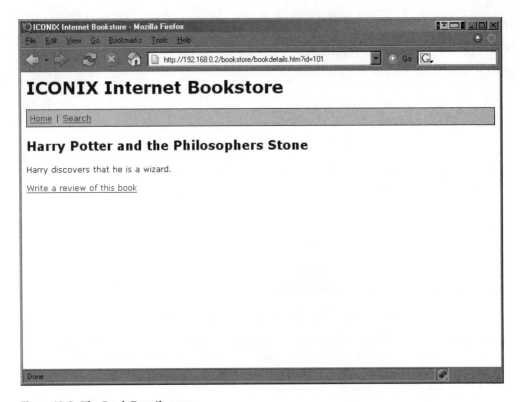

Figure 10-8. *The Book Details page*

Implementing the "Write Customer Review" Use Case

In this section, we walk through the *Write Customer Review* use case in much the same way we just did for *Show Book Details*. To refresh your memory, here's the basic course for this use case:

> On the Book Detail screen for the book currently being viewed, the Customer clicks the Write Review button. The system checks the Customer Session to make sure the Customer is logged in, and then it displays the Write Review screen. The Customer types in a Book Review, gives it a Book Rating out of five stars, and clicks the Send button. The system ensures that the Book Review isn't too long or short, and that the Book Rating is within one and five stars. The system then displays a confirmation screen, and the review is added to the Pending Reviews Queue for moderation (this will be handled by the Moderate Customer Reviews use case).

The fully reviewed, ready-to-code sequence diagram for this use case is shown in Figure 9-8. As you walk through the code, it's useful to simultaneously step through the sequence diagram and compare the two.

WriteCustomerReviewController

Scanning through the sequence diagram from left to right, top to bottom, the first class we need to implement is WriteCustomerReviewController. Figure 10-9 shows part of the static model for this class.

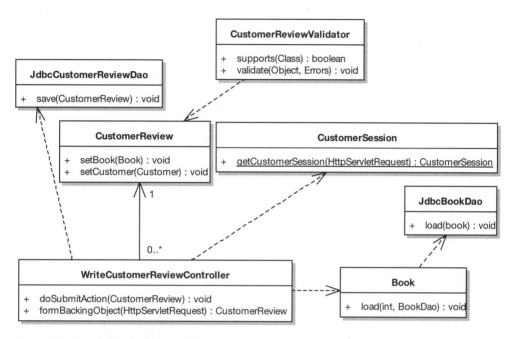

Figure 10-9. *Part of the static model for WriteCustomerReviewController*

■**Note** Peeking ahead slightly, check Figure 11-9 for an updated version of part of this diagram.

The operations assigned to the classes in Figure 10-9 have been derived by stepping mechanically through the relevant parts of the sequence diagram and turning the messages into operations on the class diagram. These in turn, of course, turn into Java methods.

If you recall from Chapters 8 and 9, there's quite a hefty sequence diagram for this use case. So we'll walk through it in several smaller segments, writing the code as we go along.

Figure 10-10 shows the first excerpt from the *Write Customer Review* sequence diagram, focused on the main "form controller" class, WriteCustomerReviewController. ***This class's purpose in life is to process the user's form containing their book review***. To achieve this, the controller must first turn the form data into a domain-level object representation (i.e., a CustomerReview object), and then it must save the new object to the database. Let's walk through the design to achieve this, and turn it into code.

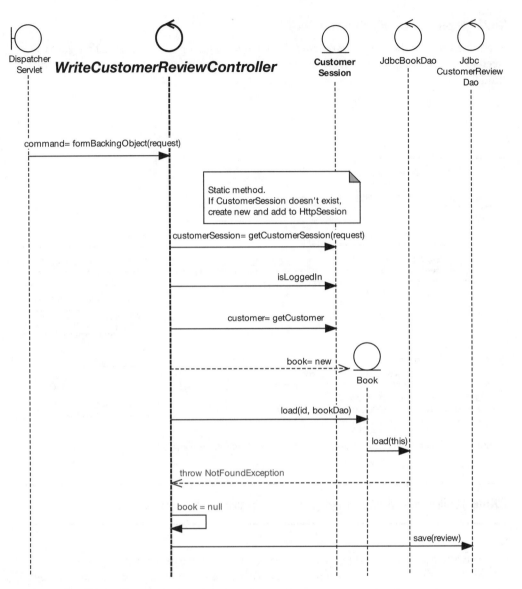

Figure 10-10. *Excerpt from the* Write Customer Review *sequence diagram focused on* WriteCustomerReviewController.formBackingObject()

Figure 10-10 makes it pretty clear what needs to be done. We need to add a method called formBackingObject() to WriteCustomerReviewController. This method will turn the user's incoming review form into a CustomerReview object.

But the class begins with a constructor that defines its command class, CustomerReview:

```
package com.iconixsw.bookstore.web;

// heaps of imports . . .
```

```
public class WriteCustomerReviewController extends SimpleFormController {

    public WriteCustomerReviewController() {
        setCommandClass(CustomerReview.class);
    }
```

■Exercise   The sequence diagram in Figure 10-10 is missing some detail that appears in the code excerpt. See if you can figure out what's missing. The answer can be found in the Code Review and Model Update in Chapter 11.

Next, here's the bulk of the new method, `formBackingObject()`, which essentially needs to return an object representation of the user's submitted form:

```
protected Object formBackingObject(
                HttpServletRequest request)
                throws Exception
{
    CustomerSession customerSession =
                CustomerSession.getCustomerSession(request);
    if (!customerSession.isLoggedIn()) {
        return null;
    }
    Customer customer = customerSession.getCustomer();

    int bookId = RequestUtils.
                getRequiredIntParameter(request, "bookid");
    Book book = new Book();
    try {
        book.load(bookId, bookDao);
    }
    catch (NotFoundException e) {
        book = null;
    }

    . . .

    }
}
```

`formBackingObject()` is passed in the HTTP request, from which we extract the book ID. As in the previous use case, we then call `book.load()` to tell it to go find itself in the database. If it isn't found (the alternate course, shown in red), then we simply set book to null.

Figure 10-11 shows the second excerpt from the *Write Customer Review* sequence diagram.

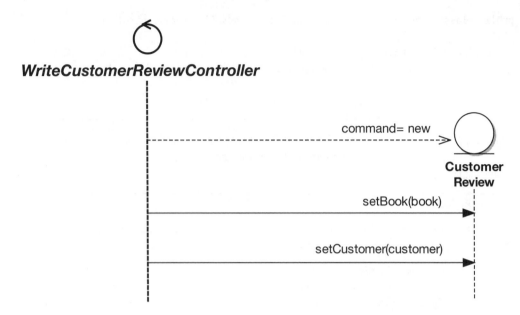

Figure 10-11. *Excerpt from the* Write Customer Review *sequence diagram finishing off* WriteCustomerReviewController. formBackingObject()

Here's the code to implement this part of the sequence diagram, finishing off the formBackingObject() method. Note that the "command" variable has been renamed as "review" in the code. This should be addressed in the following Code Review and Model Update:

```
    .  .  .

    CustomerReview review = new CustomerReview();
    review.setBook(book);
    review.setCustomer(customer);
    return review;
}
```

■**Exercise** formBackingObject has turned into quite a large method. What could be done to it in order to make the code more maintainable? We refactor this part of the code and update the design during the Code Review and Model Update in Chapter 11.

Figure 10-12 shows our third and final excerpt from the *Write Customer Review* sequence diagram.

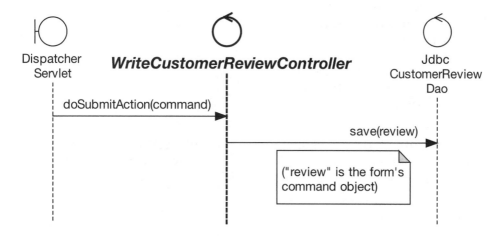

Figure 10-12. *Excerpt from the* Write Customer Review *sequence diagram focusing on* WriteCustomerReviewController. doSubmitAction()

And here's the doSubmitAction() method in its entirety:

```
protected void doSubmitAction(Object command) throws Exception {
    CustomerReview review = (CustomerReview) command;
    customerReviewDao.save(review);
}
```

As the name suggests, doSubmitAction() is called when the form is submitted and it's time to do something about it. The method is called with a command object (the CustomerReview), which we already populated in the formBackingObject() method. Because Spring passes it in as an Object, we must first cast it to a CustomerReview before we can save it.

■**Exercise** As you may recall from the responsibility-driven discussions in Chapter 9, the functions should go where the data lives. So, looking at doSubmitAction(), what should be done to make our code follow this rule of thumb? (You can find the answer in the Code Review and Model Update in Chapter 11.)

But how does this class get its reference to the customerReviewDao—and the bookDao, for that matter? These are set automatically by Spring, via its IoC mechanism. To tell Spring that we want these to be set, they're added to the WriteCustomerReviewController bean definition in bookstore-servlet.xml as follows:

```
<bean id="writeCustomerReviewController"
  class="com.iconixsw.bookstore.web.WriteCustomerReviewController">

    <property name="formView">
        <value>writecustomerreview</value>
    </property>
```

```
        <property name="bookDao">
            <ref bean="bookDao" />
        </property>

        <property name="customerReviewDao">
            <ref bean="customerReviewDao" />
        </property>
    </bean>
```

(We've already added the bookDao bean, and we'll add customerReviewDao in the next section.)

Then in the WriteCustomerReviewController class itself, there are a couple of property setters, which Spring then knows to call for us when the object is first initialized:

```
public void setBookDao(BookDao bookDao) {
    this.bookDao = bookDao;
}

public void setCustomerReviewDao(
        CustomerReviewDao customerReviewDao)
{
    this.customerReviewDao = customerReviewDao;
}

private BookDao bookDao;
private CustomerReviewDao customerReviewDao;
```

Next, let's move on to the new DAO, CustomerReviewDao.

CustomerReviewDao

Figure 10-13 shows the portion of the static model for CustomerReviewDao and its implementing class, JdbcCustomerReviewDao. The diagram also shows the entity class that is the main product of this DAO, CustomerReview.

The static model gives us the structure, but we also need to know in what context the class will be used so that we can figure out what to put in it. For this purpose, Figure 10-14 shows a detail from the *Write Customer Review* sequence diagram that deals with CustomerReviewDao (or more specifically, JdbcCustomerReviewDao).

You can see from Figure 10-14 that there isn't very much interaction with CustomerReviewDao. The only point of contact is when a CustomerReview object needs to be saved, and when it calls a method on itself (addToPendingReviewsQueue()).

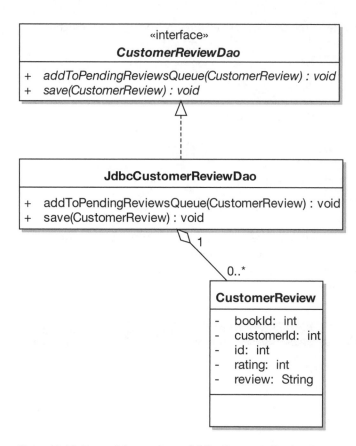

Figure 10-13. *Part of the static model for CustomerReviewDao*

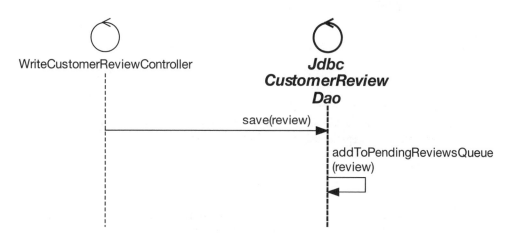

Figure 10-14. *Detail from the* Write Customer Review *sequence diagram focused on JdbcCustomerReviewDao*

Here's the `CustomerReviewDao` Java interface, generated directly from the class diagram:

```
package com.iconixsw.bookstore.dao;

import com.iconixsw.bookstore.domain.*;
import java.util.*;
import org.springframework.dao.DataAccessException;

public interface CustomerReviewDao {

    public void save(CustomerReview review)
        throws DataAccessException;
}
```

This DAO interface defines one method: `save()`. As the name suggests, `save()` writes a `CustomerReview` object to the database. It hardly seems worth defining a class for just one method, but the interface (and implementing JDBC class) will have new methods added to it as new use cases are implemented.

ADDING TO CUSTOMERREVIEWDAO

Later, depending on the use case being implemented, we would expect to add such methods as the following:

```
public CustomerReview findById(int reviewId)
    throws DataAccessException;

public Collection findByCustomerId(int customerId)
    throws DataAccessException;

public Collection findByBookId(int bookId)
    throws DataAccessException;
```

The `findById` method would look up, populate, and return a single `CustomerReview` instance for a specific review ID.

The `findByCustomerId` method, on the other hand, would return a `Collection` of `CustomerReview` objects belonging to a single `Customer`, and `findByBookId` would return a `Collection` of `CustomerReview` objects that were written for one particular `Book`.

We won't cover the `JdbcCustomerReviewDao` implementation here, as it's quite code-heavy. However, if you're interested, you can download the full source code from the book's web page.[10]

---

10. See www.iconixprocess.com.

Finally, we need to tell Spring that the `CustomerReviewDao` bean will actually be a
`JdbcCustomerReviewDao`. We do this via `bookstore-servlet.xml`:

```
<bean id="customerReviewDao"
    class="com.iconixsw.bookstore.dao.jdbc.JdbcCustomerReviewDao"
    lazy-init="true">

    <property name="dataSource">
        <ref local="dataSource"/>
    </property>

</bean>
```

CustomerSession

`CustomerSession`'s purpose in life is to track the login state (and actual `Customer` object) for an
individual `Customer`. Actually, for the purposes of this example, `CustomerSession` is just a pretend class. It does a rattlingly good impersonation of a complete customer authentication
system, as long as your name is Billy Bob and you're always expecting to be logged in.

You can see what methods need to be implemented on `CustomerSession` by checking the
sequence diagram "detail" in Figure 10-15.

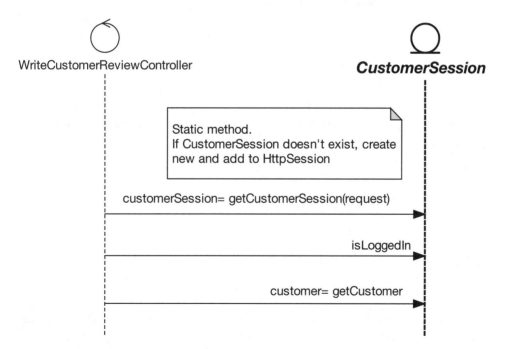

Figure 10-15. *Detail from the* Write Customer Review *sequence diagram focused on
CustomerSession*

Three operations need to be written. Here's CustomerSession with the first method, getCustomerSession(request), added:

```
package com.iconixsw.bookstore.web;

import com.iconixsw.bookstore.domain.*;
import javax.servlet.http.*;

public class CustomerSession {

    public static CustomerSession getCustomerSession(
            HttpServletRequest request) {

        CustomerSession customerSession =
            (CustomerSession) request.getSession().
            getAttribute("CustomerSession");

        if (customerSession == null) {
            // Create new CustomerSession and
            // add it to the HttpSession:
            customerSession = new CustomerSession();
            request.getSession().setAttribute(
                                "CustomerSession",
                                customerSession);
        }
        return customerSession;
    }
}
```

The other two methods, isLoggedIn() and getCustomer(), use a customer field, so we need to add that as well:

```
private Customer customer;

public boolean isLoggedIn() {
    return customer != null;
}

public Customer getCustomer() {
    return customer;
}
```

For the isLoggedIn() check, because this is a fake implementation, we just check to make sure that customer isn't null (i.e., it has been initialized).

Finally, just to reinforce the fact that this is a fake implementation, we need a way of creating a pretend customer out of thin air. To achieve that, there's a "bonus" method called makeFakeCustomer(). We call this method in the constructor to ensure that the customer is always initialized:

```
public CustomerSession() {
    makeFakeCustomer();
}

private void makeFakeCustomer() {
    customer = new Customer();
    customer.setId(1);
    customer.setFirstName("Billy Bob");
    customer.setLastName("Dupree");
    customer.setEmail("billybob@rednecks.xyz");
}
```

Of course, this method always returns the exact same customer, our old friend Billy Bob. However, it's (just about) good enough for early development and testing purposes.

■Note If you're wondering just who the heck Billy Bob is, we encourage you to peek ahead to Chapter 13 to find out.

CustomerReviewValidator

Next, let's create the class that handles the validation of the incoming customer review form. The validate() method checks to see if the review text is empty. This is one of the alternate courses, so that part of the code is shown here in red.

```
package com.iconixsw.bookstore.domain.logic;

// import statements omitted . . .

public class CustomerReviewValidator implements Validator {

    public boolean supports(Class commandClass) {
        return commandClass.isAssignableFrom(CustomerReview.class);
    }

    public void validate(Object command, Errors errors) {
        ValidationUtils.rejectIfEmptyOrWhitespace(
                errors,
                "review",
                "required",
                "Review text is required");
    }

}
```

This class was written to fit into Spring's validation framework. We're handed an Errors object, to which—assuming we find any validation errors in the form—we add one or more error messages that will then be displayed to the user, next to the offending form fields.

Exercise This implementation is missing some vital details that were specified in the use case text (see the finished use case next to its robustness diagram in Figure 6-7). We revisit this part of the code in the Code Review and Model Update in Chapter 11, but why not see if you can identify what's missing first? And, for some extra bonus points: Any guesses about *why* the detail might have been left out?

We also need to wire up this validator class to WriteCustomerReviewController, so that the validator is run automatically before the form gets processed via the doSubmitAction() method. To do that, we add a property to the writeCustomerReviewController bean in bookstore-servlet.xml:

```
<property name="validator">
  <bean
    class="com.iconixsw.bookstore.domain.logic.CustomerReviewValidator" />
</property>
```

Exercise Looking at the code for CustomerReviewValidator, what could be done to make it follow a more responsibility-driven design? You can find the answer in the Code Review and Model Update in Chapter 11.

The View: writecustomerreview.jsp

The JSP page, writecustomerreview.jsp, is the "view" in our MVC setup—that is, it creates the web page that the user sees, and it includes server-side tags that Spring uses to read in the user's form data and populate the objects we've designed thus far.

Let's walk through this JSP page piece by piece:

```
<%@ include file="include/IncludeTop.jsp" %>

<h2>
    <c:out value="${command.book.title}"/>
</h2>

<h3>
    Hello <c:out value="${command.customer.firstName}"/>,
    please enter your review for this book.
</h3>
```

The `<h2>` line provides a heading with the book's title, retrieved via the `<c:out>` JSTL tag and using the lookup text `command.book.title`. "command" refers to the name of the main object (a `CustomerReview`) that we populated the view with. `command.book.title` is the shorthand equivalent of this Java code:

```
command.getBook().getTitle();
```

The next part of the page (and the bulk of it) is the form itself. This allows the user to enter the three form fields (a title for their review, the review text, and a rating):

```
<form action="<c:url value="writecustomerreview.htm"/>" method="post">

<input type="hidden" name="bookid"
    value="<c:out value="${command.book.id}"/>" />

<table>
    <tr>
        <td>Title</td>
        <td>
            <spring:bind path="command.title">
                <input type="text"
                        name="title"
                        value="${status.value}" />
                <span class="error">
                    <c:out value="${status.errorMessage}" />
                </span>
            </spring:bind>
        </td>
    </tr>

    <tr>
        <td>Your Review</td>
        <td>
            <spring:bind path="command.review">
                <textarea name="review" cols="50" rows="10">
                    <c:out value="${status.value}"/>
                </textarea>
                <span class="error">
                    <c:out value="${status.errorMessage}" />
                </span>
            </spring:bind>
        </td>
    </tr>
```

```
<tr>
    <td>Rating (1-5)</td>
    <td>
        <spring:bind path="command.rating">
          <input type="text" name="rating"
             value="<c:out value="${status.value}"/>" />
          <span class="error">
            <c:out value="${status.errorMessage}" />
          </span>
        </spring:bind>
    </td>
</tr>
</table>

<input type="submit" value="Save Review" />
</form>
```

Notice that next to each form field is a tag for showing an error message (we've shown these in red as they're part of the alternate courses). These tags show the validation failure messages, if any. Each message is shown next to the field that failed validation. We didn't have to do any additional work to match these up—one of the benefits of using Spring's form validation framework.

Finally, we close off the page including a link back to the Book Details page, which would invoke the *Show Book Details* use case:

```
<p>
    <a href="bookdetails.htm?bookid=<c:out value="${command.book.id}"/>">
View book details
    </a>
</p>

</body>
</html>
```

Figure 10-16 shows the screenshot for the *Write Customer Review* page.

In the screenshot, Billy Bob has submitted his review but forgot to type in an actual review, so our alternate course validation failed as you'd expect, and the errant input field has an error message immediately beneath it in red text. (For those who were waiting with bated breath for the CSS "murder weapon" we introduced earlier in this chapter, that was it. We hope the wait wasn't too suspenseful.)

Notice that the Rating field allows only the values 1–5, but its initial value is 0. The default should really be one of the allowed values; we return to this in Chapter 12 when we cover testing.

■Exercise The validator didn't catch the 0 rating and highlight it on the form. We also cover this in Chapter 12. But in the meantime, looking at the sequence diagram in Figure 9-8, what could be done to catch this in the validation code? (The answer is in the Code Review and Model Update in Chapter 11.)

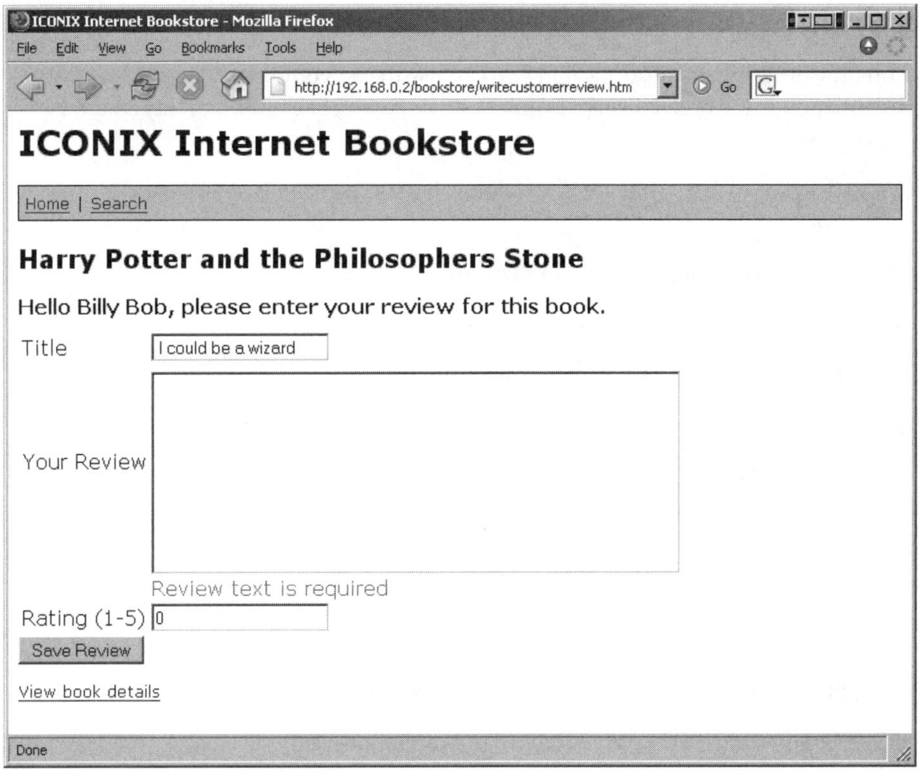

Figure 10-16. *The Write Customer Review page*

Exercise An obvious improvement in Figure 10-16 would be to use a drop-down list for the rating instead of a text field. Try modifying the *Write Customer Review* use case description to make this a specific part of the behavior description.

That about wraps up the implementation. There are a couple more pages to implement (e.g., the "success" view), but they're pretty much the same as the pages we've already done, so we won't retread old ground.

We do still need to make sure the alternate courses are all taken into account. A bullet-proof way to do this is with test cases generated directly from the controllers on the robustness diagrams, which we cover in Chapter 12.

More Practice

This section provides a list of questions that you can use to test your knowledge of use case–driven programming and delivery. If you get stuck, search back through this chapter to extract the answers.

1. Using ICONIX Process, what are the main design artifacts that you drive the source code from?

   a) Robustness diagrams and class diagrams

   b) Sequence diagrams and class diagrams

   c) Sequence diagrams and activity diagrams

   d) Robustness diagrams and sequence diagrams

2. Which of the following methods belong on an entity class? For those that should be allocated to other classes, briefly explain where (if anywhere) that the entity class would be involved in the design.

   a) A property (e.g., book title)

   b) A method containing validation logic

   c) JDBC code to write the entity's data to a database table

   d) A SOAP interface query to retrieve data to go in the entity class

3. Explain why it's good practice to implement the trickiest parts of the system first and to avoid putting the difficult parts off until the end. Try to quantify your answer.

4. Describe the differences among a `CustomerReviewDao` class, a `CustomerReview` entity, and a `CustomerReviews` database table.

5. If a DAO method takes a `Book` argument and returns a `BookReviewCollection`, should the method go on a `BookDao` or a `BookReviewDao`? Explain why.

6. If you're implementing an alternate course in which the customer's login details can't be found, what is the preferable way to implement it?

   a) Make the DAO return null so that the form handler can deduce that it should display a "not found" message.

   b) Make the form handler throw an exception so that the web application container redirects to an error page.

   c) Make the DAO throw an exception so that the form handler can display a "not found" message.

   d) Make the form handler set a null Customer bean in the JSP page so that the JSP page logic displays a "not found" message.

7. Describe why a system written in the following style would quickly become unmaintainable. After deciphering what the code is meant to do, refactor it so that it's more maintainable. (Hint: You'll need to decide which classes to reallocate the behavior to.)

```
public class ShoppingCartHelper extends AdhocUtilThings {
    public ShoppingCartHelper() {
        init();
    }
    public void doAction(Cart c, Book b) {
        if (available(b)) c.add(b);
            else throw new UnavailableException(b);
    }
}
```

8. Which of the following statements is *not* true? Explain why the statement is incorrect.

a) An entity must have a 1:1 mapping with a row in a database table.

b) A DAO can return both individual entity objects and collections of objects.

c) An entity can contain references to other entities.

d) An entity class can delegate to other "helper" classes as needed.

Summary

In this chapter, we took the sequence diagrams for two of the use cases plus the static model, and turned it all into working source code for the Internet Bookstore. Figure 10-17 shows where we are; the items covered in this chapter are shown in red.

Because the use case text is fully disambiguated and written in the context of the domain model, it's possible to walk through the use case text and match it up directly with the class and property names in the Java code.

What we haven't yet done is written any unit tests for the Internet Bookstore—an important step. Normally, you would expect to write the tests as you write the code. We've kept the unit testing step separate so that we're not explaining too many things at once, but in Chapter 12, you'll see how the unit tests can be driven directly from the controllers on the robustness diagrams.

In the next chapter, we perform a review of the code that's been written thus far and bring the model up to date in any places where the code and the model might have diverged.

Milestone 3: Critical Design Review

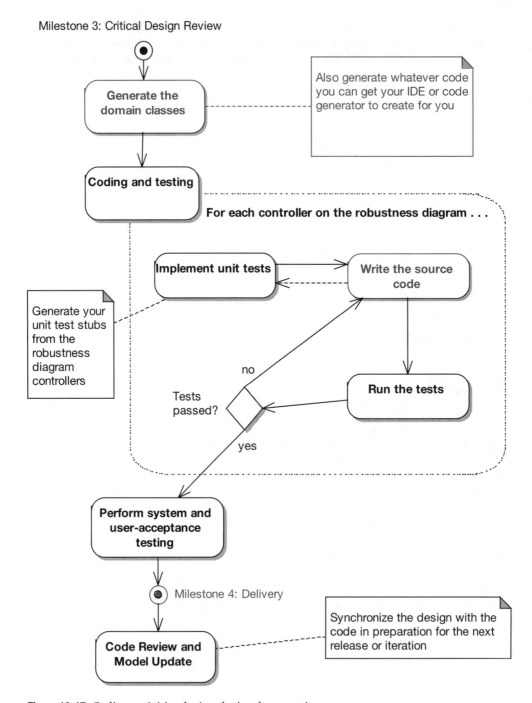

Figure 10-17. *Coding activities during the implementation stage*

CHAPTER 11

∎∎∎

Code Review and Model Update

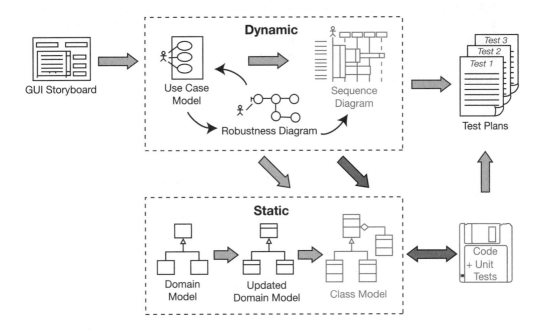

During coding, it's likely that you'll have made a few changes to the design, so the code will now be slightly out of sync with the design diagrams. A depressingly common reaction at this stage is to deem the design documentation obsolete, throw it away, and continue all subsequent development work without doing any more design work.

However, ICONIX Process (with some major tools assistance from the folks at Sparx Systems) provides an easy technique for rescuing all that design work you did and keeping it current so that it forms the basis of the design work for the remainder of the project.

The 10,000-Foot View

Why bother reviewing the code and syncing it up with the design? Here's a hypothetical conversation that we hope will shed some light on the subject.

Q: You mean I have to review the code, too? Why? Isn't working code enough?

A: The purpose of the Code Review and Model Update milestone is to bring the code and the model back into sync, ready to begin work on the next set of use cases. So, when you start developing the use cases for the next release, you can build on the design work that's already done. You'll continue to update and refine the static model, and reuse the objects that are in your domain model.

Q: What does the review involve?

A: As the name suggests, there are two parts to this review: checking the code and giving it a good shaking-up if needed, and comparing the code with the detailed design diagrams. Wherever they've diverged, either the code is brought back in line with the design, or the design diagrams are updated to be in sync with the code.

Q: How often should this review take place?

A: You'll need to tailor the timing of the Code Review and Model Update to fit your project. But the review should ideally take place at least at the end of each release (either to QA or to the end users), in preparation for the next release. Depending on the size of the release, you could also hold a review session after implementing a few use cases.

Q: I read in an agile development book that I should "update only when it hurts." Isn't all this updating going to take forever?

A: Updating only when it hurts is analogous to visiting the dentist only when you have a toothache. It might be a little late by then (unless you like root canal surgery). It might seem quite time-consuming to have to bring everything back into sync like this. But if you don't leave too much time between reviews, then it doesn't take very long at all. It's a good way to keep everyone in the team on the same page, so to speak. Keep the process fine-grained, and you'll catch design or integration issues early, before they become a problem.

Code Review and Model Update in Theory

Before we get started on the Internet Bookstore example, let's pause for a minute to examine why code reviews are even necessary—especially after doing all that up-front analysis and design work. But first, the usual top 10 guidelines.

Top 10 Code Review and Model Update Guidelines

The principles discussed in this chapter can be summed up as a list of guidelines. Our top 10 list follows.

10. Prepare for the review, and make sure all participants have read the relevant review material prior to the meeting.

9. Create a high-level list of items to review, based on the use cases.

8. If necessary, break down each item in the list into a smaller checklist.

7. Review code at several different levels.

6. Gather data during the review, and use it to accumulate boilerplate checklists for future reviews.

5. Follow up the review with a list of action points e-mailed to all people involved.

4. Try to focus on error detection during the review, not error correction.

3. Use an integrated code/model browser that hot-links your modeling tool to your code editor.

2. Keep it "just formal enough" with checklists and follow-up action lists, but don't overdo the bureaucracy.

1. Remember that it's also a Model Update session, not just a Code Review.

Let's look at these guidelines in more detail.

10. Prepare for the Review, and Make Sure All Participants Have Read the Relevant Review Material Prior to the Meeting

Alternatively, don't bother preparing and have a disorganized, time-wasting meeting. Or try it the XP way: remove all the chairs from the meeting room and give the meeting a catchy name like "early morning stand-up meeting."

9. Create a High-Level List of Items to Review, Based on the Use Cases

The high-level list of items to review should be based on the use case titles. Although it's possible to create a checklist of specific classes and methods, it's better to drive the list from the use cases, as this provides for a more structured review, which is more likely to catch behavior-related defects or missing functionality.

8. Break Down Each List Item into a Smaller Checklist (If Necessary)

Because the high-level checklist is essentially a list of use case titles, it's possible to drive the fine-grained list from the controllers on the robustness diagrams.

Note that for some projects, it may not be necessary to break the list into this level of detail; the high-level checklist (based on use cases) might be sufficient to start identifying classes and methods to review.

7. Review Code at Several Different Levels

Review the code for the usual code-level stuff: adherence to coding conventions, design style, naming, and so forth. But also compare the code with the design by walking through the sequence diagrams. In the same way that it should be possible to trace the path of a *use case* through a sequence diagram, it should also be possible to trace the path of a sequence diagram through the code.[1]

As you review the code, walk through the behavior descriptions in the use case text and compare the scenario text with the code. Sometimes this helps to catch missing functionality that might have been lost during the detailed design stage.

If it proves difficult to match up the method names with the actions in the use case text, then the code hasn't truly been written in the context of the design—or to flip the problem around, perhaps the use case and the design don't match. Either way, the problem needs to be corrected so that there's a direct correlation between the code and the use case text. If necessary, break the code into smaller methods, and use descriptive names that allow the code to be traced back to the use cases.

6. Use Data Gathered During the Review to Accumulate Boilerplate Checklists for Future Reviews

During code reviews, you tend to notice the same old issues again and again. Turning these into a checklist can save a lot of time, and it can help to make sure specific problems aren't missed. Over time, add to the list of checklists; in particular, look for insidious problems that might otherwise be overlooked, and make them explicit by adding them to the checklist.

If these checklists are in circulation around the company, then programmers can learn to avoid the same old issues in the first place, saving even more time!

5. Follow Up the Review with a List of Action Points E-mailed to All People Involved

Alternatively, have the meeting, assign action items, and never follow up to make sure the action items get done.

■Tip Have a follow-up meeting to ensure that all the action points actually did get "actioned."

---

4. Try to Focus on Error Detection During the Review, Not Error Correction

It's OK to make small updates to the model during the review, as it's a good way to make sure everyone is in agreement. However, if code needs to be updated or major design changes are required, that should be done separately and a follow-up review meeting scheduled.

---

1. Note that if you're doing aspect-oriented programming (AOP), your code may very well be organized in exactly this manner. See the sidebar "Use Cases and Aspects" in Chapter 3.

THERE'S A RIGHT WAY AND A WRONG WAY TO CONDUCT A CODE REVIEW

Preparing for the code review is important, and it involves tossing various weighty objects (baseball bats, golf clubs, skis—anything you can get a good swing with[2]) into the middle of the room, and then running for cover while the reviewer and the programmer dive for the nearest makeshift weapon in order to defend their criticisms and their code, respectively.

Well, OK, that's what happens when a code review goes wrong and is taken to its logical conclusion. The ideal code review isn't so much a fight to the death as a discussion between a programmer and an impartial observer about the code's adherence to the design. It's a review of the code rather than a personal performance review. In fact, as soon as a programmer's individual abilities are brought into question (even subtly), that programmer will go on the defensive, and the effectiveness of the review will be dramatically reduced.

3. Use an Integrated Code/Model Browser That Hot-Links Your Modeling Tool to Your Code Editor

This saves time and means that, when the programmer is updating the code later, none of the changes are forgotten about. See the sidebar "Using the UML Model to Browse the Java Code" at the end of this chapter.

2. Keep It "Just Formal Enough" with Checklists and Follow-up Action Lists

The approach described in this chapter is halfway between an informal code review and a formal code inspection. The key is to keep it "just formal enough" without overdoing the bureaucracy.

Some paperwork is necessary to ensure that individual items don't get forgotten. But, like the rest of the analysis and design process, too much documentation and too many process hoops can lead to analysis paralysis—or to *review and update paralysis*, in this case. Learn to recognize when the review has had its positive effect, and when it's time to move on.

1. Remember That It's Also a Model Update Session, Not Just a Code Review

The present state-of-the-art in development tools makes it trivially easy (at last!) to keep the model and the code in sync. It borders on the criminal to not take advantage of these capabilities.

---

2. Douglas Adams fans will recognize the similarity between a "wrongly done" code review and a violent game of Brockian Ultra-Cricket.

CODE REVIEW VS. CODE INSPECTION

The code review as described in this chapter involves checking the code base for adherence to the design and then either bringing the code back into line or updating the design. The review technique we propose here is more precisely a combined review of the model and the code. In fact, although we informally call this step the "Code Review" milestone, it has much in common with more formal code inspections.

Some differences between a code review and a code inspection are as follows.

Code Inspection	Code Review
A code inspection involves creating a checklist to focus the reviewer's attention.	A code review is more ad hoc. It typically involves printing out some code and examining it for adherence to coding standards, scanning for possible bugs and so on.
A code inspection finishes with a formal list of points to fix, usually in the form of defects entered into a defect tracking system.	A code review finishes with an informal list of to-do items, written on a sticky note or in a follow-up e-mail.
Data is gathered during a code inspection. The data gathered can be useful for identifying common types of errors, which can then be focused on in future inspections.	In a code review, gathering of metrics is less common.

The Code Review and Model Update milestone described in this chapter is really a combination of all the preceding attributes.

Why Are Code Reviews Necessary After All That Design Work?

If you perform all of the up-front analysis, up-front design modeling, and the appropriate reviews at each milestone, and you drive the code directly from the design, then the code really should be in very good shape. It should be highly cohesive, well factored, and closely tied to the use cases. As we discuss in Chapter 12, it will also be tied closely to the unit tests, which in turn are tied closely to the domain model and the use cases. So, given all that, why bother doing a review? Is it a failing of the process? Or a failure of the designers and programmers to do their job properly? Or none of the above?

We think it's none of the above. Code reviews are still important, even after you do a good job at design. Some reasons spring to mind:

- The people on your team are human (at least, we hope so); they make mistakes.

- The people on your team might well make their best effort to follow the process, but software projects are big, complex beasts, and—even with a cookbook methodology— it isn't always entirely clear what the correct next step should be.

- If the team is adopting a new process for the first time, it's likely that they will not follow the process at first, at least not completely. It takes time to adapt, to learn the subtleties and ins and outs of a new way of working. There might not even be complete buy-in to the new process, until people start to see the benefits. So in the meantime, to some degree the design will be suboptimal and the code might not have much in common with the design. To address this, the first few iterations of the design/code/review life cycle should be kept quite short, so that these disparities between code and design can be addressed quickly, before they become too great.

- Although many software projects have key similarities that you can exploit to create a repeatable process, each project has its own variations, meaning that you sometimes need to improvise, adapt the process, or just do whatever you think is best. But (to make a long story short) that might not always turn out to have been the right choice. So although it will generally be in very good shape, the design might still need to be revisited once you have working code to use as a baseline.

- An up-front design addresses the majority of design errors, but not all. In this chapter, we try to highlight the sorts of things that up-front design isn't really "designed" to catch and that you need to keep in mind both when coding and when performing the code review.

- Sometimes it's only when you begin coding that you realize there was a better way of doing something, or the technology you're using already provides a prebuilt solution for a particular function. This is why early prototyping is an essential part of the project life cycle, especially when you're working with unfamiliar technology. Another good approach is to write the unit tests while you're drawing the sequence diagrams. It's a good way of getting into the "coding frame of mind" before actually turning the detailed design into code.

With these guidelines in mind, in the next section let's see how our entirely fictional reviewer handles the Internet Bookstore code review. Note that we intentionally left a couple of design errors in our example to illustrate the sorts of mistakes that would typically be caught at this stage of the process.

Code Review and Model Update in Practice

Now it's time to put this theory into practice, and attack the Internet Bookstore code that was written in Chapter 10. As it turns out, we followed the design process quite closely and there isn't a *huge* amount of tidying up or bulletproofing that we need to do, but there is some.

For the Internet Bookstore code review, we'll follow the reviewer/programmer conversation as it unfolds. They begin with a list of the use cases and walk through them one by one. For each use case, the reviewer looks through the controllers on the robustness diagram and uses that as the fine-grained review checklist.

■**Note** During the review you'll see an occasional "Action Item"—this is a point list that the reviewer makes during the session. The list should be e-mailed to all participants and then followed up on, either after an agreed period of time or in a follow-up review session.

Code Review and Model Update Checklist

It's important to go into a review with a prepared checklist. This checklist is essentially just a list of the use cases and their basic and alternate courses (it's very easy to prepare).

For this review, the reviewer will look at two use cases (you can probably guess which two):

- *Show Book Details*

- *Write Customer Review*

The reviewer and the programmer will walk through both of these use cases, and for each one trace it to the code, via the controllers on the preliminary design and the detailed design.

■**Tip** If any code doesn't obviously trace back to the use cases using the reverse of this process, it's a surefire sign that the code and the requirements aren't tied closely enough together.

"Show Book Details" Use Case

The review begins with *Show Book Details.* *Checking the robustness diagram (see Figure 5-11), this use case has these controllers (logical software functions):

- Display links

- Retrieve List of Books

- Retrieve Book Details

- Display Book Details page

- Display Book Details Not Found page

The code for the first three functions all looks fine, so the review kicks into action with the "Display Book Details page" controller.

"Display Book Details Page" Controller

Reviewer: Here's the use case text:

> *BASIC COURSE:*
>
> *The Customer types in the URL for the bookstore's home page. The system displays a list of books from the Catalog on the home page, in the form of clickable links. The Customer clicks a link on the home page,* and the system retrieves the book details for the selected book and displays them on the Book Details page.

ALTERNATE COURSES:

Book not found: *The system displays a Book Details Not Found page.*

Programmer: We can trace the Display Book Details page controller via the sequence diagram to the BookDetailsController class. *(See Figure 9-7.)*

Reviewer: *(Pausing to get his bearings)* OK, so let's take a look at the handle() method in BookDetailsController. If I recall, this handles an incoming browser request to show the details of a Book, given its ID. *(The code that returns the Book Details view is shown in red.)*

```
protected ModelAndView handle(
            HttpServletRequest request,
            HttpServletResponse response,
            Object command,
            BindException errors) throws Exception {

    Book book = (Book) command;
    try {
        book.load(book.getId(), bookDao);
    }
    catch (NotFoundException e) {
        return new ModelAndView("booknotfound");
    }
    return new ModelAndView("bookdetails", "book", book);
}
```

Reviewer: *(Scratches his head)* Hmm, well . . . I think maybe I have a problem with the way that the book is being loaded. It seems odd that you're having to pass the book's ID in to itself, when it obviously already knows the ID.

Programmer: Yep. It's strange—when I looked on the sequence diagram *(see excerpt in Figure 11-1)*, it didn't seem to be an issue. But in the code it looks odd.

Reviewer: Here's the problem: the design is wrong!

■**Tip** Usually, you can pick up a fairly major warning sign that something is wrong from looking at the sequence diagram. From there, tracking down what's wrong is rather like following a trail of breadcrumbs (as we demonstrate in this review segment).

Reviewer: *(Glues on Poirot moustache)* Clue number 1: The load() message passes in an ID and a bookDao, but on the diagram there's not even a hint as to where these come from. It's a dead giveaway that something in that area of the design hasn't been thought through to the required level of detail.

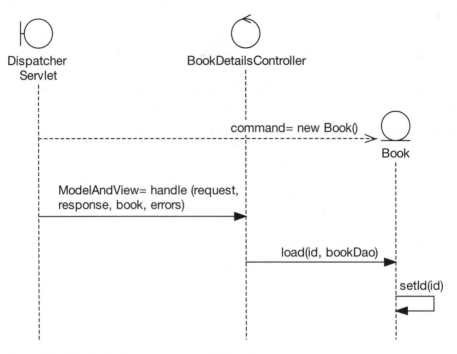

Figure 11-1. *The design is missing a crucial detail.*

Programmer: But that doesn't explain what's actually wrong with the design—just that something *might* not be right.

Reviewer: Well, then, let's follow the breadcrumbs. We need to find out where the ID and the bookDao come from. Clue number 2: You're setting the ID on the Book. But the Book is our Spring "command" object, and the ID should be set automatically for us because it's passed in via the web request. But—and this is clue number 3—this isn't shown on the diagram. We also need to show the bookDao being set. And finally, clue number 4: It isn't actually the DispatcherServlet class that creates the Command object.

Programmer: I know, it's actually ServletRequestDataBinder, one of Spring's helper classes. But we've generally used DispatcherServlet to mean "some Spring class or other"—it's a black box.

Reviewer: Sometimes it's probably OK to do that. But in this case, glossing over the details like that means that you missed a detail.

■Note `ServletRequestDataBinder` performs data binding from servlet request parameters to Java-Beans. For example, if the request includes a parameter called `id` that needs to be mapped to a `Book` JavaBean, the data binder will look for a property called `Book.setId()`, and pass in the parameter's value. In our example, `ServletRequestDataBinder` is actually used by `BaseCommandController`, an abstract Spring class that our `BookDetailsController` extends (see Figure B-2 in Appendix B).

■Action Item Update the sequence diagram to show the "command" Book ID being set where it's *really* being set, and then revise the design so that the ID doesn't have to be passed into the `load()` method.

Time-warp forward to the follow-up meeting...

Programmer: Here's the corrected diagram *(see Figure 11-2)*. In the diagram, I'm showing a lot more of the behind-the-scenes Spring detail to get to the bottom of the design error. So I've shown all the Spring classes and methods in red. `BookDetailsController` is our class, but it extends an abstract Spring class.

Reviewer: That gives a much better idea of what's really going on. It's good to map out your framework's detail like this for at least one use case, to gain an understanding of what's going on behind the scenes (but you definitely wouldn't want to repeat all this detail for every single use case).

■Tip Modern UML tools can reverse-engineer source code into sequence diagrams, which can provide an overview of what the code's doing where. However, often it's more useful to just draw the diagrams manually, as it engages the gray matter and gets you thinking about the design—by far the best way to learn how something works.

Programmer: And here's the corrected source code, in `BookDetailsController.handle()`:

```
book.load(bookDao);
```

Then in `Book`, I've changed the `load(id, bookDao)` method so that it no longer takes the redundant ID:

```
public void load(BookDao bookDao) throws NotFoundException {
    bookDao.load(this);
}
```

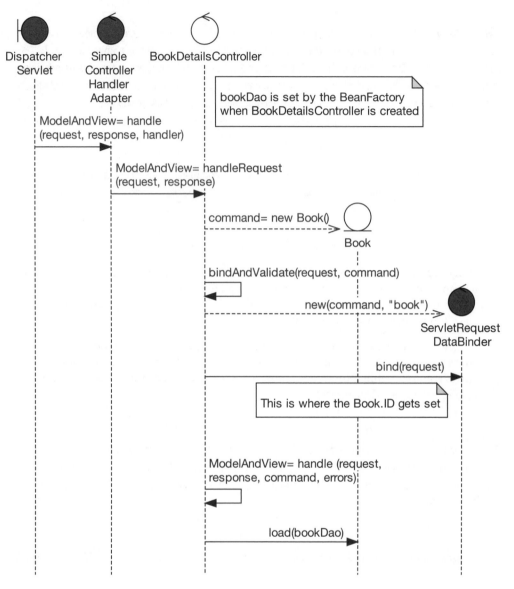

Figure 11-2. *The design was missing a crucial detail: the fact that the Book ID was being set for us*

Display "Book Details Not Found Page" Controller

Reviewer: Let's take a look at the "Book Details Not Found page" controller next.

Programmer: OK, here it is on the robustness diagram. *(See excerpt in Figure 11-3.)*

Reviewer: In the use case text on the left of the diagram, the alternate course is labeled "Book Not Found," so we need to make sure that there's a matching piece of code that obviously implements the same alternate course. And ideally, it needs to be easy to find, without too much digging and scrutinizing of the code.

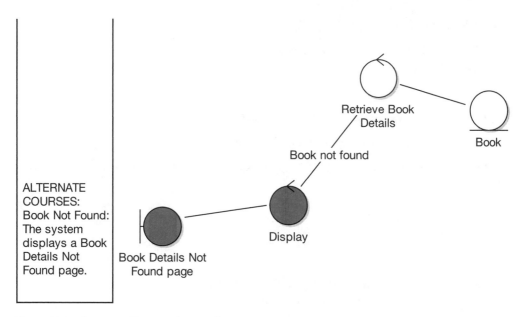

Figure 11-3. *The constellation of . . . No, hang on—it's part of the* Show Book Details *robustness diagram.*

Programmer: The code you're looking for is in the same `handle()` method that we just looked at *(the alternate course is shown in red)*:

```
try {
    book.load(bookDao);
}
catch (NotFoundException e) {
    return new ModelAndView("booknotfound");
}
```

Reviewer: Looks good to me. The fact that you're being forced to catch a `NotFoundException` is a good thing, as it shows that the alternate course is being handled correctly.

"Write Customer Review" Use Case

The team now moves on to the second use case, *Write Customer Review*. Checking the robustness diagram (see Figure 6-7), this use case has these logical functions (controllers):

- Is user logged in?

- Display Write Review page

- Enter review text

- Assign Review Rating

- Set Book ID on Customer Review

- Display Confirmation page

- The "validation" controllers "Is Book Review length OK?" and "Is Review Rating in allowed range?"

- Add Customer Review to Pending Reviews Queue

- Display "review exceeds max length" message

- Display "rating outside allowed range" message

Next, we show the highlights of the review session walking through these behavior fragments.

Finding a Starting Point

Reviewer: We may as well start at the top-left of the robustness diagram and work our way through the controllers.

Programmer: A lot of these first controllers have been implemented as methods on the WriteCustomerReviewController class, so that seems like a good place to start.

Reviewer: WriteCustomerReviewController has a constructor that defines its command class (CustomerReview). But on the detailed design, I can't see anything that shows this. *(See the sequence diagram in Figure 10-10 and the code excerpt immediately following it.)*

Programmer: Setting the command class is a function of the framework that we're using, and it didn't really figure in the design as it was being driven from the use cases.

■**Tip** Usually, leaps of logic in the design are exposed during sequence diagramming because you're designing at a very low level by that stage (especially if you're writing the unit test skeletons at the same time). However, constructor detail is commonly missed. Just something to be aware of.

■**Action Item** Update the sequence diagram to show the constructor detail for WriteCustomerReviewController.

The "Validation" Controllers, Part 1 (in Which CustomerReview Is Deemed Irresponsible)

Reviewer: Before we really get into this controller, there's a fairly major issue that I have with this part of the design.

Programmer: *(Putting down his chocolate-chip cookie)* Mmph?

Reviewer: We were discussing earlier about RDD, and how each domain class needs to be the logical starting point if you're hunting down the behaviors and responsibilities for that class. Well, the "validation" controllers are a really obvious candidate for being the responsibilities of the domain class.

Programmer: So instead of having a separate `CustomerReviewValidator` class, you'd put the validation code in the `CustomerReview` domain class itself?

Reviewer: That's exactly right. But we didn't actually make that change prior to coding. The result is that we now have a separate `CustomerReviewValidator` class that validates the data contained in `CustomerReview`.

Programmer: Yeah, to be honest, I shrugged off the issue because I couldn't see what the problem was. It's just one extra class, after all.

Reviewer: You're right, it isn't much of a problem at the moment. But it's storing up trouble for later. Remember, this is only the beginning of the Internet Bookstore project; there are still lots of use cases and heaps of domain classes to implement. If each one of those has its own validator class, that's twice the number of classes, with no central point of control for each one.

■**Note** The root cause of the "swarms of tiny classes" problem can be traced all the way back to the technical architecture. For example, see the "layers" diagram in Figure 7-7. In that diagram, the *input validators* are shown on the Controllers layer, whereas the *domain classes* are shown separately, in the Model layer. Really, these should be jammed tightly together, as the validation logic should live in the same class as the data it's validating.

Programmer: So, I guess what you're building up to is, we should fix the design now before we implement any more use cases.

Reviewer: Sounds like a plan. But before we get started, looking at the sequence diagram *(see excerpt in Figure 11-4; the original is in Figure 8-11)*, the detail for `CustomerReviewValidator` hasn't exactly been fleshed out.

Programmer: Yes, I think we just took it as having been "predesigned" by Spring, so we didn't go into detail.

■**Tip** "We didn't go into detail" really means "We didn't think it through in detail." The golden rule is, if the detail is in the use case, make absolutely sure that it also appears in the sequence diagram. Otherwise, as you can see happening in this review, it will just come back to haunt you!

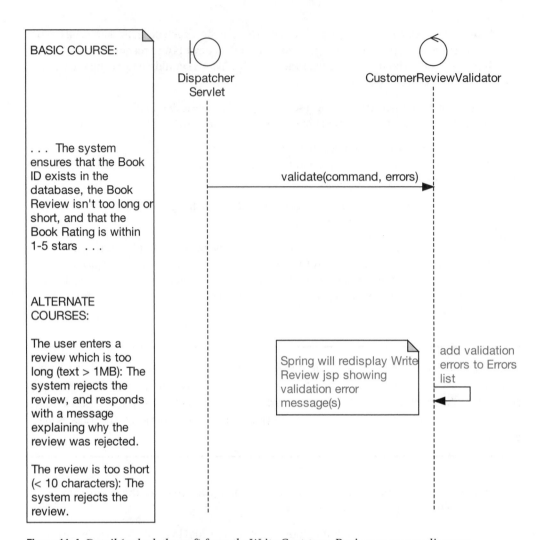

Figure 11-4. *Detail (or lack thereof) from the* Write Customer Review *sequence diagram*

Reviewer: A telltale sign is that the alternate course message "add validation errors to Errors list" is a bit vague. I think if we had included the detail, it would have looked something like this. *(Brings up sequence diagram on projector and clicks away; see Figure 11-5.)*

Reviewer: Now that gives us something we can work with.

■**Exercise**   The sequence diagram in Figure 11-5, though better, is still not quite complete. See if you can identify what's missing. (Hint: Compare the diagram with the use case text.) The answer is revealed in the next review segment.

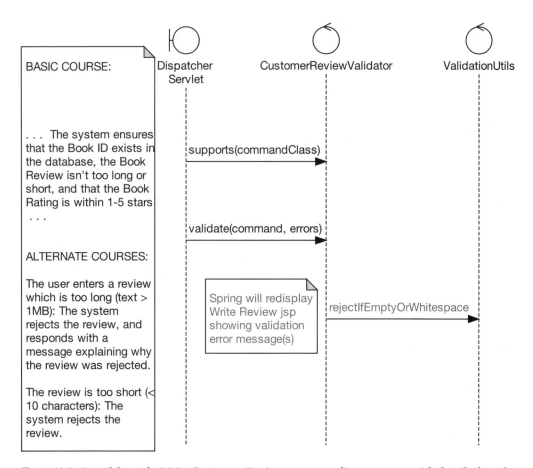

Figure 11-5. *Detail from the* Write Customer Review *sequence diagram, now with detail (though still not complete)*

Programmer: OK, to recap, we're looking for a way to avoid having to create a separate `Validator` class for every single domain class. Actually, our revamped sequence diagram gives me an idea. Before validating, Spring always calls the `supports(commandClass)` method. So what we *could* do is create a single `BookstoreValidator` class that supports *all* of our domain classes. Then when the `validate()` method is called, it just calls a `validate()` method on the respective domain class.

Reviewer: Wow, that's a mouthful. Can you sketch it out for me?

Programmer: Sure. *(See Figure 11-6.)*

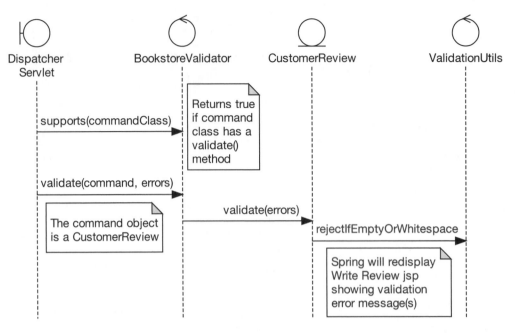

Figure 11-6. *Proposed design with a single BookstoreValidator class*

Programmer: *(Walking through the diagram)* Spring checks to see if `BookstoreValidator` supports this command class, which in this case is `CustomerReview`. The validator does a check to see if the command class has a `validate()` method. One way would be to use Java's reflection API, like this:

```
public boolean supports(Class commandClass) {
    return commandClass.getMethod(
                "validate", new Class[]{}) != null;
}
```

Reviewer: *(Drinking from a can of fizzy soda, which suddenly bubbles out of his nose)* Sorry. Well, it might be a bit more OO if you define an interface for domain object validators. Alternatively, as we don't have a common `BookstoreDomainObject` interface, we could create one of those and define a `validate()` method on it, and thus make it a requirement that every one of our domain classes has a `validate()` method.

■**Action Item** Replace `CustomerReviewValidator` with a more generic `BookstoreValidator`, and move the domain-specific validation code into `CustomerReview`. Also, create a common `BookstoreDomainObject` interface.

Time-warp forward to the follow-up meeting . . .

Programmer: Right, we now have a new interface that I've called DomainObject (BookstoreDomainObject seemed a bit too specific, as we could maybe reuse this on other projects):

```
public interface DomainObject {
    public void validate(Errors errors);
}
```

And CustomerReviewValidator has been replaced with a new, more generic validator class:

```
public class BookstoreValidator implements Validator {
    public boolean supports(Class commandClass) {
        return commandClass.isAssignableFrom(DomainObject.class);
    }

    public void validate(Object command, Errors errors) {
        DomainObject domainObj = (DomainObject) command;
        domainObj.validate(errors);
    }
}
```

Reviewer: Actually, to be consistent, you could do the same with BookstoreValidator; perhaps call it DomainObjectValidator.

Programmer: Good point—will do. And then, perhaps most important, the validation code has been moved into CustomerReview: *(Cheers of elation from Doug and Matt.)*

```
public class CustomerReview implements DomainObject, Serializable {

    . . .

    public void validate(Errors errors) {
        ValidationUtils.rejectIfEmptyOrWhitespace(
            errors,  // list of errors to show the user
            "review", // the field to validate
            "required", // it's required
            "Review text is required"); // text to add to the errors list
    }
}
```

And finally, to tie it all together, in bookstore-servlet.xml I've changed the WriteCustomerReviewController bean's validator to be BookstoreValidator instead of CustomerReviewValidator:

```
<bean id="writeCustomerReviewController"
 class="com.iconixsw.bookstore.web.WriteCustomerReviewController">


    . . .

    <property name="validator">
        <bean class=
        "com.iconixsw.bookstore.domain.BookstoreValidator" />
    </property>
</bean>
```

Programmer: I've also gotten rid of the "logic" package beneath domain, since we're now putting all of the logic directly into the domain classes.

Reviewer: Good idea. It's a useful warning sign, that if you feel the need to create an entire, separate logic *package* (let alone a separate class), something's probably gone wrong in the design.

The "Validation" Controllers, Part 2 (in Which Our Intrepid Programmer Discovers That He's Forgotten to Code an Alternate Course of Action)

Programmer: Still looking at validation for *Write Customer Review* . . . there are a couple of validation controllers on the robustness diagram: one of them checks the review length, and the other checks that the review rating is within the allowed range. *(The* validate() *logic is now in* CustomerReview, *as just shown.)*

Reviewer: Hmm, something doesn't quite seem right here. Let's compare the validation code with the relevant part of the use case text:

> *The Customer types in a Book Review, gives it a Book Rating out of five stars, and clicks the Send button. **The system ensures that the Book ID exists in the database, the Book Review isn't too long or short, and that the Book Rating is within one and five stars.***

Programmer: Well let's see, looking through the code, we check to see if the review text is empty, and . . . whoops, I see what you mean.

Reviewer: Yep, we also need to check that the text isn't too long, that the Book ID exists, and that the Book Rating is within one and five stars.

Programmer: That's actually quite a bit of missing functionality right there. I'm surprised I missed it, when it's right there in the use case text.

Reviewer: The reason you missed it is because the sequence diagram didn't have individual methods for each validation check *(see Figure 11-4)*. Instead, there was a single "blanket" validation method that was meant to contain all of the validation checks. So the problem can actually be traced back to our interpretation of the robustness diagram, which contained the validation controllers.

■Tip Each controller *must* turn into a method (sometimes several methods) on the sequence diagram. If a controller is missed, the result is that some functionality will almost inevitably be missed in the code. In some cases, your controllers might be "real control classes," which really doesn't change much because those classes have methods, too.

Being more coarse-grained on the robustness diagram is OK, but you need to "get atomic" on the sequence diagram. In the example, the programmer got atomic on the robustness diagram but reverted to "molecular" on the sequence diagram.

■Tip The "missing functionality" error would also have been caught if we'd written test cases based on the controllers (remember that these can be generated automatically) and then written unit tests based on the test cases. We revisit this example in Chapter 12 to show how this is done.

Programmer: So the sequence diagram should have looked like this . . . *(Grabs the mouse and edits the sequence diagram; see Figure 11-7.)*

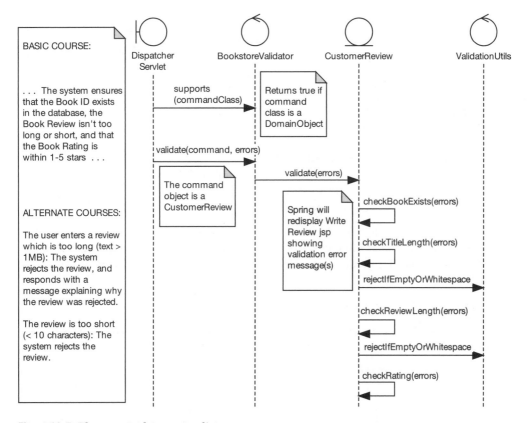

Figure 11-7. *The corrected sequence diagram*

Reviewer: I see you've also added in a checkTitleLength() message; nice catch. Checking the title length wasn't in the use case text, but it probably should have been. We should add it in now.

■**Action Item** Code the missing validation steps in CustomerReview according to the revised sequence diagram. Also, update the use case text to mention validating the review title length.

Time-warp forward to the follow-up meeting . . .

Programmer: Here's the corrected source code:

```
public class CustomerReview implements DomainObject, Serializable {

    public void validate(Errors errors) {
        checkBookExists(errors);
        checkTitleLength(errors);
        checkReviewLength(errors);
        checkRating(review, errors);
    }
```

Reviewer: OK, so you're calling four separate validation methods: checkBookExists, checkTitleLength, checkReviewLength, and checkRating. For each one, you pass in the Errors object that we cumulatively add the errors to.

Programmer: Yep. Here's the first of the new validation methods:

```
    private void checkBookExists(Errors errors) {
        if (book == null) {
            errors.rejectValue("book",
                        "BookNotFound",
                        "The selected book could not be found.");
        }
    }
```

If the Book was set to null previously by WriteCustomerReviewController, then that basically means it wasn't found (see the alternate course coded up in Chapter 10). So we can, in effect, reject the Book ID that was passed in from the browser, using errors.rejectValue().

Reviewer: Looks good so far.

Programmer: Now here's the next method, checkReviewLength(). It's remarkably similar to checkTitleLength(), so I've skipped over that one for brevity:

```
private void checkReviewLength(Errors errors) {

    ValidationUtils.rejectIfEmptyOrWhitespace(
            errors,
            "review",
            "required",
            "Review text is required");

    if (review != null && review.length() > 10000) {
        errors.rejectValue("review",
                        "too_long",
                        "The review you entered is " +
                        "a novel in itself; please try " +
                        "to shorten it");
    }
}
```

Programmer: There's a bit more to this method, as it's doing two checks on the review. The first check is unchanged from the previous version—it's using a convenience method in ValidationUtils to add an error to the list if the review text is empty. Then after that we do a manual check to make sure the review text isn't too long.

Reviewer: You might want to move the 10,000 literal into a constant. Actually, I notice you didn't include some of this detail in the sequence diagram, but we've broken the back of this now, so let's move on.

Programmer: OK. Here's the last of the four new methods, checkRating(), which makes sure that the rating is between one and five:

```
private void checkRating(Errors errors) {
    if (rating < 1 || rating > 5) {
        errors.rejectValue("rating",
                        "outofrange",
                        "The rating must be between 1 and 5");
    }
}
```

Reviewer: Good! Without this, the user would have been able to enter **0**, or indeed any old value.

■Note Validation code is a prime candidate for effective unit testing. We describe in Chapter 12 how to drive the unit tests from the (validation) controllers on your robustness diagrams.

Figure 11-8 shows a screenshot with our new `CustomerReview` validation logic in action.

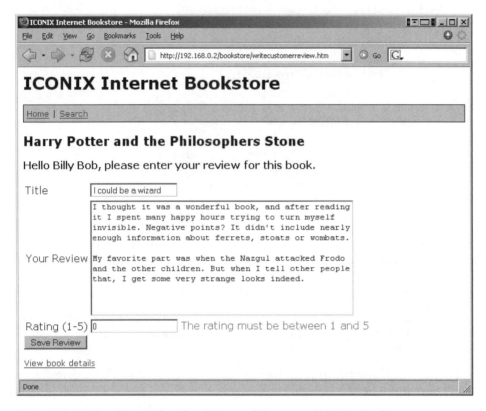

Figure 11-8. *Updated screenshot showing one of the new validation checks*

The formBackingObject() Method Is Too Complex

Reviewer: On `WriteCustomerReviewController`, the `formBackingObject()` method seems to do an awful lot. *(See the implementation in and around Figures 10-10 and 10-11.)*

Programmer: You're thinking maybe it should be divided up into smaller methods?

Reviewer: You'd be "coding by intention," which is a good thing. In other words, each method name would describe (succinctly!) in real-world terms what it does. Among other things, making this change will reduce the need for comments in your code. So, yep, dividing the code into smaller, well-named methods will make this class much easier to follow.

■**Action Item**   Divide the `WriteCustomerReviewController.formBackingObject()` method into smaller methods to make the class easier to read.

Time-warp forward to the follow-up meeting...

Programmer: I've separated out the code into separate methods. So this is what form-BackingObject() looks like now:

```
protected Object formBackingObject(
    HttpServletRequest request) throws Exception {

    Customer customer = findCustomer(request);
    if (customer == null) {
        return null;
    }
    Book book = findBook(request);
    return newBlankReview(book, customer);
}
```

Then we have individual methods, like so:

```
private Customer findCustomer(HttpServletRequest request) {
    . . .

private Book findBook(HttpServletRequest request) {
    . . .

private CustomerReview newBlankReview(Book book,
                                      Customer customer) {
    . . .
```

Reviewer: That's much easier to follow. It's virtually self-commenting.

CustomerReview Doesn't Have a save() Method

Reviewer: One of the prefactorings we made prior to coding was to add a load() method onto Book, because if you wanted to know how to load a Book instance, you'd naturally go to the Book class first. However, an obvious one that we missed was, similarly, to move save() onto CustomerReview. Currently, your form handler class has to call the DAO directly and pass it the CustomerReview. *(See the* doSubmitAction() *method just after Figure 10-12.)*

Programmer: That's easily fixed. I can just do the same thing I did for Book: add save() onto CustomerReview and make it delegate to CustomerReviewDao.

■**Action Item** Move the save() method onto CustomerReview, and make doSubmitAction() call that instead of calling the DAO directly.

(This solution is skipped over because it's basically the same as for Book.load().)

But Isn't a Book Meant to "Have" Reviews?

Reviewer: Wait a minute—something about the aggregation of some of these domain classes has been nagging away at me. I know this is a bit late in the day, but looking back at the class diagram excerpt for WriteCustomerReviewController *(see Figure 9-6)*, I'm sure that on the original domain model *(see Figure 2-7)*, the aggregation for Book and CustomerReview (or Reader Review, as it was back then) was the other way around.

Programmer: You mean that essentially a Book "has" CustomerReviews?

Reviewer: Essentially, yes. But CustomerReview suddenly now "has" a reference to its parent Book. The relationship has flipped around.

Programmer: The question is, which direction makes more sense? I know that from a design standpoint—at least for the *Write Customer Review* use case that we're implementing—it will be easier if the CustomerReview knows what its parent Book is.

Reviewer: You have to look at the bigger picture, though. If you go to an online bookstore, you zero in on a particular book and see a list of its reviews. You don't go to a review first and then find out which book it belongs to. So from a real-world perspective—which the domain model is meant to represent—it makes more sense for the Book to have a list of CustomerReviews. I bet that design-wise, in the majority of cases, it will also work out much easier that way around.

Programmer: Similarly, I suppose the Customer class would also have a list of CustomerReviews that they've written. So that one would need to be switched around as well.

■**Action Item** Reverse the relationship between Book and CustomerReview, so that a Book "has" reviews. Do the same for Customer and CustomerReview.

Time-warp forward to the follow-up meeting . . .

Programmer: Here's the updated class diagram *(see excerpt in Figure 11-9)*.

Reviewer: OK, we've walked through all of the controllers in both of the use cases. You've got some action items to bring the code in line with the design, and we've updated the design where it needed to be brought in line with the code. Nice work!

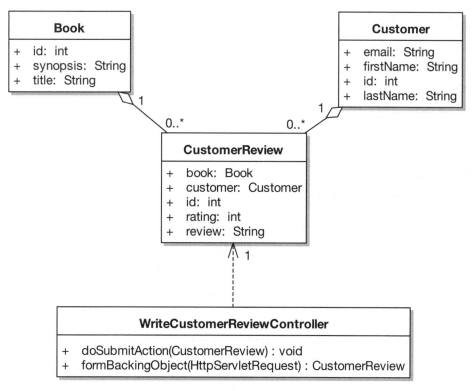

Figure 11-9. *Aggregation relationships flipped around*

ACTION LIST FOLLOWING THE REVIEW SESSION

From: Wilbert R. Shufflehammer, III (Reviewer)
To: Bim (Programmer), Ben (Programmer)
Subject: Action list following the Code Review and Model Update

1. Update the sequence diagram to show the "command" Book ID being set where it's *really* being set; then revise the design so that the ID doesn't have to be passed into the `load()` method. [Bim]

2. Update the sequence diagram to show the constructor detail for `WriteCustomerReviewController`. [Ben]

3. Replace `CustomerReviewValidator` with a more generic `BookstoreValidator`, and move the domain-specific validation code into `CustomerReview`. Also create a common `BookstoreDomainObject` interface. [Ben]

4. Code the missing validation steps in `CustomerReview` according to the revised sequence diagram. Also, update the use case text to mention validating the review title length. [Ben]

5. Divide the `WriteCustomerReviewController.formBackingObject()` method into smaller methods to make the class easier to read. [Bim]

6. Move the `save()` method onto `CustomerReview`, and make `doSubmitAction()` call that instead of calling the DAO directly.

7. Reverse the relationship between `Book` and `CustomerReview`, so that a `Book` "has" reviews. Also do the same for `Customer` and `CustomerReview`.

All items to be completed by the follow-up meeting this Wednesday.

Future Iterations

In future iterations, we'll want to add to the code base with new use cases. For example, `CustomerReviewDao` currently only saves `CustomerReview` objects to the database; there's no code there to retrieve the objects that were saved. The reason for this is simply that, so far, we haven't identified any need to retrieve saved `CustomerReview` objects.

Obviously, that will change when we get to the appropriate use case. For example, the *Moderate Pending Reviews* use case (in which a Review Moderator reads submitted book reviews and either publishes or rejects them) would need to be able to retrieve reviews. Similarly, if our client suddenly decided that the bookstore should allow users to edit their reviews, we'd create an *Edit Customer Review* use case that would need to be able to retrieve saved `CustomerReview` objects. Similarly, users would want to see the reviews that have been submitted when looking at the Book Details page.

It's because we're expecting to add new functionality that the Code Review and Model Update effort is so important. It makes it much easier to fit new design diagrams into the current design when the model is nicely in sync with the code.

USING THE UML MODEL TO BROWSE THE JAVA CODE

Historically, the separation between modeling and code has always been one of the most serious impediments to programmer acceptance of UML. When the model and the code live in separate universes (tools/environments), the model inevitably falls out of date and is perceived by the developers as an "artifact" that grows increasingly less useful over time, as changes are made in the coding environment.

What's been needed is a bridge between the modeling environment and the development environment—in other words, an extension of the IDE to include the UML model. Figure 11-10 shows an example of this "more integrated" IDE: Eclipse extended with the Sparx MDG Integration plug-in.

As you can see, the UML model for the Internet Bookstore has been "attached" to the project in Eclipse. We can now use the model to browse the code! Click on an operation on a class in the UML browser, and the source code is displayed in the editing window. Keeping the model and the code synchronized is easily accomplished by right-clicking a class and choosing "Synchronize model and code". New methods can be created in the IDE and "pushed back" into the UML model, or created within the model and "pushed forward" into code.

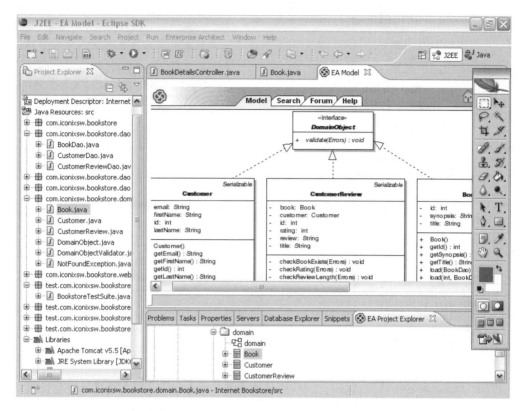

Figure 11-10. *EA integrated into Eclipse, with the Internet Bookstore project synchronized*

Summary

In this chapter, we conducted a Code Review and Model Update for the Internet Bookstore. The result was that the code was made more robust and bulletproof, and the model was updated to bring it in line with the code.

Figure 11-11 shows where we are. The activity covered in this chapter is shown in red.

In addition, by comparing the code with the behavioral descriptions in the use cases, some missing functionality was uncovered. The cause was discovered to be that one of the sequence diagrams didn't go into enough detail. So the diagram was updated and the additional functionality was added into the code. This approach of comparing the code with the use case text was possible because the code was closely tied to the domain model, a result of the robustness analysis step. All that disambiguation really paid off!

If the review results in code needing to be updated (which is likely), it's important to have some unit tests in place first. And to ensure effective test coverage, those unit tests should be driven from the controllers on your robustness diagrams. We cover the *test-driven* aspect of model-driven development in the next chapter.

Milestone 3: Critical Design Review

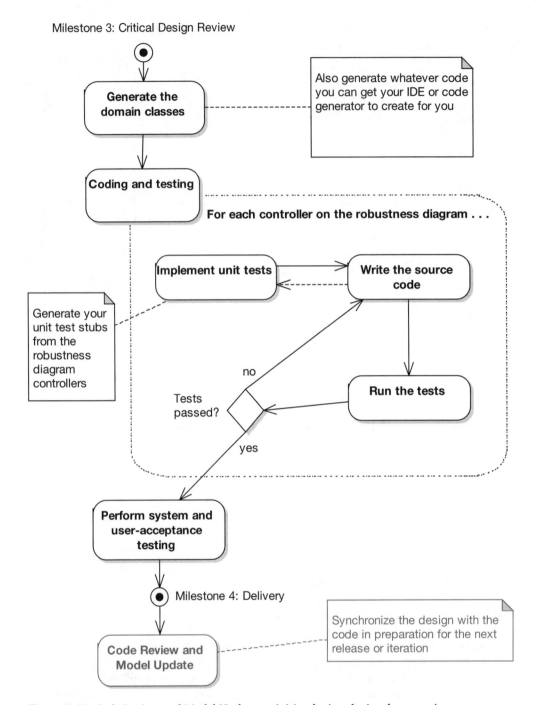

Figure 11-11. *Code Review and Model Update activities during the implementation stage*

PART 4

■ ■ ■

Testing and Requirements Traceability

CHAPTER 12

■■■

Design-Driven Testing

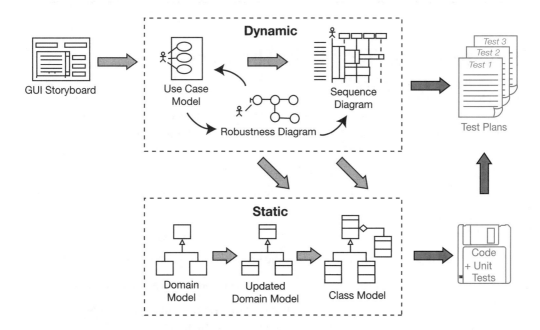

It's easy to look at a program module and say, "There, that's finished," but this sense of completion can be deceptive. How do you know for sure that the code completes all the use case scenarios—not just the basic courses, but the alternate courses, too?

Design-Driven Testing (DDT) provides a bulletproof method for producing test cases for you to verify that all the specified scenarios are complete. You can also use this process to write executable unit tests from these test cases.

Testing is a process that should begin long before coding. Beginning testing the product after it's purportedly "finished" is marginally better than a poke in the eye, but the testing process should begin long before you even start coding. Preparation for testing begins during the analysis stage, by identifying test cases using your robustness diagrams. It's possible to eliminate a lot more bugs—before they even exist—by testing early. Testing kicks in shortly after preliminary design, and then writing of unit test code takes place during implementation.

Make sure that your tests are tied closely to the requirements. That isn't to say that every test should be traced back to a requirement, but there should at least be a test to "prove" that each requirement has been implemented correctly. The process we describe in this chapter is one method for doing just that: driving the unit tests from your use cases.

■**Mind the Gap!** We should warn you in advance, there's a chapter split later on, in which Test-Driven Development (TDD) aficionados should find some useful advice on combining TDD with the up-front design approach described in this book. The rest of us may find that part of the chapter somewhat mind-bending (and also not an essential part of the process as such), so that section can be safely skipped over for non-TDD afficionados. We'll clearly signpost the chapter split when we reach it.

Design-Driven Testing in Theory

We start this chapter by looking at the premise and basic theories of DDT. We provide a few examples along the way, and the hands-on stuff will follow in the "Design-Driven Testing in Practice" section later. But it definitely helps to take in some theory first. So—no passing notes there at the back—let's put our academic hats on. First up is our top 10 list.

Top 10 Design-Driven Testing Guidelines

The principles discussed in this chapter can be summed up as a list of guidelines. Our top 10 list follows.

10. Adopt a "testing mind-set" wherein every bug found is a victory and not a defeat.

    If you find (and fix) the bug in testing, the users won't find it in the released product.

9. Understand the different kinds of testing, and when and why you'd use each one.

    Get to know the different types of testing that we describe later in this chapter (see the "V" model in Figure 12-1) and apply each test at the right time. And, just as important, use the deliverables you create along the way to prepare for each test in advance.

8. When unit testing, create one or more tests for each controller on each robustness diagram.

    Also create one or more unit tests for each operation on each class within the design. Sometimes these are the same (a controller is implemented as a single operation on a class), and sometimes a controller is realized as multiple (atomic) operations.

7. For real-time systems, use the elements on state diagrams as the basis for test cases.

    For example, test the response to various events that trigger state changes. During this kind of testing, you monitor changes that take place in an object's attributes in order to test the interactions among that object's methods. You can use the elements on state diagrams as the basis for test cases.

6. Do requirement-level verification, checking that each requirement you have identified is accounted for.

5. Use a traceability matrix to assist in requirement verification.

4. Do scenario-level acceptance testing for each use case.

3. Expand threads in your test scenarios to cover a complete path through the appropriate part of the basic course plus each alternate course in your scenario testing.

2. Use a testing framework such as JUnit to store and organize your unit tests.

1. Keep your unit tests fine-grained.

Different Kinds of Testing

You should look at testing as a full member of the iterative and incremental development life cycle, not just as something you occasionally do after you've cranked out a bunch of code. The reason for this is simple: tests prove that a product is fit for its specified purpose. But if the tests themselves aren't closely aligned with the specification, then they're not proving a huge amount except that running a test suite causes the office lava lamp to light up green.[1]

Let's run through that again: tests by themselves don't prove a huge amount. They prove that some part of your program passes some tests, but that's about it. The tests themselves need to be very closely tied in with the requirements, at a microscopic level. If the tests are closely aligned with the requirements, then passing the tests proves (to a degree) that your software is fit for its specified purpose. If the tests aren't closely aligned with the requirements, then passing the tests is, by itself, pretty meaningless.

A key to testing is to understand the different kinds of tests, and in particular when in the software life cycle each kind of test should be used.

Figure 12-1 shows which tests should be performed for each stage in ICONIX Process.

So, to test that the preliminary design has been implemented satisfactorily and to spec, you perform integration testing, and so on.

Preparation for each type of test can begin well in advance. For example, as soon as the business case (essentially the contract between you and the customer) has been signed off, QA can begin speccing out the release tests based on the contents of the business case. Similarly, as soon as each use case is written, your software testers can begin writing the system tests for that use case. (Having said that, we advise that they wait until the preliminary design for that use case is finished, as this will undoubtedly have an impact on the use case being analyzed.)

Many of the higher-level tests may be written in the form of unit tests. For example, as you'll see later in this chapter, it's desirable to drive the unit test classes and methods directly from the controllers on the preliminary design (which in turn are driven directly by the use cases).

---

1. We wish we were kidding, but now your team can set up their own eXtreme Feedback Device (XFD; aka red/green lava lamp) to provide a highly visual indication of their own build/unit test status: www.pragmaticprogrammer.com/pa/pa.html.

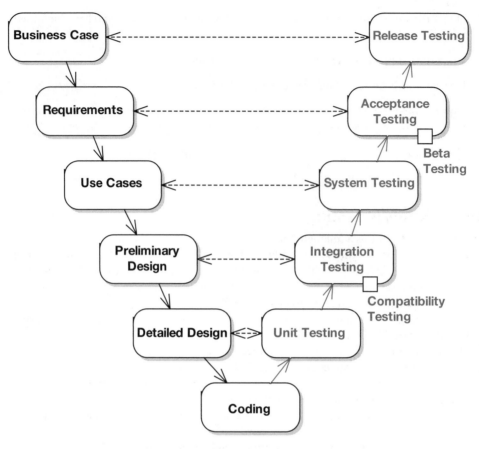

Figure 12-1. *"V" model of software testing applied to ICONIX Process*

Table 12-1 describes the different kinds of tests shown in Figure 12-1.[2]

Table 12-1. *Different Kinds of Tests and When to Apply Them*

Test	When (and Why) You Should Do It
Unit testing The testing of individual software components. Stubs may be used to simulate inputs and outputs of a component so that it can operate in stand-alone mode.	Begin unit testing before integration/system testing. Unit testing is executed on every build of the software throughout the development phase (including the bug-fixing phase after the software has been released to system test).

---

2. The definitions in Table 12-1 are adapted from the British Computer Society Specialist Interest Group in Software Testing (BCS SIGIST). Thanks to Philip Nortey for contributing heavily to this section.

Test	When (and Why) You Should Do It
Integration testing Testing performed to expose faults in the interfaces and in the interaction between integrated components. Unlike with compatibility testing (see the next test type), the classes are a part of the overall system being designed.	This is done after unit testing.
Compatibility testing Testing that the system interoperates correctly with other, "external" systems with which it is required to communicate.	This is not quite the same as integration testing, although both take place at roughly the same time.
System testing Functional and behavioral test case design. Test case selection that is based on an analysis of the specification of the component without reference to its internal workings. Functional testing consists mainly of use case and business process path tests, but also includes testing of the functional requirements.	This is done after integration testing. System testing tends to be developer focused. Its purpose is to prove that **the system that was specified has been delivered**.
Acceptance testing Formal testing conducted by (or on behalf of) the customer, to determine whether the system meets the requirements specified in the contract.	Acceptance testing operates along the same lines as system testing, but the emphasis is different. Acceptance testing is carried out to prove that **the system delivers what was actually requested**.
Beta testing Testing performed by end users who aren't otherwise involved with the development effort.	This is done before acceptance testing to exercise the software in an environment that is as close as possible to the production environment.
Release testing Verifies that the finished product accurately reflects the business case.	This is done at the point at which the software is to be delivered to the customer (or at the end of a deliverable milestone within the project), to ensure that the product has been created to spec and fulfills the goals described in the original contract.

In addition, some kinds of testing go on throughout the development process or aren't based on a specific deliverable. Table 12-2 shows the more common ones.

Table 12-2. *More Kinds of Testing and When to Do Them*

Test	When You Should Do It
Nonfunctional requirements testing Testing of those requirements that do not relate to functionality (i.e., performance, usability, etc.)	This testing should be done throughout the software life cycle (even at the unit test level) where possible. "Nonfunctional requirements testing" is really an umbrella term for performance, stress, volume, and compatibility testing.

Continued

Table 12-2. *Continued*

Test	When You Should Do It
Performance testing Testing conducted to evaluate the compliance of a system or component with specified performance requirements	This testing can (and should) be done at every opportunity, but it is usually executed after system testing.
Regression testing Retesting of a previously tested program following modification to ensure that faults have not been introduced or uncovered as a result of the changes made	This testing is executed after the code has been released to system test. Note that unit testing is a form of regression testing if it is done properly.
Stress testing Testing conducted to evaluate a system or component at or beyond the limits of its specified requirements	This testing is executed after performance testing.
Volume testing Testing where the system is subjected to large volumes of data	This testing is executed after system testing.

■**Tip** For more in-depth information on software testing and QA, we recommend two of Boris Beizer's books on the subject: *Software System Testing and Quality Assurance* (Van Nostrand Reinhold, 1984) and *Software Testing Techniques* (Van Nostrand Reinhold, 1990). They're both "golden oldies," but the techniques they describe and the *states of mind* that they get you into are still very relevant in today's agile software world, glued together as it mostly is by JUnit `assert` statements.

Driving Test Cases from Robustness Diagrams

With ICONIX Process, you invest effort in writing use cases, and you identify the objects that participate in a use case and the functions that those objects perform, on robustness diagrams (the functions are shown as controllers). Since you've made this investment in identifying the logical software functions, it would be nice to get some return on that investment in terms of a suite of test cases that remind you to test all the functionality of the use case.

Figure 12-2 shows an overview of DDT, in which the test cases are created directly from the controllers on the robustness diagrams.

As Figure 12-2 shows, you can automatically transform a robustness diagram into both a skeleton sequence diagram and a test case diagram using a simple script. Test skeleton code can subsequently be generated for unit testing frameworks like JUnit or NUnit.

Now we'll provide a more detailed explanation, which we'll illustrate step by step with an example. Since you've already identified the logical functions within a use case as controllers, it seems natural that all of these functions would need to be tested. Working from the robustness diagram, you can create a test case diagram showing a test case for each controller.

How do you do this? Easy! Copy all of the controllers from the robustness diagram onto a new diagram, and then link a test case to each one using <<realize>> connectors. We'll run through an example of this in just a moment.

```
Create a new Sequence Diagram
Create a new Test Case Diagram
Repeat for all symbols on the robustness diagram

          if (stereotype=ENTITY) or (stereotype=BOUNDARY) then
                  add it to the sequence diagram
          if (stereotype=CONTROL) then
                  add it to the testcase diagram
                  create a testcase for it, and link them

End Repeat
```

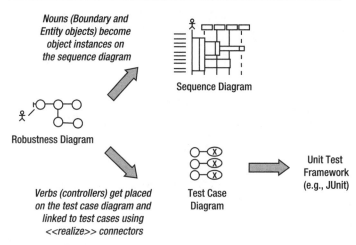

Figure 12-2. *Overview of DDT*

■**Note** The EA tool has a test case element that is a stereotyped use case.

Each test case can contain multiple test scenarios. To identify the test scenarios for each controller/test case, follow these steps:

1. Reread the use case text to remind yourself of the context in which the controller is used.

2. For each test case, create a test scenario for each use case scenario (the basic and alternate courses).

3. Name each test scenario after its use case scenario of origin. For example, for the controller Retrieve Book Details, the alternate scenario called Book Not Found would lead to a test scenario called, you guessed it, Book Not Found, in a test case called Retrieve Book Details Test.

Using the Agile ICONIX/EA Add-in

We should stress that ICONIX Process works equally well with any OO programming language, platform, CASE tool, and so on. However, the Enterprise Architect (EA) tool has an especially neat add-in that automates much of the "transitional" work when moving between diagrams in ICONIX Process. For example, the add-in will automatically create a set of robustness diagrams from a use case diagram (see Figure 12-3), and (a serious time-saver) the add-in will populate a sequence diagram using the boundary, entity, and controller objects on your robustness diagram.

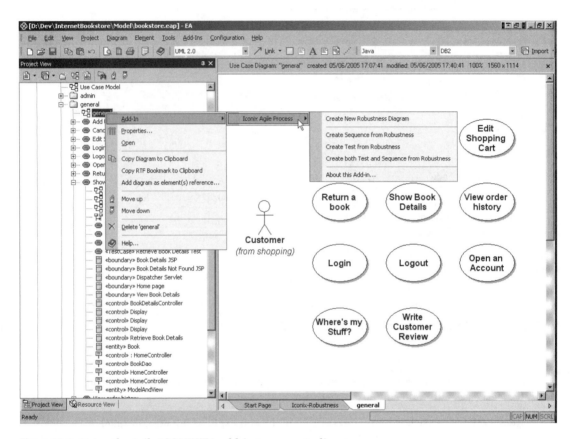

Figure 12-3. *Using the Agile ICONIX/EA add-in to generate diagrams*

For testing purposes, the add-in automatically creates a test case diagram from the controllers on your robustness diagrams (see Figure 12-4). From these controllers, it's then possible to write executable unit tests for each of the test cases.

The test case diagram in Figure 12-4 is based on the robustness diagram in Figure 5-10. Notice that each test case is linked to a controller. In other words, there's *one test case per controller*. The relationship between the test case and the controller is "realizes" (the same relationship that's used to show classes implementing/realizing an interface).

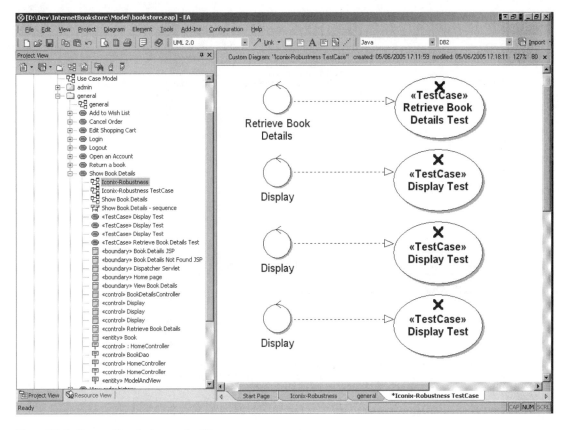

Figure 12-4. *Generating test cases in EA*

■**Exercise** The diagram in Figure 12-4 would quickly become quite difficult to work with. Any ideas why? We reveal the answer in a Note later in this chapter.

You can right-click each test case and add individual scenarios (see Figure 12-5).

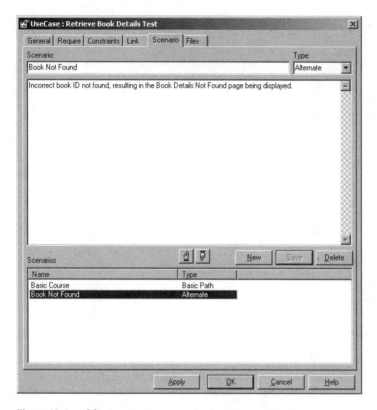

Figure 12-5. *Adding test case scenarios in EA*

Driving Unit Tests from the Test Cases

To recap, you need to model the test cases on the controllers from your robustness diagrams—that is, each controller gets exactly one test case. And for each test case, create one or more test scenarios.

Once you've created your test cases and allocated test scenarios to each one, it's time to create the unit test skeletons.

Here are some guidelines for driving unit tests from test cases:

- For each test case, create one unit test class. For example, if the test case is called Retrieve Book Details Test, then you'd create a JUnit test class called RetrieveBookDetailsTest.

- For each test scenario, create one test method in your unit test class. For example, if the test case is called Book Not Found, you'd create a test method called testBookNotFound().

- Write unit tests from the point of view of the object calling the controller.

- If you discover new *alternate courses* while thinking up test case scenarios—which is likely—*don't hesitate* to add them to the use case!

We'll walk through some examples of creating unit tests from the test cases in just a moment.

A Quick Introduction to JUnit

For the code examples later in this chapter, we'll use JUnit (www.junit.org), a popular Java-based unit testing framework. JUnit is part of the xUnit family; other members include cppUnit for C++, nUnit (www.nunit.org) for C#/.NET, and DUnit for Borland Delphi. Although the flavor of the source code can differ somewhat depending on the language/implementation, the principles discussed in this chapter are basically the same, whichever unit testing framework you use.

With JUnit, you write test cases where each test case is a single Java class. Within this class, individual test methods follow the naming convention testXYZ, where XYZ is the name of your test. This naming convention allows JUnit to automatically detect and run your test methods, without them having to be "declared" somewhere (e.g., in an external XML file). Using JUnit 4.0, test methods may also be identified using Java 5 assertions (see the sidebar "JUnit: The Next Generation" later in this chapter).

■**Tip** Using the approach described in this chapter, you can map test cases directly to JUnit test classes, and you can map test scenarios directly to individual test methods.

Within a test method, you write Java code that calls methods in the classes being tested and asserts that the result is precisely what was expected. For the assertion part, JUnit provides a number of different assert methods (e.g., to assert that a value is true, or that a value is non-null, or that two values are equal).

Your test class can consist of any number of test methods, although it's generally a good idea to keep the number below five or so. If the number of test methods in a class grows, consider dividing them into separate test cases. Similarly, it's a good idea to limit each test method to a single assert statement. This keeps the test scenario focused on testing a single thing. If you find the need to add more than one assert, it's likely that you're really looking at more than one test scenario squeezed into a single test method, so don't hesitate to separate them out.

Here's an example of a unit test class:

```
package test.com.iconixsw.bookstore.web;

import junit.framework.*;

public class AddToShoppingCartTest extends TestCase {

    public AddToShoppingCartTest (String testName) {
        super(testName);
    }

    public void testShoppingCartEmpty() throws Exception {
        ShoppingCart cart = new ShoppingCart();
        assertEquals("Cart should be empty", 0, cart.getNumItems());
    }
```

```
public void testItemAdded() throws Exception {
    ShoppingCart cart = new ShoppingCart();
    LineItem item = new LineItem();
    cart.addItem(item);
    assertEquals("Cart should contain 1 item",
                1, cart.getNumItems());
}

}
```

The AddToShoppingCartTest test case contains two test methods. The first method is
a quick sanity check to make sure that if a new ShoppingCart is created, it starts out empty.
This test would make more sense if you're dealing with DAOs that might use object caching,
in which case it might not be such a crazy notion that an object is "initially" not empty.

The second test method checks that if an item is added to the cart, then the cart contains
exactly one item. In both cases we're using assertEquals(), which takes three arguments:

- A handy description that gets displayed if the test condition fails

- A value representing what the expected value should be

- The result of the code being tested, which should, of course, resolve to the same value
  as the second argument

■**Exercise**   The test methods contain some duplicate code. What could be done to fix this? We actually
reveal the answer in the next paragraph, which makes a nice change.

Both test methods set up a ShoppingCart object. In fact, given that the test case is all
about adding items to a ShoppingCart, it would make sense for each test to use the same
setup code. Luckily, JUnit provides a setUp() method for just this purpose. To demonstrate
this, here's a new version of AddToShoppingCartTest that uses setUp() to eliminate the duplicated code. The new code is shown in red:

```
package test.com.iconixsw.bookstore.web;

import junit.framework.*;

public class AddToShoppingCartTest extends TestCase {

    private ShoppingCart cart;

    public AddToShoppingCartTest (String testName) {
        super(testName);
    }
```

```
public void setUp() {
    cart = new ShoppingCart();
}

public void testShoppingCartEmpty() throws Exception {
    assertEquals("Cart should be empty", 0, cart.getNumItems());
}

public void testItemAdded() throws Exception {
    LineItem item = new LineItem();
    cart.addItem(item);
    assertEquals("Cart should contain 1 item",
                 1, cart.getNumItems());
}

}
```

The setUp() method is run automatically, immediately before each test method is called. It's worth stressing that point: it isn't run just once for the whole test case. Instead, it's run once for each individual test method. So for each test method, you're guaranteed a nice, fresh instance of ShoppingCart (or whatever you put in your own setUp() method, naturally).

There's also a tearDown() method that does the reverse of setUp() and is useful for closing external resources like database connections or input/output streams. As you'd expect, tearDown() is called immediately after each individual test method.

JUNIT: THE NEXT GENERATION

At the time of this book going to press, the next generation of JUnit, version 4.0, is gradually beginning to see increased industry adoption (its reliance on the new language features in Java 5 may have slowed its adoption). Written by Kent Beck and Erich Gamma, it's backward-compatible with current versions of JUnit, so all your existing tests should still run, but it boasts lots of new features and refinements, making it more like NUnit with extensive support for annotations. Its new features include the following:

- Test classes do not have to extend junit.framework.TestCase.

- Test methods do not have to be prefixed with test. Instead, a test method can be tagged with the @Test annotation.

- Similarly, @Before and @After annotations provide the equivalent of setUp() and tearDown(). The benefit of the new approach is that, should you *really* need to, you can have more than one @Before and @After method in each test class.

- One-time setup and teardown for each test class can be done using the @BeforeClass and @AfterClass annotations.

- Tests can have a timeout value (passed in as a parameter in the @Test annotation).

For most of the rest of this chapter, we'll run through lots of examples to show how to drive unit test code directly from the test cases, which in turn are driven from the controllers on your robustness diagrams, which in turn are driven from the use cases. Our aim is to give you a detailed understanding of how to tie the tests closely to the requirements, at a microscopic level (the proposition that we opened this chapter with).

Writing Effective Unit Tests

Before we get started on the examples, it's worth outlining some best practices for writing good unit tests. Entire books have been devoted to unit testing, but effective unit testing techniques from a design-driven perspective can be summed up quite succinctly. So here goes:

- Keep unit tests fine-grained. Generally, you should cover a single test case with each unit test class and a different permutation or assertion of the test case (i.e., the individual test scenarios) in each test method. Which leads us to the next item . . .

- Make sure that each test method tests exactly one thing. Let's say you want to test the ability to add items to a Shopping Cart. You might have a test method that first adds an item, then asserts that the number of items in the cart is 1, and then (to *really* prove it was added successfully) asserts that if you retrieve the item, it's the same item that was added.

  But gosh, that's actually testing *two* separate things (the clue is that there are two assertions). First, it's testing that an item was definitely added; second, it's testing that retrieving an item returns the item you expect it to. Two separate test scenarios, meaning two separate test methods.

  Your first test method would be called `testAddItem()`, and the second test method would be called `testCorrectItemRetrieved()`.

- Tie the unit tests closely to the classes and methods you're testing.

- Tie the unit tests closely to the objects in the preliminary design (and therefore also to your use cases). Hopefully, you can see the connection between this point and the last point. If the unit test code is tied closely both to the preliminary design *and* to the classes and methods in the "real" production code, it ensures cohesion between the two. If it becomes troublesome to tie the unit tests at both ends, then it's a sign that the detailed design/source code might not have been driven 100% from the preliminary design. If this turns out to be the case, correct the design as soon as possible, and ***review the process*** step by step to work out where you might have gone wrong.

- Treat unit test code with the same reverence and care that you do production code. The unit test code is "designed" and needs to be maintained as much as the code that it's testing. The unit test design is driven as much from the preliminary design as the "real" detailed design is, and just as much care needs to be taken keeping the test code in trim. In particular . . .

- Avoid duplication in tests. As you're driving unit tests from your test cases (which are in turn driven from the controllers), each unit test class will consist of a lot of quite similar test methods, testing the different scenarios that pass through each controller. Whenever you see duplicated code, separate it out into shared methods or classes *as soon as you see it.*

- Make sure your tests always run at 100% success. Neglecting to fix an ailing test is an easy trap to fall into, especially in a team environment without individual code ownership, where a failing test is always somebody else's problem. If a test is failing, fix it immediately. This is especially true if you're following a test-driven methodology, in which you first write a failing test, and then write some code to make it pass. If you surge ahead writing a series of failing tests, then it becomes tempting to just turn a blind eye and concentrate on the code instead of fixing the tests.

- Use **mock objects** when you need to, but don't get too hung up on them. We provide an example of mock objects in the next section. They basically provide "stub" functionality for a real class that will be implemented later, or they act as a nonfunctional stand-in so as to avoid accessing external resources (e.g., a database), which slow down the tests and make test configuration more complex.

   We'll probably get hammered by the test-driven crowd for suggesting this but, while mock objects do have their uses, it's possible to overuse them. Their purpose is to lessen the code's dependency on external classes or resources (such as databases). However, every time you change the behavior of your code, you'll also have to fix the mock object tests. JUnit tests are pretty solid; you're testing the end behavior that doesn't change much. However, with mock objects, you're testing the flow of a method call, hence it is a lot more fragile. If you add one extra method call, or refactor the method internals, then you also have to change the mock-based tests.

   In the next section, we walk through an example for the Internet Bookstore, going all the way from the robustness diagram to the JUnit tests.

Design-Driven Testing in Practice

In this section, we illustrate the theory from the first part of this chapter, using our Internet Bookstore project. We revisit the detailed design as we left it in Chapter 9, and this time, instead of moving straight to code, we first create some test cases directly from the robustness diagrams, and match these up with the detailed design. We then use the test cases to verify that

- The detailed design matches up with the use cases.

- The code matches the detailed design and does what it's meant to.

Unit Tests for the Internet Bookstore

To write the unit tests for the Internet Bookstore, we'll take the controllers from the robustness diagrams for the *Show Book Details* and *Write Customer Review* use cases, generate test cases for them, and then write unit tests based on the test cases.

You should do this step just prior to writing the code, so that as you're coding, you have a decent set of unit tests to compile and test against. Starting to write or generate the tests is also a good way of getting yourself into the coding frame of mind, which is useful when you're doing the detailed design modeling.

Figure 12-6 shows the test case diagram. This was generated from the robustness diagram for *Show Book Details* shown back in Figure 5-10.

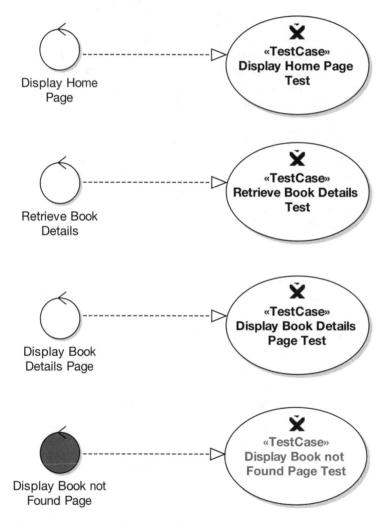

Figure 12-6. *Generated test cases for the* Show Book Details *use case*

The Display Book not Found Page controller and test case are both shown in red because they're the alternate course.

■Note We've renamed the Display controllers to be more descriptive, so that they can be differentiated (see the original version in Figure 12-4).

If some of the controllers have the same name (e.g., Display), the resultant test case diagram might be quite difficult (or impossible) to decipher. **Wherever you have controllers with the same name on the same diagram, you should rename the controllers so that you can tell them apart.** In the case of Display controllers, just add the name of the boundary object being displayed (e.g., Display Book Details Page and Display Book Details Page Test).

To recap, each controller from the robustness diagram gets its own test case, and in each test case we create one or more test scenarios. For each test case, we create a unit test class, and for each test scenario, we create a unit test method.

We'll walk through this process once for each of the test cases (in the order shown in Figure 12-6) until it's crystal clear.

Testing the Display Home Page Controller

In this section, we'll create the test scenarios for the Display Home Page controller, the simplest of the bunch, and then write its JUnit test class.

Here's the portion of the use case text that relates to this controller:

The Customer types in the URL for the bookstore's home page. The system displays a list of books from the Catalog on the home page, in the form of clickable links.

If you recall from Chapter 10, the list of books is actually just a hard-wired list, so there's no dynamic cleverness going on here. As a result, the test case for this particular controller is amazingly simple. In fact, we need to add only one test scenario to the test case, because—just this once—there's very little that can go wrong. To add a test scenario in EA, double-click the test case, and in the Properties dialog that pops up, click the Scenario tab (see Figure 12-7).

There's only actually the one test scenario for this test case, so you'd only expect to see one test method in the unit test class.

Figure 12-7. *Adding a test scenario for the Display Home Page test case*

Here's the JUnit test skeleton for this test case:

```
package test.com.iconixsw.bookstore.web;

import junit.framework.*;

public class DisplayHomePageTest extends TestCase {

    public DisplayHomePageTest(String testName) {
        super(testName);
    }

    public void testDisplayHomePage() throws Exception {
    }

}
```

The test extends TestCase, a JUnit class. In JUnit, any method whose name starts with test is automatically recognized as a test method. So in this case we have just one test method, testDisplayHomePage(), which is derived from the test scenario shown in Figure 12-7. If the test case had, say, three test scenarios, then you'd see three test methods instead of just the one.

So far it's all been quite easy—mechanical, even. However, at this stage it's difficult to say exactly what should go in the testDisplayHomePage() method. This is why it's now a good idea to go ahead and draw the sequence diagram for this use case. Figure 12-8 shows an excerpt from the *Show Book Details* sequence diagram that's relevant to this test case (see the full sequence diagram in Figure 9-8).

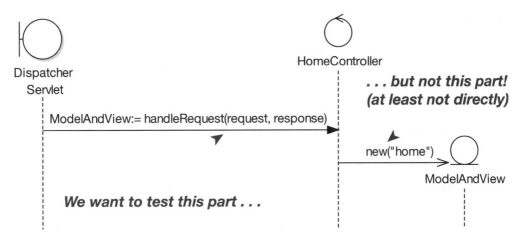

Figure 12-8. *Extract from the Display Home Page sequence diagram*

You need to write the tests from the point of view of whatever object is calling the controller that you're testing. In this case, HomeController is being tested, and the object calling it is a boundary object, DispatcherServlet (a Spring class). The unit test must verify that the result from handleRequest() is what's expected, given the values being passed in.

With that in mind, here's the test method:

```
public void testDisplayHomePage() throws Exception {
    HomeController homeController = new HomeController();
    ModelAndView modelAndView =
            homeController.handleRequest(null, null);

    assertEquals("Should be viewing home.jsp",
                 "home",
                 modelAndView.getViewName());
}
```

The test code first creates a new instance of HomeController, and then it calls the handleRequest() method. Because HomeController doesn't actually use the request or response, we can get away with just passing in null for those (in fact, that's a good habit to get into with tests, as the test explicitly shows that you're not expecting the request or response to be used).

Having retrieved the ModelAndView from homeController, the test then asserts that the view returned will indeed take us to home.jsp. (Recall from Chapter 10 that the web application is configured such that .jsp gets added to any view name, so if home is returned, it will become home.jsp.)

Now that you have your test, it's good practice to try and make it fail—this proves that the test will work if it ever encounters a *real* failure condition in the future. You can do this by first writing a blank(-ish) handleRequest() method:

```
package com.iconixsw.bookstore.web;
// import . . .

public class HomeController implements Controller {

    public ModelAndView handleRequest(
            HttpServletRequest request,
            HttpServletResponse response)
        throws ServletException, IOException {

        return new ModelAndView("");
    }
}
```

This version of HomeController returns a blank view name.[3] If you run the unit test against it, you'll get the following:

```
.F
Time: 0.015
There was 1 failure:
1) testDisplayHomePage
    (test.com.iconixsw.bookstore.web.DisplayHomePageTest)

junit.framework.ComparisonFailure:
Should be viewing home.jsp. expected:<home> but was:<>
        at test.com.iconixsw.bookstore.web.
            DisplayHomePageTest.testDisplayHomePage
            (DisplayHomePageTest.java:17)

FAILURES!!!
Tests run: 1,  Failures: 1,  Errors: 0
```

---

3. Strictly speaking, in the TDD world you would start without a handleRequest() method at all, prove that the test class doesn't compile, then add handleRequest() but make it return null in order to prove that you do indeed get a NullPointerException in your test method, *then* you would write the version that returns a blank ModelAndView and makes the test fail "properly," and *finally* you would write the working version and make the test pass. But we draw the line at seeing the test fail once, as we want each class to take less than a decade to write, plus we want to keep the page count of this book beneath 1,000!

Good, so that's proved that the test mechanism is working. We can now implement handleRequest() "properly":

```
public ModelAndView handleRequest(
        HttpServletRequest request,
        HttpServletResponse response)
    throws ServletException, IOException {

    return new ModelAndView("home");
}
```

And running the test we should now get this:

.

Time: 0.016

OK (1 test)

The one thing about the test method is that it's creating a resource in the test method itself, which is a bad habit to get into. The resource should be created in the setUp() method, which gets called prior to each test method being called.

The refactored code then looks like this:

```
package test.com.iconixsw.bookstore.web;

// import statements omitted

public class DisplayHomePageTest extends TestCase {

    private HomeController homeController;

    public DisplayHomePageTest(String testName) {
        super(testName);
    }

    public void setUp() throws Exception {
        homeController = new HomeController();
    }

    public void tearDown() throws Exception {
        homeController = null;
    }

    public void testDisplayHomePage() throws Exception {
        ModelAndView modelAndView = homeController.handleRequest(null, null);
        assertEquals("Should be viewing home.jsp.",
                    "home",
                    modelAndView.getViewName());
    }
}
```

We've turned homeController into a private variable and moved the line of code that creates it into the setUp() method. Notice that we've also added a tearDown() method (which gets called automatically *after* each test method) to set the homeController back to null. This isn't strictly speaking necessary but, even in the Java world, cleaning up after yourself is a mighty good habit to get into. Get into the habit now, and avoid spending days hunting down horrible, insidious memory leaks in the future.

A quick rerun of the test shows that none of its assertions has been broken, so that's about it for the first controller. We'll walk through the same process for the other controllers in the *Show Book Details* use case (even though it may get a bit repetitive), because ensuring proper test coverage for your controllers is an incredibly important part of the whole process, and it is worth repeating over and over until it totally clicks into place.

But just before we move onto the next controller/test case, let's do a quick bit of housekeeping.

Running the Tests from a Test Suite

We haven't yet shown how to run all the tests in one try. That's easy enough with JUnit. There's a GUI tool that can be launched from the command line, but there's also a text-based test runner that we're using for these examples.

It's possible to group all the unit test classes together into a single *test suite* and run that:

```
package test.com.iconixsw.bookstore;

import test.com.iconixsw.bookstore.web.*;
import junit.framework.*;

public class BookstoreTestSuite {

    public static Test suite() {
        TestSuite suite = new TestSuite();
        suite.addTestSuite(DisplayHomePageTest.class);
        // add more tests here . . .

        return suite;
    }

    public static void main(String[] args) {
        junit.textui.TestRunner.run(suite());
    }

}
```

If you run the BookstoreTestSuite from the command line, the main method will call suite(), which will gather together all of the individual test cases (currently just the one, DisplayHomePageTest) and return them collected together in a single object. These will then be passed to the JUnit TestRunner, which produces the "OK" and "Failures!!!" text output that you see in this chapter's examples.

As you write more test classes, you add them one by one to the test suite so that they can all be run together. It's a great way of ensuring that you haven't broken existing functionality when you add new controller logic. If your tests run quickly enough, it means you can run *all* the tests every time you change something or add something new—meaning complete end-to-end test coverage in a matter of seconds, all driven from the controllers on your robustness diagrams.

■Exercise If you have some tests that just have to take a long time (e.g., testing some long-running SQL statements), what could be done to handle this without losing the benefits of quick-running tests? We discuss some test strategies to handle this situation later in the chapter.

Now let's move on to the next controller for the *Show Book Details* use case.

HERE'S THE CHAPTER SPLIT WE WARNED YOU ABOUT!

The remainder of this "Design-Driven Testing in Practice" section is mostly of interest to developers who are currently practicing Test-Driven Development (TDD) as espoused by Kent Beck and his hard-working disciples. The rest of us can sit down for a few minutes and have a nice, relaxing cup of tea. A safe place to rejoin the chapter would be the Top 10 Design-Driven Testing Errors, on page 369.

The story told in the remainder of this chapter is true. Only the test case names have been changed to protect the innocent.

If you're not currently a "test-infected" TDD developer, the remainder of this section is . . . a lot of hard work. In fact, it might seem like a mind-boggling amount of hard work. However, it's a lot *less* work than practicing TDD without the benefit of an up-front analysis model and a set of use cases that describe alternate courses of action and itemize software behavior as controllers. If you are a TDD developer, we hope you'll agree that we can save you quite a bit of work without sacrificing the integrity of the functional testing that you're doing.

So, as the Internet Bookstore narrative continues, you'll notice that we suggest techniques for running your unit tests at a lightning-fast pace, so that they can be run repeatedly with each change or addition to the code. This will make perfect sense to keen TDDers, who essentially evolve the design as they write the unit tests and the code. But if you've followed the design process described in this book, rerunning the tests every few minutes becomes significantly less important. ICONIX Process makes a serious attempt to get as much of the refactoring done before coding as possible, and so therefore may also allow a more minimalist approach to testing than what you'll be reading about in the remainder of this section.

Having said that, we've kept the advice in the chapter because it can still be important if you're combining TDD with a use case–driven up-front design approach. The key here is to apply and adapt the process according to the needs (and agile philosophy) of your own project.

We'll make a few suggestions for more minimalist ("test smarter, not harder") alternatives as the chapter proceeds.

Testing the Retrieve Book Details Controller

In this section, we create the test scenarios for the Retrieve Book Details controller, and then write (and run!) its JUnit test class.

What do we want this particular unit test to do? If we match the Retrieve Book Details controller to the following use case text:

> *The Customer clicks a link on the home page . . . and the system retrieves the book details for the selected book . . .*

then this suggests that the test should assert that books are being retrieved correctly from the database.

To add test case scenarios in EA, double-click the test case and then, when the Properties dialog pops up, click the Scenario tab. You can then add basic and alternate scenarios to the test case. Figure 12-9 shows the two test scenarios that we'll add for the Retrieve Book Details controller/test case.

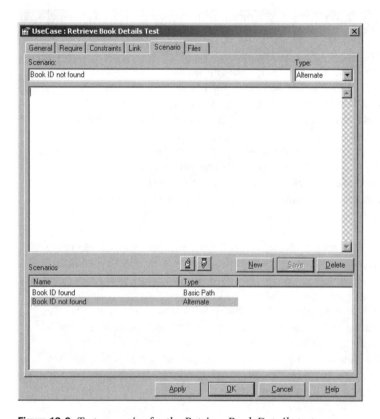

Figure 12-9. *Test scenarios for the Retrieve Book Details test case*

Now that you've added the test scenarios and further updated the use case and robustness diagram if needed, you draw the sequence diagram. The sequence diagram for *Show Book Details* is shown back in Figure 9-8. The next stage, then, is to create the unit test skeleton for this test case, using the scenarios you've just added (see Figure 12-9).

Here's the test class skeleton for the Retrieve Book Details controller/test case. The actual test methods (derived from the test case scenarios) are in red:

```
package test.com.iconixsw.bookstore.dao;

import junit.framework.*;

/**
 * Test case for the Retrieve Book Details controller.
 */
public class RetrieveBookDetailsTest extends TestCase {

    public RetrieveBookDetailsTest(String testName) {
        super(testName);
    }

    public void setUp() throws Exception {
    }

    public void tearDown() throws Exception {
    }

    public void testBookIdFound() {
    }

    public void testBookIdNotFound() {
    }
}
```

The two empty test methods, testBookIdFound() and testBookIdNotFound(), are derived directly from the two test scenarios shown in Figure 12-9.

As we discussed at the start of this section, we want to test that the Book ID is found (or not found) correctly in the database. However, a golden rule for unit tests is that they need to be able to run *really* quickly. **If the unit tests don't run really quickly, then people won't bother to run them at all while they're programming.** For this reason, it's good practice to try to avoid writing tests that create connections to external resources (e.g., databases). Connecting to databases (even locally) and running queries or updates can make unit tests run disproportionately slowly, especially when the same setup or teardown code is iterated over hundreds of times.

■**Tip** Sometimes you do need some longer-running tests that connect to databases or run lengthy processes (e.g., testing a system's ability to import and parse large files). It's useful to set up a separate test suite for these, and schedule the tests to run automatically overnight or (even better) on a build/test PC that runs hourly.

But if you can't include database code in your speedy tests, how do you actually *test* anything? One answer is to use so-called mock objects.[4] For example, we could replace our JDBC-specific DAO classes with "mock" versions, whose sole purpose in life is to provide the same unit test data, over and over, albeit very quickly.

You shouldn't go crazy and rewrite the entire JDBC data access layer in one attempt; instead, just add the "mock" code that you need, one method at a time, as and when you find that you need it. In other words, *use mock objects sparingly*!

Let's add some code to the test class to retrieve a Book given an ID, and to assert that it's been received:

```
private BookDao bookDao;

public void testBookIdFound() {
    Book book = bookDao.findById(1);
    assertNotNull("ID 1 should be found", book);
}
```

If you try to run the unit test now, you'll get a NullPointerException, as the BookDao hasn't been initialized. A good place to do that is in the setUp() method:

```
public void setUp() throws Exception {
    bookDao = new MockBookDao();
}
```

Obviously this won't compile, as there isn't yet a MockBookDao class. This is a good time to add it:

```
package com.iconixsw.bookstore.dao.mock;

// import statements omitted . . .

public class MockBookDao implements BookDao {

    private HashMap booksById;

    public MockBookDao() {
        initData();
    }
```

---

4. As we discussed in the "Writing Effective Unit Tests" section of this chapter, mock objects are overused in the test-driven world, but in certain very specific cases they do prove useful.

```java
    public List findAll() throws DataAccessException {
        return (List) booksById.values();
    }

    public Book findById(int bookId) throws DataAccessException {
        return (Book) booksById.get(new Integer(bookId));
    }

    private void initData() {
        Book favWidgets = new Book();
        favWidgets.setId(1);
        favWidgets.setTitle("My Favorite Widgets");

        Book uncommon = new Book();
        uncommon.setId(2);
        uncommon.setTitle("The Uncommon Event");

        booksById = new HashMap();
        booksById.put(new Integer(1), favWidgets);
        booksById.put(new Integer(2), uncommon);
    }

}
```

BookDao does the simplest thing possible (this isn't production code after all; it's just a development tool purely for internal use), which is to create a couple of Book objects and stick them into a HashMap keyed by the book ID. The data never gets saved out to disk; it's all done in-memory.

Now that we have a compiling test, we should run this through JUnit. But we really want to see the test fail first, to prove that the test works. So to do that, just briefly change the initData() method as follows:

```java
        Book favWidgets = new Book();
        favWidgets.setId(5);
        favWidgets.setTitle("My Favorite Widgets");
```

We've simply changed the 1 to a 5, so that the mock DAO doesn't return a book with an ID of 1. Running this test now, we get the following results:

```
.F
Time: 0
There was 1 failure:
1) testBookIdFound
   (test.com.iconixsw.bookstore.dao.RetrieveBookDetailsTest)
```

```
junit.framework.AssertionFailedError:
ID 1 should be found
at test.com.iconixsw.bookstore.dao.
   RetrieveBookDetailsTest.
   testBookIdFound(RetrieveBookDetailsTest.java:29)

FAILURES!!!
Tests run: 1,  Failures: 1,  Errors: 0
```

It seems strange to cheer and holler when you see a test fail, but it should make you feel good about the test because you now know for sure that, if there's a time when it really *should* fail, then it will do its job properly.

Now if we change the value back to 1 and rerun the test, here's the result:

```
.
Time: 0

OK (1 test)
```

Currently, we're only testing "one way"—that is, that a Book was found. We also need to test the alternate course:

```
public void testBookIdNotFound() {
    Book book = bookDao.findById(-1);
    assertNull("ID -1 should not be found", book);
}
```

What's wrong with this picture so far? You win a pork pie if you noticed that currently this test class isn't actually testing any of our *real* code. Test cases for data-retrieval controllers tend to end up like this, because they're not doing very much in the way of serious code logic, and because we don't want to test the actual data access (at least not in these particular unit tests), that doesn't leave very much left to test.

However—and this is the thing—it's the controllers **linked** to the data-retrieval controllers that will get the benefit of all this mock-object effort. For those controllers, we're not interested in testing the database access; we want to test the controllers themselves, so it doesn't matter whether the data came from a mock object, or a real database, or even from a pork pie.

The result of this effort is that we now effectively have a very simple, controlled, in-memory data source (with its own unit tests!), which the other controllers will be able to use. And, to top it all, our tests should now run blazingly fast and have zero configuration because they don't have to hit a real database.

Let's move on to the next controller.

Testing the Display Book Details Controller

The use case text that relates to this test case is as follows:

> *... the system retrieves the book details for the selected book and displays them on the View Book Details page.*

That should be a nice, bite-sized piece of work to write a test case for. Figure 12-10 shows the test scenarios added into EA for this test case.

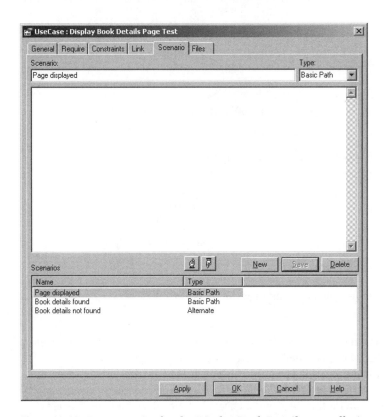

Figure 12-10. *Test scenarios for the Display Book Details controller/test case*

There are three test scenarios: "Page displayed," "Book details found," and "Book details not found." However, one of these isn't quite right.

Impostor alert: We've added a "Book details not found" test scenario, which seems like a good idea. However, checking back to the test cases shown in Figure 12-6, there's already a separate alternate course (and accompanying test case) for the case where the book details aren't found.

■**Tip** When you're adding "alternate" test scenarios, always check that you're not just duplicating an alternate course in the use case itself.

So for this test case, there are really only two test scenarios: "Page displayed" and "Book details found." Both of these are "basic path" test scenarios, which makes sense, because the test case itself is for one of the controllers in the use case's basic course.

Let's pause to get our bearings. Figure 12-11 shows an excerpt from the *Show Book Details* sequence diagram.

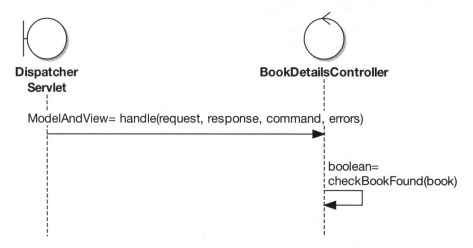

Dispatcher Servlet   **BookDetailsController**

ModelAndView= handle(request, response, command, errors)

boolean=
checkBookFound(book)

Figure 12-11. *Excerpt from the* Show Book Details *sequence diagram*

Remember that you should write the test from the point of view of the object that is calling the controller. The calling object is usually a boundary object, though it may also be another controller. We only want the calls going *into* the controller being tested. As you can see from Figure 12-11, this means testing two methods: handle() and checkBookFound().

Here's the test class skeleton for the Display Book Details controller/test case (the test methods are shown in red):

```
package test.com.iconixsw.bookstore.web;

import junit.framework.*;

/**
 * Test case for the Display Book Details Page controller.
 */
public class DisplayBookDetailsPageTest extends TestCase {
```

```
    public DisplayBookDetailsPageTest(String testName) {
        super(testName);
    }

    public void setUp() throws Exception {
    }

    public void tearDown() throws Exception {
    }

    public void testPageDisplayed()throws Exception {
    }

    public void testBookDetailsFound()throws Exception {
    }
}
```

Checking Figure 12-11, we'll want to create a BookDetailsController object to push and prod, and it would make sense to put this in setUp() so that the same setup code can be shared by both the test methods:

```
public void setUp() throws Exception {
    bookDetailsController = new BookDetailsController();
    bookDetailsController.setBookDao(new MockBookDao());
}
private BookDetailsController bookDetailsController;
```

In setUp(), we're now creating a new BookDetailsController and telling it to use the MockBookDao class that we created earlier.

setBookDao() is a simple setter method on BookDetailsController:

```
public void setBookDao(BookDao bookDao) {
    this.bookDao = bookDao;
}
private BookDao bookDao;
```

The following code shows the beginnings of the first of the two test methods, testPageDisplayed():

```
public void testPageDisplayed() throws Exception {
    Book command = new Book();
    command.setId(1);
    ModelAndView modelAndView =
            bookDetailsController.handle(null, null, command, null);

    // assert...
}
```

We can now add the `handle()` method to `BookDetailsController`:

```
protected ModelAndView handle(
                HttpServletRequest request,
                HttpServletResponse response,
                Object command,
                BindException errors) throws Exception {


    return null;
}
```

Initially it just returns null, because we want to be able to run the test first and see it fail cataclysmically. (Well, perhaps not *completely* cataclysmically, but a simple "test failed" would be nice.)

Unfortunately, the `testPageDisplayed()` test code won't compile as it stands, because the `handle()` method on `BookDetailsController` is, rather annoyingly, `protected`—not `public` (it overrides a Spring method). So we would need to make the overriding method `public` (in Java, it's legal to increase an overriding method's visibility). But another problem is that the `handle()` method accepts several objects that are difficult to create outside their respective APIs without a lot of boilerplate code. This is one of those wrinkles in the fabric of the otherwise perfect space-time continuum that surfaces to taunt us from time to time.

One solution is to pass null values into the method, but the method is now starting to look and behave less and less like it should in the real world, all for the purposes of testing.

For now, because we can, we'll leave `handle()` unaltered and with `protected` visibility, and instead add a separate, `public` method to `BookDetailsController` so that the test can call it. We'll prefix the method with "test" so that later we'll know that it is for a unit test:

```
public ModelAndView testHandle(Book command)
throws Exception {
    return handle(null, null, command, null);
}
```

The new method simply delegates to the real `handle()` method. `handle()` doesn't actually use the `request`, `response`, or `errors` parameter, so we can pass in null for these. In fact, the only parameter that really matters is `Book`. Now we can rewrite the test method to use this new method:

```
ModelAndView modelAndView =
        bookDetailsController.testHandle(command);
```

Checking the sequence diagram in Figure 12-11, we can see that the second method, `checkBookFound()`, is actually a private method called by `handle()`, so we don't need to write a specific test method for it.[5] Instead, the output from `checkBookFound()` will contribute to the eventual output of `handle()`, which we *do* need to test.

Now we can compile the test, run it against `BookDetailsController` (with its empty `handle()` method that returns null), and watch it fail. Hurrah—sort of.

---

5. If you wanted to *really* embrace the micro-grained, test-driven spirit of things, you could make `checkBookFound()` public and write an additional test method for it; it probably wouldn't do any harm.

The next step is, one would hope, to write the real code for the handle() method. Except we haven't added any assert statements into the two test methods yet, so currently we're not testing for anything. Best to be good test-driven citizens and do that first. It's quite a weighty ream of code with lots of duplication, so brace yourself. We'll turn it into something a bit more compact later.

```java
public class DisplayBookDetailsPageTest extends TestCase {

    public DisplayBookDetailsPageTest(String testName) {
        super(testName);
    }

    public void setUp() throws Exception {
        bookDetailsController = new BookDetailsController();
        bookDetailsController.setBookDao(new MockBookDao());
    }
    private BookDetailsController bookDetailsController;

    public void tearDown() throws Exception {
        bookDetailsController = null;
    }

    public void testPageDisplayed() throws Exception {
        Book command = new Book();
        command.setId(1);
        ModelAndView modelAndView =
                BookDetailsController.testHandle(command);

        assertEquals("The bookdetails page should be displayed",
                "bookdetails",
                modelAndView.getViewName());
    }

    public void testBookDetailsFound() throws Exception {
        BookDetailsCommand command = new BookDetailsCommand();
        command.setId(1);
        ModelAndView modelAndView =
                bookDetailsController.testHandle(command);

        Map model = modelAndView.getModel();
        Book book = (Book) model.get("book");
        assertEquals("The book should have been found",
                1,
                book.getId());
    }
}
```

As you can see, each test method initially does more or less the same thing: it sets up a Book command object, assigns it an ID, and then passes it to the BookDetailsController and gets a ModelAndView object back. The two methods, testPageDisplayed() and testBookDetailsFound(), each assigns an ID of 1, an *existing* Book ID (because these two methods are testing the basic course).

It seems like it would make sense to move this code into setUp() so that it gets called just prior to each test method. Each test method then starts by calling bookDetailsController.testHandle(), so that the resultant ModelAndView can be pushed and prodded by the test method. Note that bookDetailsController.testHandle() itself doesn't go in setUp(), as strictly speaking it isn't really setup code—it's part of the actual test. By putting the code in setUp(), we would effectively be saying to anyone who reads the code, "This is test *setup* code, not test code," which is a tad misleading. So instead, we've moved it into a separate method so it can be shared by both test methods.

Here's the resultant test code (the refactored code is shown in red):

```
private Book command;

public void setUp() throws Exception {
    command = new Book();
    command.setId(1);
}

public void testPageDisplayed() throws Exception {
    ModelAndView modelAndView = callTestHandle();
    assertEquals("The bookdetails page should be displayed.",
                 "bookdetails",
                 modelAndView.getViewName());
}

public void testBookDetailsFound() throws Exception {
    ModelAndView modelAndView = callTestHandle();
    Map model = modelAndView.getModel();
    Book book = (Book) model.get("book");
    assertEquals("The book should have been found.",
                 1,
                 book.getId());
}

private ModelAndView callTestHandle() {
    return bookDetailsController.testHandle(command);
}
```

Running this test class, we get red lights everywhere (aka test failures) because the handle() method is still returning null; we'll fix that in a second.

So, to round off this test case, *now* we can safely add the real code into the handle() method on BookDetailsController:

```
protected ModelAndView handle(
                    HttpServletRequest request,
                    HttpServletResponse response,
                    Object command,
                    BindException errors) throws Exception {

    Book book = (Book) command;
    book.load(bookDao);
    return new ModelAndView("bookdetails", "book", book);
}
```

Running this code through the voracious unit tester, we get green lights, meaning the tests pass. But you'd be right to feel uneasy, because this code doesn't handle the possibility that the book might not have been found. So, somewhat fortuitously, let's move on to the next test case.

Testing the Display Book Not Found Page Controller

In the final test case, we test the alternate course in which a book ID is passed in that doesn't exist. The use case text that relates to this test case is as follows:

ALTERNATE COURSES:

Book not found: *The system displays a Book Details Not Found page.*

Figure 12-12 shows the test scenarios added into EA for this test case.

There are two test scenarios: "Book Not Found page displayed" and "Book details not found." Both of these are categorized as Alternate test scenarios, which makes sense because this is a test case for a controller on an alternate course in the use case.

Figure 12-13 shows an excerpt from the sequence diagram that covers the design for this alternate course. (See the full sequence diagram in Figure 9-7.)

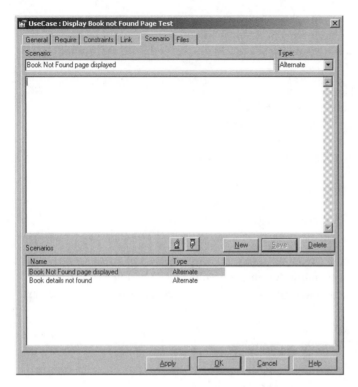

Figure 12-12. *Test scenarios for the Display Book Not Found controller/test case*

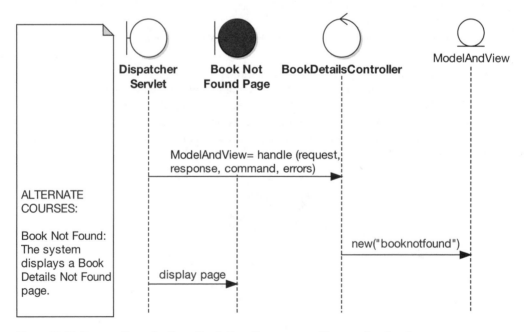

Figure 12-13. *Excerpt from the* Show Book Details *sequence diagram for the alternate course*

As you've probably gathered by now, writing the skeleton code for the unit test class (assuming it isn't being generated automatically for you) is a simple matter of walking through the test scenarios for this test case and adding a test method for each scenario. The test methods are shown in red in the following code:

```
public class DisplayBookNotFoundPageTest extends TestCase {

    public DisplayBookNotFoundPageTest(String testName) {
        super(testName);
    }

    public void setUp() throws Exception {
    }

    public void tearDown() throws Exception {
    }

    public void testBookNotFoundPageDisplayed() throws Exception {
    }

    public void testBookDetailsNotFound() throws Exception {
    }
}
```

The setup code for this class will be identical to the setup code for the previous test case, DisplayBookDetailsPageTest. In fact, the code that goes into each of the test methods is also very similar; we could even make use of that callTestHandle() method. In fact, it *appears* to make sense that DisplayBookNotFoundPageTest should be a subclass of DisplayBookDetailsPageTest. Of course, we would need to make callTestHandle() protected so that the methods in the subclass can call it directly. Another, slight complication is that this test case is testing for invalid book IDs (whereas DisplayBookDetailsPageTest was testing for valid IDs, so the callTestHandle() method was simply using the ID 1 each time). In order to reuse callTestHandle(), then, we'll need to modify it to take an argument, so that we can pass in a different book ID.

WHY BOTHER DESIGNING THE UNIT TESTS?

You might wonder why we're spending time on the design of the unit test classes instead of the "real" production code. Surely the unit tests are "second-class citizens"?

We've noticed a tendency for programmers to write unit tests in an ad hoc fashion, paying virtually zero attention to their design (the thought process seems to be, "Hey, they're not part of the main code base, so why waste our time on them?"). The result is that once the project contains more than a few small unit tests, it becomes just as difficult to maintain or extend the tests as with "proper" functional source code.

The result also is that the test classes tend to become monolithic, thousand-line beasts. You may also find that there will be less and less correlation between the test, the code that it's testing, and what the test's assertion was originally meant to be proving. It becomes very difficult to match up a test failure with the root cause of the failure. A bit like the "fog of war," you end up with the "fog of test failure." Rather than the failed test naturally pointing to the point of failure, you instead have to debug it, spend a while trawling through poorly designed test code, and then trace it through the code being tested, eventually tracking down the root cause of the failure.

But just being aware that some attention must be paid to the test design goes a long, long way toward alleviating this problem. And *that's* why you need to keep an eye on the unit test code, and keep its design nice and clean!

Figure 12-14 shows how the two classes should fit together (TestCase is shown in red as it's an external JUnit class).

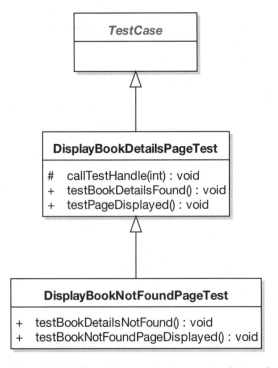

Figure 12-14. *Class diagram for the two Book Details test cases (first attempt)*

However, the problem with this design is that when `DisplayBookNotFoundPageTest` is run, the tests from the parent test class will also be run. It isn't a big problem, but it's a bit messy. In effect, we're saying that `DisplayBookNotFoundPageTest` is-a `DisplayBookDetailsTest`, which really it isn't. Also, using an inheritance relationship in this way could limit the code's extensibility: what if you find that some other test cases could also share the helper method, but are otherwise unrelated (i.e., where an is-a relationship *really* wouldn't make any sense)? Similarly, you might want `DisplayBookNotFoundPageTest` to share some functionality in some other abstract parent class, but Java doesn't support multiple inheritance (thank goodness!).

So this design still isn't quite right. Whatever to do?

You could take the "postmodernistic" approach[6] and avoid inheritance in favor of aggregation. In other words, you could move the common code into a separate helper class shared by both test cases (see Figure 12-15).

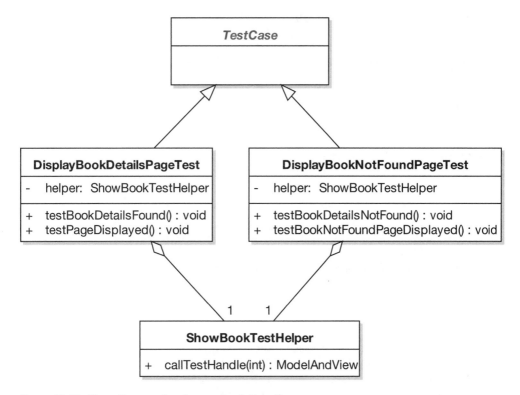

Figure 12-15. *Class diagram for the two Book Details test cases*

---

6. Shortly after the "Gang of Four" book was published, inheritance was all the rage—everyone who was anyone was doing it. However, it didn't take long for people to encounter the sorts of problems we've described here. So nowadays, aggregation (and copious use of interfaces) is generally seen as a neater, less problematic approach.

Here's our sleek, postmodernistic test helper class:

```
public class ShowBookTestHelper {

    public ModelAndView callTestHandle(int bookId) throws Exception {
        BookDetailsController bookDetailsController =
                                new BookDetailsController();
        bookDetailsController.setBookDao(new MockBookDao());

        Book command = new Book();
        command.setId(bookId);
        return bookDetailsController.testHandle(command);
    }
}
```

And finally, here's the new version of DisplayBookNotFoundPageTest, refactored to use the new shared helper class (the code that uses the helper class is shown in red):

```
public class DisplayBookNotFoundPageTest extends TestCase {

    public DisplayBookNotFoundPageTest(String testName) {
        super(testName);
    }

    public void setUp() throws Exception {
        helper = new ShowBookTestHelper();
    }
    private ShowBookTestHelper helper;

    public void testBookNotFoundPageDisplayed() throws Exception {
        ModelAndView modelAndView = helper.callTestHandle(-1);
        assertEquals("The booknotfound page should be displayed",
                    "booknotfound",
                    modelAndView.getViewName());
    }

    public void testBookDetailsNotFound() throws Exception {
        ModelAndView modelAndView = helper.callTestHandle(-1);
        Map model = modelAndView.getModel();
        Book book = (Book) model.get("book");
        assertNull("The book should not have been found", book);
    }
}
```

DisplayBookDetailsPageTest will also look quite similar to this class after refactoring it to use ShowBookTestHelper. If you're interested, you can download the finished code from this book's website.

That about wraps it up for the testing element of the use case–driven process. We'll finish this chapter with our top 10 list of Design-Driven Testing errors.

■**Note** Non-TDDers who opted to skip over this more mind-bending part of the chapter for the much safer option of a nice cup of tea may safely rejoin the chapter here.

Top 10 Design-Driven Testing Errors (the "Don'ts")

To break with tradition, we're presenting a top 10 list of the **things you shouldn't do** when Design-Driven Testing, in addition to the top 10 "do's" from the start of the chapter.

10. Go overboard with mock objects.

While mock objects do have limited usefulness to "grease the skids" of your testing process, they suffer from a law of diminishing returns. It's all too easy to end up with code that does this sort of thing:

Unit test: Assert that the mock object returns 3.0

Mock object: Return 3.0

Of course, that isn't testing for anything—your unit tests and your mock objects are just giving each other mutual kisses and cuddles. While you may get a warm feeling because you have 1,000+ mock objects returning the values that your tests are expecting, it doesn't do much for the quality of your software.

9. Duplicate alternate course scenarios in the alternate test scenarios for basic course controllers.

(Pause for a moment to reread that last line.) When you're brainstorming test case scenarios, it's easy to think up rainy-day scenarios that were already thought of when you were brainstorming alternate scenarios for your use cases. It's important to make sure you don't duplicate these scenarios. Make sure the rainy-day test scenarios go into the appropriate alternate course test case.

8. Forget to tie the tests closely to the requirements.

7. Leave testing until after the code has been written.

If there's one thing we have in common with the XP crowd, it's that we firmly believe that testing should begin before you start writing the code. In fact, you should begin thinking about testing and preparing the way, long before that. Retrospective testing (i.e., sitting down and testing the code after it's been written) is better than no testing at all, but it's possible to eliminate a lot more bugs, before they even exist, by testing early.

6. Confuse testing with designing.

Well, OK, this one is a bit tongue-in-cheek. But hopefully in the course of this book, we've brought home to you the importance of designing *before* you begin coding and testing. It is possible to design your code by writing unit tests (the basic premise of

Test-Driven Development [TDD]), but we feel that it's much more efficient and more "bulletproof" to design using the process we've described, and then write the tests to validate and further hone the design.

5. Ignore problem hot spots.

When you find patches of buggy code, find out why they're there, and try to fix the problems at the source. Remember that the probability of finding a bug in a given piece of code increases with the number of bugs already found in that piece of code.

Tip   When fixing a bug, always start by writing a test that will fail if the bug reoccurs.

---

4. Use **brute force testing** instead of identifying and then targeting "test hot spots" from your preliminary design.

3. Use the wrong kind of testing for the wrong situation.

2. Forget to do any testing at all.

1. Test so thoroughly that you never release the product.

More Practice

This section provides a list of questions that you can use to test your knowledge of DDT.

1. Which of the following would you use to specify your system tests?

   a) Robustness diagrams

   b) Use cases

   c) Sequence diagrams

   d) Conceptual design

2. What's the main difference between integration testing and compatibility testing?

   a) Integration testing exposes faults in the interaction between "internal" classes, whereas compatibility testing checks that the system interoperates correctly with other, "external" systems and components.

   b) Integration testing checks that the system interoperates correctly with other, "external" systems and components, whereas compatibility testing exposes faults in the interaction between "internal" classes.

   c) Integration testing proves that the system that was specified has been delivered, whereas compatibility testing proves that the system delivers what was actually requested.

   d) Integration testing proves that the system delivers what was actually requested, whereas compatibility testing proves that the system that was specified has been delivered.

3. Unit tests are derived from, and check the processing logic contained in, which of the following?

   a) Controllers

   b) Boundary classes

   c) Entity classes

   d) Use cases

4. What's the maximum number of test methods you should have in each unit test class? What can happen if the test class (or the individual test methods) grows too large?

5. Which of the following statements is true?

   a) You should tie the boundary classes in the preliminary design to the setup methods in the unit test classes.

   b) You should tie the controller method names closely to the unit test class names.

   c) You should keep your unit test methods coarse-grained.

   d) You should tie the unit tests closely to the classes and methods you're testing.

6. Describe when mock objects are beneficial, and also describe the "point of diminishing returns" when they cease to be useful.

7. Why is aggregation a preferable design strategy to generalization when creating test classes?

8. For each use case, should the alternate courses be tested in the same test class as the basic course? Explain your answer.

Summary

In this chapter, we covered the various forms of use case–driven testing and described when you would want to use each of them. We also ran through an example of Design-Driven Testing (DDT) for the Internet Bookstore and wrote some unit tests to cover the *Show Book Details* use case.

Figure 12-16 shows where we are. The activities covered in this chapter are shown in red.

If you want to further explore the possibilities of combining use case–driven development with Test-Driven Development (TDD), we provide an in-depth discussion and detailed example in *Agile Development with ICONIX Process* (Apress, 2005).

One of the key points in this chapter is that tests don't prove a huge amount if they aren't tied microscopically closely in with the requirements (though not so closely that the requirements *are* the tests—that would be silly!). In the next and final chapter, we talk about requirements and show how they fit into the overall process.

Milestone 3: Critical Design Review

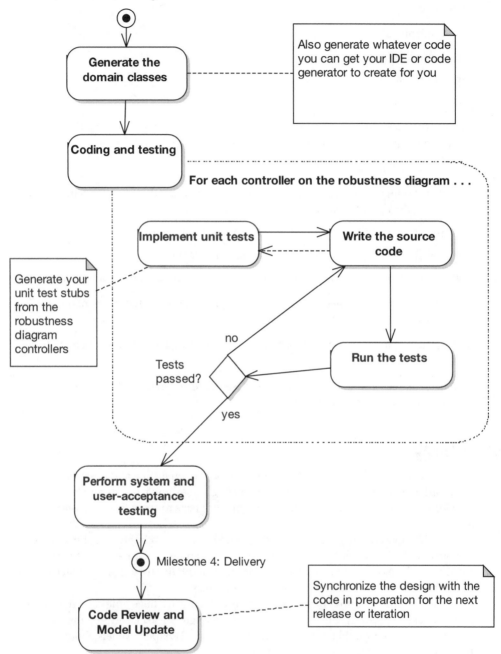

Figure 12-16. *Testing activities during the implementation stage*

CHAPTER 13

■■■

Addressing Requirements

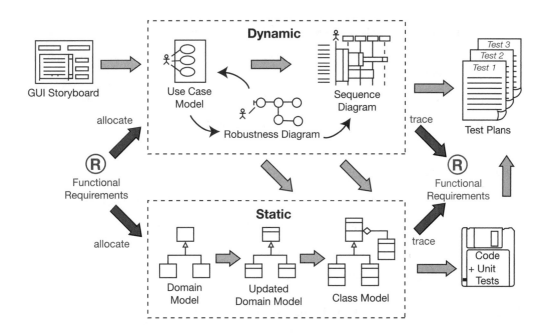

Dynamic

GUI Storyboard

Use Case Model

Robustness Diagram

Sequence Diagram

allocate

trace

Test Plans

Test 1
Test 2
Test 3

Ⓡ Functional Requirements

allocate

Ⓡ Functional Requirements

Static

Domain Model

Updated Domain Model

Class Model

trace

Code + Unit Tests

We've held off on discussing requirements until the end of the book for a couple of reasons. First off, there seems to be a lot of confusion about the differences between requirements, use cases, and behavior (operations). Since we talked about use cases in Chapter 3, allocating behavior in Chapter 8, and a whole series of techniques driven by use cases and operations in the subsequent chapters, it's easier to talk about requirements in terms of how they contrast with those items.

The requirements process described in this chapter isn't a core part of ICONIX Process as such, so that's another reason this chapter is at the end. It's not a core part of the process simply because different organizations have different strategies for handling requirements. In some companies, the requirements are just handed down from on high, and for political or other reasons, there's no ability to change the requirements elicitation process. In fact, sometimes it seems as if there are as many ways of addressing requirements as there are software development projects. But we believe that if you take the ideas in this chapter to heart, you'll find your customers will be more satisfied with what you deliver.

Requirements Gathering in Theory

In this section we describe the theory behind requirements gathering in a use case–driven project. First up are our top 10 requirements gathering guidelines.

Top 10 Requirements Gathering Guidelines

The principles discussed in this chapter can be summed up as a list of guidelines. Our top 10 list follows.

10. Use a modeling tool that supports linkage and traceability between requirements and use cases.

9. Link requirements to use cases by dragging and dropping.

8. Avoid **dysfunctional requirements** by separating functional details from your behavioral specification.

7. Write at least one test case for each requirement.

6. Treat requirements as first-class citizens in the model.

5. Distinguish between different types of requirements.

4. Avoid the "big monolithic document" syndrome.

3. Create estimates from the use case scenarios, not from the functional requirements.

2. Don't be afraid of examples when writing functional requirements.

1. Don't make your requirements a technical fashion statement.

Let's look at each of these items in more detail.

10. Use a Modeling Tool That Supports Linkage and Traceability

As irrational as it sounds, there was a time when visual modeling tools didn't have built-in support for allocation and traceability "out of the box" (at least not without purchasing six additional software modules at a cost of eleventy-million dollars, and then hiring a team of consultants to manage the interfaces between the tools). These days, however, matters have improved, and we can adopt a much more rational process.

For example, Enterprise Architect (EA) provides support for drag-and-drop allocation of requirements and automatic generation of a requirements traceability matrix. We show an example of that later in this chapter.

9. Link Requirements to Use Cases by Dragging and Dropping

We show an example of this in the second part of this chapter, but in a nutshell you can link any element in your model back to a requirement by dragging the requirement onto the element. Naturally, we recommend doing this with use cases (i.e., **drag the requirement onto the use case**), as you can then automatically generate and display a traceability matrix to see how all of your behavioral requirements link back to the customer's original high-level requirements.

8. Avoid Dysfunctional Requirements

A recent trend we've seen that's a bit disturbing involves mixing the functional requirement statements in with use case text. We're not sure whose advice has led so many different organizations to this style of writing use cases, but it certainly seems to be in fashion as we're writing this chapter. We've seen it often enough during recent Jumpstart classes that we decided to invent a new term to describe it: we call it *intermangling* of requirements and scenario text.

In other words, the (passive voice) requirements statements become intermixed and mangled up—*intermangled*—with the (active voice) scenario text. So you can't quite tell if you're reading a use case or a requirements document. You're just not sure: *Is it a functional requirement? Is it a nonfunctional requirement? Is it a behavioral requirement . . . what is it that I'm reading here?* The use cases are rendered . . . well, useless, actually.

We believe it's much better to separate out the active voice (use case) stuff from the passive voice (requirement) stuff. When they're all intermangled together, they aren't really very useful in our experience. So we've begun referring to this style of requirements spec as *dysfunctional requirements*. They're dysfunctional because of their schizophrenic nature. The specification is unsure if it's a list of functional requirements or a list of use case steps; it has a split personality.

One of the reasons that intermangled requirements and use cases are dysfunctional is that **you can't disambiguate the use cases and put them in the context of the object model when they're intermangled with the functional requirements**. All the use case text has to be active voice text that describes how the users interact with the system as the program is running. So **you have to disintermangle them before you can disambiguate them**. It's quite important, actually.

■**Note** We hope you've gotten a real-world feeling about ICONIX Process from this book. Doug spends up to 20 weeks a year (sometimes more) out in the field, applying this process on real projects, with more than half of the projects being new developments from existing clients. Having done this for over a decade, we have a pretty good idea of what works and what doesn't.

DISINTERMANGLING DYSFUNCTIONAL REQUIREMENTS FROM THE SCENARIO TEXT

As previously mentioned, dysfunctional requirements are functional requirements that appear in the use case scenario text (which, as you know by now, should contain only *behavioral* requirements). Here's an example, with the dysfunctional text in red. (Please, don't try this at home.)

BASIC COURSE:
The user clicks the Advanced Search button on the hub page.
The system displays the Advanced Search page.
[REQUIREMENT] On this page, there are two search fields: Search by Title, Search by Author; and search options:
[REQUIREMENT] Order results by sales rank;
[REQUIREMENT] Order results alphabetically by Title;
[REQUIREMENT] Order results alphabetically by Author;

[REQUIREMENT] Order results by date.

The user enters a book title and clicks the Submit button.

[REQUIREMENT] The search results should be fine-tuned to be displayed to the user in no more than five seconds.

The system displays the Search Results Page.

(We also slipped a nonfunctional requirement in there to show how easy it is to fall into the trap!)

The text in red *is* important and it needs to be specified *someplace*, but the use case just isn't that place. One of the purposes of robustness analysis, in addition to disambiguation, is to remove the intermangled requirements from the use case text and put them somewhere more appropriate (i.e., in separate requirement elements that are linked to the use cases).

If that doesn't seem to make sense, perhaps this will help:

*We remove **dysfunctionality** from the requirements by **disintermangling** them from the scenario text and then **disambiguating** them, in preparation for prefactoring the design.*

Hopefully that clears things up a little . . .

■**Note**   Intermangling has a dangerous cousin that we might call *vicious intermangling*. A classic example of vicious intermangling is to repeat the functional requirements inline within each and every use case that has anything to do with satisfying the requirement. We once met someone in Phoenix who, when we pointed out repeated inline instances of functional requirements (each with a unique number!) within the use cases, replied, "Oh, definitely. Some of these are repeated 70 or 80 times." Whereupon we asked him how he knew whether he had 80 distinct requirements or a single requirement repeated 80 times. We wish we were making this stuff up.

---

7. Write at Least One Test Case for Each Requirement

Make sure that your tests are tied closely to the requirements. That isn't to say that every test should be traced back to a requirement, but there should at least be a test to "prove" that each requirement has been implemented correctly.

In Chapter 12, we describe several techniques for tying your requirements closely to your test cases.

6. Treat Requirements As First-Class Citizens in the Model

Give each requirement a short, catchy name, just as you would a use case or a class.

5. Distinguish Between Different Types of Requirements

Requirements specs tend to be a mixture of high- and low-level requirements, of business requirements and technical notes—whatever the driving force is that has pushed the project into existence. But it's worth separating the requirements into different sections delineated by the types of requirements (e.g., functional, data, performance, capacity, and test requirements).

4. Avoid the "Big Monolithic Document" Syndrome

Treat the functional spec as a collection of short, highly focused, interlinked documents linked back to from the use cases, instead of one big impenetrable 200-page tome.

3. Don't Create Estimates Directly from the Functional Requirements

Break the requirements down into use cases first (see Chapter 3), and then create estimates from the use cases. Even better, draw the robustness diagrams (see Chapter 5) and create estimates from the list of controllers.

2. Don't Be Afraid of Examples When Writing Functional Requirements

When writing functional requirements specs, use examples copiously throughout, as a brief, concrete example often illustrates a point much more succinctly than a normative explanation. Also remember to keep the examples interesting, to hold the reader's attention.

1. Don't Make Your Requirements a Technical Fashion Statement

In this age of trendy open source web frameworks and fashionable coding methodologies, it's easy to drive the project from such "requirements" as "Must use EJB 3.0," "Must use AOP," "Must use Spring Framework," and so forth. Similarly, projects can end up being delayed because the developers wanted to spend longer "improving the design" before releasing to the customer.

Projects that are driven by technical requirements like these are out of step with the real-world forces that drive the business world. The number 1 business motivator is, of course, profit—**not** design patterns. As soon as the developers take over, and design patterns become more important than the business' profit, the project has lost touch with reality.

■**Tip** When gathering requirements, ask the right questions of the right people (project stakeholders, end users), and keep on asking until you get the specific answers that the project needs.

Why Bother Tracking Requirements?

You may wonder whether the approach described in this chapter is overkill or whether only, say, big aerospace companies need to trace requirements to any level of detail. We can see how you might think that.

We'll try to shed some light on the topic by telling you a true story about a training workshop that found Doug at a major corporation in Chicago with a small team (about five developers) and a really tight deadline. In fact, the code was being written in parallel with the modeling workshop, that's how tight the deadline was:

The project had about 30 named requirements. We had allocated them to the use cases during analysis, and we were in the process of verifying that our sequence diagrams met those requirements. Suddenly, as we were tracing the first requirement, the lead engineer got, well, red in the face with embarrassment and said, "I just coded this last night, and I completely forgot about that exception condition."

It can happen to you, too.

Requirements Allocation and Traceability in Theory

■Note Our thanks to Jeff Kantor for contributing this section.

When you look forward in the life cycle, you perform *allocation* of requirements to use cases, classes, operations, states, and so forth. When you look backward, as you would in a verification/validation phase of the project, the term *traceability* comes into play. The two terms are different perspectives on the same relationship, but you traverse the relationship from each perspective under different circumstances.

When you move from analysis to design, you perform allocation in order to assign requirements to the design elements that will satisfy them. When you test and integrate code, your concern is with traceability, to determine which requirements led to each piece of code, and to provide criteria for testing that code. Thus allocation/traceability is a concern across the entire life cycle, not just from system requirements to software requirements, but also from software requirements to preliminary design, from preliminary design to detailed design, and from detailed design to implementation, testing, and integration.

You need to address several aspects of the allocation/traceability problem before you start serious coding.

- **Data capture** has to do with finding efficient ways to capture the analytical elements of each phase of the life cycle (requirements, functional analysis, functional allocation, hardware/software design, code, test, documentation, data) and the allocation/traceability relationships among these elements. You also need to consider how you will manage this information over several iterations of the life cycle phase activities, and how you will manage updates and changes to the elements and relationships.

- **Data analysis and reduction** encompasses ensuring that all the allocation/trace pointers are valid, that all requirements are allocated, and that all requirements trace. This aspect also presents management questions as iterative and incremental development occurs. In addition, you need to be aware of the impact that changes have on elements throughout the system, and work to ensure that the results leave your design consistent with the users' needs.

- **Data reporting** involves the ability to report efficiently on the results of data capture and data analysis/reduction. This typically takes the form of large tables that should be included in ongoing project documentation.

Requirements Gathering in Practice

In this section, we dispense with the Internet Bookstore example, and instead reintroduce everyone's favorite redneck, Billy Bob (a character from Doug's first book on ICONIX Process, coauthored by Kendall Scott). We'll use the requirements from the original Billy Bob example to illustrate how to organize your functional requirements in EA.

■**Note** The remainder of this chapter focuses on requirements management using EA. Non-EA users should still find this section helpful, if only because it illustrates just how easy requirements management and traceability have become these days, using the right tools.

Organizing Requirements in EA: BillyBob 2.0

In Doug's first book on ICONIX Process,[1] he and coauthor Kendall Scott introduced to us the infamous Billy Bob. In the original example, Billy Bob was driving down the road at 80 miles an hour while drinking beer, scratching, and tossing the empty beer cans out the window of his pickup truck. From these actions, a set of behavioral requirements was identified: "Drive Pickup Truck," "Drink Beer," and "Toss Can Out of the Window."

As this seems to be the storytelling chapter, and since we're pretty close to the end of the book, here's one more. Doug was teaching a class in Oak Ridge, Tennessee, a few years back and one of the students came up at a break and introduced himself as being from Mississippi (or was it Alabama?). At any rate, he proceeded to confess that the Billy Bob story was the only part of the book he had actually understood, and then explained that Doug and Kendall had it all wrong, as follows:

> *You throw the cans into the back of the pickup, but you throw the bottles out of the window because they make a much more satisfying noise when they hit the signs.*

You just can't make this kind of stuff up, folks. But at any rate, we can use Doug's student's explanation to explore the further adventures of Billy Bob. We can define the requirements for BillyBob 2.0 as follows:

1. Billy Bob shall throw his cans into the back of the pickup.

2. Billy Bob shall recycle his beer cans so he can buy an additional six-pack.

3. Billy shall throw only the bottles out the window.

4. *(Performance requirement)* The bottles must hit the signs with an accuracy ratio of at least 63.5%.

We'll return to these requirements later in this chapter and give a practical demo of how they can be organized and linked to use cases in EA.

---

1. Doug Rosenberg and Kendall Scott, *Use Case Driven Object Modeling with UML: A Practical Approach* (New York: Addison-Wesley, 1999).

Figure 13-2 shows the updated domain model, with the domain objects that we've identified from the new requirements (the new 2.0 objects are shown in red). The behavior of the system will be distributed across these objects.

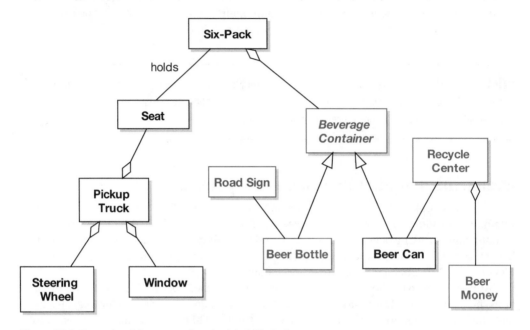

Figure 13-1. *Domain objects associated with Billy Bob*

Figure 13-2 shows the use cases we can identify from our new requirements, as well as the declarations we can make about how these use cases are related.

■Exercise Can you spot an additional <<precedes>> relationship that's missing from Figure 13-2?

Here's a possible use case for *Drink Beer* (adapted from Doug's first book with Kendall, now with our new requirements added):

BASIC COURSE:

Billy Bob removes one hand from the steering wheel and grabs a can of beer from the six-pack on the seat next to him. He drains it in one prolonged gulp, and then invokes the Toss Cans in back of Pickup Truck *use case.*

ALTERNATE COURSE:

Bottle instead of Can: *The* Toss Bottles out of Window at Signs *use case is invoked instead.*

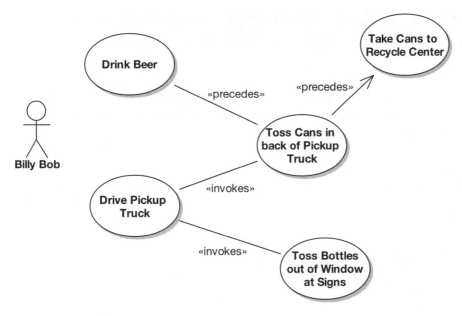

Figure 13-2. *Billy Bob's refactored behavior*

Here's the basic course for the *Toss Cans in back of Pickup Truck* use case:

Keeping his eyes on the road at all times, Billy Bob tosses the drained Can over his shoulder into the back of the Pickup Truck.

■Exercise Should Drained Can be a separate domain object, or should it be an attribute of Beer Can?

And finally, here's the *Toss Bottles out of Window at Signs* use case:

BASIC COURSE:

Keeping his eyes on the road at all times, Billy Bob tosses the drained Bottle out the window, at an approaching sign; the system makes the Bottle hit the sign with a satisfying noise.

ALTERNATE COURSE:

Bottle misses sign: *Satisfying noise not heard.*

Using a Visual Modeling Tool to Support Requirements

In this section, we describe EA's support for allocating and tracing requirements.

■Note This section is rather EA-specific, but if you're using a different modeling tool, we think you'll still pick up some good ideas about how you can link your functional requirements to your use cases.

Figure 13-3 shows the Require tab that will appear on your use case and class specifications within EA. We've linked two requirements to it by dragging the requirements directly onto the use case (as you'll see in the next section, these are *external* requirements). In the screenshot, a new Testing requirement is being added directly to the use case.

Figure 13-3. *Require tab within EA*

EA has a number of built-in features to help you manage requirements. These features include the ability to

- Define requirement elements ("external" requirements)

- Link requirements to model elements that implement that requirement

- Link requirements together into a hierarchy

- Report on requirements and move requirements into and out of model element responsibilities

■**Tip**   If you're starting out with a set of requirements in an external document, it's possible to import these requirements into EA from a comma-separated value (CSV) file.

Internal and External Requirements

EA supports two basic types of requirements: internal and external. *Internal* means "internal to a UML element" (such as a use case or class), whereas *external* means "independent of any specific UML element."

Most commonly, you'll want to associate internal requirements (aka ***responsibilities***) with use cases. You can double-click a use case to open its Properties dialog, and then click its Require tab and enter a list of requirements that are then inherently "part of" the use case (see Figure 13-3).

Alternatively, you can create *external* Requirement elements and place them on diagrams. These are custom UML elements, so they can be connected to each other and to other UML elements.

It's possible to turn internal requirements into external requirements. For example, you might begin by adding requirements directly into a use case, but then later discover that you want to associate the same requirements with other use cases. The "simplest thing that can possibly work" would be to recreate a carbon copy of the requirements in the other use cases, but we don't want to do that, as duplication of *anything* (except fat royalty checks) is bad. So, let's walk through the process of turning internal requirements into external requirements. Along the way, we'll discuss some of the ways in which requirements can be organized in EA.

In Figure 13-3, we defined a use case called *Toss Bottles out of Window at Signs*, and within it we've defined a new internal requirement (requirement 5). To turn this requirement into an external requirement (i.e., to "unshackle" it from a specific use case), click the Move External button on the Require tab. This pops up a dialog (see Figure 13-4), from which you can select a package to move the requirement to.

Figure 13-4. *Choosing where to put the newly "externalized" requirement*

Once you have a sizeable batch of external requirements, you can create a new diagram to place the requirements on and organize them a bit more. The diagram we'll create is an *extended class diagram,* the reason being that this diagram type allows custom elements (such as Requirement elements) to be placed on it. To place the Requirement elements onto a diagram, drag them over from the Project View (see Figure 13-5).

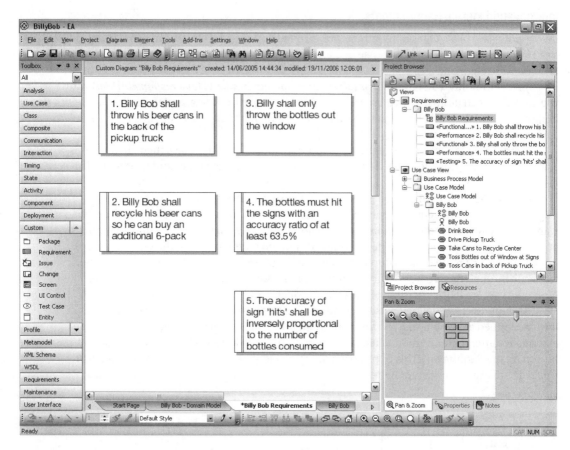

Figure 13-5. *Placing the external requirements on a new diagram*

If you recall from earlier in this chapter, there's a hierarchical aspect to these requirements: requirement 5 was derived from 4, and 4 was derived from 3. It would be useful to show this "tree" relationship graphically, so let's do that next.

Tree of Requirements

Requirements can be linked to show construction of a complete requirements "tree" using aggregation (see Figure 13-6).

■**Caution** For some projects, creating a requirements tree might be overkill, but the capability is there if you need it. However, it's more important to allocate the requirements to the use cases and classes than it is to organize them into pretty tree structures.

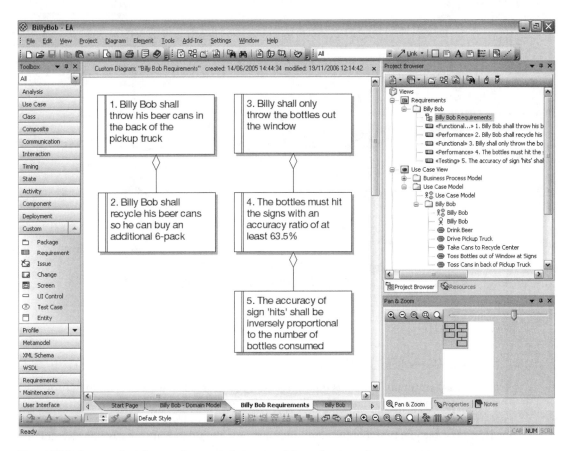

Figure 13-6. *Structuring the requirements into a tree hierarchy*

Once the links are established, the Hierarchy window will display the complete requirement implementation/composition detail (see Figure 13-7).

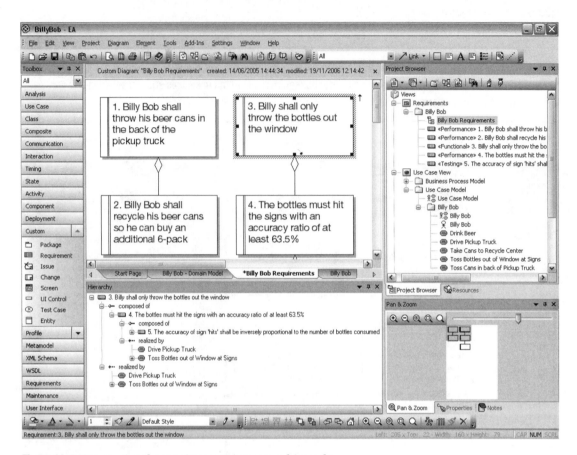

Figure 13-7. *Structuring the requirements into a tree hierarchy*

Linking Requirements to Use Cases

If you create your requirements as *internal* requirements inside a use case and then turn
them into external requirements, they'll already be linked automatically to the original use
case. However, you might also want to approach the problem from the other direction: start
by defining some external requirements and then link 'em up to your use cases (as we did for
the first four requirements we showed earlier).

In fact, use cases aren't the only model elements that you can link external requirements to. Pretty much any model element can be linked up to a requirement: classes, interfaces, components, and so forth. In EA, you link requirements to model elements using the
Realization relationship (see Figure 13-8).

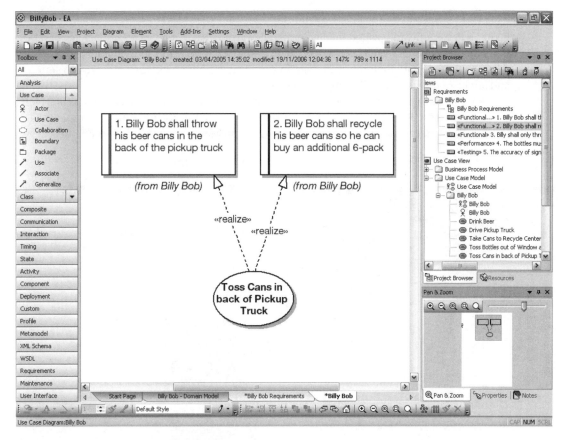

Figure 13-8. *Linking an external requirement to a use case*

As you can see in Figure 13-8, a model element is marked as "realizing" a requirement. Once this link exists, EA will display the requirement in the element's Require tab, in the requirement hierarchy window, and in the dependency and implementation reports, as well as in the standard RTF output.

■**Tip** A quick method of generating a Realization link is to drag a Requirement element from the Project Browser over an element in a diagram that is to be the implementing element. EA will interpret this as a request to create the realization link and do so automatically. To confirm this, perform the action, and then go to the Require tab page of the target element. There should now be an external relationship to the requirement that was dragged over the target.

External requirements have their own properties and are reported on separately in the RTF documentation.

Pain-Free Requirements Traceability

EA has a rather nifty tool called the Relationship Matrix. It's a spreadsheet-like display of relationships between model elements. You select a source package and a target package, the relationship type and direction, and then EA will display all the relationships between source and target elements by highlighting a grid square.[2]

You can also use the Relationship Matrix to create and manage the relationships between requirements (see Figure 13-9). This is a convenient way of quickly building up complex relationships and hierarchies. Choose View ➤ Relationship Matrix from the main menu to access this window.

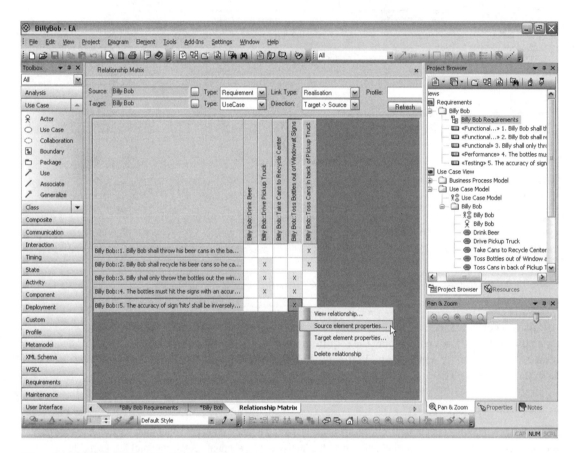

Figure 13-9. *EA's Relationship Matrix feature*

A point to note when using requirements and the Relationship Matrix is that multiple elements can be selected and realized to a Requirement element (or any other element) by dragging the mouse across a set of cells or Ctrl-clicking individual cells. When you right-click

---

2. This brings a nice, satisfying closure to the allocation/traceability discussion we had at the beginning of the chapter. Allocate the requirements to the use cases by dragging them, and the tool produces the traceability matrix automatically. Can it get any easier? Life is good. (Thank you, Geoff Sparks.)

one highlighted cell and select Create New Relationship, the relationships are set up for all selected cells. This can be very useful when a requirement has impact on a number of elements within a diagram.

More Practice

This section provides a list of questions that you can use to test your knowledge of requirements analysis and traceability in a use case–driven project.

1. Describe the differences between a functional requirement and a data requirement.

2. Which of the following is a behavioral requirement?

   a) The user must be allowed to select from the following three invoice types: . . .

   b) The speed limit of the road along which Billy Bob is driving is 65 mph.

   c) If more than 3,000 users connect simultaneously, the system should respond by redirecting excess users to a "busy" page.

   d) The user selects one item from the list of available invoice types and clicks Submit . . .

3. Which of the following statements is true?

   a) A use case describes the laws that govern a function's behavior.

   b) Requirements describe the individual actions that occur within a use case.

   c) Functions are the individual actions that occur within a use case.

   d) A use case describes the laws that govern a requirement's functions.

4. If you turn an internal requirement into an external requirement, how does that change its relationship with a use case?

5. Disintermangle the following use case scenario so that the nonbehavioral requirements are separated out:

On the Maintain Seller Catalog page, the user clicks Add New Catalog. The user should only be allowed to do this if she is already logged in. The system displays the Add New Catalog page, showing a Catalog Name field, a book search field, and a list of recently accessed Books. The system shows the user's login name so that if she is a different user, she logs out. The user enters a Book's ISBN and clicks Add; the system updates the Catalog to show the new Book. Then the user repeats this for as many Books as she wants to add. She shouldn't be allowed to enter more than 20 Books in one Catalog, or to enter 0 Books. Finally, the user clicks the Save button; the system saves the new Catalog and takes the user back to the Maintain Seller Catalog page.

6. Describe the differences between *data capture* and *data analysis and reduction*.

Summary

In this chapter, we looked at how requirements fit into the development process. We distinguished between different types of requirements. We also demonstrated how to use Enterprise Architect to help support the requirements effort.

We're about at the end of the book, so we'd like to leave you with this final thought: all humans are fallible, and one of the best ways to reduce error rates is to focus on one thing at a time. "One thing at a time" is one of the central themes that's woven throughout ICONIX Process. Even if you take nothing else from this book, we think you'll be more successful if you try to at least keep that simple fact in mind.

Figures 13-10 and 13-11 show (in red) the items that were covered in this chapter.

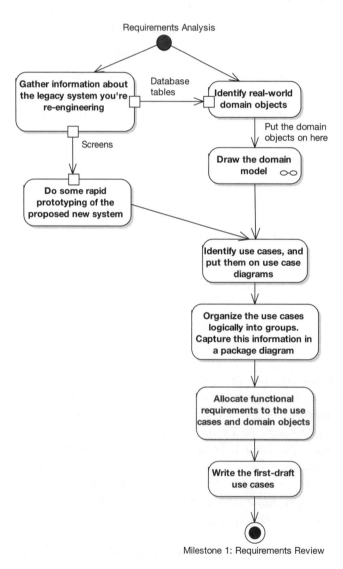

Figure 13-10. *Requirements Analysis Checkpoint 3*

Milestone 2: Preliminary Design Review

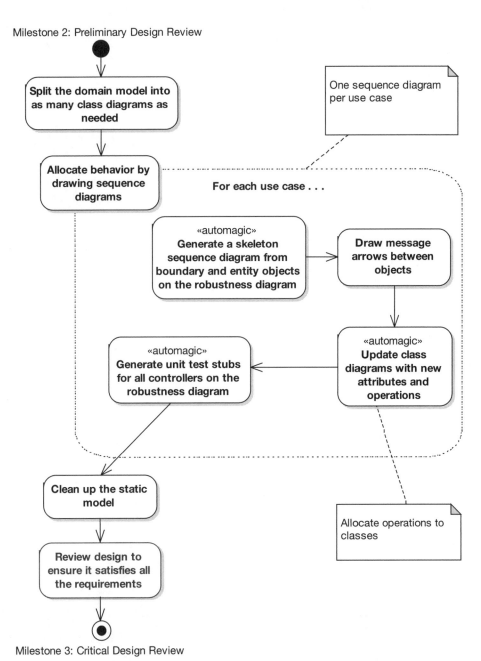

Figure 13-11. *Design Checkpoint 2*

PART 5

Appendixes

■■■

What's New in UML 2.0

In this appendix, we look at what's new in UML 2.0, with a keen eye on how (if at all) it affects ICONIX Process. We step outside the "core UML subset" that we've defined in this book and look at all the new diagram types in UML 2.0.

Overview of Changes in UML 2.0

The main "theme" for the UML 2.0 update appears to be increased support for precision in diagrams, improving UML's suitability for modeling real-time embedded systems.

UML 2.0 now consists of the following diagram types (some of these are subdivided into more types of diagrams, which we cover later in this appendix):

- Use case diagrams

- Package diagrams

- Structure diagrams

- Object diagrams

- Composite structure diagrams

- Communication diagrams

- Activity and state machine diagrams

- Interaction and interaction overview diagrams

- Timing diagrams

- Component and deployment diagrams

There's still no sign of robustness diagrams, as you can see, so we'll have to make do with UML's extension mechanism (UML profiles and stereotype icons) for now. Luckily, support for UML extensions in tools such as EA is pretty advanced these days.

Similarly, there's no sign of test case diagrams, although the test case notation we describe in Chapter 12 is supported in EA and can also be modeled in other tools using UML extensions. (At the time of this writing, EA is the only tool that can actually generate test cases automatically from your robustness diagrams.)

Of the new diagram set, the main ICONIX diagrams remain unchanged: use case diagrams, structure diagrams (aka class diagrams), and—although there's some additional notation—sequence diagrams (one of the four types of interaction diagrams) also remain largely unchanged. In fact, there haven't been major changes to use cases, packages, class diagrams, or object diagrams in UML 2.0. So, you might say that the UML 2.0 extensions don't really affect ICONIX Process at all. To borrow a phrase, YAGNI (You Aren't Gonna Need It) applies to a lot of the new stuff in UML 2.0 for the majority of projects that we've seen. Of course, if you do need this stuff, by all means use it.

A number of new modeling constructs can be shown on composite diagrams. These include *parts*, *ports*, *exposed* and *required interfaces*, *connectors*, *assemblies*, and *collaborations*.

Communication diagrams used to be called collaboration diagrams.[1] They still show the interactions between elements at runtime in much the same manner as a sequence diagram.

Activity diagrams are used to model the behavior of a system and the way in which these behaviors are related in an overall flow of the system, while state machine diagrams illustrate how an element can move between states classifying its behavior, according to transition triggers, constraining guards, and so on.

UML 2.0 has four different kinds of interaction diagrams: *timing diagrams*, *sequence diagrams*, *interaction overview diagrams*, and *communication diagrams*.

A timing diagram defines the behavior of different objects within a time scale. It provides a visual representation of objects changing state and interacting over time. Timing diagrams are typically used for defining hardware-driven or embedded software components.

A component diagram illustrates the pieces of software, embedded controllers, and so forth that will make up a system. In UML 2.0, components can be linked by assembly connectors. As before, a deployment diagram shows how and where the system will be deployed. Physical machines and processors are reflected as nodes, and the internal construction can be depicted by embedding nodes or artifacts.

UML profiles provide a generic extension mechanism for building UML models in particular domains. A *profile* is a collection of stereotypes and tagged values that together describe some particular modeling problem and facilitate modeling constructs in that domain.

Let's go through these changes in more detail.

Composite Structure Diagrams

A *composite structure diagram* reflects the internal collaboration of classes, interfaces, or components to describe some functionality.

Composite structure diagrams are similar to class diagrams, except that they model a specific usage of the structure. Class diagrams model a static view of class structures, including their attributes and behaviors. Composite structure diagrams are used to express runtime architectures, usage patterns, and the participating elements' relationships, which might not be reflected by static diagrams.

---

1. Actually, they were originally called "object diagrams" in Booch method, then they were renamed to "collaboration diagrams" in UML 1, and they have now become "communication diagrams, a flavor of interaction diagrams" in UML 2. This explains why Doug refuses to join any standards committees. There are better things to do in life than to rename diagrams 12 times. Sequence diagrams, by the way, were originally called "object interaction diagrams" in the Jacobson Objectory method. If you're not confused yet, you win another pork pie.

In UML 2.0, the changes to composite structure diagrams center on parts and ports, interfaces, connectors and assemblies, and collaborations.

Parts and Ports

In a composite structure diagram, classes are accessed as *parts,* or runtime instances fulfilling a particular role. These parts can have multiplicity, if the role filled by the class requires multiple instances. When parts need to communicate with entities outside of their enclosing class, they will usually do this through a port. The *port* defines an interface that communicating parts are required to implement.

There is extensive flexibility and an ensuing complexity that comes with modeling composite structures. To optimize your modeling, consider building collaborations that represent reusable patterns.

Figure A-1 shows an example of a composite structure diagram.

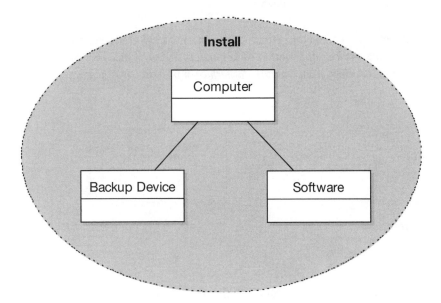

Figure A-1. *Composite structure diagram*

Interfaces

An *interface* is a specification of behavior that implementers agree to meet. It is a contract. By implementing an interface, classes are guaranteed to support a required behavior, which allows the system to treat nonrelated elements in the same way, through the common interface.

An interface cannot be instantiated (i.e., you cannot create an object from an interface). You must create a class that "implements" the interface specification and place operations in the class body for each of the interface operations. You can then instantiate the class.

Interfaces may be drawn as a stereotyped class, with operations shown. They may also be drawn as a circle with no explicit operations detailed (see Figure A-2).

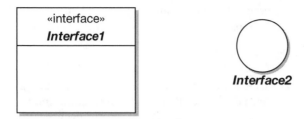

Figure A-2. *Interface notation*

Assembly Connectors

An *assembly connector* bridges a component's required interface with the provided interface of another component (see Figure A-3).

The UML 2.0 specification states the following:

> *An assembly connector is a connector between two components that defines that one component provides the services that another component requires. An assembly connector is a connector that is defined from a required interface or port to a provided interface or port.*

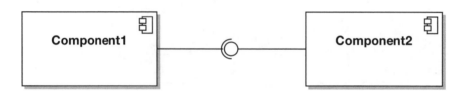

Figure A-3. *Assembly connector*

Collaborations

A *collaboration* defines a set of cooperating roles and their connectors (see Figure A-4).

Collaborations are used to collectively illustrate a specific functionality. A collaboration should specify only the roles and attributes needed to accomplish a specific task or function. A collaboration often implements a pattern to apply to various situations, and it is drawn as a dashed oval that surrounds the elements that are collaborating.

Figure A-4. *Collaboration*

Activity and State Diagrams

Activity diagrams are used to model the behaviors of a system and the way in which these behaviors are related in an overall flow of the system.

Activity diagrams are similar to flowcharts, but they allow the specification of concurrent parallel processing paths. Activities on an activity diagram can be partitioned into regions, which are usually called *swimlanes* because of their visual appearance (regions separated by solid lines on the diagram).

New Activity Diagram Elements for Communication Actions

UML 2.0 adds some new elements to activity diagrams that are primarily useful for defining real-time systems, very precise business processes, and detailed execution logic (see Figure A-5). These include action pins and new special symbols for certain types of communication actions.

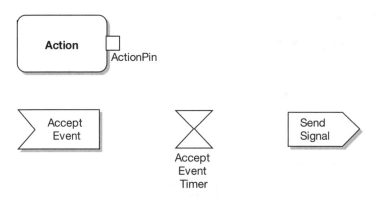

Figure A-5. *New activity diagram elements*

An *action pin* is used to define the data flow into and out of an action. An *input pin* provides values to the action, whereas an *output pin* contains the results from that action. Action pins can be further characterized as defining exception parameters, streams, or states. Associating a state with a pin defines the state of input or output values.

UML 2.0 includes symbols for accept event, accept time event, and send signal actions. The call behavior and call operation actions are used to reference other activities and class methods within an activity diagram.

Expansion Regions

UML 2.0 also provides a construct called an *expansion region*, which is used to denote processing that occurs in parallel (see Figure A-6). These are shown by a segmented box appearing on the top and bottom of the activity symbol. According to *The Unified Modeling Language Reference Manual, Second Edition*,[2]

---

2. James Rumbaugh, Ivar Jacobsen, and Grady Booch, *The Unified Modeling Language Reference Manual, Second Edition* (New York: Addison-Wesley, 2004).

An expansion region is the expansion of computation containing a multiple value into a set of computations executed in parallel.

Each input to the expansion region receives a collection value, shown by the segmented box icon. One execution of the expansion region is performed for each element of the collections. For each output position in the expansion region, the output values from all of the executions are assembled into a single collection value. An expansion region represents a "forall" construct.

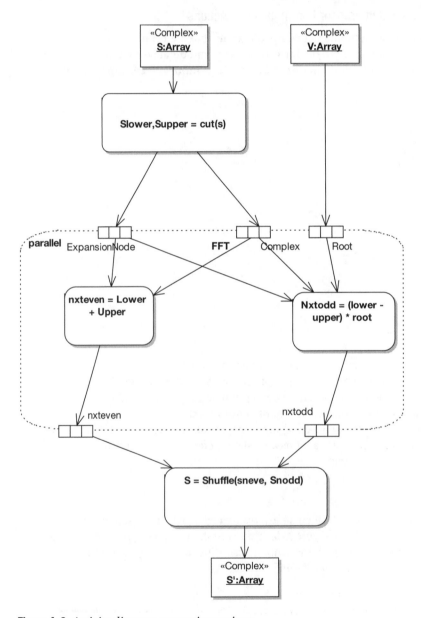

Figure A-6. *Activity diagram expansion regions*

New State Diagram Elements

Continuing with the theme of enhancing real-time modeling capability, UML 2.0 extends state diagrams with entry and exit connection points (see Figure A-7) and junctions. An *entry point connection* is shown by a small circle on the boundary of a substate machine symbol. A transition can be connected from a state to the entry point connection. An *exit point connection* is shown in a similar manner by a small circle containing an "X". A transition can be connected from the exit point connection to another state.

The *Unified Modeling Language Reference Manual, Second Edition* defines a *junction* as "a pseudostate that is part of a single overall transition step in a state machine," and further states that a junction state "makes it possible to build a single overall transition from a series of transition fragments" and that it is "a dummy state to structure transitions and not a state that can be active for any finite time." Junction states are drawn as small filled circles on a state diagram.

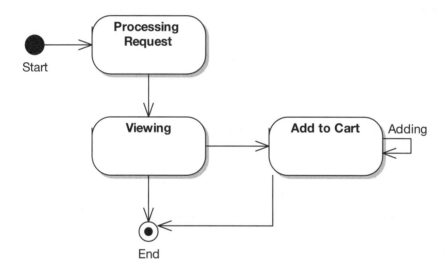

Figure A-7. *State diagram entry/exit points*

Sequence and Interaction Overview Diagrams

An *interaction* is a generalization for a type of interaction diagram. UML 2.0 has four kinds of interaction diagrams: timing diagrams, sequence diagrams, interaction overview diagrams, and communication diagrams. We discuss timing diagrams later in this appendix.

Sequence Diagrams

You know by now that sequence diagrams are a rather important building block in ICONIX Process. The basic notation for sequence diagrams hasn't changed in UML 2.0; however, some new elements have been introduced, including fragments, gates, states, and message endpoints. These new elements collectively make it easier to draw structured control constructs on sequence diagrams (see Figure A-8).

Complex flow of control on a sequence diagram can be shown using combined fragments. A *combined fragment* has a keyword and one or more subfragments, which are called *interaction operands*. Examples of fragments are LOOP, CONDITIONAL, and PARALLEL. Guard conditions and loop conditions may be shown within fragments.

It's a philosophical question as to whether drawing flowcharts on sequence diagrams is a good idea or not. (Hint: We vote no.) But if you don't want to draw your flowcharts using activity diagrams, you can now draw them on sequence diagrams.

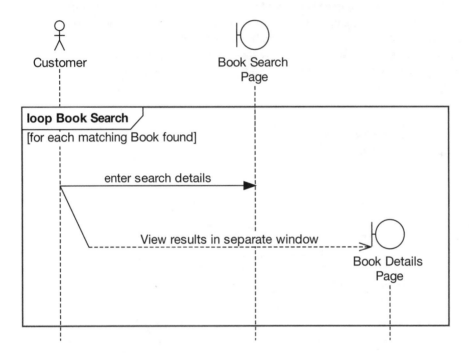

Figure A-8. *New sequence diagram elements*

Interaction Overview Diagrams

Interaction overview diagrams are used to visualize the cooperation between other interaction diagrams to illustrate a control flow serving an encompassing purpose (see Figure A-9).

Since interaction overview diagrams are a variant of activity diagrams, most of the diagram notation is similar, as is the process in constructing the diagram. Decision points, forks, joins, start points, and end points are the same. The diagram appears very similar to an activity diagram and is conceptualized the same way: as the flow moves into an interaction, that respective interaction's process must be followed before the interaction overview's flow can advance.

Instead of activity elements, however, rectangular elements are used. There are two types of these elements: interaction elements and interaction occurrence elements. *Interaction elements* display an inline interaction diagram, which can be a sequence diagram, communication diagram, timing diagram, or interaction overview diagrams. *Interaction occurrence elements* are references to an existing interaction diagram. They are visually represented by a frame, with "ref" in the frame's title space. The diagram name is indicated in the frame contents.

■**Note** If you've been craving a notation that lets you do functional decomposition in UML (like you used to do it on DFDs 15 years ago), the interaction overview diagram makes a strong candidate.

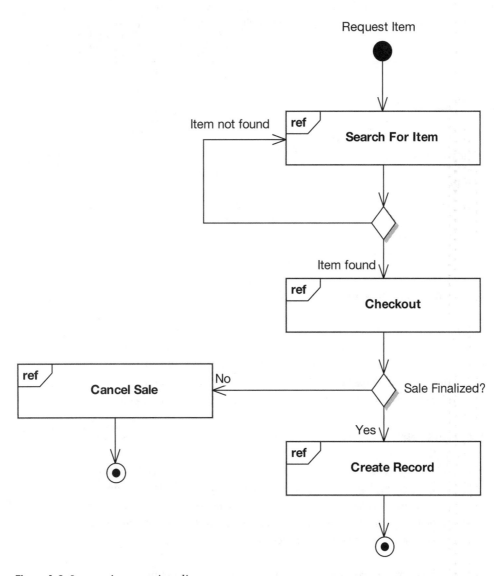

Figure A-9. *Interaction overview diagram*

Timing Diagrams

As with many of the UML 2.0 extensions, *timing diagrams* came from the world of electrical engineering and are most useful if you are modeling real-time, embedded systems (e.g., embedded software such as that used in a fuel injection system, a microwave controller, etc.). They can also be used for specifying time-driven business processes, although this would be a less typical usage.

Timing Diagram Basics

A timing diagram defines the behavior of different objects within a time scale (see Figure A-10). It provides a visual representation of objects changing state and interacting over time.

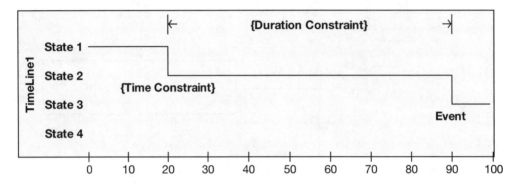

Figure A-10. *Timing diagram showing a state lifeline*

The UML 2.0 specification states the following:

Timing diagrams are used to show interactions when a primary purpose of the diagram is to reason about time. Timing diagrams focus on conditions changing within and among Lifelines along a linear time axis. Timing diagrams describe behavior of both individual classifiers and interactions of classifiers, focusing attention on time of occurrence of events causing changes in the modeled conditions of the Lifelines.

The UML 2.0 specification also states,

The primary purpose of the timing diagram is to show the change in state or condition of a lifeline (representing a Classifier Instance or Classifier Role) over linear time. The most common usage is to show the change in state of an object over time in response to accepted events or stimuli. The received events are annotated as shown when it is desirable to show the event causing the change in condition or state.

A timing diagram can have either a state lifeline or a value lifeline.

State Lifeline

The diagram in Figure A-10 shows an example of a state lifeline. The scale along the bottom indicates the passage of time, and the possible states are represented as the vertical scale. The stepped lifeline shows the state changes that occur over time.

Value Lifeline

The diagram in Figure A-11 shows an example timing diagram with both a state lifeline and a value lifeline. (The top two items, User and AC System, are state lifelines, and the bottom item, User Accepted, is a value lifeline.)

The scale along the bottom again indicates the passage of time, but for the value lifeline the possible states are represented as named sections of the lifeline. Where two named states transition, the value lifeline narrows to a single point.

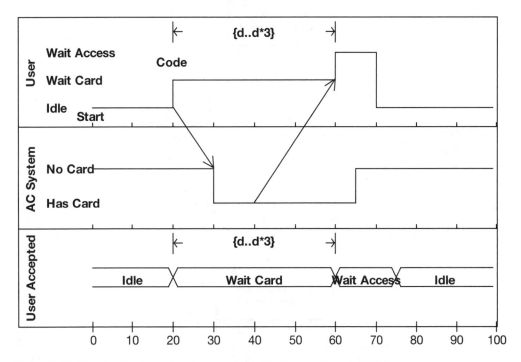

Figure A-11. *Timing diagram showing two state lifelines and a value lifeline*

Messages Between Lifelines

Multiple lifelines can be shown on the same timing diagram. The lifelines stack vertically with each lifeline in a separate compartment on the diagram. Messages can be drawn across compartments, thereby linking events on different lifelines (see the diagonal arrows in Figure A-11).

Component and Deployment Diagrams

Finally, we look at the differences in component diagrams and deployment diagrams in UML 2.0.

Component Diagrams

A *component diagram* illustrates the pieces of software, embedded controllers, and so forth that will make up a system (see Figure A-12). A component diagram has a higher level of abstraction than a class diagram—usually a component is implemented by multiple classes (or objects) at runtime. Components are building blocks and often encompass a large portion of a system.

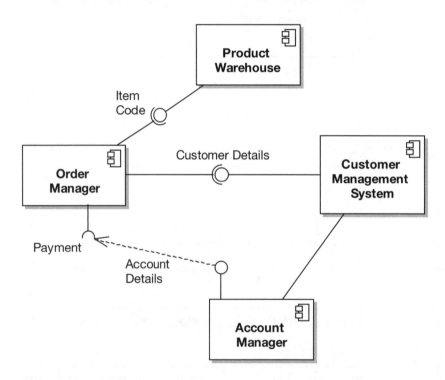

Figure A-12. *Component diagram*

In UML 2.0, components can have ports. A port is shown as a small rectangle on the boundary of the component rectangle. Interfaces may be connected to the ports.

There are two types of interfaces: provided and required. A *provided* interface is represented by a small circle on the end of a short line, which is sometimes referred to as a "lollipop" symbol. A *required* interface is shown similarly to a provided interface, but with an open semicircle at the end of the lollipop stick.

Deployment Diagrams

A *deployment diagram* shows how and where the system will be deployed (see Figure A-13). Physical machines and processors are reflected as nodes, and the internal construction can be depicted by embedding nodes or artifacts. *Artifacts* model physical entities such as files, scripts, database tables, web pages, JAR files, and the like, while *nodes* model computational resources such as computers and disk drives.

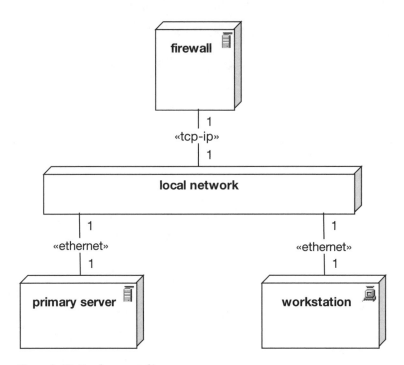

Figure A-13. *Deployment diagram*

The allocation of artifacts to nodes is guided by the use of deployment specifications, each of which contains a specification of a deployment location within a node and an execution location. A deployment specification is shown as a rectangle with a stereotype of `<<deployment spec>>`. Parameter values can be listed within the symbol. A dashed arrow is drawn from the specification to the artifact whose deployment it describes.

What's Still Missing in UML

UML 2.0 represents a step forward in some ways, but in certain other ways, we get the impression that it's just marching in place.

In particular, there is still no standard notation in the UML for defining user interfaces or "screen flows" (or "page flows" if you're creating a web-based system). Also surprising is that there is still no dedicated diagram for showing data models (whether as an entity-relationship diagram or, well, as anything else for that matter).

These two omissions are surprising because the majority of IT projects involve creating both a system with a user interface and a system with a back-end database of some sort. There are plenty of diagram types out there to fill these gaps, but they really should be part of the UML itself. Here's hoping that the next revision of the UML standardizes on these much-needed diagram types.

APPENDIX B

■ ■ ■

Spring Bin

At several points throughout this book, we wanted to describe more about what we were doing with Spring Framework, but doing so would have detracted from the flow of the main discussion (i.e., use case–driven object modeling). So, if you thrive on the technical details, we've put the Spring-based implementation notes in this appendix and referred to it in the text.

Note that none of this material is vital if your main goal here is to learn about use case–driven object modeling, though. We guess that's why this material is in an appendix . . .

Spring in More Detail

In Chapter 7, we introduced Spring from a technical architect's perspective. In this section, we expand on some of the technical discussions from that chapter.

A (Very) Brief Example of IoC

We introduced Inversion of Control (IoC) and its cousin, Dependency Injection (DI), in Chapter 7. To illustrate IoC, here's a straightforward Java bean with one property, propertyA:

```
package com.iconixsw.example;

public class MyBean {

    private YourBean propertyA;

    public String getPropertyA() {
        return propertyA;
    }

    public void setPropertyA(YourBean propertyA) {
        this.propertyA = propertyA;
    }
```

Our property, propertyA, is of type YourBean.

JAVA NAMING CONVENTIONS: A 30-SECOND CRASH COURSE

If you're unfamiliar with Java, be aware that it uses some special conventions:

- Variables (references to an object) start with a lowercase letter (e.g., `propertyA`, `customerReview`).

- Classes start with an uppercase letter (e.g., `YourBean`, `CustomerReview`).

- Variables (i.e., attributes) are typically private, meaning they can be accessed only within the class that they belong to.

- To access (and write to) a variable from outside its class, you add a get method and a set method (e.g., `getPropertyA()`, `setBook()`).

- Once a variable has get and set methods, it's known as a *property*.

- And (to finish our ultra-packed crash course) Java classes are organized into *packages*, where a package is basically a folder. Packages can contain classes and other packages. Package naming is kind of a weird thing, but it makes sense: so that different Java libraries can coexist in the same program space, packages universally follow the *reverse URL* convention. In our case, the company domain is `iconixsw.com`. So the package name for all our classes always begins with `com.iconixsw`. And the product name is "Bookstore," so all the classes in this product go under `com.iconixsw.bookstore` (note the lowercase "bookstore"). There will most likely also be subpackages—for example, DAO classes could go into `com.iconixsw.bookstore.dao`. And so on . . .

Here's the `YourBean` class that `MyBean` refers to via its `propertyA` property:

```
package com.iconixsw.example;
public class YourBean {

    private String title = "Ethel the Aardvark Goes Quantity Surveying";

    public String getTitle() {
        return title;
    }
}
```

YourBean simply defines one read-only property called `title`, which always returns "Ethel the Aardvark Goes Quantity Surveying" (a vastly underrated page-turner). To wire these two beans together, you'd define them in some Spring-friendly XML as follows:

```
<bean name="myBean" class="com.iconixsw.example.MyBean">
    <property name="propertyA ">
        <ref bean="yourBean" />
    </property>
</bean>

<bean name="yourBean" class="com.iconixsw.example.YourBean" />
```

This XML fragment defines an instance of the MyBean class called myBean, and an instance of the YourBean class called yourBean. By default, each bean declared in a Spring XML file is a singleton (i.e., only one instance of it can exist). It's possible to override this for each bean, but most of the time it makes life much easier to know that there's only one instance of each class flying around.

■Note *But aren't Singletons unfashionable these days*? True, the Singleton design pattern has come under heavy scrutiny because it imposes some questionable constraints on your software design.[1] The Singleton design pattern ensures that only one instance of a class can exist by making the constructor private and having a static factory method that always returns the same instance of the class.

While they do work, Singletons are notoriously difficult to test. It's impossible for a unit test class to create and dispose of the same Singleton class, because only the Singleton itself controls its life cycle. On the other hand, simply specifying that there should be only one instance of a class (i.e., making it a "singleton," lowercase "s") is fairly harmless, and in a server environment it is useful. As long as the class still has a public constructor and can be tested, then there's no harm in it being a singleton.

When Spring initializes our one instance of MyBean, it populates the propertyA property with a reference to yourBean (the one instance of the YourBean class). You could therefore add some code to MyBean that actually does something with yourBean:

```
public class MyBean {
    . . .

    public void doSomething() {
        System.out.println(
            "The title of our one mysterious bean is: "
            + propertyA.getTitle()
        );
    }
}
```

Notice that you don't need to actively go and find an instance of YourBean, and you don't need to explicitly set a value for propertyA—you've "wired up" myBean to yourBean in the XML, so you know that Spring will initialize myBean's propertyA with yourBean.

That's the essence of IoC: "bean wiring" is fundamentally how the different components in Spring work with each other. In fact, if you use Spring primarily for its IoC features, it's possible to use it in a stand-alone Java program; it doesn't *have* to be part of a J2EE server. However, we are, of course, using it as part of a web application, so in the next section we'll introduce Spring's web features.

---

1. For example, see www.softwarereality.com/design/singleton.jsp.

■Note The "flavor" of IoC that we just described is known as *Dependency Injection*. More specifically it's actually *Method Injection* (also known as *Setter Injection*), because the framework "injects" the values into the bean via their set methods. Another form of Dependency Injection (which is also supported by Spring) is *Constructor Injection*, in which the values are passed into the bean's constructor. For the Internet Bookstore, we only use Method Injection.

Models, Views, and Controllers

In Chapter 7, we introduced Spring Web MVC and described the concepts of controllers, command objects, views, and DAOs.

For the Internet Bookstore, the view is handled by JavaServer Pages (JSP) coupled with the Java Standard Tag Library (JSTL). In the next section, we look at Spring's support for JSP.

Controllers

Controller support in Spring is both flexible and extensive. However, it's all based ultimately around a single interface, as follows:

```
public interface Controller {

    /**
     * Process the request and return a ModelAndView object
     * which the DispatcherServlet will render.
     */
    ModelAndView handleRequest(HttpServletRequest request,
                               HttpServletResponse response)
                        throws Exception;
}
```

The Controller interface defines a single method, handleRequest, which accepts a request and response, and returns an appropriate model and view. The request and response objects are both part of the J2EE Servlet API. In fact, this method should look familiar to most server-side Java programmers—the main difference between this and the HttpServlet interface is the ModelAndView class it returns. In many ways, this fixes a major flaw in the original Servlet API, by decoupling the model and view from the controller. As a result, your choice of view technology can vary from controller to controller.

Views

The *view* is the JSP page that will generate the HTML that the user sees. Controllers in Spring generally return a ModelAndView object, which tells Spring which view to send back to the browser and what model data to populate it with.

Let's say you have a "book details" page that shows the details for a specific book (identified by its ID). You'd have a BookDetailsController class that finds the Book matching the ID, and then returns a ModelAndView:

```
Book book = [ find book from somewhere . . . ]
return new ModelAndView("bookdetails", "book", book);
```

The first line of code goes off and finds the Book, most likely via a BookDao class (see the next section). The second line tells Spring to map the view to a JSP file called bookdetails.jsp (the .jsp part gets added by Spring, depending on how you've configured your web application). The second argument passed into the new ModelAndView, book, indicates that the model for the view will consist of a variable called book, and the third argument is the book object itself. The book variable will then be accessible from the bookdetails.jsp page.

DAO and JDBC Support

For the Internet Bookstore, we've used Spring's support for creating "raw" JDBC DAO implementations. The advantage of this approach is that we can write our own SQL to query and write to the database, and map the result set to our JavaBeans (i.e., our domain objects). A potential disadvantage, however, is that code using JDBC directly tends to become quite verbose and repetitive (with lots of similar code for creating and discarding database connections, handling update transactions, etc.).

Luckily, Spring provides some useful JDBC support classes that handle most of this tedious plumbing for you. This means that your JDBC DAOs can focus on the SQL, and on the mapping between the result set and the domain objects.

Figure B-1 shows an example DAO and how it fits in with the overall design.

In Figure B-1, the BookDao is used by BookDetailsController's handle() method to find Book objects. The DAO's concrete implementation, JdbcBookDao, is actually mapped to BookDetailsController via the XML configuration shown earlier, and it is automatically set via the setBookDao() method when the controller object is created (another example of IoC in action).

■Note Our final implementation may or may not need findById() and findByTitle() methods—we'll find out when we draw the sequence diagrams (see Chapter 8).

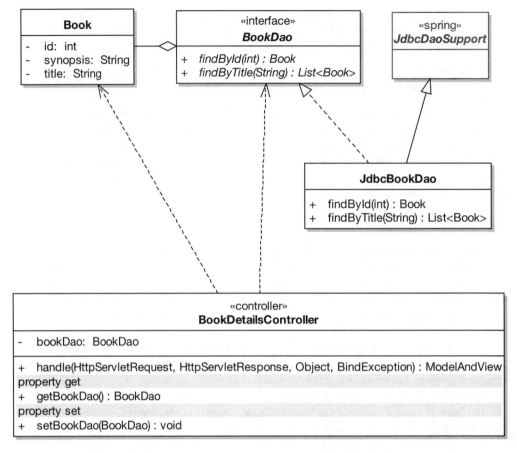

Figure B-1. *Example Internet Bookstore DAO (the external Spring class is shown in red)*

Internet Bookstore Design: Spring Details

This section provides additional Spring details for the Internet Bookstore design described in Chapter 8.

"Show Book Details" Use Case

Here we describe the sequence of events shown in the sequence diagram for the *Show Book Details* use case, shown in Figure 8-2 (see Chapter 8).

First, the Customer clicks the link for a Book, and the browser sends an HTTP request to Spring's DispatcherServlet (running in Tomcat). This request would be something like the following:

```
http://localhost/bookstore/bookdetails.htm?bookid=101
```

The request tells Tomcat to hand the request to the "bookstore" web application. The bookstore web application is configured to use Spring's DispatcherServlet. Because of the bookdetails.htm part of the URL, Spring hands the request to BookDetailsController via the handle(request, response, command, errors) method.

■Note The handle(..) method is actually a concrete implementation of an abstract method defined in AbstractCommandController, which our own BookDetailsController extends (see Figure B-2).

Spring also extracts the bookid parameter and puts it in a Command object, which is also passed into the handle(..) method. (We haven't shown the details of Spring extracting the request parameters and so forth, because this is already implemented in the Spring code, plus it takes place for every request that comes in. Showing this on all of our sequence diagrams would become redundant very quickly.)

Next, BookDetailsController uses its BookDao to get an instance of Book for whatever book has the ID 101 ("Ethel the Aardvark Goes Quantity Surveying," perhaps). Still following the basic course, the Book instance is returned, so BookDetailsController then creates a new ModelAndView object with the parameter bookdetails (a String literal) and the new Book object. The handle(..) method then exits, returning the ModelAndView. The bookdetails parameter tells Spring to find a page that matches the name bookdetails.jsp and invoke this so that the book details are displayed to the user. Spring also hands bookdetails.jsp the Book (because we passed it into the ModelAndView). Still with us? Good!

■Note ModelAndView is a Spring class (notated by the fact that it's shown in red in Figure B-2). It's the object returned by the Controller to indicate to the DispatcherServlet which view (JSP page) to use and what data to feed the view with. So it literally is the model and view (or, at least, references to the model and view).

Our one alternate course (shown in red in Figure 8-2) handles the case where the book details weren't found (e.g., the user might have fiddled with the URL and changed it to a non-existent book ID, or it might simply be an old link and the book no longer exists [shudder]). To handle this alternate course, BookDetailsController creates a new ModelAndView object, but instead of passing it "bookdetails", it passes it "booknotfound". This will tell Spring to find a matching "booknotfound" page, which as you'd expect tells the user that the book ID wasn't found.

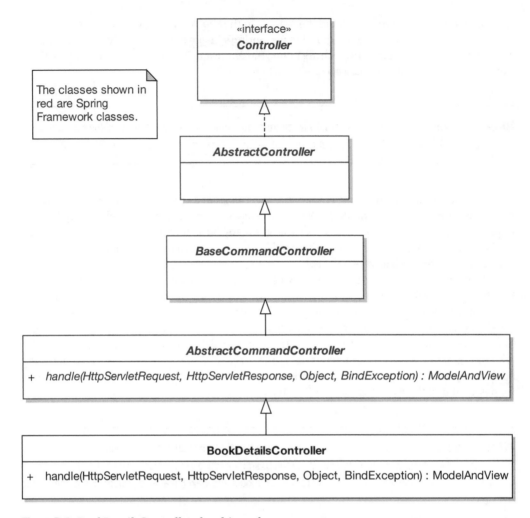

The classes shown in red are Spring Framework classes.

Figure B-2. *BookDetailsController class hierarchy*

"Write Customer Review" Use Case

Here we describe the sequence of events shown in the sequence diagram for the *Write Customer Review* use case shown in Figure 8-11.

In Figure 8-11, the Customer clicks the Write Review button (or link), which has the effect of making a request to Spring's DispatcherServlet running in Tomcat. DispatcherServlet uses the application's XML configuration to work out which Controller to hand the request to (we haven't shown this detail in the sequence diagram as it's a feature of Spring, already implemented). The servlet then calls the formBackingObject() method on WriteCustomerReviewController. This method runs some checks to make sure the Customer is logged in, and then it creates and populates the WriteCustomerReviewCommand object. Note that if the Customer/user isn't logged in, he or she is redirected to the Login page. (We haven't shown the details for this as it would have complicated an already complex sequence diagram, but you get the general idea.)

WriteCustomerReviewController calls a static factory method on CustomerSession, which in turn attempts to get a CustomerSession instance from the servlet's HttpSession. If the instance doesn't exist, it creates a new one and adds it to the session.

To model this, we've simply added a note in Figure 8-11. Note, however, that this lack of detail causes a problem later and is picked up on during the example Code Review and Model Update in Chapter 11.

At this stage, we're also updating the static model as we go along. So, for example, we've decided that WriteCustomerReviewController will extend the Spring class SimpleFormController. We'll show the completed class diagram near the end of the chapter.

Still following Figure 8-11, the *Write Customer Review* page is now being displayed to the Customer. The Customer fills in the review details and clicks the Submit button (or the button might be titled Save Review, since we don't want our customer to willingly submit to anything). The form is submitted, picked up by Spring's DispatcherServlet, validated, and finally handed to WriteCustomerReviewController via the doSubmitAction() method. This method passes in the WriteCustomerReviewCommand object that was created earlier by the formBackingObject() method (effectively providing state between the HTTP GET request, which created the form, and this POST request, which submitted the form).

Note that the form validation process is handled automatically for us by Spring. The CustomerReviewValidator is actually wired up to our form controller in the XML config. In the sequence diagram we gloss over this slightly, because this side of things is already implemented for us in the Spring code.

After that, it's smooth sailing: the form controller calls the CustomerReviewDao to save the CustomerReview domain object, and the DAO in turn adds it to the Pending Reviews Queue in the database.

■**Note** It's debatable whether the form controller should do this by calling a ReviewsQueueDao object—is it a function of the form controller or the CustomerReviewsDao to handle the application logic? In this case, it seems to simplify things if the DAO handles it. This way, if some other part of the system were to save a CustomerReview via the DAO, the logic of adding it to the queue would be already encapsulated in the DAO, not in a UI form handler elsewhere.

Internet Bookstore Implementation: Spring Details

This section ties in closely with the Internet Bookstore implementation described in Chapter 10. Here we describe the way in which the Internet Bookstore code and supporting files are organized.

First, we'll look at the overall folder structure. Then in the next section, we'll examine the package hierarchy that we'll use to organize our Java classes.

Folder Structure

At the very top level we have an InternetBookstore folder. Let's put this in D:\Dev:

```
D:\Dev\InternetBookstore
    .classes
    db
    dist
    lib
    src
    war
```

Beneath D:\Dev\InternetBookstore we have .classes, db, and so on. This is a pretty standard folder structure for Spring web applications: the .classes folder is the target folder where the compiled classes will go; db contains the HSQLDB database; dist is where the built release archives will go, ready to be deployed to the application server; lib contains various library files needed for compilation; and war (which stands for "web archive") contains all the bits and pieces that go into making the web application (JSP files, CSS file, XML config, etc.).

Most important, however, is src, where we'll spend most of our time, as this folder will contain the Java source code that we've derived from all of our analysis and design efforts leading up to this point.

We'll delve into some of these folders in more detail in the next couple of sections.

Contents of the war\WEB-INF Folder

WEB-INF contains two rather important files, web.xml and bookstore-servlet.xml. These are central to the way that our Internet Bookstore application will be configured to work within Spring, so (even though digging around in XML files takes us slightly outside the scope of this book) it's worth visiting them briefly here.

web.xml

The web.xml file is used by Tomcat, and it defines the Internet Bookstore web application. In particular, it defines a servlet called bookstore, which (due to a naming convention, as we'll see in a moment) will lead Spring to bookstore-servlet.xml.

Here's what web.xml looks like:

```
<?xml version="1.0" encoding="ISO-8859-1"?>

<!DOCTYPE web-app PUBLIC
    "-//Sun Microsystems, Inc.//DTD Web Application 2.3//EN"
    "http://java.sun.com/dtd/web-app_2_3.dtd">

<web-app>
```

```
<servlet>
    <servlet-name>bookstore</servlet-name>
    <servlet-class>
        org.springframework.web.servlet.DispatcherServlet
    </servlet-class>
    <load-on-startup>1</load-on-startup>
</servlet>

<servlet-mapping>
    <servlet-name>bookstore</servlet-name>
    <url-pattern>*.htm</url-pattern>
</servlet-mapping>

<welcome-file-list>
    <welcome-file>index.jsp</welcome-file>
</welcome-file-list>
```

```
</web-app>
```

The `<servlet>` tag and its contents define the `bookstore` servlet. The class for the `bookstore` servlet isn't actually one of our classes—it's Spring's `DispatcherServlet`. `DispatcherServlet` will use the servlet name to determine where to get its configuration from; basically it appends `-servlet.xml` to the name, in this case giving us `bookstore-servlet.xml`.

The `<servlet-mapping>` tag tells Tomcat that any browser requests whose page ends in `.htm` should be handed over to the `bookstore` servlet (in other words, to `DispatcherServlet`). This is an important point: our application doesn't actually contain any files ending in `.htm`. These are "virtual" files, used purely for mapping browser requests to Controllers. The actual mapping is done in `bookstore-servlet.xml`, which we'll get to in just a moment.

The third and final part of `web.xml` is the `<welcome-file-list>` tag. This simply tells Tomcat that if a request doesn't specify a filename, then it should default to `index.jsp`.

bookstore-servlet.xml

The main purpose of `bookstore-servlet.xml` is to collectively define all the various beans (Java classes) needed in order to make the `bookstore` servlet hang together. So for the most part, it consists almost entirely of `<bean>` tags. We return to it periodically in Chapter 10 and add more configuration to it as we create the new classes (aka beans).

```
<?xml version="1.0" encoding="UTF-8"?>
<!DOCTYPE beans PUBLIC "-//SPRING//DTD BEAN//EN"
    "http://www.springframework.org/dtd/spring-beans.dtd">

<!--
  - Application context definition for "bookstore" DispatcherServlet.
  -->
```

```xml
<beans>
    <bean id="dataSource"
        class="org.springframework.jdbc.datasource.DriverManagerDataSource">
        <property name="driverClassName">
            <value>org.hsqldb.jdbcDriver</value>
        </property>
        <property name="url">
<value>jdbc:hsqldb:file:D:\Dev\TravelBookstore\db\data\test</value>
        </property>
        <property name="username">
            <value>matt</value>
        </property>
        <property name="password">
            <value>pass</value>
        </property>
    </bean>

    <bean id="viewResolver" class=
"org.springframework.web.servlet.view.InternalResourceViewResolver">
        <property name="viewClass">
            <value>org.springframework.web.servlet.view.JstlView</value>
        </property>
        <property name="prefix">
            <value>/WEB-INF/jsp/</value>
        </property>
        <property name="suffix">
            <value>.jsp</value>
        </property>
    </bean>

    <bean id="homeController"
        class="com.iconixsw.bookstore.web.HomeController"/>

    <bean id="urlMapping"
class="org.springframework.web.servlet.handler.SimpleUrlHandlerMapping">
        <property name="mappings">
            <props>
                <prop key="/home.htm">homeController</prop>
            </props>
        </property>
    </bean>
</beans>
```

The first bean, dataSource, defines the JDBC data source: the DataSource class that will manage the whole database connecting thing for us, the driver class, a URL pointing to our local HSQLDB file, and the database username and password.

The second bean, `viewResolver`, overrides the default Spring `InternalResourceView` class. Instead, we want to use the `JstlView` class, which allows us to put JSTL tags in our JSP pages. `viewResolver` also defines a couple of other properties, `prefix` and `suffix`:

- `prefix` is given the value `/WEB-INF/jsp/`, meaning that the view files (our JSP pages) will be kept in the `WEB-INF/jsp` folder.

- `suffix` is given the value `.jsp`, meaning that all the view files will end in `.jsp`.

For example, if a view is identified as "home," then the actual view file will be /WEB-INF/jsp/home.jsp.

The third bean, `homeController`, is (at last!) one of our classes, and was identified during the design for the *Show Book Details* use case. The declaration is saying that we want a single instance of the class `HomeController`, and if it's to be referred to by other beans in the XML configuration, it will be referred to using the ID `homeController`. `HomeController` is simply there to return the main ("home") view page, so it doesn't do a huge amount.

The fourth bean, `urlMapping`, uses one of the Spring classes to map HTTP requests to Controllers. Currently there's only one mapping set up: we're telling the `HandlerMapping` class that if a request arrives for a virtual page called `home.htm`, then the request should be handed to a bean called `homeController`. Hey, and as luck would have it, we've just defined a bean called `homeController`.

Back to the remaining folders.

Contents of the war\WEB-INF\jsp and war\WEB-INF\jsp\include Folders

`WEB-INF\jsp` contains the JSP files (the "view"). Because the JSP files are located beneath `WEB-INF`, they can't be accessed directly by the user's web browser. Instead they are invoked in a controlled fashion by Spring, which sends the output from the JSP back to the browser.

`WEB-INF\jsp\include` currently just contains one file, `IncludeTop.jsp`. This is "included" by each one of our JSP files, and it contains the standard stuff that goes at the top of each page, to avoid repetition.

Here's what `IncludeTop.jsp` looks like:

```
<%@ page contentType="text/html" %>
<%@ taglib prefix="c" uri="http://java.sun.com/jstl/core" %>
<%@ taglib prefix="fmt" uri="http://java.sun.com/jstl/fmt" %>
<%@ taglib prefix="spring" uri="http://www.springframework.org/tags" %>

<html>
<head>
    <title>ICONIX Internet Bookstore</title>
    <meta content="text/html; charset=windows-1252" http-equiv="Content-Type" />
    <link rel="stylesheet" href="elements/bookstore.css" />
```

422 APPENDIX B ■ SPRING BIN

```
    <META HTTP-EQUIV="Cache-Control" CONTENT="max-age=0">
    <META HTTP-EQUIV="Cache-Control" CONTENT="no-cache">
    <meta http-equiv="expires" content="0">
    <META HTTP-EQUIV="Expires" CONTENT="Tue, 01 Jan 1980 1:00:00 GMT">
    <META HTTP-EQUIV="Pragma" CONTENT="no-cache">
</head>

<body bgcolor="white">
<h1>ICONIX Internet Bookstore</h1>

<div class="navbar">
    <a href="home.htm">Home</a> |
    <a href="search.htm">Search</a>
</div>
```

It's worth stepping through this file, as it contains a bunch of interesting stuff. The first line, a JSP tag, simply states that this will be an HTML file. The next two lines import the JSTL tag libraries, and the line after them imports Spring's tag libraries.

■**Note** JSTL stands for *JSP Standard Tag Library*, and it provides core functionality common to many web applications. Common tasks such as iteration (for/while loops), conditionals (if...then...else), XML manipulation, and internationalization are included and can be dropped into your JSP page as simple tags. You can find out more about JSTL at http://java.sun.com/products/jsp/jstl.

Next, the top part of the page is begun, with familiar HTML tags such as <html>, <head>, and <body>.

You'll notice that there are five lines that begin with <META HTTP-EQUIV=. These collectively tell the web browser not to cache any of these pages, but always to request the latest version from the server.

Because this is all defined in a shared include file, all of our pages will have the same title, heading, navigation bar, cache settings, and so on.

Java Package Hierarchy

All of the classes we've identified in our design need to be organized into Java *packages*.

Each package is a folder in the local file system. The choice of package structure is pretty much up to you, though it makes sense to follow whatever conventions are used by the framework that you're coding to.

For the Internet Bookstore, the package hierarchy looks like this (located directly beneath the src folder):

```
com
    iconixsw
        bookstore
            dao
                jdbc
            domain
                logic
            web
```

Packages are referred to in Java using *dot notation* so, for example, the full name for the dao package is `com.iconixsw.bookstore.dao`. The physical folder structure for this package (at least in the Windows file system) would be `com\iconixsw\bookstore\dao`.

As we described in the "Java Naming Conventions: A 30-Second Crash Course" sidebar earlier in this appendix, package names follow a reverse URL convention, so the company's domain name is `iconixsw.com` and the application name is `bookstore`, hence `com.iconixsw.bookstore`.

Here's a quick rundown of each of the packages beneath `bookstore`:

- The `dao` package contains the DAO interfaces (the "home objects" for retrieving domain objects from the data source).

- The `dao.jdbc` subpackage contains a concrete implementation of the DAO interfaces for HSQLDB via JDBC. The DAO design pattern makes it relatively easy to migrate your application to some other database with relatively little rework.

- The `domain` package contains the domain classes, which in our design are doubling as Controller classes. Form validators go in the `domain.logic` subpackage.

- The `web` package contains all of the `Controller` classes.

Now that we've set up our package structure and basic configuration, we can start to create the "real" implementation (see Chapter 10).

Index

◼A

AbstractCommandController class, 274
acceptance testing, 333
Acegi Security, 179
actors
    adding a Customer actor to a robustness
        diagram, 117
    as external to the system, 54
    as fulfilling several roles, 54
    modeling external systems as, 35
    placing on use case diagrams, 32
    representing nonhuman external systems, 54
    roles of, in use case diagrams, 53
Add External Books to Catalog use case, 128,
    218
adding operations to domain objects, 4
addToPendingReviewsQueue(), 284
AddToShoppingCartTest test case, 340
advices, 74
aggregation (has-a) relationship, 24, 27, 33
algorithms, differentiating from use cases, 76
alternate courses
    displaying in a different color on robustness
        diagrams, 110
    Login use case, example robustness diagram,
        110
    modeling in a robustness diagram, 122
analysis and preliminary design phase, 3, 9
analysis paralysis, 175
anemic domain model, 242
architectural layering
    architectural diagrams, examples of, 162
    definition of, 162
    horizontal vs. vertical layers, 163
    UML class diagrams, 164
architectural paralysis, 180
arrows
    as communication associations on
        robustness diagrams, 108
    showing data flow or control flow, 108
aspect-oriented programming (AOP), 74
    defining cross-cutting concerns through
        code, 171
    as extending object-oriented programming
        (OOP), 171
    problems with, 172
assert methods, in JUnit, 339
assertEquals(), arguments used, 340
attributes, discordant, 205
avoiding dysfunctional requirements, 6

◼B

Beck, Kent, 351
behavioral requirements, 3–4, 7
Beizer, Boris, 334
beta testing, 333
BillyBob 2.0, requirements for, 379
Book class
    distribution of responsibilities in, 238
    as an unused object on a sequence diagram,
        246
Book.java, code example, 266
BookDao, 243, 255
bookdetails.jsp, 274, 277
BookDetailsCommand, 240
BookDetailsController, 240, 243, 272–273, 275,
    305, 359–360, 362
bookstore-servlet.xml, 287, 290, 315, 419–421
bookstore.css, 265
boundary objects, 8, 187
    definition of, 103
    disambiguated nomenclature of, 108
    referencing by name in use cases, 52, 61
    treating as nouns, 103
building a project glossary, 7

◼C

callTestHandle(), 365
Carnegie Mellon Software Engineering Institute,
    161
CASE tools, 57, 105, 193, 203, 260
CDR guidelines, 15
checkBookFound(), 358
checkRating(), 319
checkReviewLength(), 318
checkTitleLength(), 318
class attributes, relationship to database tables,
    29
class diagrams, 4
    adding getters and setters to, 211
    conventions of, 164
    domain model and, 24, 28–29
    finishing the updating of, 127
    keeping static and dynamic models in sync,
        211
    tidying up for a clearer layout, 255
    updating and refining, 210
    using to find errors on sequence diagrams,
        238
class notation, types of, 27
classes
    allocating behavior to, 188
    assigning operations to, 125
    distribution of responsibilities among, 239

organizing around key abstractions in the problem domain, 28
relationship to use cases, 51
searching for classes without attributes, 236
subclasses and superclasses, 37
cleaning up the static model, 14
Code Review and Model Update
    accumulating boilerplate checklists for future reviews, 299–300
    avoiding review and update paralysis, 299, 301
    breaking down list items into a smaller checklist, 299
    catching design or integration issues early, 298
    code review vs. code inspection, 302
    comparing the code with the design diagrams, 298
    conducting a productive code review, 301
    creating a high-level list of review items (use case titles), 299
    emailing action points to all participants, 299–300
    focusing on error detection, not error correction, 299–300
    frequency of, 298
    guidelines, 299
    keeping the review just formal enough, 299, 301
    not forgetting the Model Update session, 299, 301
    preparing for, 299
    purpose of, 298
    quickly addressing disparities between code and design, 303
    reusing objects in the domain model, 298
    reviewing code at different levels, 299–300
    syncing code with design, 297
    updating and refining the static model, 298
    using an integrated code/model browser, 299, 301
    value of up-front design, 303
    why code reviews are necessary, 302–303
Code Review and Model Update guidelines, 18
coding and testing, 4, 15
collaboration diagrams
    function of, 109
    not confusing with robustness diagrams, 107–108
    purpose of, 107
Command objects, definition of, 168
commenting code, 259, 262
compatibility testing, 333
Constructor Injection, 412
Controller interface, 412
controller objects
    lack of, on sequence diagrams, 187
    using sparingly, 108
controllers, 3, 11, 412
    creating test cases for, 109
    definition of, 103
    ensuring proper test coverage for, 350
    as logical software functions, 11

as methods on the boundary and entity classes, 109
names of, 120
as real control objects, 11
renaming those with the same name on a diagram, 345
running test cases for data-retrieval controllers, 356
Show Book Details use case, 351
treating as verbs, 103
Create New Book use case, 219
Create New Customer Account use case, 128
Critical Design Review (CDR), 4, 15
    allocating operations to classes appropriately, 235–236
    centralizing responsibility in a class, 240
    checking for continuity of messages, 234
    checking for entity classes without attributes, 251
    checking that operations are complete and correct, 235, 237
    coupling object-oriented encapsulation with RDD, 239
    covering both basic and alternate courses of action, 235–236
    determining if the sequence diagram matches the class diagram, 250
    discovering unexplored areas in the analysis space, 251
    distribution of responsibilities in the Book class, 238
    ensuring that the sequence diagram matches the use case text, 234–236
    generating and inspecting the code headers for classes, 235, 237
    generating skeleton tests from the robustness diagram, 238
    guidelines, 235
    having all patterns reflected on the sequence diagram, 235, 237
    identifying a stable set of abstractions, 249
    identifying attributes from functional requirements, 251
    ironing out leaps of logic between objects, 234
    limiting to designers and developers, not customers, 234
    minimizing code breakage and refactoring, 249
    performing a sanity check on the design, 235, 237
    primary goals, 234
    reviewing the attributes and operations on classes, 235–236
    reviewing the quality of the design, 234
    reviewing the test plan for the release, 235, 237
    searching for classes without attributes, 236
    setting the starting time for, 235
    Show Book Details use case, 238
    tracing functional requirements to use cases and classes, 235, 237

using class diagrams to find errors on
    sequence diagrams, 238
Write Customer Review use case, 245
cross-cutting concerns
    extension use cases, 74
    infrastructure use cases, 74
    peer use cases, 74
CustomerReview, 247, 311
CustomerReviewValidator class, 311
CustomerSession class, 179, 287

■D

Data Access Objects (DAOs), 165, 169–170, 175
data analysis and reduction, definition of, 378
data capture, definition of, 378
Data Definition Language (DDL), 259
data model, 161
data reporting, definition of, 378
database tables, relationship to class attributes,
    29
Dependency Injection (DI), 409, 412
deployment model, 161, 173, 175
design as building the system right, 9
Design-Driven Testing (DDT)
    acceptance testing, 333
    adding a tearDown() method, 350
    AddToShoppingCartTest test case, 340
    adopting a testing mind-set, 330
    aligning tests closely to requirements, 331
    avoiding duplicating alternate course
        scenarios, 369
    avoiding duplication in tests, 343
    beginning testing before coding, 369
    beta testing, 333
    compatibility testing, 333
    covering basic and alternate courses in
        scenario testing, 331
    creating a resource in the test method itself,
        349
    creating unit tests for each controller on a
        robustness diagram, 330
    DDT errors, list of, 369
    different types of testing, 330
    discovering alternate courses during, 338
    doing requirement-level verification, 331
    doing scenario-level acceptance testing, 331
    driving unit tests from test cases, 338
    driving unit tests from use cases, 330
    ensuring that each test method tests exactly
        one thing, 342
    finding and fixing buggy code, 370
    function of, 329
    generating test skeleton code for unit testing,
        334
    guidelines, 330
    identifying and targeting "test hot spots", 370
    identifying test cases using robustness
        diagrams, 329, 334
    identifying the test scenarios for each
        controller/test case, 335
    integration testing, 333
    keeping unit tests fine-grained, 331, 342
    linking one test case to each controller, 336

mapping test cases directly to JUnit test
    classes, 339
mock objects, testing with, 354
neglecting to fix a failing test, 343
nonfunctional requirements testing, 333
not writing tests that connect to external
    resources, 353
performance testing, 334
practice questions to test your knowledge,
    370–371
preparing for, during the analysis stage, 329
programmers' attitudes toward, 331
proving a test by trying to make it fail, 348
regression testing, 334
release testing, 333
running tests from a test suite, 350
stress testing, 334
system testing, 333
testing paralysis, 370
transforming a robustness diagram into a
    test case diagram, 334
treating unit test code with reverence, 342
tying closely to requirements, 329
tying unit tests to the preliminary design
    objects, 342
understanding the tests required at each life
    cycle stage, 331
unit test skeletons, guidelines for creating,
    338
unit testing, 332
using "realize" connectors, 334
using a testing framework, 331
using a traceability matrix, 331
using mock objects sparingly, 343, 369
using the Agile ICONIX/EA add-in to
    generate diagrams, 336
volume testing, 334
why bother with designing unit tests, 366
writing effective unit tests, 342–343
writing tests from the calling object's point of
    view, 338, 347, 358
writing tests to validate and hone the design,
    369
detailed design phase, 3, 12, 186
discordant attributes, 205
DispatcherServlet, 167, 174–176, 178, 269, 271,
    306, 347, 415–416, 419
Display Book Not Found page controller, 345
Display controllers
    initialization behavior and, 111
    necessity for, on robustness diagrams, 111
DisplayBookDetailsPageTest, 365
doesBookIDExist(), 247
domain classes, 7, 24, 27, 30
    candidates for the Internet Bookstore, 33
    referencing by name in use cases, 52, 59
domain model, 11
    assumed to be incomplete, 28
    class diagrams and, 24, 28–29
    creating before use cases, 29
    definition of, 24
    deliberate simplicity of, 29
    disambiguating, 29

domain classes and, 24, 30
feeding updated information and changes
    back into, 51
identifying attributes to be added to classes,
    125
not mistaking for a data model, 28
refining and updating throughout a project,
    23
relationship to use cases, 25
removing UI elements from, 32
showing aggregation and generalization
    relationships, 24, 27
updating after identifying a new domain
    object, 122
updating incrementally while drawing
    robustness diagrams, 125
using as a project glossary, 24, 26, 29
when to update, 51
domain model diagrams
    creating, 33, 35
    ensuring coverage of the problem domain,
        85
    showing generalization and aggregation
        relationships, 86
    using a link class, 86
domain modeling, 3
    creating the initial model in two hours, 28
    definition of, 7
    distinguishing domain models from data
        models, 7
    exercises and solutions for spotting
        modeling errors, 39–42, 44–45
    focusing on real-world objects within the
        problem domain, 26
    guidelines, 7, 26
    identifying and eliminating duplicate terms,
        32
    practice questions in modeling, 45–46
    static and dynamic parts of, 25
DomainObject interface, 315
doSubmitAction(), 283, 290
dot notation, 423
drawing a robustness diagram, 3, 11
driving test cases from the analysis model, 20
DUnit, 339
dynamic workflows, 2
dysfunctional requirements, definition of, 375

■E

Edit Customer Review use case, 324
Edit Shopping Cart use case, 220
Enterprise Architect (EA), 57, 89, 105, 112, 238,
    260
    adding a test case scenario in, 345, 352
    built-in features for managing requirements,
        382
    creating a requirements tree, 385
    creating an extended class diagram, 384
    custom UML elements, 383
    dragging elements from the Project View, 384
    dragging requirements onto the use case,
        382
    external requirements, definition of, 383

generating a requirements traceability
    matrix automatically, 374
Hierarchy window, 386
importing requirements from a comma-
    separated value (CSV) file, 383
internal requirements, definition of, 383
linking any model element to a requirement,
    386
Move External button, 383
opening the Properties dialog, 383
organizing functional requirements in, 379
Relationship Matrix, using, 388
Require tab, 382–383
requirements for BillyBob 2.0, 379
supporting requirements using a visual
    modeling tool, 382
turning internal requirements into external
    ones, 383
use cases and domain model for BillyBob
    2.0, 380
using the Agile ICONIX/EA add-in to
    generate diagrams, 336
using to generate Spring-ready Java code,
    165
Enterprise JavaBeans (EJB), disadvantages of,
    166
entity objects, 187
    definition of, 103
    treating as nouns, 103
entity-relationship (ER) diagrams, 214
Errors object, 290
extended class diagrams, creating, 384
"extends" association, 64, 66, 69
external requirements, in Enterprise Architect
    (EA), 383
external systems, modeling as actors, 35

■F

facilitator/moderator, benefits of, 88
findByCustomerId(), 286
findById(), 243, 286
flowcharts, not drawing on sequence diagrams,
    189
focus of control, 187–188, 192
formBackingObject(), 280–283, 320–321
Fowler, Martin, 242
functional requirements, 3

■G

generalization (is-a) relationship, 24, 27
    notation for, 37
getCommandClass(), 241
getCustomer(), 288
getCustomerSession(), 288
GUI prototypes, 51, 56, 87

■H

handle(), 272, 305, 358
handleRequest(), 347–348
Hibernate, 166, 260
Hierarchy window, 386
home.jsp, 269, 271

HomeController, 268, 347–348
HSQL database, 176
    use of, in-memory persistence mode, 165
HttpServlet interface, 412
HttpUnit, 179

■

iBATIS, 166
ICONIX Process
    acceptance testing, 333
    adding operations to the domain objects, 4
    allocating behavior to classes, 188
    analysis and preliminary design phase, 3, 9
    analysis as building the right system, 9
    avoiding dysfunctional requirements, 6
    behavioral requirements, 3–4, 7
    beta testing, 333
    boundary classes, 8
    CDR guidelines, 15
    class diagram, 4
    cleaning up the static model, 14
    Code Review and Model Update guidelines,
        18
    coding and testing, 4, 15
    compatibility testing, 333
    completing refactoring before coding, 351
    controllers, 3, 11
    Critical Design Review (CDR), 4, 15
    depicting how objects interact, 188
    design as building the system right, 9
    detailed design phase, 3, 12
    domain modeling, 3, 7, 11
    drawing a robustness diagram, 3, 11
    driving test cases from the analysis model, 20
    dynamic workflows, 2
    entities, 4
    extensions to, 19
    finalizing the distribution of operations
        among classes, 188
    functional requirements, 3
    implementation (coding) guidelines, 17
    implementation phase, 4, 15
    improving by ongoing iteration and
        refinement, 35
    initial domain model as normally
        incomplete, 106
    integration and scenario testing, 4, 18, 333
    as an intensely feedback-driven process, 96
    interaction scenarios, 19
    iterative nature of, 2
    Model-View-Controller (MVC) architecture,
        167
    naming the logical software functions
        (controllers), 3
    nonfunctional requirements testing, 333
    organizing use cases into packages, 9
    overview of, 2
    performance testing, 334
    performing a Code Review and Model
        Update, 4
    persona, definition of, 19
    prefactoring designs, 14
    Preliminary Design Review (PDR), 3, 12

    preliminary design steps, 9
    preventing entropy (code rot), 18
    regression testing, 334
    release testing, 333
    requirements definition phase, 4
    requirements gathering guidelines, 6
    Requirements Review, 3, 8
    robustness analysis, 3, 11
    as a scenario-based approach, 7
    screen mockups, 8
    sequence diagramming, 3, 14, 188
    showing generalization and aggregation
        relationships, 9
    static model, 4
    static workflows, 2
    storyboarding the GUI, 3, 7
    stress testing, 334
    suitability to agile projects, 2
    syncing code with design, 297
    system testing, 333
    Test-Driven Development (TDD), 19
    types of tests and when to apply them, 332
    UML 2.0 extensions and, 396
    understanding the tests required at each life
        cycle stage, 331
    unit testing, 17, 332
    updating the domain model, 3
    use case modeling guidelines, 8
    volume testing, 334
implementation, 4, 15
    coding as a design review stage, 272
    correcting wrong coding, 258
    driving the code directly from the design, 259
    fixing design problems immediately, 259–260
    following the same coding conventions, 260
    guidelines, 17, 259
    holding regular code inspections, 259–260
    including alternate courses on sequence
        diagrams, 259, 263
    keeping the design and code in sync, 259,
        261
    not leting framework issues drive business
        issues, 259, 261
    overcommenting code, 259, 262
    practice questions in programming and
        delivery, 294–295
    preventing code from getting out of control,
        259, 261
    programmer-driven design, 258
    questioning a framework's design choices,
        259, 261
    Show Book Details use case, 268
    Write Customer Review use case, 278
    writing code and unit tests at the same time,
        259, 262, 329
"includes" association, 64, 69
initData(), changing, 355
integration and scenario testing, 4, 18, 333
interaction scenarios, 19
intermangling, definition of, 375
internal requirements, in Enterprise Architect
    (EA), 383

Internet Bookstore
    accounting for alternate courses of action, 93
    action list following the Code Review and
        Model Update, 322
    actors, 53
    Add External Books to Catalog use case, 128
    adding a MockBookDao class, 354
    adding a tearDown() method, 350
    adding assert statements into the test
        methods, 361
    adding individual tests to the test suite, 351
    adding new properties and operations to
        entity classes, 267
    adding save() onto CustomerReview, 321
    addToPendingReviewsQueue(), 284
    analyzing basic and alternate courses, 72–73
    anemic domain model, 242
    avoiding overly abstract use case text, 93
    Book class, 238, 266
    Book Details Not Found page controller, 308
    Book Not Found page displayed test
        scenario, 363
    Book.java, code example, 266
    BookDao, 243, 255, 275
    bookdetails.htm, 270
    bookdetails.jsp, 274, 277
    BookDetailsCommand, 240, 255
    BookDetailsController, 240, 243, 270,
        272–273, 275, 305, 360, 362
    bookstore-servlet.xml, 275, 283, 287, 290,
        315, 419–421
    bookstore.css, 265
    boundary classes and display(), 212
    bridging the modeling and development
        environments, 324
    browser request, flow of events, 178–179
    callTestHandle(), 365
    candidate domain classes, 33
    catching a NotFoundException, 309
    changing statements from passive to active
        voice, 95
    checkBookFound(), 358, 360
    checkRating(), 319
    checkReviewLength(), 318
    checkTitleLength(), 318
    cheering a failing test, 356
    clarifying relationships between domain
        classes, 38
    code generation and CASE tools, 260
    Command classes, 216
    completed sequence diagram, 208
    constructor detail as commonly missed, 310
    Controller classes, 216
    controller layer, 175
    Create New Customer Account use case, 128
    creating a BookDetailsController object, 359
    creating a first domain model diagram, 33
    creating a persistent object model using
        JavaBeans, 169
    creating a resource in the test method itself,
        349
    creating a second domain model diagram, 35

    creating a single BookstoreValidator class,
        313
    creating the database, 263
    Customer class, 266
    CustomerDao, 255
    CustomerReview, 216, 247, 255, 266, 279, 284,
        311
    CustomerReviewDao class, 284
    CustomerReviewValidator class, 311
    CustomerSession class, 179, 206, 287
    Data Access Objects (DAOs), 165, 169–170,
        175, 216, 413
    dataSource property, 275
    defining and separating architectural layers,
        172, 174–176
    delegating behavior into helper classes, 243
    deployment model, 175
    determining if the sequence diagram
        matches the class diagram, 250
    direct mapping between JavaBeans and
        domain classes, 169
    discovering additional domain objects, 35
    DispatcherServlet, 167, 174–176, 178, 216,
        271, 306, 347
    Display Book Details controller, test class
        skeleton, 358
    DisplayBookDetailsPageTest, 365
    DisplayBookNotFoundPageTest, refactored,
        368
    dividing code into smaller, well-named
        methods, 320
    doesBookIDExist(), 247
    domain classes and database dependencies,
        176
    DomainObject interface, 315
    doSubmitAction(), 283, 290
    Edit Customer Review use case, 324
    ensuring proper test coverage for controllers,
        350
    entity classes and database tables, 266
    .error style, 265
    Errors object, 290
    examining the handle() method, 305
    expecting to add new functionality, 324
    exposing leaps of logic in the design, 310
    extracting domain classes from high-level
        requirements, 30–33
    filling in implementation details on
        sequence diagrams, 208
    findByCustomerId(), 286
    findById(), 243, 286
    forgetting to code an alternate course of
        action, 316
    formBackingObject(), 280–283, 320–321
    generating the entity classes for Spring, 260
    getCommandClass(), 241
    getCustomer(), 288
    getCustomerSession(), 288
    getting "atomic" on the sequence diagram,
        317
    handle(), 272, 358
    handleRequest(), 347–348

handling an unused object on a sequence diagram, 246
handling the "validation" controllers, 311
home.jsp, 269, 271
HomeController class, 268, 271
how the home page is displayed, 271
HSQL database, 165, 176
identifying a stable set of abstractions, 249
implementing the home page (home.jsp), 268
IncludeTop.jsp, 270, 277, 421
index.jsp, 271
initData(), changing, 355
insufficiently detailed sequence diagram, 243
invoking a use case from a sequence diagram, 245
isLoggedIn(), 288
isUserLoggedIn(), 206, 212
Java package hierarchy, 422–423
Java Standard Tag Library (JSTL), 412, 422
JavaServer Pages (JSP), 165, 179, 412
JdbcBookDao class, 275
JdbcCustomerReviewDao class, 284
JSP Tag Library (JSTL), 165
load(), 240, 243
Login use case, 105, 122
Login use case, example robustness diagram, 110
mapping browser requests to Controllers, 419
mapping entity classes to implementation classes, 266
minimizing code breakage and refactoring, 249
Model-View-Controller (MVC) architecture, 165, 167
ModelAndView object, 178, 216, 272
Moderate Customer Reviews use case, 122
Moderate Pending Reviews use case, 324
moving the validation code into CustomerReview, 315
naming participating domain objects, 92
not creating a Validator class for every domain class, 313
not generating SQL from the domain model, 259
organizing use cases into packages, 61
overall folder structure, 418
picking up warning signs from sequence diagrams, 305
prefix and suffix properties, 421
preparing the style sheet, 265
problems with a single "blanket" validation method, 316
proving a test by trying to make it fail, 348
removing out-of-scope information, 90
Retrieve Book Details controller, test class skeleton, 353
reversing the relationship between Book and CustomerReview, 322
reviewing the Show Book Details use case, 304

reviewing the Write Customer Review use case, 309
root cause of the "swarms of tiny classes" problem, 311
running test cases for data-retrieval controllers, 356
running the BookstoreTestSuite from the command line, 350
save(), 286
Search for Books use case, 131
setBookDao(), 243, 359
setUp(), 354
Show Book Details sequence diagram, 347
Show Book Details use case, 268, 292, 344, 414–415
Show Book Details use case, CDR example, 238
Show Book Details use case, robustness diagram, 115, 126
Show Book Details use case, updated sequence diagram, 252
ShowBookTestHelper, 368
showing HttpSession on the sequence diagram, 206
showValidationErrors(), 213
Spring Framework, 165
Spring Web MVC, 165, 167
testability, 179
testBookDetailsFound(), 362
testBookIdFound(), 353
testBookIdNotFound(), 353
testDisplayHomePage(), 346
testing HomeController, 347–348
testing that a book was not found, 356
testing the Display Book Details controller, 357
testing the Display Book Not Found page controller, 363
testing the Display Home Page controller, 345
testing the Retrieve Book Details controller, 352
testing to retrieve a book using its ID, 354
testPageDisplayed(), 359–360, 362
tracing individual requirements to use cases, 96
tracking the source of the book's ID, 305
turning controllers into methods on sequence diagrams, 317
UML model for, 324
updated static model, 126, 210–211
user authentication/authorization, 179
using a Code Review and Model Update checklist, 304
using Java for, 165
using Java's reflection API, 314
validate(), 289, 313
validation controllers, 133
view (presentation) layer, 173, 175
view page (bookdetails.jsp), 274, 277
web security, 179
WEB-INF folder, 418, 421
web.xml, 418–419

when the use case text and robustness diagram don't match, 246
why bother with designing unit tests, 366
Write Customer Review use case, 278, 344, 416–417
Write Customer Review use case, CDR example, 245
Write Customer Review use case, reviewing the controllers, 309
Write Customer Review use case, robustness diagram, 117
Write Customer Review use case, updated sequence diagram, 252
Write Reader Review use case, 70–71
writecustomerreview.jsp, 290
WriteCustomerReviewCommand, 247, 255
WriteCustomerReviewController class, 279, 284, 290, 310
WriteReviewScreen class, 213
writing tests from the calling object's point of view, 338, 347, 358
writing unit tests prior to coding, 344
Inversion of Control (IoC)
Dependency Injection (DI), 409, 412
design pattern, 166, 283
Java bean example with one property, 409
wiring beans together, 411
"invokes" association, 63, 69
isLoggedIn(), 288

■J

J2EE Servlet API, 412
Java
classes, 410
dot notation, 423
naming conventions, 410
object naming conventions, 275
packages and subpackages, naming conventions, 410
property, 410
reverse URL convention, 410, 423
variables, 410
Java Data Objects (JDO), 166
Java Standard Tag Library (JSTL), 412, 422
Java Swing, 166
JavaBeans, 165
JavaServer Pages (JSP), 165–166, 412
testing, 179
JDBC, 166, 258
JdbcBookDao class, 275
JDO, 260
JGenerator, 260
JSP Tag Library (JSTL), 165
Jumpstart training workshops, 88
JUnit, 18, 331, 334
adding individual tests to the test suite, 351
AddToShoppingCartTest test case, 340
assert methods, 339
assertEquals(), arguments used, 340
introduction to, 339
limiting each test method to a single assert statement, 339

mapping test cases directly to Java test classes, 339
naming convention followed, 339
new features in version 4.0, 341
operation of, 339
running tests from a test suite, 350
setUp(), 340–341
suite(), 350
tearDown(), 341
test skeleton, 346
testDisplayHomePage(), 346
TestRunner, 350
unit test class, code example, 339
website of, 339

■L

link class, 86
linking use cases to objects, 11
load(), 240, 243
Login use case, 105, 110, 122

■M

manager classes, 108
MDG Integration, 195, 262
messages
differentiating among programming languages, 189
labeling on sequence diagrams, 188, 194
passing, 187
Method Injection, 412
Microsoft Visual Studio 2005, 262
miscommunication in IT projects, 23
mock objects
testing with, 354
using sparingly, 343, 354, 369
MockBookDao class, 354
Model-View-Controller (MVC) architecture, 165, 167
ModelAndView object, 168, 178, 412, 415
modeling aggregation and generalization relationships, 28
Moderate Customer Reviews use case, 122
Moderate Pending Reviews use case, 324
multiplicity, using, 214

■N

naming the logical software functions (controllers), 3
nonfunctional requirements testing, 333
NotFoundException, 309
NullPointerException, 354
NUnit, 334, 339

■O

object discovery, 106
object instances, 59
object lifelines, 187
object model, use cases and, 25
object-oriented design (OOD), sequence diagrams and, 185
object-relational mapping (ORM), 166

objects
   classification of, 101
   definition of, 25
operation, UML definition of, 189
organizing use cases into packages, 9, 85–86

■P

package/component model, 161, 173
packages, 410, 422
   definition of, 61
performance testing, 334
performing a Code Review and Model Update, 4
persona, definition of, 19
Plain Old Java Objects (POJOs), 165
pointcuts, 74
"precedes" association, 63, 66, 69, 91
prefactoring designs, 14
preliminary design, 51
   robustness analysis and, 102
Preliminary Design Review (PDR), 3, 12
preliminary design steps, 9
preventing entropy (code rot), 18
problem domain, 26, 249
problem space, describing, 29
problem space classes, 201
project glossary, 24, 26
project requirements, ongoing changeability of, 28
Properties dialog, Enterprise Architect (EA), 383
property (in Java), 410

■R

Rational Rose, 57, 196
Rational XDE, 260
real-time systems
   using elements on state diagrams to build test cases, 330
Realization relationship, 386
refactoring, 351
regression testing, 334
Relationship Matrix, 388
release testing, 333
requirements gathering
   allocation and traceability as a life cycle concern, 378
   avoiding dysfunctional (intermangled) requirements, 374–375
   avoiding the "big monolithic document" syndrome, 374, 377
   creating estimates from use cases or controllers list, 374, 377
   data analysis and reduction, definition of, 378
   data capture and data reporting, definitions of, 378
   different corporate strategies for handling, 373
   distinguishing between types of requirement specs, 374, 376
   drag-and-drop linking of elements back to requirements, 374

   driving requirements from business needs, not design patterns, 374, 377
   giving each requirement a short, catchy name, 374, 376
   guidelines, 6, 374
   intermangling of requirements and scenario text, 375–376
   practice questions in, 389
   removing dysfunctionality from requirements, 376
   separating active-voice use cases from passive-voice requirements, 375
   traceability of requirements, 378
   using examples when writing functional requirements, 374, 377
   using modeling tools supporting linkage and traceability, 374
   why requirements tracking is vital, 377
   writing at least one test case for each requirement, 374, 376
Requirements Review, 3, 8
   accounting for alternate courses of action, 93
   achieving basic agreement among all stakeholders, 88
   actively describing user interactions and system responses, 95
   allocating functional requirements to use cases, 89
   avoiding overly abstract use case text, 93
   avoiding passive-voice functional requirements in use cases, 85–86
   benefits of a facilitator/moderator, 88
   changing statements from passive to active voice, 95
   as a collaborative review among project stakeholders, 83
   creating clear illustrations of user and system behavior, 87
   decomposing a system along usage scenario boundaries, 93
   describing basic and alternate courses in active voice, 86
   eight steps to a better use case, 88–89
   guidelines, 8, 85
   keeping use case terminology concise and consistent, 92
   linking the GUI model to the narrative behavior descriptions, 87
   making the sign-off process collaborative, 84
   naming mock-up screens, 87
   naming participating domain objects, 92
   organizing use cases into packages, 85–86
   performing collaboratively with the right people, 88
   placing use cases in the user interface context, 87
   rationale for, 84
   referring use case text to the appropriate domain objects, 87
   removing out-of-scope information, 90
   tracing individual requirements to use cases, 96
   use case diagram, purpose of, 87

using storyboards and GUI prototypes, 87
writing coherent, specific, and unambiguous use case text, 95
writing use cases in the context of the object model, 87
requirements tree, creating, 385
Resin, 166
Responsibility-Driven Design (RDD), 194, 204, 247
reverse URL convention, 410, 423
robustness analysis
    adding a Customer actor to the robustness diagram, 117
    boundary objects, 103
    bridging the gap from analysis to design, 101
    controllers, 103
    creating a new, blank robustness diagram, 117
    enforcing a noun-verb-noun pattern in use case text, 104
    entity objects, 103
    exercises and solutions for fixing modeling errors, 128, 131–133, 136–137, 139
    guidelines, 11, 104–105
    linking use cases to objects, 101
    as the middle ground between analysis and design, 102
    modeling the alternate courses, 122
    performing for a use case, 114
    practice questions in modeling, 140–141
    as preliminary design, 102
    rules for noun–verb interaction, 103
    technical architecture (TA), 102, 160
    using to disambiguate use case text, 102
    walking through the Write Customer Review use case, 117
robustness diagrams
    adding a Customer actor, 117
    adding missing entity classes to the domain model, 104, 106
    arrows as communication associations on, 108
    avoiding drawing individual UI elements, 118, 136
    boundary objects, 103
    CASE tools, 105
    catching rule violations, 112–114
    controllers, 103–104, 108
    creating a new, blank diagram, 117
    definition of, 101–102
    disambiguated nomenclature of boundary objects, 108
    discovering hidden functionality and missing domain classes, 137
    doing a preliminary sketch on paper, 102
    enforcing a noun-verb-noun pattern in use case text, 104
    entity objects, 103
    expecting to rewrite (disambiguate) the use case, 104, 107
    generating skeleton tests from, 238
    GUI, 107
    learning to draw the use case text, 117

main purposes of, 108
making a boundary object for each screen, 104, 108
manager classes, 108
modeling alternate courses, 122
morphing of objects into the detailed design, 105, 109
naming screens unambiguously, 104
not allocating operations to classes, 133
not confusing with a collaboration diagram, 107–108
not including sections of use case text, 136
not redrawing endlessly, 208
not specifying validation checks in detail, 139
not worrying about arrow directions, 104, 108
object discovery, 106
object messages as verbs, 104
as an object picture of a use case, 101, 105, 109
objects as nouns, 104
page names as nouns, 116
pasting the use case text onto, 104–105
performing the highlighter test, 122, 136
as a preliminary conceptual design of a use case, 105, 109
problems arising from ambiguous use case text, 136
reading like an activity diagram or a flowchart, 103
representing the flow of action between two objects, 103
requirement for matching use case text precisely, 101
rules for noun–verb interaction, 103
Show Book Details use case, 115, 126
showing invoked use cases, 104, 109
showing valid and invalid relationships, 113
software functions, 107
taking entity classes from the domain model, 104, 106
technical architecture (TA) and, 160
three class stereotypes, 103
time requirements of, 102
using controller classes sparingly, 108
working through a use case one sentence at a time, 105, 107, 114
Write Customer Review use case, 117

■S
save(), 286
screen mock-ups, 8, 51, 56
Search for Books use case, 131
sequence diagrams
    actor, 187
    adding implementation details to, 211
    allocating behavior among collaborating objects, 192
    allocating behavior to classes, 188
    assigning operations to classes, 188, 194, 202
    behavior allocation error, 218

boundary and entity classes becoming object instances, 109
boundary object, 187
cleaning up the static model before the CDR, 188, 194
completed example of, 208
controller classes, 187–188
controllers becoming messages, 109
converging the problem space and solution space, 211
converting controllers from robustness diagrams, 203
copying boundary objects and actors from robustness diagrams, 200
copying entity objects from robustness diagrams, 199
copying use case text directly onto a diagram, 197
depicting how objects interact with each other, 188
determining which controllers go on which classes, 204
difficulty in drawing, 193
direct link to use cases, 186
discordant attributes, 205
drawing notation, 186
drawing one diagram for every use case, 58, 187, 189
entity object, 187
exercises and solutions for fixing errors, 217–218, 220–221, 223–224, 227
expanding upon the robustness diagram, 187, 190
filling in the implementation details before coding, 208
finalizing the distribution of operations among classes, 188
fixing leaps of logic in, 227
focus of control, 187–188, 192
four criteria of a good class, 205
four essential steps for drawing, 195
getting "atomic" on, 317
guidelines, 14, 187
invoking a use case from, 245
keeping the static and dynamic models in sync, 211
lack of controller objects on, 187
mapping use case text to messages, 188, 192
not drawing flowcharts on, 189
as noun-verb-noun in nature, 104
object lifelines, 187
object-oriented design (OOD), 185
overallocating a class, 205
overapplying design patterns, 204
passing messages, 187
pasting the entire use case text onto, 190
practice questions in modeling, 228–230
prefactoring designs, 188, 194
putting the functions where the data lives, 251
real design vs. conceptual design, 109
reviewing frequently, 188, 194
Show Book Details, 347, 353, 358, 363

showing basic and alternate courses on the same diagram, 187, 189
showing how objects accomplish use case behavior, 188, 190
turning a controller into a control class, 204
turning controllers into operations on classes, 188
understanding the primary goals of, 187–188
use cases and, 59
using CASE tools, 193
using incorrectly as just a flowchart, 223
using to drive the detailed design, 186
ServletRequestDataBinder class, 306
setBookDao(), 243, 359
setUp(), 354
Show Book Details use case, 89, 91, 190–191, 238, 252, 268, 292, 344, 414–415
ShowBookTestHelper, 368
showing generalization and aggregation relationships, 9
singletons, 411
software architecture. *See* technical architecture (TA)
software functions, 107
solution space classes, 201, 211
Sparx Systems, 112, 195–196, 297
    MDG Integration plug-in, 262
Spring Framework, 20
    AbstractCommandController class, 274
    Acegi Security, 179
    anatomy of, 165
    aspect-oriented programming (AOP) and, 172
    choosing a view technology, 167
    Command classes and domain classes, 168
    Command objects, definition of, 168
    Constructor Injection, 412
    Controller classes, 216
    Controller interface, 412
    controller, definition of, 167
    creating a persistent object model using JavaBeans, 169
    DAO and JDBC Support, 413
    Data Access Objects (DAOs), 165, 169–170, 175
    definition of, 165
    Dependency Injection (DI), 409, 412
    differentiating Spring and UML controllers, 168
    direct mapping between JavaBeans and domain classes, 169
    DispatcherServlet, 167, 174–176, 178, 269, 415–416, 419
    Enterprise JavaBeans (EJB), disadvantages of, 166
    Errors object, 290
    form validation, 417
    Hibernate, 166
    HttpServlet interface, 412
    iBATIS, 166
    Inversion of Control (IoC), 166, 283, 409, 411
    J2EE Servlet API, 412
    Java Data Objects (JDO), 166

Java Swing, 166
JavaBeans, 165
JavaServer Pages (JSP), 166
JDBC, 166, 258
lack of a security framework, 179
learning more about, 172
lightweight framework approach, 267
as a lightweight J2EE application framework, 166
mapping entity classes to implementation classes, 266
Method Injection, 412
model, definition of, 167
Model-View-Controller (MVC) architecture, 165, 167
ModelAndView object, 168, 178, 412, 415
object-relational mapping (ORM), 166
Plain Old Java Objects (POJOs), 165
Resin, 166
running in a Java servlet/JSP container, 166
separating the view from the MVC framework, 167
ServletRequestDataBinder class, 306
Show Book Details use case, 414–415
singletons and the Singleton design pattern, 411
Spring Rich Client, 166
Spring Web MVC, 165, 167, 258
Struts, 166
Tomcat server, 166–167
using XML files for JavaBean dependencies, 165
Velocity, 166
view, 167–168, 412
wiring beans together, 410–411
Write Customer Review use case, 416–417
YourBean class, code example, 410
Spring Rich Client, 166
Spring Web MVC, 165, 167
Controller interface, 412
DAO and JDBC Support, 413
HttpServlet interface, 412
J2EE Servlet API, 412
ModelAndView class, 412, 415
view, 412
SQL and the domain model, 259
state diagram, 108
static model, 4
static workflows, 2
stereotypes
assigning to a UML element, 63
"extends" association, 64, 66, 69
"includes" association, 64, 69
"invokes" association, 63, 69
"precedes" association, 63, 66, 69, 91
table of common use case relationships, 67–68
storyboards, 3, 7, 51, 56
stress testing, 334
Struts, 166
stubs, using to simulate component inputs/outputs, 332
subject matter experts, 29

subtyping
definition of, 37
subclasses and superclasses, 37
Sun Microsystems
Java, 165
JavaBeans, 165
JSP Tag Library (JSTL), 165
Plain Old Java Objects (POJOs), 165
system architecture. See technical architecture (TA)
system testing, 333
system topology, 160

■T

tearDown(), 350
technical architect
Carnegie Mellon Software Engineering Institute, 161
duties of, 160
leadership skills required, 161
pushing for TA adoption, 162
role in documenting and communicating system architecture, 160
technical architecture (TA)
analysis paralysis, 175
analyzing usage and transaction requirements, 160
architectural paralysis, 180
basing the architecture on objective requirements, 161
business-level system requirements, 160
common errors to avoid, 180–181
communicating and disseminating, 160
completing before detailed design, 160
considering the system's scalability, security, and availability, 162
data model, 161
definition of, 160
deployment model, 161, 173, 175
documenting, 159–160
domain classes containing no behavior, 175
examining the maintainability of a design, 242
guidelines, 161
HttpUnit, 179
identifying a stable set of abstractions, 249
interfacing with external systems, 162
internationalization and localization factors, 162
making models minimal yet sufficient, 175
minimizing code breakage and refactoring, 249
overnormalizing a design, 242
package/component model, 161, 173
planning ahead for testing, 162
purpose of, 159
scalability, 180
separating functional, data, and system architecture, 161
service-level system requirements, 160
testing application logic, 179
understanding the purpose of, 161
writing JUnit tests, 179

terminology, ambiguous, 29
Test-Driven Development (TDD), 19, 330
  Beck, Kent, 351
testBookDetailsFound(), 362
testBookIdFound(), 353
testBookIdNotFound(), 353
testing
  aligning closely to requirements, 331
  beginning as the code is being written, 329
  discovering alternate courses during, 338
  driving unit tests from use cases, 330
  identifying test cases using robustness
        diagrams, 329, 334
  identifying the test scenarios for each
        controller/test case, 335
  linking one test case to each controller, 336
  not writing tests connecting to external
        resources, 353
  preparing for, during the analysis stage, 329
  programmers' attitudes toward, 331
  proving a test by trying to make it fail, 348
  tying closely to requirements, 329
  unit test skeletons, guidelines for creating,
        338
testPageDisplayed(), 359–360, 362
TestRunner (JUnit), 350
Together, 260
Tomcat server, 166–167, 173, 270
traceability, 96, 374, 378–379, 388–389

U

UML
  assigning a stereotype to a UML element, 63
  custom elements, 383
  model for the Internet Bookstore, 324
  operation, definition of, 189
  package mechanism, 61
  stereotypes, 63–64
  synchronizing model and code, 262
  syntax, 39
  tools that reverse-engineer code into
        sequence diagrams, 307
  understanding the generalization and
        extends concepts in use cases, 66
UML 2.0
  action pins, 399
  activity diagrams, 396, 399
  artifacts, 396, 407
  assembly connectors, definition of, 398
  class diagrams, 396
  collaborations, definition of, 398
  combined fragments, 402
  communication diagrams, 396
  component diagrams, 396, 406
  composite structure diagrams, 396
  deployment diagrams, 407
  diagram types, list of, 395
  entry and exit point connections, 401
  expansion regions, definition of, 399
  extension mechanisms, 395
  functional decomposition, 403
  ICONIX diagrams remaining unchanged, 396

increased support for precision in diagrams,
        395
  input and output pins, 399
  interaction diagrams, 396, 401–402
  interaction elements and operands
        (subfragments), 402
  interaction, definition of, 401
  interfaces, definition of, 397
  junction states, definition of, 401
  linking components by assembly
        connectors, 396
  new modeling constructs on composite
        diagrams, 396
  new state diagram elements, 401
  nodes, 396, 407
  omissions in, 407
  overview of changes in, 395
  parts and ports, definitions of, 397
  profiles, definition of, 396
  provided and required interfaces, 406
  robustness diagrams, lack of, 395
  sequence diagrams, 401
  state lifeline, 405
  state machine diagrams, 396
  stereotyped class, 397
  swimlanes, 399
  test case diagrams, lack of, 395
  timing diagrams, definition of, 396, 404
  value lifeline, 405
unit testing
  avoiding duplication in tests, 343
  creating tests for each controller on each
        robustness diagram, 330
  driving from use cases, 330
  driving unit test classes and methods from
        controllers, 331
  driving unit tests from test cases, 338
  ensuring that each test method tests exactly
        one thing, 342
  generating test skeleton code for, 334
  guidelines, 17
  keeping unit tests fine-grained, 342
  neglecting to fix a failing test, 343
  running unit tests quickly, 353
  treating unit test code with reverence, 342
  tying unit tests to the preliminary design
        objects, 342
  using mock objects sparingly, 343, 369
  why bother with designing unit tests, 366
  writing effective unit tests, 342–343
use case diagrams
  actor, role of, 53
  definition of, 53
  placing actors on, 32
use cases
  actively describing user interactions and
        system responses, 95
  allocating functional requirements to, 89
  analyzing basic and alternate courses, 50, 53,
        72
  answering the three magic questions, 52, 72
  aspect-oriented programming (AOP), 74
  avoiding analysis paralysis, 63

avoiding overly abstract text in, 93
avoiding passive-voice functional
    requirements, 85–86
avoiding vagueness and ambiguity, 60
capturing user actions and associated
    system responses, 50
creating after the domain model, 29
describing both sides of the user/system
    dialogue, 51, 55
describing system usage in an object model
    context, 51, 59
describing system validation, 71
differentiating from algorithms, 76
disambiguating, 11
driving the design from, 51
eight steps for improving, 88–89
enforcing a noun-verb-noun pattern in use
    case text, 104
errors in first-draft use case text, 108
exercises and solutions for fixing errors,
    77–79
"extends" association, 64, 66, 69
factoring out commonality to avoid
    duplication, 67
following the two-paragraph rule, 51–52
as fragments of a user guide, 67
function of, 49
functional requirements and specifications,
    50
grounding in reality, 25
guidelines for writing, 51
identifying a first-pass list for
    implementation, 3
importance of linking to objects, 59
"includes" association, 64, 69
"invokes" association, 63, 69
keeping terminology concise and consistent,
    92
linking to objects, 11
modeling guidelines, 8
nouns as object instances, 59
organizing into packages, 61, 85–86
organizing with actors and use case
    diagrams, 51, 53
pasting use case text onto robustness
    diagrams, 104–105
placing in the user interface context, 87
practice questions in modeling, 80–81
"precedes" association, 63, 66, 69, 91
referencing boundary classes by name, 52, 61
referencing domain classes by name, 25, 52,
    59
referencing to the domain model, 71
referring text to the appropriate domain
    objects, 87
relationship of actors to responsibilities, 54
removing ambiguity from, 107
removing preconditions and postconditions,
    91
robustness diagram as an object picture of,
    101, 105, 109

as a runtime behavior specification, 51, 58
sequence diagrams, 59
similarity to end-user documentation, 58
state diagram, 108
sunny day vs. rainy day scenarios, 53, 72
table of common stereotypes and
    relationships, 68
templates and their misuse, 74–76
terseness of, 70
understanding the generalization and
    extends concepts, 66
use case diagram, purpose of, 87
using an event/response flow, 51, 55
using robustness analysis to disambiguate
    use case text, 102
using storyboards, GUI prototypes, and
    screen mock-ups, 51, 56
validating the behavior requirements of, 109
verbs as messages between objects, 59
Write Reader Review scenario, 70–71
writing coherent, specific, and unambiguous
    text, 95
writing first-draft use cases, 3
writing from the user's perspective, 54
writing in the active voice, 51, 54
writing using a noun-verb-noun sentence
    structure, 52, 59
writing within the domain model context,
    50, 102
writing within the object model context, 25,
    87
user authentication/authorization, 179

V

validate(), 289, 313
validation controllers, 133
Velocity, 166
view, 412
Visual Studio 2005, 262
volume testing, 334

W

Web Archive (WAR), 270
web security, 179
web.xml, 418–419
Wirfs-Brock, Rebecca, 237
Write Customer Review use case, 175, 195, 206,
    245, 252, 278, 344, 416–417
Write Reader Review use case, 70–71
writecustomerreview.jsp, 290
WriteCustomerReviewCommand, 247
WriteCustomerReviewController class, 279, 290,
    310

X

XDoclet, 260
XML, 180
    Spring XML file, 411
    using with JavaBeans, 165
xUnit, 339

You Need the Companion eBook

Your purchase of this book entitles you to buy the companion PDF-version eBook for only $10. Take the weightless companion with you anywhere.

We believe this Apress title will prove so indispensable that you'll want to carry it with you everywhere, which is why we are offering the companion eBook (in PDF format) for $10 to customers who purchase this book now. Convenient and fully searchable, the PDF version of any content-rich, page-heavy Apress book makes a valuable addition to your programming library. You can easily find and copy code—or perform examples by quickly toggling between instructions and the application. Even simultaneously tackling a donut, diet soda, and complex code becomes simplified with hands-free eBooks!

Once you purchase your book, getting the $10 companion eBook is simple:

❶ Visit **www.apress.com/promo/tendollars/**.

❷ Complete a basic registration form to receive a randomly generated question about this title.

❸ Answer the question correctly in 60 seconds, and you will receive a promotional code to redeem for the $10.00 eBook.

2560 Ninth Street • Suite 219 • Berkeley, CA 94710

eBookshop

THE EXPERT'S VOICE™